CLOSING THE PRODUCTIVITY GAP

TO RICHARD,
HEINZ,
AND THE MEMORY OF JOHN

Closing the Productivity Gap

A comparison of Northern Ireland, the Republic of Ireland,
Britain and West Germany

D.M.W.N. Hitchens
The Queen's University, Belfast

K. WAGNER
Technische Universität, Berlin

J. E. BIRNIE
The Queen's University, Belfast

Avebury

Aldershot · Brookfield USA · Hong Kong · Singapore · Sydney

Published by
Avebury
Gower Publishing Company Limited
Gower House
Croft Road
Aldershot
Hants GU11 3HR
England

Gower Publishing Company
Old Post Road
Brookfield
Vermont 05036
USA

ISBN   1 85628 098 5

Printed and Bound in Great Britain by
Athenaeum Press Ltd., Newcastle upon Tyne.

Contents

List of tables   viii

Preface   xii

**PART 1: THE UNITED KINGDOM'S PRODUCTIVITY GAP:
         ITS SIZE AND CAUSES**   1

1   Comparisons of productivity levels in Britain,
    America and Germany   3

2   Explanations of Britain's poor productivity   12

**PART 2: THE COMPARATIVE PRODUCTIVITY OF NORTHERN IRELAND
         AND GREAT BRITAIN**   27

3   Methods and data sources   29

4   Levels of output per head in Northern Ireland as
    compared to Great Britain   35

5   Explanations 1: Structural differences   44

6   Explanations 2: Prices, ownership, capital
    and plant size   54

7   Does Northern Ireland have a lower quality of
    labour force and management?   72

8   Northern Ireland's performance
    in international perspective: Conclusions to Part 2   82

**PART 3: MATCHED PLANT COMPARISONS OF NORTHERN IRELAND
         WITH WEST GERMANY**   91

9   Introduction   93

10 Design of the inquiry   102

11 Indicators of company performance   110

12 The quantity and quality of machinery and equipment   129

13 Overmanning in Northern Ireland   139

14 Management and labour force qualifications
    and training   146

15 Other labour force characteristics   159

16 Characteristics of the firms relevant to productivity   168

17 Growth, market failure and policy failure   174

18 The comparative productivity of a sample of matched
    manufacturing plants: Conclusions to Part 3   180

**PART 4: THE COMPARATIVE PRODUCTIVITY OF NORTHERN IRELAND
         AND THE REPUBLIC OF IRELAND**   187

19 Levels of output per head in the Republic of Ireland
    compared to Northern Ireland   189

20 Performance of the small firm sector in Britain and
    Ireland   220

21 Improving productivity: Obstacles, policy issues,
    and recommendations   228

APPENDICES   273

A   Northern Ireland's declining cost competitiveness
    relative to Great Britain and international competitors 275

B   Public subsidisation of Northern Ireland
    manufacturing: a comparison with other areas   278

C   The adjustment of the comparative productivity
    measurements to a per employee-hour basis   282

D   Manufacturing productivity differences within
    the United Kingdom: Northern Ireland compared
    to Scotland, Wales and the English regions   285

E   Description of the data used   288

F   Northern Ireland's comparative gross value-added:
    The results for 1979 and 1984   294

G   Long run trends in output per head   299

BIBLIOGRAPHY   302

List of tables

1.1 Long-term changes in comparative productivity: US/UK   5
1.2 Long-term changes in comparative productivity:
    Germany/UK   6
1.3 Industries in which UK net output per head was higher
    than Germany in 1967-68   7
1.4 International comparative productivity growth   8
1.5 German/UK comparisons of productivity levels in 1985   9
2.1 Gross non-residential fixed capital stock   13
2.2 Civilian R and D as a percentage of GDP   20
3.1 A comparison of productivity estimates for Northern
    Ireland drawn from two census sources   33
4.1 The Northern Ireland level of productivity in all
    manufacturing as a percentage of
    the Great Britain level   36
4.2 The percentage distribution of manufacturing output
    and employment by relative
    Northern Ireland/Great Britain performance   37
4.3 Northern Ireland's GVA per head relative
    to Great Britain, 1985   39
4.4 Northern Ireland's GVA per head relative
    to Great Britain, 1980-1985   40
4.5 Historical comparison of net output per head,
    NI relative to GB   42
5.1 Contribution of structure to Northern Ireland's
    productivity shortfall   46
5.2 Structural change in NI and the UK   47

5.3	The relative growth of the high productivity level industries in Northern Ireland	48
5.4	Individual industry contributions to the productivity gap	50
5.5	Number of firms in given industries in NI and GB, 1984	51
6.1	The effects of differences in unit prices on comparative productivity, 1968	55
6.2	Branch-plants and multinational plants, and comparative productivity by standard region	57
6.3	Transport costs as a percentage of gross output	58
6.4	Relative electricity prices paid by NI manufacturing	58
6.5	Comparative labour productivity and investment in foreign owned plants in the UK, 1985	59
6.6	(a) Comparative productivity by ownership type	60
6.6	(b) Relative productivity of foreign owned firms in NI	60
6.6	(c) Relative productivity of foreign owned firms in GB	60
6.7	Relative importance of foreign owned manufacturing plants in NI and GB	61
6.8	NI's comparative productivity and investment relative to GB	63
6.9	NI's comparative sectoral productivity and investment	64
6.10	Share of investment in value-added	65
6.11	Trends in comparative productivity and comparative capital intensity	66
6.12	Relative factory size and comparative productivity	68
7.1	Occupational structure of the labour force in NI and GB in 1981	73
7.2	Numbers of residents Northern Ireland and Republic of Ireland (ROI) with birthplaces outside of Ireland	74
7.3	Composition of total employment, 1983	75
7.4	Educational qualifications of the manufacturing labour force, 1981	77
7.5	Northern Ireland's strike rate compared to United Kingdom	78
7.6	Comparison of strike rates in Northern Ireland and United Kingdom, 1980-85	79
7.7	Relative rates of absence	80
8.1	Comparative productivity levels NI, Britain and Germany, 1985	83
8.2	NI's growth in output, employment and output per head compared to the OECD economies	84
9.1	Comparative manufacturing productivity, 1860 to 1986	95
10.1	Number of plants visited and products matched by sector	103
10.2	(a) Distribution of plants by size	103
10.2	(b) Average size of plant by sector	104
10.3	Comparison of sample and population	104
10.4	Percentage of shop-floor workers with formal qualifications	109
11.1	Comparative employment growth by sectors	111
11.2	Employment change 1982-87 sample compared to population	112

11.3   Comparative export performance   113
11.4   Methods of productivity measurement   114
11.5   WG physical productivity as a % of NI, 1987-88   115
11.6   WG value-added per head as a % of NI and UK, 1985   117
11.7   Importance of differences in product quality   118
11.8   Reject rates   122
11.9   NI assessment of reason for shortfall
       relative to Germany   126
11.10 Percentage of firms reporting productivity growth   127
11.11 Sources of productivity growth in NI companies   128
12.1   Comparisons of capital stock   130
12.2   Comparative levels of technology and the extent of
       its adaptation to the specific circumstances
       of the firm   131
12.3   Payback periods   133
12.4   Rate of grant support for capital in NI   134
12.5   Comparative size of the maintenance labour force   136
12.6   Comparative capacity utilisation   137
13.1   Number of detailed observations of matched processes
       by sector   141
13.2   Percentage of NI companies reporting overmanning   141
13.3   Size of indirect employment   144
14.1   Higher level qualifications   146
14.2   Percentage of the shop-floor labour force
       with a skill   153
15.1   Absenteeism   160
15.2   Labour turnover   161
15.3   Incidence of strikes and disruptions in NI   162
15.4   Poor attitudes to work   164
16.1   Age of companies   171
17.1   Main constraints on growth   175
17.2   Selective financial assistance (SFA) to
       sample companies in NI   177
19.1   Manufacturing productivity growth   191
19.2   ROI's net output per head relative to NI   192
19.3   ROI's net output per head relative to the UK   193
19.4   ROI's comparative productivity level 1980, 1984,
       and 1985   195
19.5   ROI's comparative productivity using PPPs, 1985   197
19.6   ROI's comparative productivity by nationality of firm   199
19.7   Productivity of foreign owned plants in the ROI as a
       percentage of domestically owned plants, 1984   198
20.1   Components of employment change in
       small firms 1973-86   221
21.1   Comparative GDP per capita of NI and ROI   229
A.1   NI's manufacturing unit labour costs relative to GB   276
A.2   International comparisons of NI's relative unit costs   276
B.1   Rates of subsidy   279
B.2   Rates of subsidy with and without shipbuilding and
       aerospace   279
B.3   Rate of subsidy to German manufacturing   279
B.4   Rates of subsidy in Britain and Ireland   280
C.1   Comparison of average weekly hours worked, 1960-83   283

D.1   Productivity of GB Standard Regions as a % of NI   286
F.1   Comparative GVA per head of NI industries   294
G.1   Manufacturing output and productivity growth
       during the post-war period   300

Preface

The central concern of this book is to examine the causes of
Northern Ireland's poor manufacturing productivity. The approach
is comparative: performance of industry in Northern Ireland is set
against the yardstick provided by manufacturing in Great Britain
and a longstanding 20 per cent shortfall in labour productivity is
identified.

The sources of that productivity gap are explored and it is
notable that little of the differential poor performance can be
attributed to problems arising from the location such as transport
costs or energy costs etc. Even having a disadvantageous
industrial structure is excluded as an important explanatory
factor: Northern Ireland's labour productivity is low relative to
Great Britain on an industry by industry basis.

Recognition of Britain's lagging international productivity
performance led the authors to make international plant
comparisons between more than forty companies in Northern Ireland
and their matched counterparts in West Germany. These comparisons
provide detailed examples and lessons as to how productivity might
be improved.

The book is divided into four parts. Part 1 examines Britain's
productivity shortfall relative to Europe and the USA and the
reasons for this poor performance. Part 2 employs the official
statistics to analyse the causes of Northern Ireland's
productivity shortfall relative to Great Britain. Part 3 considers
Northern Ireland-West German inter-plant comparisons.

Part 4 is drawn from the results of two separate studies by two
of the present authors. Chapter 19 considers the sources of the

differences in relative Republic of Ireland/Northern Ireland and Republic of Ireland/Great Britain value-added. Does the peripheral Republic of Ireland perform as badly as Northern Ireland? This chapter is derived from Esmond Birnie's forthcoming doctoral dissertation. Chapter 20 examines the comparative performance and sources of failure of small firms in Britain and Ireland. It draws on the findings of parallel work undertaken by D.M.W.N. Hitchens with P.N. O'Farrell in their set of inter-regional comparisons of small firms in the different regions of the British Isles.

The study was directed by Dr David Hitchens at the Northern Ireland Economic Research Centre whilst on half-time secondment from the Department of Economics at the Queen's University of Belfast (1986-88) (subsequently developed, enlarged and completed at the University), with Esmond Birnie as research assistant (now lecturer in economics at the Queen's University) and Dr Karin Wagner of the Technische Universitat, Berlin as consultant in Germany. Both David Hitchens and Karin Wagner have worked on similar international productivity studies at the National Institute of Economic and Social Research.

Some of the material from which this book developed also formed the basis for two articles: "The United Kingdom's Productivity Gap: Its size and causes", Omega (1989), vol. 17, no. 3, pp. 209-221; "Productivity levels in Northern Ireland Manufacturing Industry: A Comparison with Great Britain", Regional Studies (1989), vol. 23, no. 5, pp. 447-454.

The authors would like to thank Tony Smith of the National Institute of Economic and Social Research London, and Professor Kieran Kennedy of the Economic and Social Research Institute Dublin for reading early drafts of a large part of this book. We are also grateful to Graham Gudgin and Professor Black for their comments. The assistance of Kieran Kennedy and John McMahon (Industrial Development Authority of Ireland) is greatly appreciated for Chapter 19 especially.

Richard Harris (formerly of the Department of Economics at the Queen's University) kindly supplied some estimations of data for 1968 used in the statistical comparisons. Some statistical advice was also received from George O'Doherty, George Campbell, Sid Stalford and others at the Department of Economics (Northern Ireland), Statistics Branch. Not least, the authors would like to thank the senior management of the companies visited in Northern Ireland and West Germany for the hundreds of hours of time which they gave to the study.

A report such as this cannot see the light of day without a great deal of administrative and secretarial support and the contribution, in this area, of many individuals at the Queen's University is readily acknowledged (as well as Elaine Gordon and Christine Gordon at the Northern Ireland Economic Research Centre). Of particular note were proof reading provided by Mary Trainor and Colin Coulter and advice on type-setting by Georgina Holmes and Carol Richmond.

To all these individuals the authors are greatly obliged whilst absolving them, of course, from any defects which the finished product retains. The judgments, analyses and views expressed are those of the authors and are not necessarily those of the Northern Ireland Economic Research Centre nor its Committee of Management.

D.M.W.N.H.
K.W.
J.E.B.
31 March
1990

Note

As often in books about Ireland a note on terminology is in order. The terms Northern Ireland (NI) and Republic of Ireland (ROI) are usually used to refer to the two political units on the island. Sometimes, for the purposes of variety, the shorthand of north and south is used. "Ireland" is used to refer to the island of Ireland and is employed in a purely geographical sense. Likewise, when the term Irish is employed this should be taken to imply all the inhabitants of Ireland (both Protestant and Catholic, unionist and nationalist, northern and southern). Once again, this use of terminology should not be taken as an endorsement of any particular view on the so-called constitutional question. Northern Ireland and Republic of Ireland are also usually applied anachronistically (i.e. pre-1921 and pre-1948) to those areas equivalent to the present political entities.

PART 1

THE UNITED KINGDOM'S PRODUCTIVITY GAP: ITS SIZE AND CAUSES

[higher productivity is responsible] "... for the superior affluence and abundance commonly possessed even by [the] lowest and most despised member of Civilised Society".

Adam Smith (1776), The Wealth of Nations

PART 1
THE UNITED KINGDOM'S PRODUCTIVITY GAP: ITS SIZE AND CAUSES

1 Comparisons of productivity levels in Britain, America and Germany

"Anyone who can suppose that it is possible to raise the standard of living without the necessary production must be living in a world of fantasy or cloud-cuckoo land".

Dr Ludwig Erhard on the German "Economic Miracle"

Introduction

The interest of economists, businessmen, trade unionists, politicians and other commentators in Britain's comparative productivity is not a new phenomenon and has been present to some extent throughout the twentieth century (Williams, 1896; Marshall, 1919). However, the recent attention to Britain's comparative productivity performance is unusual in that it has broken with the traditional pessimism and proclaims that Britain is now undergoing a "productivity miracle" (Pratten, 1985; HM Treasury, 1987; Sunday Times, 1988, May 1, May 8 and May 15). One of the aims of this Chapter is to place this assertion into perspective by showing how far the UK had already fallen behind other industrial economies by the beginning of the 1980s, and the limited extent of the gains achieved since 1981. Chapter 2 will consider whether it is possible to explain the UK's long run comparative productivity performance.

The productivity gap: its size and development through time

An impressive array of international productivity comparisons suggest that current British productivity levels are now substantially below those attained by almost all other industrial economies. In this section we will argue that it is useful to think of two sets of comparisons; those with the United States, and then with other industrial economies. Before the Second World War concern as to Britain's comparative productivity was usually expressed through comparison with the United States, which probably overtook the UK before the start of this Century (Maizels, 1963; Phelps-Brown 1973; Maddison, 1982). Official studies were undertaken at an aggregate manufacturing level (HM Treasury and CSO, 1943) and the sectoral level (Platt Report, 1944) in order to ascertain the size of the productivity gap behind the US, and to recommend policy measures to close this gap. Some policy makers still felt that achievement of American levels was a realistic goal. However, others thought that it was inevitable that the US should have surpassed British productivity levels and that it was not the existence of the gap but its size which was worrying (Marshall, 1919).

Table 1.1 shows the results of the major academic studies of Anglo-American differences in productivity levels. It is striking that in every case from 1899 onwards the United States is found to have levels of output per head more than double those of the UK and in some studies the superiority is not far from being a factor of three.

Given the widely different methodologies used the results shown lack the degree of comparability necessary to identify precise trends in the Anglo-American productivity gap. However, it does seem safe to make the following generalisation; the US advantage relative to the UK widened to one of almost three-to-one during the Great Depression and Second World War and any narrowing since then has been slow (Matthews, 1988). The depressing conclusion is that despite of the amount of research lavished on the subject and the efforts of industrial policy, there was very little catch up relative to America during the post-war period.

That comparisons were made with other economies may itself be indicative of a recognition that United States productivity levels were unattainable. Unfortunately, even when the UK was matched with an economy of comparable population, natural resources and industrial structure, Britain was still a laggard in productivity terms. The major Anglo-German comparisons are detailed in Table 1.2 (references to Germany post-1945 apply to the Federal Republic[1]).

Whilst Germany overtook Britain much later than did America, the pioneering study by Rostas (1948) suggests that Germany achieved a temporary superiority as early as the 1930s and this superiority was reasserted during the "economic miracle" of the 1950s and 1960s so that the UK productivity level was surpassed at some point close to 1960. Doubt remains as to the present size of the productivity gap for, although Smith, Hitchens and Davies (1982) suggest German productivity may be about 50 per cent higher than that of the UK, three other studies also undertaken at the National Institute of Economic and Social Research (Jones, 1976; Roy, 1982; Ray, 1987) show German levels of output per head at about twice that achieved in Britain. Most of the divergence arises from the different methodologies used. Smith, Hitchens and Davies (1982) made detailed comparisons of physical outputs in 1967-68 (respectively, the years of German and British Industrial Censuses) and brought these forward to later years using official volume indices of output growth. Jones and Roy employed home currency estimates of the national censuses of production and converted these to a common currency through the final expenditure purchasing power parities calculated by Kravis et al (International Comparisons Project, 1973, 1977, 1982). The use of the latter is problematic since Purchasing Power Parities may not reflect factory gate prices[2] (National Institute Economic Review, 1982).

Table 1.1
Long-term changes in comparative productivity: US/UK

	US/UK UK=100	Methodology[a]	Authors
1899	218	Index from 1937	Maizels (1963)
1909	226	Exchange rate	Flux (1933)
1913	209	Index from 1937	Maizels (1963)
1929	293	Exchange rate	Flux (1933)
1937	216	Physical output	Rostas (1948)
1937	222	Exchange rate	Maizels (1963)
1947	269	Physical output	Frankel (1957)
1950	272	Physical output	Paige and Bombach (1958)
1955	254	Purchasing power parities	Maizels (1963)
1968	289	Physical output	Smith, Hitchens Davies (1982)
1973	242	Purchasing power parities	Jones (1976)
1977	291	Index from 1968	Smith, Hitchens Davies (1982)
1980	249[b]	Purchasing power parities	Roy (1982)
1986	259[b]	Purchasing power parities	Ray (1987)

Notes: Productivity defined as value-added (usually net output) per employee.
[a] and [b] Refer to Appendix E.3.

Despite these technical uncertainties it seems safe to conclude that a substantial productivity gap has opened up relative to Germany, albeit not as large as the one behind the US. Moreover, wider multilateral comparisons suggest that the Anglo-German difference has parallels with most Western European economies[3].

Table 1.2
Long-term changes in comparative productivity: Germany/UK

	Germany/UK UK=100	Methodology	Authors
1855-64	70[a]	Exchange rate	Crafts (1988b)
1875-84	79[a]	Exchange rate	Crafts (1988b)
1890-99	66[a]	Exchange rate	Phelps-Brown (1973)
1895-1904	98[a]	Exchange rate	Crafts (1988b)
1900	75[b]	Index from 1937	Maizels (1963)
1905-13	118[a]	Exchange rate	Crafts (1988b)
1913	109[c]	Index from 1937	Maizels (1963)
1929	127[d]	Index from 1937	Maizels (1963)
1936	104	Physical output	Rostas (1948)
1937	120	Exchange rate	Maizels (1963)
1942-45	133[e]	Physical output	Various[e]
1950	71	Index from 1955	Maizels (1963)
1955	90	Purchasing power parities	Maizels (1963)
1968	135	Physical output	Smith, Hitchens Davies (1982)
1970	155	Purchasing power parities	Jones (1976)
1973	168	Purchasing power parities	Jones (1976)
1977	152	Index from 1968	Smith, Hitchens, Davies (1982)
1980	215[f]	Purchasing power parities	Roy (1982)
1986	200[f]	Purchasing power parities	Ray (1987)

Notes: Productivity defined as value-added (usually net output) per employee. For other notes refer to Appendix E.3.

In certain engineering sectors the exemplar of best practise is now Japan (Guinchard, 1984), but overall Japanese output per head is still lower than the US whilst being about four-fifths higher than the UK's (Kurosawa, 1982; Ray, 1987).

Having established how poor the UK's comparative productivity record is by international standards, we now review the results of previous studies at a disaggregated level. Is there any systematic tendency for Britain to do better or worse in certain types of industries?

Britain's comparative productivity level: individual industries

Rostas (1948) provides one of the earliest examples of sectoral comparisons of British and American performance; of 31 industries considered for 1935-37 America had higher productivity in every case. This advantage varied from having two-and-a half times the

British level in engineering and metals, to the "worst" American performance of 156 per cent of the UK level in food, drink and tobacco.

Rostas' Anglo-German comparisons were restricted to 13 broad sectors and used market exchange rates in nearly all cases. Germany appeared to be doing better in eight of these in 1935-37. These included all engineering, metals, chemicals, leather, clothing and textiles. British superiority was restricted to minerals, timber, furniture, paper, printing and publishing,and food, drink and tobacco.

Paige and Bombach (1958) compared UK and US productivities in 44 industries during 1950. Once again, the US had the advantage across the entire field (varying from 111 per cent of the British level in shipbuilding to 600 per cent in fuel refining). Smith, Hitchens and Davies (1982) have provided the most up-to-date detailed, disaggregated comparison. They compared the UK and the US for 117 industries (approximately equivalent to Minimum List Headings of the UK 1968 SIC) in 1967-68. Once again, the US had superiority in every case. There were 24 industries where the UK did relatively well in the sense that the US achieved less than twice the British level. Of these, three were in food sector and eleven in paper, mineral products, textiles and clothing. Broadly speaking one might characterise these better British performers as low in technological intensity (per cent of turnover devoted to R and D being low; Midland Bank Review, 1986) and as low in value-added. Smith et al found that of 69 possible comparisons in 1967-68 Germany had better output per head in four-fifths of the cases. Table 1.3 shows the fifteen industries where the UK had a better productivity than Germany in 1967-68.

Table 1.3
Industries in which UK net output per head
was higher than Germany in 1967-68

Grain milling
Bread, and flour confectionery
Biscuits
Bacon, meat and fish
Sugar
Electrical engineering (average, disaggregation not available)
Shipbuilding and marine engineering
Cutlery
Jewellery and precious metals
Hosiery and knitted goods
Bedding and soft furnishing
Footwear
Clothing (average, disaggregation not available)
Rubber and asbestos
Miscellaneous manufacturing

As with the Anglo-American comparison it seems possible to detect a systematic pattern. The comparatively "low-tech" food, textiles and clothing industries are predominant while the more complex engineering industries appear to be under-represented. That conclusion might be qualified if we had more finely disaggregated data; Patel and Pavitt (1987, 1988) working with alternative data sources (trade and patent performance) show that the UK has a revealed comparative advantage in some niches within the engineering sectors such as mining machinery, aerospace and nuclear engineering.

Having considered the historical development of the UK's comparative performance in terms of the levels of productivity for all manufacturing and individual sectors, the next two sections will consider to what extent the so-called "productivity miracle" has succeeded in narrowing the productivity shortfall.

The acceleration in United Kingdom productivity growth

It is worth considering what has been the impact of the much vaunted "productivity miracle" upon the UK's status as a low productivity economy (Pratten, 1985). Table 1.4 shows that UK productivity growth since 1979 is comparable to that achieved prior to the world economic recession which began in 1973, and above the average for the OECD as a whole.

Nevertheless, this advantage in recent growth has not been enough to close the large productivity gap which existed in 1979. This is shown in the next section.

Table 1.4
International comparative productivity growth
Output per head in manufacturing, average % per annum

	1964-73	1973-79	1980-88
Japan	9.8	4.0	3.1
Italy*	5.5	2.5	3.5
France*	5.4	3.0	3.1
Canada	4.3	2.5	3.6
West Germany	3.9	3.3	2.2
United Kingdom	3.8	0.7	5.2
United States	3.4	3.5	4.0
Weighted average	5.0	3.2	3.6

* Includes mining and utilities as well as manufacturing.

Source: HM Treasury (1987, 1989)

The extent to which the productivity gap has been closed

The limits to what the so-called "miracle" has so far achieved can be illustrated with reference to Germany. Smith, Hitchens and Davies (1982) brought their results for 1967-68 forward to 1976 using national volume series of production and employment at the broad sectoral level. For all manufacturing and individual sectors

we have extended this procedure so as to estimate comparative
productivity levels in 1985 (these procedures must be regarded as
fairly crude since a detailed harmonisation of the German and
British industrial classifications was not attempted)[4]. Table 1.5
outlines the components of the results.

Table 1.5 shows that for all manufacturing and for six of eleven
broad sectors the UK productivity has been grown more rapidly than
Germany during 1976-85. Nevertheless, the German lead still
remains substantial[5]. As a Financial Times leader (1987, May 27)
put it "UK manufacturing is enjoying a very modest miracle in that
its productivity performance has outpaced that of its main
competitors ..[but].. it would take the best part of half a
century to reach the average (of the OECD economies)".

Table 1.5
German/UK comparisons of productivity levels in 1985

	WG/UK 1976 UK=100	Growth 1976-85 % WG	Growth 1976-85 % UK	WG/UK 1985 UK=100
Food, drink, & tobacco	117	35	35	117
Mech. eng. & metal goods	163	17	19	161
Instrument eng.	95	34	44	89
Electrical eng.	103	45	59	94
Shipbuilding, & vehicles	209	12	29	180
Textiles, & clothing	145	22	23	144
Paper, printing, & publishing	207	41	13	257
Timber, & furniture	229	5	2	236
Glass, & pottery etc.	190	18	4	215
Chemicals, & man-made fibres	162	24	38	146
Rubber, & plastics etc.	151	29	28	152
All manufacturing	147	27	31	142

Sources: Smith, Hitchens and Davies (1982); Statistisches
Bundesamt, 1988; and various Monthly Digest of Statistics (Central
Statistical Office).

Levels and trends: a summary

At the beginning of the 1980s productivity levels in American
manufacturing were between two and three times higher than those

in Britain whilst Germany had an advantage of about 50 per cent. Almost every other Western European economy (including the Republic of Ireland; see Chapter 19) had built-up a substantial lead relative to the UK, as had Japan[6]. Britain's comparative performance has historically been weaker in parts of the engineering industries and stronger in food, textiles and clothing. This is suggestive of the UK having acquired a structural bias towards those industries which have required lower levels of worker skills, management competence and technological sophistication.

Such is the scale of the UK's productivity shortfall that even the past eight years of rapid growth had little impact. The persistence of such a large gap is one reason why we will not consider in any depth the hypotheses suggested to explain the "productivity miracle". These include; shifts in the relative price of energy, better industrial relations, new technology, shedding of the below average plants, scrapping of obsolete capital and a better utilisation of the remaining stock, and the reduction in labour hoarding; (Berndt and Wood, 1986; Muellbauer, 1986). Whilst it is true that explanation of the comparatively rapid productivity increase since 1980-81 would go some way by implication to explain those factors which were arresting productivity improvement prior to that date, the size and persistence of the UK's productivity gap is such that one might expect most of its explanation to lie with factors too deeply-rooted to have been removed within the last decade. We will now attempt to detect what are the fundamental flaws in Britain's social and industrial systems which result in low productivity.

Notes

1. While the comparative productivity of East Germany has been the subject of less investigation, a recent calculation prepared for the European Commission estimates that East German industrial productivity was 39 per cent of that in West Germany in 1987 (Financial Times, 1990, February 12).

2. Kravis, Kennesy, Heston and Summers (International Comparisons Project, 1973, 1977, 1982) provide international comparisons of the prices of several hundred finely defined categories of final expenditure. As far as is possible the price comparisons are such that like is compared with like. Since the prices are intended to be used in comparisons of Gross Domestic Product they are not the same as the factory-gate prices one would wish to use in making international comparisons of manufacturing value-added. They will differ to the extent that there are international variations in retail margins and rates of indirect taxation. Researchers wishing to use purchasing power parities (PPPs) to compare manufacturing value-added have the further problem that they must aggregate together a large number of single product PPPs to produce an average PPP for all of manufacturing output. Kravis et al have themselves generated sectoral PPPs for the purpose of Gross

Domestic Product comparisons and the studies quoted have applied some of these to manufacturing output even though the Kravis prices give weight to imported products as well as those made in Britain. For these reasons of indirect taxation, retail profits and improper weighting one should regard the comparative productivity estimates which are made using purchasing power parities as approximations only.

3. Jones (1976) calculated Belgian, French and Italian and Dutch outputs per head in 1970 as 155 per cent, 164 per cent, 105 per cent and 183 per cent respectively of the UK level in manufacturing, and these gaps had if anything widened by 1986 (Ray, 1987).

4. We have used the results of the Smith, Hitchens and Davies, (1982) Anglo-German comparison as our foundation in preference to those of Jones (1976) or Roy (1982) which were based on a methodology of purchasing power parities. It should be noted that a PPP-based comparison (Ray, 1987) has given Germany a current productivity level double that of the UK as opposed to our estimate of a superiority of around 40 per cent. Given the technical difficulties with PPPs we feel the latter to be a more reasonable estimate even though the procedure of bringing forward earlier comparisons over a long period of years by using volume indices of output is itself subject to unreliability (Appendix G).

5. And this gap would be even wider if the Anglo-German productivity differences had been estimated using the methodology of purchasing power parities (see Note 3).

6. There has been a perception that the relatively slow rate of productivity growth of US manufacturing since the early 1970s is a symptom of an American productivity "problem" to parallel the British problem. Whatever the validity of this thesis the US case is distinguished from the British in that it is an example of a relatively slow rate of growth in an economy which is already at the frontiers of international best practise as oppposed to one where that poor growth performance occurred before international productivity standards were achieved (i.e. the UK example). It is also clear that despite the inroads made by the Japanese and Germans in certain sectors, the US maintains technological and product quality superiority (e.g. micro-computers, aviation and defence) across a wider range of industries than does Britain (Financial Times, 1987, May, Surveys on US Competitiveness).

2 Explanations of Britain's poor productivity

"The English disease is not the novelty of the past ten or even twenty years... but a phenomenon dating back more than a century".

Corelli Barnett (1976, January 26), "Obsolescence___and Dr Arnold", Sunday Telegraph

Capital stock: historical comparisons

It has been suggested that Britain has lower productivity because capital equipment is deficient in either a quantitative or qualitative sense. Flood and McCloskey (1981) show that in both the 1870-1914 and 1950-73 periods Britain had a lower proportion of gross net capital formation in GNP than either the US or Germany (also demonstrated by Crafts, 1988a, 1988b). Table 2.1 shows that there was a close correspondence in timing between the loss of Britain's leadership as far as capital stock per head was concerned, and that in output per head.

However, these statistics are confined to the whole economy and do not tell us about the level and rate of change of the capital stock in manufacturing. There are however estimates which suggest that the post-war growth of the UK's manufacturing capital stock was relatively slow such that during 1954-72 the UK's growth rate in constant prices of the gross stock in all manufacturing was estimated at 3.9 per cent per annum compared to 7.2 per cent for Germany (Panic, 1976). It is highly probable that the UK stock of capital per capita is inferior to that of its major competitor economies (on the basis of postal survey findings Prais (1986) estimated that the capital intensity of the British metal working industries in the early 1980s was roughly one-fifth lower than that of its counterparts in Germany, France and Japan). Nevertheless, most of the difference between German and British rates of growth of output in manufacturing during 1954-72 has been attributed by Panic (1976) to factors other than a differential rate of growth of factor (principally capital and employment) inputs. Moreover, Prais (1986) indicated that the difference between British and USA capital intensity in the metal working industries was in the wrong direction to explain the Anglo-American productivity gap (i.e. in spite of having about one-fifth more machines per head the British plants still had lower labour productivity).

Table 2.1
Gross non-residential fixed capital stock
per person employed 1870-1978, whole economy

($, 1970 US purchasing power)

	1870	1890	1913	1950	1973	1978
Germany	3,597	5,311	7,888	9,386	26,733	34,877
USA	5,066	6,838	13,147	18,485	30,243	32,001
UK	6,068	6,658	7,999	9,204	17,718	20,931

Source: Maddison (1982).

Capital: Recent inter-plant comparisons

Detailed inter-plant comparisons have suggested that the quantity of capital is not necessarily an important factor. Pratten (1976) thought that more than four-fifths of the differences between the productivity of plants of international firms operating in both Germany and Britain could be explained by factors other than the quantity of capital. Daly, Hitchens and Wagner (1985) matched a set of metal working firms in GB with plants in Germany. The German's had substantially better productivity but not many more machines per operative.

Capital quality

The quality of capital affects comparative productivity too. The lower its average age the more likely that it will incorporate the most up-to-date specifications. Britain's capital stock is not substantially older than that of its competitors. In metal cutting machines in 1982, the biggest single group of machines, 40 per cent were less than five years old compared with a smaller 35 per cent less than seven years old in Japan (in 1981), and 30 per cent less than nine years old in the US (for 1978) (The Economist, 1983). This is reinforced by Daly, Hitchens and Wagner (1985) in their matched plant comparison which found no evidence that showed that the British metal workers had older machines and similar conclusions were reached by earlier studies (Rostas, 1948; Anglo-American Council on Productivity, 1950; Bacon and Eltis, 1974; and Prais, 1986).

A factor relating to the vintage of the machinery is its technical up-to-dateness. One particularly important recent process innovation has been the introduction of Computer-Numerically Controlled machine tools (CNC) and the development of Flexible Manufacturing Systems (FMS) whereby whole clusters of related machine processes are placed under common automatic control. FMS and CNC may raise labour productivity not only through displacing labour but by achieving economies in materials, floor-space and time (in change-over from one product line to another). Given the recentness of these developments, the data on the international application of these innovations is poor. However, it seems that the usage of CNCs in German industry is greater than that in Britain (the results of postal surveys as well as matched plant comparisons; Daly, Hitchens and Wagner, 1985; Prais, 1986; Steedman and Wagner, 1987). Furthermore it is estimated that Japanese factories average 2.5 times the American application of CNCs which in turn is ahead of the Europeans (Jaikumar, 1986).

Miscellaneous capital-related factors

Even if the capital is technically advanced there may be a number of other capital-related factors which limit productivity relative to international rivals. Economies may differ in the degree to which they manage to keep their capital at relatively full utilisation. In part the rate of capital utilisation will depend upon the level of aggregate demand in the economy (Pratten, 1976) and in part on factors more directly under the firms' control such as material feeding and loading systems adopted to machines and the incidence of breakdowns. Prais (1981a), and Daly, Hitchens and Wagner (1985) have identified a tendency for the British systems of transport of goods and materials in the factory to be more primitive than those used in Germany. Linked machinery (used for example in kitchen furniture making) is more common in German factories. Matched plant comparisons suggest that breakdowns are more frequent in Britain than in Germany and that British manufacturers may have more difficulty in repairing these (partly because the British tend to avoid doing planned maintenance and partly because the Germans can more often use home-produced machines, while the British have to deal with suppliers in Japan or Continental Europe (Daly, Hitchens and Wagner, 1985; Steedman and Wagner, 1987). Problems of machine maintenance may also be related to some labour skill and attitudinal problems.

Whilst the quantity of capital available almost certainly contributes to the explanation of comparatively low UK productivity it is not the sole, or even the most important, explanation of the comparative productivity level (Matthews, 1988). The counterpart of the lag in labour productivity is probably some deficiency in capital productivity (Prais, 1981a). Statistical comparisons of capital stocks and vintages are problematic but a number of detailed comparisons at the factory level are indicative of Britain having such problems as under-utilisation, lack of CNCs, under-developed feeding systems and frequent breakdowns. None of these problems should be seen in isolation from the questions of labour force and management quality which we will now consider.

Labour force

The alleged deficiencies of the British labour force have probably received even more attention from commentators than those of capital. The British education and training system fails in at least three ways: the technical and vocational training given to school-leavers, the on-the-job training given by companies, and the quality and quantity of managers, engineers and scientists available.

Historical comparisons

For over a century the British educational system has been criticised as failing to educate the British work-force for industrial competitiveness; "The one point in which Germany is overwhelmingly superior to England is in schools" (Second Report of the Royal Commission on Technical Instruction, 1884, Command Papers). A similar message came from three other Royal Commissions during the late nineteenth century as well as the Emmott Report, 1927; Balfour Report, 1928; Spens Report, 1938; Norwood Report, 1943; and the Percy Report, 1945 (Barnett, 1986).

The current British education system seems to have none of the economic advantages which may accrue to either the Japanese, American or German approaches. In the USA and Japan the majority of school-leavers stay in school until they are 18-19 years old. This enables them to receive a broad education which later aids labour flexibility. By contrast, the bulk of young Germans (like the British) leave school at 15-16 and then receive compulsory apprenticeship training (National Economic Development Council and Manpower Services Commission, 1984). This has the advantage of giving the work-force a very high level of technical skill. Like the Germans most of the British leave school at 16, but unlike the Germans very few of them then receive apprenticeships. Daly (1984) estimates that about half of the UK work-force have no formal qualifications whereas Prais (1981a) shows that just one-tenth of German 15-16 year olds enter the labour market without any vocational skills.

It is certainly significant in this connection that British foremen are almost always only time-served whereas the German Meister has a formal qualification; Prais and Wagner (1988) show that the annual German output of examined apprentices is more than seven times that of Britain, and the German courses are superior in duration, scope and rigour. The chief productivity-related benefits of this corps of highly trained foremen include; adaption of machinery to the specific needs of the firm, repair of machinery without call on mechanics, and the maintenance of work-flow up to delivery dates. Whilst, youth training has been the subject of various government initiatives since the start of the 1980s Finegold and Soskice (1988) doubt if these programmes (particularly the Youth Training Scheme) have the coherence and the intensity necessary to raise the British to levels of competence achieved by American, French, Scandinavian and German youths. (The impact of government policy on productivity is considered below.)

It appears that the British enter the work-force relatively unskilled and there is little indication that this is compensated for by superior on-the-job training. All training spending by private and public sectors in the UK was estimated to be 1.9 per cent of GNP compared with 2.3 per cent in Germany (Financial Times, 1987, September 3). However, if the comparison was restricted to private sector adult training the advantage to Germany would look very much better. German employees probably spend at least two times longer each year in training than their British counterparts (according to LWT, 1987, private German industrial training spending was £5 billion compared to £1 billion in Britain and another estimate put the training expenditure of German industry as high as £12 billion; Financial Times, 1988, August 25)[1].

The comparative qualifications of British managers

Britain may have a skill problem not only at the lower end of the skill range but also at the top. In Germany and the US at least half of senior managers have a degree (Lawrence, 1980; Financial Times, 1987, September 3). The recent Handy Report (Handy, 1987) suggests that only a fifth of British managers have a university degree. In addition there is a qualitative difference. Accountancy and marketing seem to be more strongly represented amongst British managers than engineers or technicians. In Germany engineering and technical qualifications are important leading to a commitment to Technik as opposed to short-term financial results which is a further boost to labour productivity. It has been alleged that British manufacturing is short of engineers and scientists[2] (Finneston, 1980) but the supply is likely to be related to the comparatively poor pay for engineers as compared with finance and marketing personnel, which may suggest that firms have a low level of demand for engineers and technicians (Silberstone, 1987). What is certain is that a much smaller proportion of the total supply of UK scientists and engineers is working in the civilian sector. Most are engaged in military research which is comparatively more important in Britain than almost any other Western economy outside America (Kaldor, Sharp and Walker, 1986; and below).

Questions have also been raised about the structure of

management in the UK since British companies have tended to be more de-centralised than those in Germany (Child and Keiser, 1979). There was a lag behind America in the development of clear management hierarchies and also in the direct management of the production process in highly mechanised assembly line industries (Crafts, 1988a, 1988b). The social background of British managers has also been the subject of comparative investigation. Swords-Isherwood (1980) suggested that as compared to managers in France, Germany and America, which generally had a well educated middle class background, British managers were more likely to have worked their way up from the shop-floor. If this were true it might be argued that British factories should have been characterised by more solidarity and better industrial relations than was in fact the case. Yet it has been suggested that the highly skilled German shop-floor labour force, in contrast to its unskilled British counterpart, shares with its management middle class values and aspirations which are conducive to the achievement of rapid improvement in productivity (Lawrence, 1980; Johnson, 1984).

Overmanning and loss of working time

Apart from skill levels, the work force affects productivity through absenteeism, labour relations, labour flexibility and overmanning. Other things being equal, labour productivity would be expected to be lower when absences, strikes, inflexibility and overmanning are widespread.

Labour time lost through sickness is the main cause of lost working hours. There is some evidence that the UK loses comparatively more time through illness. In 1978 8.1 per cent of working days were lost compared with 6.1 per cent in France, 5.6 per cent in Germany and under 5 per cent in the USA (Maddison, 1982). It is not clear how his comparatively high estimate for the UK can be reconciled with the much smaller rates obtained by various recent surveys of British firms (Industrial Society, 1985; CBI, 1987).

Days lost through strikes are only a small proportion of those from illness. International comparisons of strike rates are important since they may indicate the degree to which a country has relatively favourable or poor industrial relations, itself depressing labour productivity through such mechanisms as overmanning and restrictive practises. The aggregate strike rate in Britain is very much higher than that of Germany, Switzerland and Japan, and yet is not dissimilar to the US, and is lower than Italy and Canada; all of which have higher manufacturing productivity than the UK (Employment Gazette, 1984). Caves (Caves and Krause, 1980), and Davies and Caves (1983, 1987) have used econometric techniques to test whether there is any causal link between the extent of unionisation and stoppages in an industry, and the comparative productivity which that industry achieves relative to the US. The variables are by themselves not statistically significant, however, they do become significant if

17

a regional location variable is included, this indicated that labour relations were more of a problem in the "North" than the "South" of Britain. Prais (1981a) showed how large plants in the UK were particularly strike-prone when compared with comparable companies in Germany or the US. Britain could be handicapped he adds, in those industries (e.g. metals, engineering and chemicals) where plant size economies are important; industries in which Britain's comparative productivity appears to be especially poor.

It is difficult to make quantitative comparisons of labour flexibility in various economies, however, it may be indicative that since 1979 there have been substantial changes in British working practises (Wenban-Smith, 1982; Boakes, 1988) and at the same time productivity growth has exceeded that of almost all other OECD economies. The very rapid growth of real wages in Britain since 1980 may represent the "bribe" given by employers in order to extract improvements in working practises. Not the least of these improvements has been a reduction in the extent of overmanning from the levels reported by earlier studies (Hutton, 1953; Pratten and Atkinson, 1976; Prais, 1981a).

Labour force: summary

The UK labour force appears deficient in almost every dimension. The flows of technically or vocationally trained are smaller than in other advanced economies. British managers are more likely to be unqualified or, if qualified are unlikely to have any technical background. There are comparatively few scientists in civilian R and D. Historically absenteeism and strike rates have exceeded those of other industrial economies. Whilst previous studies have demonstrated the very wide range of deficiencies of British labour and management, they have generally not been able to show how, at a practical level specific characteristics are translated into productivity shortfall. Part of the problem is that questions of labour force training, motivation and competence of management become mixed with those of the appropriateness and utilisation of machinery and plant size economies of scale. It is still unclear, for example, whether the last eight years have seen a permanent supply side improvement in British labour relations and flexibility and hence in the prospects for productivity growth.

Demand

The level, variability, and growth in demand have all an important impact on productivity. In post-war Britain a relatively low level of aggregate demand (Eatwell, 1982; Pollard, 1982) was held to discourage investment and hence productivity growth. Pratten (1976) has argued that the level of output per head has a strong positive association with the rate at which output is produced. A higher level of demand allows a higher rate of output, although Daly, Hitchens and Wagner (1985) found little variation in running speeds of German and British metal working machines. Variable demand can discourage investment and therefore productivity and the UK had an exaggerated "stop-go" cycle during 1945-73, although Whiting (1976) doubts if demand variability in the UK was any different from other Continental economies.

Plant size

It has been suggested that in most industries unit costs will decline as the size of total plant output increases and fixed costs are better spread. Whilst there are diseconomies arising from increased scale of operation, Pratten (1971) argued that existing British plants were generally smaller than the size at which diseconomies outweighed economies. However Caves and Davies (1983, 1987) found no statistically significant association between the UK/US comparative productivity and the UK industry median plant size. They suspected that this was because poor industrial relations were swamping the benefits of large plant operation. Prais (1981a) used national statistics to show that median plant sizes were not very different in Britain, Germany, and the US. In 1970-73 they were; 440 in the UK; 410, in Germany; 380, in the USA. However, the size distributions are different and Germany is marked by a preponderance of giant plants in certain industries. In motor vehicles, iron and steel, chemicals, machine tools and office equipment, the German medians were two to three times greater than the equivalent British industries. Yet the Germans also had a proportionately larger number of Handwerk plants of less than four employees. In some sectors, conspicuously food and tobacco, Britain had the size advantage.

Firm size

Costs such as administrative, financial, marketing, distribution and research can be better spread in the larger firm yet it has been argued that UK manufacturing took longer than either its American or German counterpart to enter the era of the large corporation. This has been attributed to an indifference to scientific application and new production methods amongst poor quality British managers who were reluctant to challenge the unions' close control of work organisation (Sanderson, 1972; Coleman and Macleod, 1986). Imperfections in UK capital markets may also have been an obstacle to the development of large firms (Hannah, 1974; Kennedy, 1987). Pratten (1986) has noted that whereas the largest companies in the UK take a large proportion of total output of manufacturing, they are still relatively small by international standards. He compared British Leyland with Volkswagen, and GEC with Siemens and in both these cases the Germans had a turnover size advantage of a factor of two to three. While ICI was approximately the same size as its German competitors, there were three German firms of this size; BASF, Bayer, Hoescht (other examples of a firm size disadvantage could include Jaguar relative to BMW and Daimler-Benz, or Rolls-Royce relative to General Electric and Pratt and Whitney). However, larger firm size need not be associated with better productivity. In an earlier study Pratten matched 50 firms in Sweden with the same number in the UK. The Swedes averaged only half the British size and yet had 50 per cent better productivity.

Research and development

Lower productivity in Britain could reflect a low rate of technological innovation of either products or processes. There is evidence that the UK commits a smaller amount of resources to R and D than do other major advanced economies. In 1983 the UK spent 2.3 per cent of GDP on R and D compared with 2.7 per cent in the US, 2.6 per cent in Germany and 2.5 per cent in Japan and all these economies had the advantage of having higher GDP's per head than Britain (The Times, 1987, February 16). The picture looks worse for civilian R and D alone, as Table 2.2 demonstrates.

Table 2.2
Civilian R and D as a percentage of GDP

	1979	1982
UK	1.6	1.6
USA	1.8	2.0
France	1.4	1.6
Sweden	1.7	1.7
Germany	2.2	2.5
Japan	2.5	2.5

Source: Kaldor, Sharp, and Walker (1986).

The high proportion of defence R and D in the UK it has been argued crowds out civilian development, and the defence-orientated industries tend to have low productivity growth (because of lack of competition and cost-plus contracts, Levitt, 1985; Kaldor et al, 1986). Patel and Pavitt (1987, 1988) have demonstrated that British manufacturing's poor input of R and D is matched by an inferior output of innovation (as measured by the national origin of patents taken out in the USA).

It is not clear why British manufacturing places a low priority upon civilian research nor why this should have been such a persistent phenomenon (Sanderson, 1972; Pavitt and Soete, 1982). It may reflect the "short-termism" of City financial institutions or perhaps it is a cultural trait; the cult of the "practical man" traced by Wiener (1981) and Barnett (1986). The 1928-29 Balfour Commission (Final Report of The Committee on Industry and Trade, Command Papers) complained "nothing less than a revolution is needed in their (i.e. British industrialists and educationalists) general outlook on science". The findings of The House of Lords Select Committee in 1987 were not very different

(The Times, 1987, February 16).

Cultural and institutional factors

It has been argued that the decisive reason for lower productivity
in Britain lies with its culture (Caves and Krause, 1980; Wiener,
1981). For some reason the supply of entrepreneurship (defined as
the ability to realise new possibilities as regards products,
processes and markets) is held to be more inelastic than   in
competitor economies. It has also be claimed that other countries
have a better "work ethic" or "ethos" in the   sense that the
labour force as a whole sees good work as an end in itself quite
apart from any monetary rewards they may receive for doing it
(Morishima, 1984; and Yankelovich, 1984). Since it has also   been
argued that Britain   industrialised first for distinctive cultural
reasons, this leaves the problem of why these cultural advantages
faded away.

Perhaps the Empire encouraged complacency about safe markets
(Barnett, 1987)? Or, maybe the industrial middle class succumbed
to gentrification by the ancient upper class and so lost the
profit motive (Wiener, 1981)? Unlike the Continental and Japanese
economies, the twentieth century British economy never had to
undergo the shock of defeat in war or conquest. Olson (1982) has
argued that such a settled environment could lead to the
development of strong collective interest groups which give the
economy the disease of "institutional schlerosis". Amongst such
groups he would number trade unions. Olson's thesis would explain
the post-1979 burst of productivity growth as the product of the
shock created by the 1979-81 recession. It is undoubtedly true
that the experience of 1933-45 played a part in prompting German
trade unions and management to seek a "social peace" through a
common acceptance of a social market economy (Dahrendorf, 1957;
Lawrence, 1980). There is also some irony in the fact that the
British occupational authorities and TUC were instrumental in
imposing on Germany the highly successful system of a small number
of industrial unions (Johnson, 1984) in contrast to the continued
proliferation in post-war Britain of the early industrial craft
unions.

The financial system represents another institutional factor
which has immense influence over economic destiny and during the
nineteenth century finance capital in the UK became more and more
concentrated in the City of London. It has been argued (Glyn and
Harrison, 1980) that the keepers of British finance in the City
are fundamentally out of sympathy with the industrialists in the
north of the country who require their finance. This is explained
in terms of different educational and social backgrounds. It may
be for this cultural reason that British financial institutions
invest so much abroad as opposed to in UK manufacturing, or it may
just be that UK manufacturing has historically had too low a rate
of return. Britain has evolved a very different system of
industrial financing than that found in Germany, France or Japan.
In the UK banks are reluctant to take equity investment in

manufacturing firms. There is no equivalent to the German industrial banks which have proved effective at monitoring management for high risk, high pay off projects (Tilly, 1986). The result is that UK firms are much more reliant upon stock market funding than are their competitors. The investors may be short sighted and may be too much concerned with short-term profits (Nickell and Wadhani, 1987). It should however be noted that it has also been claimed that British management efficiency was impeded prior to 1948 (and the Companies Act of that year) for because the take over mechanism was held to be too weak (Hannah, 1974).

The cultural contribution to relative low productivity is inherently difficult to quantify. Nevertheless, its existence is not in doubt (though a rare dissident view is provided by Rubinstein, 1988). One of the best "experimental" demonstrations of its importance is the fact that the British plants of foreign-controlled multinational enterprises generally have lower productivity than the non-UK plants of the same international firms. After allowing for the "economic" factors (rate of output, capacity utilisation, output mix and labour mix) Pratten (1976) reckoned that half of the intra-company Anglo-German difference had to be explained by "behavioural" causes and about one-third of the Anglo-American gap. Problems of strikes, absenteeism, labour inflexibility, poor attitudes and inadequate training of management have already been discussed and these may be symptoms of a deeper social malaise (Finegold and Soskice, 1988). If British society has in some sense been a brake on the achievement of higher productivity levels it is obviously a very important question as to whether some of these attitudinal and institutional obstacles have been removed since 1979. Unfortunately it is still too early to judge the success of the so-called enterprise culture.

Multinationals

It has been argued that in-coming multinational enterprises (MNEs) are beneficial to the productivity of the host economy (Pratten, 1976;Dunning, 1985). This is because in a world of imperfect markets they may be the most efficient way of transferring superior knowledge about technology or working practises. In recent years the UK has become the prime site for American and Japanese firms wishing to locate within the European Community. According to the above theoretical argument, this trend should be encouraged as being likely to lead to long run productivity gains (and this seems to have been the policy stance of the Conservative Administrations since 1979). However, foreign ownership per se may not improve productivity. There is evidence that foreign owned plants in the UK have frequently been out-performed by their Continental and US counterparts. The alleged under-performance of UK Ford[3] and General Motor's plants in the 1970s became notorious (Hill, 1985, and Pratten 1976, instance other examples) and emphasises once again the importance of labour and management[4] (albeit some foreign owned subsidiaries in the UK do claim to have achieved productivity comparable to the home country; German Chamber of Commerce and Industry, 1989).

Industrial structure

Industrial structure could effect the UK's comparative productivity if the UK has proportionately more of those industries which have low levels of absolute productivity everywhere. Smith, Hitchens and Davies (1982) took data for 1967-68 and asked the question what the UK's average manufacturing productivity would be if it had the same industrial structure as the US or Germany. They could find no substantial difference between the actual and the structurally adjusted productivity. Thus the UK's "productivity problem" would appear to be one of having a lower productivity across almost all industries rather than having the "wrong" mix of industries.

Government policy

The final factor which we review is government policy. Policy can impact upon productivity through a wide variety of means. The general macro-economic stance may make conditions more or less favourable to productivity growth through the level, stability and growth of demand. According to such a view, a restrictive monetary or fiscal policy should be damaging to productivity growth. In almost every Western economy the dis-inflationary policies instituted after the 1973 OPEC shock were accompanied by a severe slow-down in the rate of productivity growth (Matthews, 1982). There were almost certainly other forces at work but demand restriction must bear some responsibility for the deceleration. However, during 1979-81 fiscal policy in the UK was highly restrictive and yet this was a prelude to what has sometimes been called "Mrs Thatcher's productivity miracle" (Pratten, 1985). If there is any connection between government macro-policy and the recent rapid productivity growth it is largely an unintended effect of what may have been policy mistakes. The real appreciation of sterling exchange rate during 1979-81 acted as a shock to British manufacturing which removed extensive overmanning.

Through acting on capital markets, industrial relations, education, innovation and incentives to MNEs, public policy could also have an effect upon productivity but the literature concerning these areas suggests that state action has so far failed to do much to remove the factors which inhibit the attainment of foreign productivity levels. Morris (1985) and Eatwell (1982) argue that post-war Britain failed to develop a consistent industrial policy comparable to that said to have been administered by the French Commissariat Generale du Plan or the Japanese MITI. The recent Conservative Administrations to some extent reflect a reaction against earlier interventionist attempts[5] to achieve higher British output and productivity growth.

However, in the field of vocational education and training they have taken an increasingly interventionist and centralising line. Whilst the aim has been to create the conditions for faster industrial growth there is a lack of coherence in the proliferation of initiatives. The Technical and Vocational Education Initiative is designed to keep youths in the full-time educational system beyond the age of sixteen so as to attain a technical education, but the Youth Training System offers them stronger incentives (allowances and better prospects of eventual employment) to leave school at sixteen. The City Technology Colleges offer a further strand in an already confusing picture. Are these an attempt to succeed where the Technical Schools of the 1944 Education Act failed (Finegold and Soskice, 1988)? Neither educational policy nor industrial policy offers the magic lever which government simply has to pull to produce an immediate improvement in the standards of manufacturing performance. Japanese and French "industrial policies" may only have succeeded because of factors unique to their economic, political and cultural histories. At the same time, the post-war productivity growth in Germany and Italy probably owes little to direct public intervention in industry (indeed, Britton, Eastwood, and Major (1986) argue Italian growth was achieved in spite of government policy). Finegold and Soskice (1988) suggest that in the absence of the peculiar German institutions (strong employer organisations and centralised unions) the German system of apprenticeship training could not work in Britain. Campbell, Sorge and Warner (1990) emphasise that British engineering companies give their workers comparatively limited and specialised training because this is what their product strategies require. Those strategies are in turn driven by those realities of the UK finance market (short-term profits) and labour market (fear of trained labour being poached) which are not present in Germany. Thus there be may little return from slavish imitation of foreign counterparts unless this is preceded by a much greater convergence between the Britain's economic and administrative institutions and those in the relatively more successful Continental countries.

Conclusions

While the perception of Britain's relatively poor performance in manufacturing has been sufficiently widespread to cause the term the "British disease" to be applied (Allen, 1979; Caves and Krause, 1980; Crafts, 1988b), forty years of investigation have not yet provided a complete understanding of the causes of Britain's productivity shortfall. General statistical analyses such as those by Davies and Caves (1987) have shown that the productivity gap is correlated with deficiencies such as in labour training, the organisation of production and levels of managerial sophistication but they have not been able to discriminate between the impact of each factor individually. An alternative methodology of comparative factory visits (exemplified by the work of the National Institute of Economic and Social Research which involved two of the authors, and that of the Northern Ireland Economic Research Centre involving all of the authors) may be a more fruitful means of uncovering the mechanisms through which specific characteristics of British capital and labour are translated into lower productivity. This method is adopted in Part 3 where we review the performance of matched pairs of companies in Northern Ireland and West Germany.

Prior to consideration of these matched plant comparisons, Part 2 provides the foundation for our consideration of Northern Ireland's comparative performance by applying the methodology of international productivity comparisons to an inter-regional comparison between Northern Ireland and Great Britain. Parts 2 and 3 indicate that the performance of NI manufacturing is of special interest since it displays particularly severe symptoms of the general British manufacturing disease which has been noted in this Chapter (with stress being on deficiencies on the supply side and in human resources). Despite the "productivity miracle" since 1981 it is not clear to what extent market profit signals give UK firms the incentive to correct the shortfall relative to Germany in their shop-floor training, management skills, product quality and research and development (Crafts, 1988a). In the absence of such signals it is not possible to be sanguine about the long run capability of UK manufacturing to close the productivity gap with Germany and other advanced industrial economies. The situation in Northern Ireland is even more complex because, as we will show in Chapters 17, very high rates of grant aid dampen the incentive to make productivity improvements relative to either Great Britain or Germany. Such considerations form the basis of the policy recommendations which are made in Part 4 with a view to improving NI's comparative productivity performance (these recommendations are also informed by a comparison of productivity in NI and the Republic of Ireland; Chapter 19).

Notes

1. Whilst it is Britain's educational shortfall relative to Germany which has received the most prolonged attention it also true that the British technical and vocational training system is deficient compared to almost every other industrial economy; Britton, Eastwood and Major, 1986; Campaign for Work, 1988; Steedman, 1988.

2. The Engineering Council suggests that Japan in 1987 had an in-take of 82,000 persons to higher education engineering courses whereas Britain had only 16,000; five times the input but only double the UK's population.

3. Even in 1989, after several years of generally rapid growth in the British motor industry, the output per head of Ford's continental plants was estimated to be 40-65 per cent higher

than that of the Dagenham plant (Financial Times, 1989, January
30). At the same time there was one shop steward for every 55
manuals in Dagenham compared to one for every 373 in Genk
(Belgium).

4. As does the performance of Britain's own, home-grown
multinationals. It may be significant that British MNEs are
unusual in the extent to which they have re-located output and
employment away from their home country. A second notable
characteristic is the relative under-representation of UK MNEs in
the high-technology, high value-added areas. The aggregate
performance of UK manufacturing may suffer from the bias towards
retailing, clothing, food, drink and tobacco.

5. As shown by the attack on regional policy (the real value of
Regional Development Grants has been halved since 1980 as
automatic assistance is phased out), investment subsidies (tax
allowances scrapped in 1984), indicative planning (National
Enterprise Board abolished) and "corporatism" (NEDO and MSC
marginalised).

PART 2

THE COMPARATIVE PRODUCTIVITY OF NORTHERN IRELAND AND GREAT BRITAIN

"And he gave it for his opinion, that whoever could make two ears of corn or two blades of grass to grow upon a spot of ground where only one grew before, would deserve better of mankind, and do a more essential service to his country than the whole race of politicians put together".

Jonathan   Swift, Gulliver's Travels, " Brobdingnag"

3 Methods and data sources

"Political economists should ... produce figures which are roughly right instead of precisely wrong".

Samuel Brittain (1987, October 22), Financial Times

Introduction

The comparison of manufacturing productivity levels achieved in Northern Ireland (NI) and Great Britain (GB) is set out under three main headings;

1. measurement of differences in the level of manufacturing productivity between NI and GB;

2. measurement of the change in NI's comparative productivity performance over time;

3. investigation of a number of possible sources of explanation of the observed differences in levels.

   The justification for the examination set out in this paper arises from the implications which low comparative productivity have for competitiveness, employment and output (Chapter 21). In NI, as we shall show, levels of productivity lie below those achieved in GB and while it is possible for a low productivity industry to remain competitive by maintaining relatively low costs, there is evidence that such costs in Northern Ireland in the absence of subsidies are at least as great as those incurred in GB; Appendix A focuses particularly on unit costs and shows that these have risen in NI in the last decade and are now higher than in GB. This disadvantage is modified by a higher rate of grant aid which reduces costs relative to GB. Appendix B compares the level of grant aid and shows this is greater than for other peripheral regions within the British Isles.

Consideration is restricted to the productivity of manufacturing alone as opposed to that of the the whole economy including services (private and public) and the extractive sector (mining and agriculture). Whilst the preponderance of non-manufacturing activities in Gross Domestic Product (GDP) and their supply linkages with the manufacturing sector makes the service sector worthy of attention, justification for examination of manufacturing alone is partly pragmatic; productivity levels and growth in services are usually difficult to measure (Smith and Hitchens, 1985; and Murfin, 1987; provide examples of statistical studies of service sector productivity). The more substantive reason is that international comparisons have shown that the bulk of the UK's lag behind American and Continental standards of income per capita (Gross Domestic Product per person) is attributable to a productivity shortfall in manufacturing (Smith, Hitchens, and Davies, 1982; Smith and Hitchens, 1985; Roy, 1987; HM Treasury, 1989). That is, if UK manufacturing could achieve the same levels of output per head as West Germany or the USA much of the gap in material living standards would disappear. Northern Ireland is a low GDP per capita regional economy even by the standards of the average UK income per head (Chapter 21). Thus substantial income gains could be expected from a closing of the manufacturing productivity gap with Great Britain (though the gain would be smaller than that for the UK as a whole if UK manufacturing achieved international productivity levels).

In making comparisons the present study updates that of Isles and Cuthbert (1957). They measured and compared labour productivity in NI with GB for the 1930s using the then available Censuses of Production and basic methodology follows that adopted by Smith, Hitchens and Davies (1982).

Since Isles and Cuthbert's investigations Britain's position in the international productivity league table has dropped sharply (thereby affecting the standard of comparison) and it is important to place the comparisons of Northern Ireland to Great Britain against the background of the UK's comparatively poor productivity position as summarised in Part 1. NI's lag behind the rest of the UK must be interpreted as a poor performance even by the standards of a poor performer. American manufacturing productivity levels are three-to-four times higher than those achieved in NI and German levels at least 75-100 per cent greater. That position is worse than the gap obtaining between those countries and the UK even though over the long run of the last sixty years NI has achieved a faster productivity growth rate than GB. In Chapter 8 the international perspective on comparative productivity is considered more fully (while Chapters 19 and 20 compare NI with the Republic of Ireland).

It might be asked why it is of interest to compare Northern Ireland with another economy (that is, GB) which is clearly so far behind the frontier of international best practise. Policy makers would wish to know to what extent the reasons for the generally low productivity of the UK (described in detail in Part 1) also provide the explanation for NI's comparatively low productivity within the UK; is NI only the most severe case of the "British Disease"?[1] (Appendix D shows that Northern Irish manufacturing output per head is substantially lower than not only the South East of England but also Northern England, Scotland and Wales; this suggests comparatively low NI productivity cannot be explained solely in terms of the general problems of peripheral, structurally disadvantaged, depressed regions). Northern Ireland's productivity performance relative to the rest of the UK is important because at the very least NI firms have to be competitive within the UK administrative context (to be, for example, price competitive at a given sterling exchange rate). Policy makers would also wish to know if NI's higher rate of grant aid has boosted the corporate performance of NI or whether larger subsidies have cushioned NI firms against the consequences of inferior productivity. It is for these reasons very important to find how NI firms perform in comparison with the average in Great Britain. The proposed completion of the the European Community's Internal Market by 1992, the possible entrance of the UK into the European Monetary System[2] and the increasing role of Brussels[3] in shaping regional policy mean that the arguments for comparison with GB apply even more powerfully to comparisons with Western European best practice; usually West Germany. Part 3 makes such comparisons with Germany.

Methods and measurements

Labour productivity rather than some measure of the combined productivity of labour and capital (total factor productivity[4]) is the concern of this study. It is defined as value added in production divided by the total number of persons engaged in that production.

The Census gives data on the number of persons engaged in production and includes both full and part-time employees, managers, and working proprietors (in establishments employing more than 20 persons, together with an estimate for the numbers employed at smaller establishments). Two measures of, "value-added", are recorded: net output and gross value-added. Each is calculated by subtracting from the annual sales value of firms' production (net of indirect taxes) the cost of industrial materials and services (including the cost of materials, fuels and sub-contracting). Gross value-added (GVA) differs from net output by additionally excluding non-industrial services (e.g. rents, rates, transport payments to outside organisations, professional services, and marketing). Gross value-added is a closer measure of the required value-added generated by the firm itself than is net output but has only been calculated since 1973, for that reason gross value-added has been the preferred measure when calculating comparative productivity levels while net output is employed to estimate productivity trends.

Calculation of trends in productivity growth and comparison of productivity levels over long runs of years involves Census data based on several Standard Industrial Classifications (SICs); during the 1951-86 period four are involved (1948, 1958, 1968 and 1980). Given the aim of as much consistency as possible in the definition of a given industry several approaches are employed to maintain comparability.

First, in some cases there are sufficiently detailed Census data to allow productivity levels to be adjusted for the change in SIC. Data for all manufacturing in 1980-85 can be adjusted from the 1980 SIC to the 1968 SIC to give a consistent longitudinal run of data.

However, the problem of definitional changes is minimised if one restricts long run productivity growth analysis is restricted to a few very broadly defined industrial groups (this is because most definitional changes affect closely allied industries but not large groups such as engineering). Thus long run growth rate analysis is restricted to the four sectors of food, drink and tobacco, textiles, clothing and all engineering which in aggregate did not experience significant classificational modifications during 1951-86 (the official statistics remove man-made fibres from textiles after 1980 but we were able to add it back to maintain long run consistency). In any case some limitation to the data from the longitudinal point of view is acceptable if the primary interest is in a cross-sectional comparison, that is if mineral products in 1935 is defined differently from mineral products in 1985 as long as the NI and GB definitions are consistent in each year.

Data sources and productivity measures

Data sources Two major sources of the data employed are: The Report on The Census of Production (UK) and The Report on the Census of Production of Northern Ireland.

In the main data are taken from a single regional table of the UK Census (either those in the summary volume or those in the individual industry Business Monitors) in order to ensure comparability. More detailed data down to the individual industry level are provided by the Business Monitors which are published annually by Minimum List Headings (1968 SIC) and Group/Activity (1980 SIC). Occasionally comparisons required the use of the NI Census which, unlike the UK Census, restricts its analyses to larger firms (of greater than 20 employees). Table 3.1 gives an indication of the extent to which it is legitimate to compare data drawn from the two different Censuses. It shows the size of the difference between estimates of GVA per head for NI based on the NI and the UK Censuses in 1983.

Table 3.1
A comparison of productivity estimates for
Northern Ireland drawn from two census sources

Estimates in the NI Census expressed as a
percentage of that shown in the UK Census

Manufacture of non-metallic mineral Products	105.1
Chemicals	98.7
Metal goods not elsewhere specified	95.3
Mechanical engineering	99.1
Office equipment, data processing, electrical, and electronic engineering	99.9
Motor vehicles	100.0
Other transport vehicles	99.5
Instrument engineering	121.6*
Food, drink and tobacco	100.9
Textiles	100.8
Leather, footwear and clothing	97.5
Timber and furniture	93.0
Paper, printing and publishing	99.5
Rubber, plastics and other manufacturing	91.9*
All manufacturing	99.0

Notes: SIC Groups 21, 22 and 26 are not shown separately in the NI Census.

* See Appendix E.3.

Source: Unless otherwise stated the Tables in Part 2 derive from the Census of Production.

If the qualifications noted in Appendix E.3 are applied so that the results for instrument engineering and rubber and plastics etc. are excluded as reflecting some major inadequacy in the data, then in most of the remaining cases it does not matter much whether the NI or the UK Census is used.

Productivity measures Productivity calculations are based on output per worker-year otherwise known as output per head. A preferred measure of labour input would take account of the number of hours worked but this measure is acceptable because average weekly hours worked in NI and GB are almost identical. Full-time manual males in all manufacturing in NI averaged weekly hours which were 97.7 per cent of those worked in GB (for the years 1973 to 1985). Appendix C compares the comparative productivity ratios obtained by using per head as opposed to per hour measures.
Net output or GVA per head are calculated from the Annual Census of Production. Data drawn from the Census have the disadvantage of being based on an incomplete sample of firms excluding the smallest firms and most of the self-employed. No

ideal measure of output per employee is otherwise available and this is the best source of consistent data covering a reasonable span of years as well as one which measures manufacturing output and employment together.

Notes

1. This view is implied by Lord Kaldor's comment that the United Kingdom was in danger of becoming to the EEC what NI was already within the UK, i.e. a chronically depressed region.

2. At present NI firms try to retain international price competitiveness within the context of the real Sterling exchange rate. If the UK became a full member of the EMS Northern Ireland firms would have the problem of trying to align their wage and productivity movements within what is in effect a Deutsche Mark zone. Southern Irish firms have had this difficulty since 1978.

3. The European Commission already limits the maximum rate of subsidy on major shipbuilding orders (currently 28 per cent). Thus Harland and Wolff's price competitiveness is very much determined by its relative productivity.

4. GVA will therefore include that part of transport costs which is internal to the firm, e.g. if the firm has its own fleet of delivery vans. Since the data for total transport costs in 1968 (the last year in which it is available from the Census) suggests that "internal" transport costs are a significant proportion of the whole, the implication is that NI's comparative GVA per head is being biased upwards (because it includes part of transport costs and these are probably higher in NI than GB; see Chapter 6).

4 Levels of output per head in Northern Ireland as compared to Great Britain

"The modes of thought of men, the whole outlook on affairs, the grouping of parties, all encountered violent and tremendous changes in the deluge of the world, but as the deluge subsides and the waters fall short, we see the dreary steeples of Fermanagh and Tyrone emerging once again".

Winston Churchill (1922)

Comparative productivity performance

Table 4.1 sets out the comparative NI/GB manufacturing productivity levels for the years 1973 to 1985. In all years the NI level of value-added per head lies below that for GB and ranges from a shortfall of 6 per cent in 1973 to one of 26 per cent in 1978. The average productivity shortfall is seventeen per cent over the whole period.

The comparative productivities of individual industries

The best available data for testing whether a productivity gap also exists at the individual industry level in recent years is that shown in the Census for the Groups and Activities of the 1980 SIC in 1979 and 1984. In 1979 GVA per head comparisons are possible in 99 cases and in 1984 in 84. (Appendix E discusses the sources of this data and its reliability. Appendix F tabulates it).

These data on industrial comparative productivities have been used to test whether it is possible to characterise in a general sense the type of industries where NI has high comparative productivities and those where NI has low comparative productivities. Does NI perform better, in comparative terms, when the industry in question has a high absolute level of productivity and is of large size in NI? The importance of size of individual industries, and the absolute level of productivity achieved are examined using the 1979 Census data for which the greatest number of divisions of activities are available.

Table 4.1

The Northern Ireland level of productivity in all manufacturing as a percentage of the Great Britain level

	Gross Value-added per employee (GB=100)
1973	94
1974	83
1975	93
1976	88
1977	81
1978	74
1979	79
1980	79
1981	88
1982	79
1983	81
1984	81
1985	78
1973-79 Average	85
1980-85 Average	81
1973-85 Average	83

Note: All Manufacturing definition follows the 1968 SIC classification and the Census data for 1980-85 is converted to this.

The theoretical case for examining the size of industry (in output terms) rests on the scope for gains from external economies and specialisation leading to better productivity (Smith, Hitchens and Davies, 1982; Smith, 1985). In attempts to account for variations in industrial comparative productivities between America and Britain the size variable has sometimes been specified as the industry output in one economy as a proportion of that in the other (Smith, 1985; Davies and Caves, 1987). In the case of NI relative to GB it was felt more appropriate (given that almost all the NI proportional sizes would be under 2 per cent of

GB) to use the absolute level of value-added in Northern Ireland as the measure of size. The strength of any economies of scale was investigated by an ordinary least squares regression of NI's absolute level of GVA in that industry against its comparative productivity ratio with GB. In fact some of the largest industries in Northern Ireland, namely man-made fibres, rubber and milk did register productivity levels in excess of their GB counterparts. However, taking all 99 industries the association whilst positive was not statistically significant.

The absolute level of productivity achieved in an industry has sometimes been used as a proxy for the degree of technology intensity and there is some evidence (albeit, the results found by previous studies have usually not been statistically significant) that this may be negatively associated with the UK's productivity compared to either Germany or the USA (Smith, Hitchens and Davies, 1982; Smith, 1985). It is sometimes suggested that Britain's industrial performance is most outclassed by competitors in the more technologically intensive sectors (Midland Bank Review, 1986). We therefore postulate a negative association between the comparative productivity achieved by NI in an industry and the level of GVA in GB[1]. In a regression of comparative productivity with the absolute productivity level in GB a non-significant negative association is obtained. Thus regression estimates suggest that industry size and the level of productivity are non-significant in statistical terms but the regression coefficients indicate the same direction suggested by theory.

Distribution of NI industries according to their comparative productivities

NI has lower productivity in a majority of cases (68 of the 99 industry groups in 1979, and 64 of the 84 in 1984). Table 4.2 shows that in both years most NI employees in manufacturing are concentrated in industries which have lower output per head than GB.

Table 4.2
The percentage distribution of manufacturing output
and employment by relative
Northern Ireland/Great Britain performance

	1979 Output (%)	1979 Employment (%)	1984 Output (%)	1984 Employment (%)
GVA per capita less than GB	57	64	67	73
GVA per capita greater than GB	43	36	33	27
	100	100	100	100

Note: The sample industries represent 98 per cent of NI manufacturing employment in 1979 and 93 per cent in 1984 (refer to Appendix E and F).

Between two-thirds and three-quarters of NI employees are in Activities with productivities lower than their GB counterparts. Not only are most NI employees in industries which have productivities lower than those attained in GB but the majority of employees are concentrated in industries where comparative productivity levels are between 75 per cent and 100 per cent of those achieved by the counterpart industry in GB. Only a small minority are in industries which either have extremely poor or extremely good relative performances. In 1979 only six per cent of employees were in activities with productivity levels less than half of those attained by counterparts in GB and less than two per cent were in those which have levels more than one-and-a-half times those of GB. In 1984 the magnitudes were 1.7 per cent and 2.2 per cent respectively.

The most important conclusion to be drawn is that NI has lower productivity in all but a minority of cases. Taking the two measurement years together NI had better productivity than GB in only 20-30 industries out of a total of 80-100 comparisons made in each of the years. Between two-thirds and three-quarters of NI manufacturing workers are in industries which have comparative productivities less than GB and half of employees are concentrated in industries achieving 75 to 100 per cent of the GB level. The number of industries with extremely poor comparative performances (i.e. achieving less than 75 per cent of the GB level) is small and comparable to the number which have higher levels than GB.

Sectoral comparative productivities in 1985

Table 4.3 shows the most recent comparative productivity data available at the time of writing. Data are for 1985 and are at a high level of aggregation compared with those used in the preceding analysis. The calculations show that NI's GVA per head for all manufacturing industries was 80 per cent that of the GB level in 1985.

Reliability of the results

Data for all manufacturing The question of the reliability of the results arises because of the large year-on-year variability observed in some of the comparative productivity calculations. Comparative productivity for all manufacturing varied between a best performance of 94 per cent in 1973 and a worst performance of 74 per cent in 1978. Some of the variation can be accounted for by trends in comparative productivity (long run historical trends are considered below). However, some of the large year-on-year changes observed (the greatest being a gain in the comparative productivity from 83 per cent in 1974 to 93 per cent in 1975) may reflect an underlying unreliability in the data. Nevertheless, though the precise magnitude of NI's comparative productivity in any given year may be subject to uncertainty, one can be satisfied that NI's productivity level is in fact lower than GB given that it is lower in each of the years 1973 to 1985.

Table 4.3
Northern Ireland's GVA per head relative to Great Britain, 1985

(GB=100)

Metal manufacture	98
Extraction of minerals	63
Manufacture of non-metallic mineral products	91
Chemicals	96
Man-made fibres	133
Metal goods not elsewhere specified	88
Mechanical engineering	102
Office equipment and data processing	44
Electrical and electronic engineering	78
Motor vehicles	100
Other transport equipment	40
Instrument engineering	81
Food, drink, and tobacco	103
Textiles	83
Leather	87
Footwear and clothing	88
Timber and furniture	82
Paper, printing and publishing	83
Rubber and plastics	96
Other manufacturing	91
All manufacturing	80

Data for finest disaggregation of industries: 3 to 4-digits Data
problems underlying the highly disaggregated comparative
productivity estimates for 1979 and 1984 are described in Appendix
E. While the comparative productivity estimates are more reliable
than those which could be made for earlier years when many
industry values were undisclosed on grounds of company
confidentiality, two data problems presented themselves. The first
arose from NI's productivity being estimated from a "residual"
which includes another UK region. The second imprecision was
caused by rounding errors. These two data problems are considered
in more detail in Appendix E, and Appendix F where industries
are listed with their comparative productivity attainment in 1979
and 1984 together with an assessment of the basic reliability of
the data.

Data for broad industrial groups: 2-digits disaggregation The
Census estimates of comparative gross value-added per head are
examined for individual years between 1973 and 1985, for each of
fifteen broad industrial sectors (see Table 4.4). While the range
of estimates is wide in many sectors, for example in chemicals
this varies between a 22 per cent Northern Ireland advantage in
1973 to a disadvantage of 55 per cent relative to GB in 1981,
there is a high degree of consistency in the direction of the
estimates. Where average productivity is below that of the

39

comparable GB sector we find that in most years the measured productivity gap continues this trend, and conversely, where Northern Ireland's productivity exceeds that found in Great Britain again annual observations show this trend continuing.

Given that value-added largely consists of wages and profits one might expect some variation in GVA being driven by annual fluctuations in profits (the wage bill is likely to be more stable). Examination of the annual changes in nominal value-added in NI and GB suggests that it is variability in the NI growth rate rather than that in GB which is primarily responsible for the instability in the comparative productivity ratio noted above (and shown in Table 4.4). Explanations for such variability in the NI data arise from the small number of firms in each industry in NI and hence the scope for an impact arising from plant opening or closures or from the unusually good or poor performance by individual firms. Moreover the lack of homogeneity of the comparison between NI and GB so that the NI industries are making different products compared to those in GB means that shifts in demand for NI products are not synchronised with those in GB.

Table 4.4
Northern Ireland's GVA per head relative to Great Britain, 1980-85

(GB=100)

SIC (1980)	1980	1981	1982	1983	1984	1985	Average 1980-85
All manufacturing	80	90	81	84	82	80	83
Food, drink, tobacco	93	130	106	110	102	103	107
Chemicals	49	45	57	64	78	96	65
Mechanical engineering	89	106	97	87	98	102	97
Electrical engineering	65	84	94	80	91	78	82
Instrument engineering	96	98	86	104	80	81	91
Ships, aircraft	58	70	41	55	74	40	56
Metal goods nes.	82	81	83	86	88	88	85
Textiles	96	98	94	94	89	83	93
Man-made fibres	149	131	65	195	142	133	136
Leather & fur	89	108	99	80	90	87	93
Clothing & footwear	82	80	81	83	86	88	83
Timber & furniture	77	77	90	86	83	82	83
Paper, print & publish	85	86	91	93	80	83	86
Bricks, pottery and glass, and cement	110	97	110	123	91	91	104
Rubber, plastics and other manufacturing	125	102	102	86	92	96	101

Notes: nes. Not elsewhere specified. See Appendix E.3 for additional notes.

In fact taking the period 1973-85 as a whole (1980-85 is shown in Table 4.4), of the 173 annual readings at this broad level of industrial aggregation 147 lie in the same direction indicated by the average (i.e. if the average NI/GB comparative productivity

for 1980-85 lies below 100 per cent the result for a given year
also lies below 100 per cent). We would not wish to examine the
data in any other way because of: (a) the high level of
aggregation at which the comparison is made; (b) trends in
productivity differences which we examine below and (c) the
productivity impact of the entry and exit of large firms in
sectors which are otherwise small.

Historical comparison, 1912-85

Having established that in recent years labour productivity in NI
lies about 20 per cent below that of GB we now consider whether
there has been any tendency for this gap to change over time. How
has NI's productivity changed in comparison with the rest of the
UK? Table 4.5 examines comparative productivity performance since
1912.
    The historical data contained in the table illustrates the
extent of aggregate convergence in productivity levels, the
characterisation of industries according to movements in their
comparative productivity (converging, diverging, stable, volatile)
and whether there has been any long run stability in the pattern
of industrial comparative productivities. These issues of
aggregate and sectoral comparative productivity level convergence,
and of stability in the ranking of industries are considered in
turn.
    Perhaps the most striking conclusion to be drawn from the table
is that the extent of long run productivity convergence between NI
and GB manufacturing has been very limited (and Figure 4.1 shows
that NI's comparative performance has deteriorated since the early
1970s). Recent productivity levels of around four-fifths of GB
are not very different from those achieved in 1949 (71 per cent)
and 1912 (79 per cent). To the extent that post-war industrial
development policy in NI was trying to achieve parity with GB
levels of productivity it failed by a large margin.
    A more optimistic picture is given by the trends in some of the
individual industries. In mechanical engineering, aerospace,
metal goods, other manufacturing, textiles and clothing there was
a clear trend improvement (in textiles and clothing it was
concentrated from the mid-1970s onward whereas in mechanical
engineering the improvement began earlier, the data for the other
industries are insufficient to allow the beginning of the
convergence to be identified with certainty). The behaviour of the
relative productivity level in clothing etc. and textiles is also
striking. After having been stuck at about 70 per cent of the GB
level, a powerful improvement began in the 1970s. In contrast to
these industries which were improving relative to GB in only one
was there a clear downward trend; shipbuilding. Most other
industries experienced stability in their comparative
productivity; instrument and electrical engineering, leather,
bricks etc., timber and furniture, and paper etc. Food, drink,
tobacco and chemicals were rather volatile performers which in
some years lay above the GB productivity level. As a new industry

41

the scope for examination of historical trends in man-made fibres is limited but it can be noted that since its emergence it has consistently shown higher productivity levels in NI than in GB.

Table 4.5
Historical comparison of net output per head, NI relative to GB
(GB=100)

	1912	1924	1930	1935	1949	1958	1963-73 Average	1973-85 Average
All manufacturing	79	68	62	62	71	68	84	81
Food, drink, and tobacco	97	75	61	81	80	87	106	96
of which:								
Tobacco	..	..	..	..	..	84	..	78
Chemicals	75	47	75	73	88	..	121	77
Metals	..	..	..	..	..	41	72	87
Mech. engineering	54	..	..	77	65	77	89	89
Instr.engineering	53	..	..	..	91	89	76	88
Electrical eng.	54	..	..	..	75	83	79	76
Transport equip.	..	..	..	..	..	..	67	61
of which:								
Shipbuilding	109	..	..	..	..	..	59	50
Aerospace	..	..	..	..	..	..	70	101
Motor vehicles	..	..	..	..	..	..	71	78
Metal goods	78	..	..	..	..	91	89	94
Textiles	70	73	72	71	67	71	73	89
Man-made fibres	..	..	..	..	..	..	138	120
Leather and fur	..	..	..	..	..	84	78	78
Clothing, and footwear	..	70	63	63	70	71	71	80
Bricks, pottery, glass & cement	..	108	118	107	93	91	95	100
Timber, and furniture	100	78	73	73	73	95	80	91
Paper, and printing	87	77	78	75	73	75	79	82
Other manufacturing	..	..	..	..	..	60	80	103

Notes: .. : Data undisclosed. See Appendix E.3 for additional notes.

Apart from attempting to characterise industries according to the trends in their comparative productivity level there is also the question of whether there is any pattern in the ranking of industries according to their comparative productivities; are the industries which do well relative to GB always the same (and are the ones which do badly always the same)? This question is given force by the findings of international comparisons which show stability in the pattern of Anglo-American industrial comparative productivities (Smith, 1985; and Chapter 1). In fact there is only limited stability in the pattern of NI comparative productivities.

The table shows how, for example, in 1912 shipbuilding, timber etc. and food, drink and tobacco were at the top of the ranking by comparative productivity, whereas mechanical, electrical and instrument engineering came in the last three positions of this ranking. In later years timber etc. stayed in the top half of rankings whereas shipbuilding fell so as to become one of NI's worst performers in comparative terms (in 1963-73, and 1973-85 it had the worst comparative productivity of any industry). Bricks and mineral products had a high ranking in both 1958 (second) and 1973-85 (third). Food, drink and tobacco had a position in the top half of the ranking in every year. New industrial development was illustrated by man-made fibres having the best comparative productivities in 1963-73 and 1973-85, and also by chemicals (second in the ranking in 1973-85) and aerospace (third in the ranking in 1973-85). Textiles and clothing occupied a fairly stable position in the bottom half of the rankings.

The improvement in comparative net output per head between NI and GB over this time period suggest that NI has experienced a slightly faster rate of productivity growth, in real terms, over the period. Appendix G explores this conclusion further.

Notes

1. The absolute productivity level in GB is a better indicator of the technological intensity of the industry given that in most cases NI's productivity level will be below GB.

5 Explanations 1: structural differences

"Historical analysis involves different levels of precision and imprecision, and once we have become more aware than is common at present of the considerable margin of error in many of our statistical series: we shall perhaps be less worried about admittedly more difficult problems of evaluating cultural, social or ideological factors".

J. Saville, "The Development of British Industry and Foreign Competition" (1978), 1875-1914, Business History 12

Introduction

There are two features of NI's comparative productivity level which we seek to explain; first, is there any indication of why it is significantly lower than that for GB and, second, why has the differential hardly narrowed in seventy years?

The search for explanations is mainly confined to the relevant statistical data shown in the Census. Analyses are divided into two broad types; first, those arising from NI having proportionately more industries which are inherently of a low productivity type relative to other industries perhaps for technological reasons, than GB. The second group of factors explored in Chapter 6 examines potential explanations for comparatively low productivity when individual industries are matched with GB; these factors include, economies of scale (both at the level of the firm or establishment and at the industry level), ownership type, comparative levels of capital stock per head, and labour and management quality.

Industrial structure

NI's productivity shortfall is the outcome of two forces; first, in matched sector comparisons NI has lower productivity and, second, NI has proportionately more of those industries which in absolute terms are of a low productivity type. This section attempts to measure the relative strength of these forces.

The separation between the effects of structure and those of shortfall at a matched industry level is not a straightforward matter (Smith, Hitchens and Davies, 1982). Isles and Cuthbert (1957) estimated an "expected value" of what NI's aggregate level of manufacturing productivity would be if each industry within NI kept its actual level of output per head (in 1935) but contracted or expanded in size so as to have the same proportional employment size as its GB counterpart. In other words, they estimated manufacturing in NI assuming a similar industrial structure to GB. Where the estimated value exceeds the actual then NI is said to suffer from a poor structure which is more dependent on low productivity industries. The ratio of the gap to the actual productivity indicates the size of that structural effect.

In Table 5.1 we include Isles and Cuthbert's estimate of the structural effect in 1935 together with those calculated for the years 1968, 1979 and 1984 using their method. Although the "Isles and Cuthbert" method has an appeal from the policy makers perspective (for the relevant question is what would happen if lead to NI's industrial structure being more like GB's, it is much more unlikely that policies would be adopted which attempted to shift the industrial structure in GB towards that found in NI) it is not the only way in which to estimate such a structural effect.

An alternative estimates what NI's average manufacturing productivity would be if in each individual industry NI has the same level of output per head as its counterpart in GB whilst the industrial structure in NI remains the same. This so-called shift-share method removes the effect of productivity shortfall at the matched industry level and attributes the residual productivity gap at the all manufacturing level to differences in industrial structure. In other words, one is asking the question by how much is NI's manufacturing productivity lower than that of GB because of industry size and range.

Table 5.1 shows estimates based on each method and three main conclusions follow from these results. Firstly, NI does indeed have a negative structural effect. Secondly, the size of the structural effect in recent years is smaller than in 1935. Finally, there is a substantial difference in the estimated size of the effect according to which method of measurement is employed[1].

Table 5.1
Contribution of structure to Northern Ireland's
productivity shortfall

(Percentage of the total gap in average
manufacturing productivity between NI and GB)

Method	1935	1968	1979	1984
(a)	55	27	15	7
(b)	66	49	39	24

Notes: Method (a) follows that of Isles and Cuthbert (1957).
Method (b) uses a shift-share technique (as described in text).
See Appendix E for additional information on sources and
construction. The calculation for 1968 is based on a data set
kindly provided by Harris (1987).

Whereas Isles and Cuthbert were confident that NI's industrial
composition was the most important explanation of comparatively
lower productivity in NI in 1935 since it accounted for more than
one half of the productivity gap. In recent years even if the
larger shift-share values are taken for 1968, 1979 and 1984 the
structural effect whilst still substantial is no longer
predominant.

Whilst the structural effect is less important in the 1980s than
it was in the 1930s the NI and GB structures of manufacturing
employment still demonstrate substantial contrasts. Table 5.2
gives the percentage shares in total manufacturing employment of
over a dozen broadly defined industries in 1939 and 1986 for both
NI and GB and shows that by a crude measure of change the two
employment structures are still very different. This is the
absolute (disregarding negative signs) sum of the differences in
percentage shares. While at most this will take a value of 200,
the 1939 sum of differences of 74.4 and the 1986 sum of 63.7
indicate that although structures were becoming more alike, the
convergence on this measure is small. That conclusion is in
marked contrast to results obtained by a similar comparison for
the UK and West Germany where, using comparable aggregation
techniques, the sum of differences was found to be only 26.2 and
21.6 in 1952 and 1972 (Panic, 1976). The structural effect is in
fact determined by the combination of differences in the relative
productivities of industries with differences in the size of those
industries in the two regions. Hence, substantial structural
differences by themselves do not make a large structural effect
on comparative productivity inevitable.

One could hypothesise that the decrease in the importance of the
structural effect observed in Table 5.1 has involved the relative
contraction of some low productivity industries which were
over-represented in NI (such as clothing, textiles and
shipbuilding), the relative expansion of some high productivity
industries which were under-represented in NI (such as parts of
electrical, electronics, mechanicals engineering and chemicals)

and increases in the size of high productivity industries (such as man-made fibres, tobacco and aerospace).

Table 5.2
Structural change in NI and the UK

Employment in industries as % of total
in manufacturing, 1939 and 1986

	1939		1986	
	NI	GB*	NI	GB
Mineral products	1.2	4.3	5.7	4.4
Chemicals	0.2	4.1	3.3	6.6
Metal manufacture	0.0	5.2	0.3	3.3
Engineering	8.5	14.1	13.9	29.2
Motor vehicles & aircraft and other vehicles	7.5	8.4	10.1	8.6
Miscellaneous metal goods	2.2	11.8	1.9	5.9
Shipbuilding	6.9	2.3	4.1	1.6
Textiles excluding man-made	42.1	16.4	10.6	4.6
Leather and clothing	16.5	10.7	17.2	5.9
Food, drink and tobacco	9.4	9.3	19.4	10.8
Woodworking	1.8	3.6	4.7	4.0
Paper, printing, publishing	3.5	7.1	5.3	9.4
Other manufacturing	0.2	2.5	3.5	5.6

Notes: * In 1939 data was not available for GB separately. UK data is used as a very close approximation. In 1986 chemicals are defined to includes man-made fibres.

Sources: Data for 1939, Isles and Cuthbert (1957). Data for 1986, Census of Employment.

The three major low productivity industries, textiles, clothing and shipbuilding did indeed decline in their proportional importance in NI, whilst they represented almost two-thirds of NI employment (65.3 per cent) in 1939 they had a weight of less than one-third (31.9 per cent) in 1986. Whilst these industries also experienced relative decline in Great Britain this was by a lesser amount (28.3 per cent to 12.1 per cent) and so in respect to these low productivity industries NI did experience a structural convergence with GB.

NI's structural effect may also have declined because certain under-represented high productivity industries became more represented. However, it can be seen from Table 5.2 that this was not the case. The NI chemicals and engineering group grew from 8.7 per cent to 17.2 per cent over the period but the GB proportions grew by more; from 18.2 per cent to 35.2 per cent. Thus structural change was insufficient to remove the under-representation of these industries relative to GB.

47

The third potential explanation for the decline in the structural effect was an increased over-representation of such high productivity industries as man-made fibres, aerospace and tobacco. This is shown in Table 5.3.

Table 5.3
The relative growth of the high productivity level
industries in Northern Ireland
Percentage of manufacturing employment

	1951/2		1985/6	
	NI	GB	NI	GB
Aerospace	3.3	2.0	7.3	3.3
Tobacco	1.8	0.6	2.4	0.4
Man-made fibre	0.7[a]	0.4[b]	1.1	0.2

Notes: [a] 1958 Census of Production.
       [b] 1963 Census of Production.
All other data from Ministry of Labour (NI) and Census of Employment.

Thus this bloc of high productivity industries grew from being around 5 per cent of NI employment to over one-tenth. In GB however they stayed at between 3 per cent and 4 per cent of total manufacturing employment. This differential had a beneficial impact upon NI's comparative productivity[2].

The structural part of the explanation of lower productivity in NI relative to GB is therefore substantial but NI's industrial structure is now much less of an obstacle in the way of the achievement of high average productivity than it was in the 1930s. Overall NI's structure of manufacturing industries has become more like that of GB as the low productivity industries of shipbuilding, textiles and clothing have suffered relative decline. Although the NI development of certain high productivity industries, such as in engineering and chemicals, has lagged that of GB, NI has been relatively advantaged in comparative productivity terms by the strength of representation of tobacco, aerospace and man-made fibres. Consideration of the strength of the compositional effect upon comparative productivity suggests that the productivity shortfall at the matched industry level is now a more significant explanation of the gap in productivity achieved at the aggregate level. This conclusion is not surprising given that the earlier analysis of comparative productivity at the level of industries suggests that NI has lower productivity in most individual comparisons. Next we examine a subject related to the importance of structure and measure how much individual industries contributed to the aggregate shortfall in the productivity of NI manufacturing.

Contribution of individual industries to Northern Ireland's productivity shortfall

In attempting to find the contribution of individual industries to the aggregate shortfall we follow the technique used by Smith, Hitchens and Davies (1982) who asked the question for each individual industry what would have been the aggregate manufacturing productivity ratio if in every other industry productivity levels were achieved which were equal to those of the comparison country while the industry in question retained its existing comparative productivity ratio. In other words, the contribution of an individual industry is its productivity shortfall weighted by its share in total NI manufacturing employment. Thus the "worst offenders" from the point of view of contributors to the gap will tend to be those industries which are of a substantial size in NI and also have a significant productivity shortfall. Table 5.4 lists industries in each of the years which contributed more than 0.5 percentage points to the aggregate productivity shortfall.

Even with allowance for inadequacies in the data Table 5.4 does suggest that "blame" for lower productivity in NI has become less concentrated over time. Thus in 1935 seven industries explained about half of the aggregate shortfall and in 1968 eleven industries explained about two-thirds, but in 1979 and 1984 only 5 industries made contributions of over half of a percentage point each. In these two latter years the aggregate shortfall is primarily because most individual industries have lower productivities rather than a consequence of the dismal performance of a select band of worst cases. Ceteris paribus, the above analysis would suggest that even if the shipbuilding industry shut down (so removing the single largest industrial contribution to lower productivity) the aggregate productivity gap would close by only around a seventh. Apart from the conclusion that "blame" for lower productivity is fairly widely spread, Table 5.4 suggests that in addition to shipbuilding the most significant contributions tend to come from industries within textiles and clothing. Even with allowance for definitional changes comparison of 1935 with 1984 suggests that these industries have greatly decreased their contribution to shortfall. This is consistent with improvement in comparative productivities which occurred in these sectors in the 1970s and 1980s. The other reason why they made much smaller contributions to the productivity gap is that their relative size was declining (part of the explanation for the lessening importance of the structural effect, see above). From a policy making point of view it is important to stress that failure, in comparative productivity terms, is widely spread.

Consideration of individual industry contributions to the shortfall suggests that most of NI's aggregate productivity gap behind GB cannot be accounted for by a handful of industries. Rather "the problem" is that there is a similar shortfall for most individual industries. At the same time a few percentage points of the aggregate gap can be accounted for by a few industries such as tobacco and shipbuilding which in turn contain only two firms and one firm respectively. As the next section makes clear the performance of individual firms has implications for the average productivity of industries in NI.

Table 5.4
Individual industry contributions to productivity gap

(as % points of the total gap between NI and GB levels)

1935			1968	
Linen and hemp	7.9		Shipbuilding	3.0
Ready-made clothing	2.0		Aerospace	2.1
Mechanical engineering	2.0		Overalls, men's shirts	1.8
Building & contracting	1.5		Spinning, doubling	1.8
Shirts and collars	1.4		Weaving cotton, linen & man-made fibres	1.3
Textile finishing	0.8			
Printing, newspapers	0.5		Dresses, infants' wear	0.8
			Household textiles	0.7
Above combined	16.1		Men's & boys tailored	0.7
Total gap	35.0		Hosiery & knitted	0.6
			Miscellaneous building materials	0.5
			Textile machinery	0.5
			Above combined	13.8
			Total gap	16.0

1979			1984	
Shipbuilding	3.5		Shipbuilding	2.5
Household textiles	0.9		Milk	1.3
Tobacco	0.6		Clothing	1.3
Basic electrical equipment	0.5		Tobacco	0.9
Jute and polypropylene	0.5		Miscellaneous building materials	0.6
Above combined	6.0		Above combined	6.6
Total gap	19.0		Total gap	18.0

Notes: Some results are estimates (described in Appendix E). Comparisons between years should only be made with caution given classification changes.

The importance of individual firms

A very important difference between manufacturing industry in NI and GB is that the total population of firms in NI is relatively small (in 1978 and 1986 only around 700 companies employed more than 20 persons). One implication of this is that there will be many industries in NI which are represented by just a couple of firms. This paucity of firms is illustrated in Table 5.5 which compares the numbers of enterprises in certain industries with those in GB according to whether they display comparatively high or low productivity.

Table 5.5
Number of firms in given industries in NI and GB, 1984

Industries where NI productivity was greater than
or equal to that of GB in both 1979 and 1984

	Number of firms in NI by location of ownership			Number of firms in GB
	(NI)	(GB)	(Foreign)	
Clay products	4	0	0	189
Man-made fibres	0	0	3	19
Constructional and earth-moving equip.	3	1	2	316
Poultry slaughtering	5	1	1	130
Fruit, vegetables	1	0	0	259
Bread, flour	8	3	0	3811
Leather goods	1	1	0	948

Industries where NI productivity was less
than three-quarters that of GB in both 1979 and 1984.

	Number of firms in NI by location of ownership			Number of firms in GB
	(NI)	(GB)	(Foreign)	
Synthetic rubber	0	0	1	19
Fertilisers	1	1	0	103
Pedal cycles	0	0	1	80
Shipbuilding	2	0	0	1410
Leather tanning	1	1	0	233
Pharmaceuticals	3	0	0	323
Basic electrical equipment	5	1	1	1582

Sources: NIERC Database and UK Census of Production.

It can be seen that in both the "good" and "bad" comparative productivity groups individual industries are represented by only a very small number of firms in NI. Hence it follows that the source of comparatively good or poor performance can be traced to individual firms. The variability in comparative productivity

51

levels by industrial activity observed in Chapter 4 reflects both these small numbers and is a ray of hope for a remedy to the problem of poor comparative performance. This is because the fact that some firms do manage to attain GB productivity levels indicates that there are able managers in NI who are capable of overcoming the various supply side difficulties which contribute to NI's chronic productivity gap. Furthermore a fuller understanding of the comparative productivity failure lies with a close examination of individual firm specific features such as peculiarities of labour and especially of management. Appendix F reminds us that in a minority of industries NI has attained GB productivity levels and it is to achieve that standard that policy makers should aspire for a wider range of NI industries. The next step would be to make detailed plant studies (preferably with a control in the form of a matched factory in another region and country) to gather the information necessary to evaluate the role of pricing, scale economies, ownership, capital, labour and management quality and such a matched plant comparison is described in Part 3. The following chapter examines the statistical data relating to the explanation of lower productivity in NI.

Notes

1. Partly because it includes those industries where NI has no output (and hence a zero productivity level). The Isles and Cuthbert method weights the differences in employment proportions by the NI productivity level and so an industry which has no output in NI will have no measured impact upon the structural effect. However, in the shift-share method such an industry will have an impact equal to:

(Wni-Wgb) X Prodgb <u>or</u>
(- Wgb) X Prodgb

Where; Wni: weight of given industry in NI (i.e. per cent of total manufacturing employment represented by it), Wgb: weight of given industry in GB, and Prodgb: level of output per head in GB.

The 1968, 1979 and 1984 data show that NI has negligible output and productivity in some of the chemical, iron and steel, non-ferrous metal and metal goods industries as well as railway and tramway vehicles and wines etc. Given that some of these industries have high absolute levels of productivity in GB it would be proper that the "lack" of such activities is included within the estimated NI structural effect.

A second explanation of the larger negative compositional effect using shift share analysis is that Northern Ireland has a lower absolute level of productivity than GB in many of the industries which are smaller in NI. For example, the "under-representation" of chemical industries in Northern Ireland "matters more" when GB rather than NI productivity levels are used (Northern Irish

productivity levels may be absolutely low precisely because the
industry is operating on a small scale in Northern Ireland).

2. These industries make a positive contribution to the structural
effect because they have higher than average levels of
productivity.   It is not necessary that they also have higher
levels of productivity in NI than GB though this is generally the
case in man-made fibres and in some years in aerospace.   NI
benefits from the high absolute level of output per head in
tobacco even when this is less than that attained in GB.

6 Explanations 2: prices, ownership, capital and plant size

"In St. Petersburg, there were by 1914, over 900 very large factories working well within the city's perimeter, using the most advanced German technology with a recalcitrant labour force, an inefficient factory lay-out and elements of very backward technology, to the bewilderment of foreign observers".

Norman Stone (1984), Europe Transformed 1878-1919

Introduction

In this chapter we consider four factors as explanations of the productivity shortfall, namely; comparative NI/GB input prices and product prices; ownership; capital intensity; and plant size.

Price differences

Following Isles and Cuthbert (1957) a distinction is drawn between productivity differences arising from price differences between GB and NI in factor and product markets and physical productivity differences when identical industries are compared. The purpose is to separate NI physical productivity (that is, say, millions of cigarettes, or tonnes of cement, or bales of cotton) from the effects on measured net output per head of selling a given product at a different price or buying inputs at a different price (this distinction is discussed in Pratten, 1976).

The Census affords little direct evidence on this matter and 1968 is the last year for which some comparisons of NI and GB product prices are possible. For illustrative purposes Table 6.1 shows what NI comparative net output per head would have been in food, textiles and clothing if NI unit prices had been the same as those in GB (since price comparisons are only possible on a sample of products it is necessary to assume that the price ratio for all the disclosed products is the same as that for the undisclosed).

Table 6.1
The effects of differences in unit prices on comparative productivity, 1968

NI's comparative net output per head (GB =100)

	Without price adjustment	Adjusted for price difference
Grain milling & animal foodstuffs	71	67
Bread, biscuit & flour confectionery	100	82
Bacon, meat, fish	96	124
Milk	79	80
Weaving	66	72
All clothing etc.	70	87

The table suggests that even if GB unit prices were used NI's comparative productivity would hardly change in grain etc., milk, and weaving. On the other hand, there would be a large fall in bread etc. which would be indicative of NI's actual bread prices being substantially dearer than GB (interestingly the Reward Regional Survey (1987) suggested that a loaf of bread in NI cost 10 pence more than in GB). In meat etc. and clothing NI's comparative productivity would probably gain from the use of GB unit prices. The available data does not allow us to say whether within a given principal product category, say cured bacon or men's suits, NI is concentrating upon the lower end of the price/quality range. There is some evidence that in the case of meats etc. and clothing, NI was in 1968 concentrating upon principal products which on average had lower unit prices than others. To extrapolate to more recent years from these limited pieces of evidence for 1968, would be hazardous. However, there are indications that NI product prices in certain sectors exceed those of GB. Hitchens and O'Farrell (1987, 1988a, 1988b) in their matched comparisons of small NI manufacturers with those in three other UK regions found that the NI prices were almost always higher in a number of industries. They suggested this was part cause, and part effect of the dependence of NI producers on the local NI market within which there may be less price competition than in mainland Britain. It also seems to be fairly well established that the prices of most foods and consumer durables are higher in NI than GB; Reward Regional Survey (1987). This may be a result of higher profit margins in a retail sector which is more monopolistic than its GB counterpart, or it could reflect higher factory gate prices for goods made in NI and transport costs on those imported from elsewhere.

However an equally plausible theoretical case can be put for NI having a systematic tendency towards lower prices because of a greater prevalence of branch-plants in NI. (These may sell at cost to their head offices in GB or abroad and so reduce the value of NI's nominal GVA. Since NI does not share the Irish Republic's liberal corporate tax regime it is unlikely that the international plants in NI, in contrast to those in the South, have any incentive to artificially inflate their internal transfer prices; see Chapter 19).

Table 6.2 shows that the proportion of the Northern Irish manufacturing labour force in foreign owned plants is higher than that of several English Regions (Yorks-Humberside, East and West Midlands, South West and the North) all of which have higher GVA per head than NI. However, East Anglia, South East, North West, Wales and Scotland combine greater foreign ownership than NI with a level of productivity which is also higher. The degree of foreign ownership is considered in its own right in a following section as an explanation of NI's comparative productivity (one might expect the organisational, capital or technological advantages of the foreign plants as compared to the UK owned ones to outweigh any negative transfer pricing).

Turning to the plants in NI which are controlled from Great Britain it is notable that despite the characterisation of NI as a branch-plant economy NI appears to have a lower representation of such plants than any other UK peripheral region. Indeed no strong association between dependence on branch-plants and poor comparative productivity can be noted. Scotland and the North have large proportions of employment in branch-plants and yet good comparative productivity. The two Midland Regions have low proportions of employment in branch-plants and yet poor comparative productivity. The problem of transfer pricing with multi-regional and multinational firms would reward further research through better employment data and individual case studies.

Similarly, little direct evidence is available to compare input prices. From the data which is available, we know that energy and transport costs are higher in NI but expressed as a percentage of gross output the difference is not large; for all manufacturing transport is no more than 2 per cent points (see Table 6.3) and for energy less than this. Differential transport costs cannot be a major explanation for the substantial gap between Northern Ireland and Great Britain. Table 6.3 shows that in 1963 and 1968

the difference in costs was usually small and sometimes in NI's
favour (i.e. tending to boost NI's net output relative to that of
GB). Even the worsening in NI's relative transport costs in the
1970s shown in the Table cannot be the explanation for the
substantially lower level of net output per head observed in NI.
The reason for this is statistical, after 1973 transport costs
were no longer defined as part of the industrial costs of Census
firms and so total payments on transport in both NI and GB were
included in the measured "net output" of the firms. Thus the
statement that NI's average comparative net output per head
during 1973-85 was 81 per cent (see Table 6.6) exaggerates NI's
true comparative "value-added" per head (that is, value-added
exclusive of all transport costs incurred)[1]. In other words,
higher transport costs cannot be blamed for the lower level of
productivity in NI because the official measure of net output does
not allow for regional differences in transport costs. A more
realistic value-added measure which did adjust for total transport
costs would show NI to have a worse comparative productivity than
that shown in our previous analysis (the GVA measure only
partially adjusts for differential transport costs since spending
by a firm's own transport department still remains within
"value-added")[2].

Table 6.2
Branch-plants and multinational plants
and comparative productivity by standard region

	% of employment: "Branch-plants"*	% of employment: Foreign-owned	GVA per head
	1980	1985	1985 (NI=100)
North	53.7	13.1	134
Yorks-Humberside	31.0	7.6	114
East Midlands	17.1	6.3	109
East Anglia	33.2	20.0	132
South East	12.7	18.4	135
South West	45.2	10.9	125
West Midlands	26.7	8.3	113
North West	55.5	14.5	127
Wales	68.1	20.5	125
Scotland	65.9	17.3	132
Northern Ireland	42.2	13.5	100

* This measure is the percentage of regional manufacturing
employment in plants which are located more than 100 miles from
their head office (data for NI derived from a measure of
employment in externally controlled firms (Gudgin, Hart, Fagg,
Keegan and D'Arcy, 1989)).

Sources: Census of Production and Harris (1987).

The relative unimportance of energy costs occurs in spite of NI electricity prices being about one-fifth higher (Table 6.4). Since total energy costs, in 1983, in NI manufacturing industry amounted to only 2.5 per cent of gross output, the scope for a difference with GB is in any case small. The minimal impact of differential energy pricing on comparative productivity can be demonstrated by asking the question what would happen to NI's net output if energy costs came into line with GB. Assuming average energy costs for NI industry to be one-fifth higher NI's productivity level would be raised by less than 2 per cent.

Table 6.3
Transport costs as a percentage of gross output

All manufacturing		Food drink tobacco		All engineering		Textiles		Clothing	
NI	GB	NI	GB	NI	GB	NI	GB	NI	GB
1963									
1.6	2.1	1.5	3.2	1.3	1.7	2.4	1.7	1.2	0.9
2.1	2.2	2.0	3.5	1.7	1.4	2.4	1.4	1.7	1.1
4.2	2.6	4.1	2.9	3.0	1.7	3.0	1.9	2.8	1.4

Sources: 1963 and 1968, Census of Production. For 1979, PEIDA (1984) (result for Scotland used as a proxy for GB).

Table 6.4
Relative electricity prices paid by NI manufacturing (GB=100)

1968	93.6
1969	106.2
1970	118.5
1971	113.9
1972	107.2
1973	105.8
1974	114.1
1975	148.5
1976	173.8
1977	142.7
1978	116.6
1979	126.0
1980	117.8
1981	108.1
1982	113.6
1983	120.1

Sources: Census of Production and Digest of Energy Statistics[3].

While no conclusive evidence is available on materials cost differences the work of PEIDA Consultants (1984) suggests that the majority of materials suppliers charge a common rate regardless of a customer's location within the UK (Hitchens and O'Farrell (1987) found the same for a sample of input supplies into NI).

Further research is required into the extent of differential output and input pricing. Nevertheless, the available data suggests that these can explain little of the productivity difference.

Extent of foreign ownership

Table 6.5
Comparative labour productivity and investment in foreign owned plants in the UK, 1985
(British owned=100)

	Foreign GVA per head	Foreign investment per head
Metal manufacturing	106	118
Extraction of minerals	97	143
Mineral products	109	115
Chemicals	121	95
Man-made fibres	100	234
Metal goods nes.	135	144
Mechanical engineering	127	149
Office equip., data processing	115	256
Electrical, electronic eng.	113	177
Motor vehicles and parts	132	200
Other transport	116	124
Instrument engineering	110	157
Food, drink, tobacco	158	146
Textiles	124	132
Leather and leather Goods	116	495
Footwear and clothing	105	110
Timber and furniture	125	494
Paper, printing, publishing	121	104
Rubber and plastics	136	79
Other manufacturing	114	170
All manufacturing	140	170

Note: nes. Not elsewhere specified.

Source: Census of Production.

The Census of Production shows that for the UK as a whole foreign owned enterprises have substantially higher GVA per head than their British owned counterparts. Table 6.5 reveals that value-added per head at foreign owned companies averaged 40 per cent more than that of indigenous companies across all manufacturing. Only in the extraction of minerals was value-added per head greater at the British owned firms.

Not only is productivity generally higher in the foreign owned firms in the UK but investment per worker is also considerably higher (70 per cent). The multinational enterprises (MNEs) can therefore be characterised as high productivity and capital intensive.

No similar disaggregation is possible from published statistics for NI and Table 6.6 shows how NI's comparative productivity in all manufacturing varies according to the origin of ownership.

Table 6.6
(a) Comparative productivity by ownership type
(GB=100)

	Foreign owned (NI/GB)	UK owned (NI/GB)	All firms (NI/GB)
1973	118	79	92
1979	72	77	80
1981	103	84	90
1983	78	85	84
1984	93	77	82
1985	81	80	80

(b) Relative productivity of foreign owned firms in NI
Foreign owned/UK owned (UK owned=100)

1973	1979	1981	1983	1984	1985
209	146	158	125	174	143

(c) Relative productivity of foreign owned firms in GB
Foreign owned/UK owned (UK owned=100)

1973	1979	1981	1983	1984	1985
140	157	128	135	145	140

Source: Census of Production.

The performance of the foreign owned firms in NI can be analysed in two ways; by comparison with other firms in NI (i.e. those under local ownership or with owners in mainland UK) and, secondly, compared to the foreign owned firms in GB.

Comparison of foreign owned firms within NI with domestically owned companies shows (Table 6.6 (b)) that in every year the MNEs in NI have substantially better productivity. The extent of this superiority is however very unstable so that in 1973 the MNEs have more than double the productivity level of the domestically owned firms but in 1983 their productivity is only one quarter higher than the domestic. By contrast the superiority of MNEs over UK owned in GB is more stable (between one third and one half higher). Table 6.6 (c) shows that MNEs in GB also have higher productivity than their domestically owned counterparts. However, the extent of this superiority has been relatively stable over time (the largest productivity advantage for the MNEs was 57 per cent in 1979 and the smallest advantage was 28 per cent in 1981).

Table 6.6 (a) shows that in two years (1973 and 1981) the NI foreign owned firms had higher productivity than their counterparts in GB. This can be contrasted with the performance of the UK owned firms in NI which in every year falls short by about 20 per cent of the productivity level of the British owned plants in GB. In 1979, 1983, 1984 and 1985 all NI plants regardless of ownership type have lower productivity than those in GB.

Given that foreign controlled firms have higher labour productivity and capital investment (investigated in more detail below) than their British owned counterparts (Pratten, 1976; Dunning, 1985), the key question from a comparative productivity stand point is whether NI or GB has proportionately more of these plants. Table 6.7 shows that Northern Ireland had a larger proportion of employment in foreign owned plants than had GB in every year except 1985.

Table 6.7
Relative importance of foreign owned manufacturing
plants in NI and GB
(% of all manufacturing)

	Gross value-added		Employment		Investment	
	NI	GB	NI	GB	NI	GB
1973	31.2	14.3	17.9	10.6	33.3	15.1
1979	30.0	20.3	22.7	13.9	37.4	21.2
1981	30.1	18.1	21.5	14.7	42.7	25.1
1983	19.6	18.6	16.3	14.5	35.7	22.7
1984	27.7	19.6	18.1	14.1	26.3	20.2
1985	18.2	18.1	13.5	13.6	20.4	21.1

Source: Census of Production.

The available statistics show that in a crude sense NI's potential for a high level of productivity was not disadvantaged by a "lack" of MNEs relative to GB[4]. The greater importance of MNEs in the Northern Ireland economy was most marked in the 1970s and early 1980s. The implication of this is that since 1981 the MNEs in NI have shed labour (or closed completely) at a greater rate than that of UK owned firms (Fothergill and Guy, 1989). By contrast, the data suggests that the GB decline in the employment of international firms has been very similar to that for the work force as a whole (maintained at about one-in-seven of the manufacturing work-force).

One question which the present data cannot adequately answer is to what extent the convergence between NI and GB productivity levels which occurred in the 1960s was caused by the increasing importance of international firms in the NI economy (the arrival of high productivity plants would pull up NI's aggregate output per head level and so cause measurable productivity growth even if there was no productivity growth at all in the existing stock of plants). And whether the stagnation (or even decline) in NI's comparative productivity since 1973 (Tables 4.1 and 4.5) is associated with the contraction and closure of MNEs in NI; employment in MNEs in NI rose from 4515 in 1958 to 26141 in 1975 and fell back to 14500 in 1985 (1985 Census of Production; Teague, 1987). To the extent that the gains in Northern Ireland's comparative productivity have been the result of the attractions of MNEs certain very important policy conclusions follow.

First, it would be implied that NI's more rapid productivity growth during 1951-73 was more "artificial" than "organic" given that it derived more from the arrival of entirely new firms than from the growth of efficiency within the existing stock of firms (comparative rates of productivity growth are illustrated in Appendix G along with a discussion of the reliability of the chosen measures). "Artificial" because many of these firms would not have located in NI but for the unusually high level of grant aid available.

It is notable that NI productivity growth has fallen behind GB since 1973 which suggests that organic efficiency improvement is lower. If the comparatively rapid NI productivity growth of the 1960s was largely the result of the inward investment then this implies that such rapid growth can only be repeated if the industrial development authorities are prepared to spend very large sums in attracting a second wave of investment by international firms. This is a second major conclusion to be derived from this classification of the NI productivity growth as artificial. Such a prospect may not appeal to policy makers and in any case the high investment and hence productivity growth of the 1960s was carried on the back of the general golden age of growth throughout the Western economies. Thus the scope for "artificial" productivity growth in the early 1990s appears to be limited.

Capital per worker

The level of capital per worker in NI relative to that in GB has a direct influence on productivity. Isles and Cuthbert (1957) inferred that in 1935 NI manufacturing was less capital intensive than GB since the profit share in income was lower, despite wages also being lower. Neoclassical economic theory suggests that it would be rational for NI companies, to the extent that they face lower wage costs than their GB counterparts, to have relatively less capital and hence to have a lower level of labour productivity. We now review the evidence as to whether NI's comparative productivity can largely be explained by differences in the factor ratios.

No official capital stock measures exist but several studies have produced estimates. Gleed and Rees (1979) and Harris (1983) are consistent in finding that whilst NI has a lower stock of capital per worker than GB the difference has been narrowing over time and in 1978 stood at 94.9 per cent of the UK level.

This increase in NI's stock of capital per worker is the result of a higher rate of investment in NI and this is illustrated by the Census data for net[5] investment per employee as recorded by the Censuses since 1968. In spite of the limitations of the data a number of firm conclusions are possible.

First, at the all manufacturing level NI has combined a long-run superiority in investment rates with an inferiority in labour productivity. This is shown in Table 6.8.

Table 6.8
NI's comparative productivity and investment relative to GB
(GB=100)

	Net output per head	Net capital expend. per head
1968	84	155
1970	78	100
1971	89	100
1972	83	100
1973	92	133
1974	81	125
1975	90	120
1976	87	100
1977	80	86
1978	74	88
1979	87	90
1980	79	110
1981	87	133
1982	79	110
1983	81	117
1984	80	114
1985	77	107

Notes: SIC 1968 used for 1968-79; SIC 1980 used for 1980-85. No comparisons were possible for 1969 because there was no Census of Production for GB in that year.

This Table shows that since 1978, Northern Irish investment per employee has averaged 9 per cent above the GB rate. Given that the authorities adjust neither the NI nor GB investment data for losses due to plant closures it cannot be guaranteed that NI's stock of capital per employee is now actually higher than that in GB. Nevertheless this does seem probable given that the Census data tends to under-estimates NI's investment relative to GB by virtue of its omission of capital expenditure in pre-production plants[6] and factories constructed by the government[7].

NI has surpassed GB investment rates in most individual industries too, as shown in Table 6.9 for the period 1973-85. The most important implication of Table 6.9 is that the perverse relationship between comparatively low productivity and comparatively high investment holds good regardless of whether one is considering sectors such as textiles and clothing which could be characterised as predominantly UK owned, or sectors such as chemicals where the ownership by NI is small. Unfortunately disaggregated investment data is not available for the MNE's in NI but in aggregate they have had an investment rate higher than either the UK owned firms within NI or the MNEs in GB[8].

The corollary of the differential rate of investment combined with low productivity, is that NI spends more in value-added terms on investment that does GB. This is illustrated by Table 6.10.

Table 6.9
NI's comparative sectoral productivity and investment
(NI/GB, GB=100)

		1973-79	1980-85	1973-85
All manufacturing	GVA[a]	85	83	84
Net capital expenditure[a]		106	115	110
Food, drink, tobacco	GVA	105	107	106
Net capital expenditure		105	131	118
Chemicals	GVA	88	65	77
Net capital expenditure		148	209	176
Mechanical engineering	GVA	90	97	93
Net capital expenditure		111	144	125
Electrical, & electronic engineering	GVA	75	82	77
Net capital expenditure		84	137	108
Instrument engineering	GVA	92*	91	91
Net capital expenditure		224	160	194
Shipbuilding, marine engineering, and other vehicles	GVA	47*	56	57
Net capital expenditure		139	49	97
Metal goods nes.	GVA	91*	85	88
Net capital expenditure		70	114	90
Textiles	GVA	86*	93	90
Net capital expenditure		105*	146	130
Man-made fibres	GVA	109*	191	158
Net capital expenditure		128*	136	133
Leather and fur	GVA	na	77	na
Net capital expenditure		na	93	na
Clothing and footwear	GVA	80	83	81
Net capital expenditure		93	130	110
Timber and furniture	GVA	97	83	90
Net capital expenditure		153	133	144
Paper, printing, and publishing	GVA	84	86	85
Net capital expenditure		114	141	126
Bricks, pottery, glass, cement, & other mineral products	GVA	94	104	98
Net capital expenditure		155	147	151
Rubber, plastic, and other manufacturing	GVA	106	101	103
Net capital expenditure		144	131	138

Note: * 1976-79 only.
[a] GVA and net capital expenditure per employee.
SIC 1968 used for 1973-79; SIC 1980 used for 1980-85.

NI manufacturing spends about £14 of every £100 of value-added on additional land, buildings, vehicles, plant and machinery whereas GB manages with only £10. This raises the suspicion that NI may be less efficient in the use of these assets (this would be consistent with the findings of Hitchens and O'Farrell (1987, 1988a, 1988b) for small, indigenous firms. In Appendix B we show that state grants to Northern Ireland manufacturing enable NI firms to survive in spite of having lower productivity than GB. The higher rate of subsidies in NI also allow NI firms to spend a higher proportion of their value-added on additional capital. Chapter 12 indicates that NI firms had a very much lower capital productivity than their matched counterparts in Germany.

Table 6.10
Share of investment in value-added
(net capital expenditure as % gross value-added)

	NI	GB
1973*	13.7	8.5
1974*	15.0	9.2
1975	15.0	10.9
1976	10.0	10.0
1977	11.8	10.8
1978	13.4	12.0
1979	14.7	12.3
1980	15.8	11.3
1981	12.8	9.4
1982	11.8	9.0
1983	13.6	9.2
1984	14.7	10.6
1985	15.2	11.4
Average 1973-85	13.7	10.4

* Percentage of net output.

Harris (1983) calculates the rate of capital utilisation and shows a comparatively low rate for NI. Such a finding is suggestive of NI having "too much" capital and also that capital productivity, like labour productivity, has fallen below the GB average. Matched indigenous small firm comparisons by Hitchens and O'Farrell (1987, 1988a, 1988b) indicated more modern plant in NI and matching of MNE plants by Hood and Young (1983) showed that NI was not handicapped by a lack of capital (this is also strongly implied by the results of the matched plant comparison with Germany; see Chapter 12).

Even if it is still the case that NI's stock of capital falls short of that in GB it is doubtful if such a deficiency is a major explanation of the productivity gap. Whilst the neoclassical argument that the level of labour productivity is determined by the relative factor prices (feeding through to the capital/labour ratio) receives some support there is some evidence which suggests support for it should be qualified. As Table 6.11 shows, the strong convergence in levels of capital per head between 1950 and 1978 was not matched by any comparable improvement in the relative productivity level i.e. their correlation is a weak one.

Moreover, capital stock was far from being a likely major explanation for the longitudinal narrowing of the productivity gap observed in Table 6.11. The improvements in Northern Ireland's industrial structure were probably a stronger force.

Table 6.11
Trends in comparative productivity and capital intensity

	Comparative net output per head NI/GB (GB=100)	Comparative capital per head NI/UK (UK=100)
1949/50	71	79
1958	68	71
1963	75	68
1968	84	75
1978	74	95

Sources: Gleed and Rees (1973), Harris (1983) and Census of Production.

Whilst the comparatively low labour productivity of the 1910s to 1960s may have been the outcome of relatively cheap labour the question remains as to why the productivity gap has persisted into the early 1980s when wages in NI were almost equal to the GB level and with the higher rate of subsidisation on capital the capital-labour ratio has been pushed to the GB level.

There are two different hypotheses as to the role of capital in the explanation of comparatively low productivity. According to the neoclassical approach the persistence of the productivity gap testifies to a long term difference in regional capital-labour ratios i.e. low NI productivity is the result of a lower capital labour ratio. An alternative hypothesis would be that there is no longer a significant difference in the ratio and that other explanations must be sought for the persistence of the productivity gap. Without further research we cannot be certain as to the contribution of capital to the productivity gap. Nevertheless, given the weak association historically between levels of capital and output per head, we suggest that capital is not now a major explanation of lower productivity (this conclusion receives further support in Part 3 where the modernity and technology of machinery in NI is not found to be generally inferior to that of the equipment found in matched German counterparts).

Plant size

Plant size in NI is compared with GB in order to examine the importance of economies of scale in manufacturing (Pratten, 1971, 1988). If economies of scale at the plant level are significant then it is possible that one explanation for lower value-added per head in NI is that factories tend to be smaller. In examining the potential for plant size economies the most relevant measure of size would be one of factory output. Unfortunately output data are not readily available at the factory level and so employment is used instead. Given that the distribution of employment by plant is probably highly skewed towards a few very large establishments medians are more representative indicators of plant size than simple averages. Table 6.12 compares median employment sizes in NI and GB in 1986 (the most recent year for which published firm size estimates are complete).

This Table suggests that the median size for all manufacturing units in NI is about three quarters that of GB. In the majority of individual industries where comparisons are possible NI has a smaller median employment. However, does it matter that NI has generally smaller plants? We investigated the effect of the size deficiency on value-added per head by establishing a "best-fit" relationship between establishment size and level of GVA per head in GB. With such a relationship we can estimate the loss in GVA per head arising from the smaller plant size found in NI. The loss is expressed according to a GB size-productivity relationship for which data are available. The difference between the two levels of productivity can be thought of as potential scale economies which would be realised if NI had the same median plant size as GB (assuming NI has the same size-to-productivity relationship as GB). Table 6.12 shows NI's actual comparative productivity and the comparative productivity implied by the incorporation of the GB scale effect.

This Table indicates that for all manufacturing and most individual industries there are positive economies of scale to be achieved but that in total they would boost NI's comparative productivity by only a small amount[9]. The potential positive effect is largest in glass (a gain of 11 percentage points), office equipment and data processing (gain of 6 percentage points), drink (8 percentage points) and paper etc. (gain of 7 percentage points). However, in a few industries NI actually has the advantage of scale economies, motor vehicles parts, instrument engineering, footwear and clothing, shipbuilding, and so NI's comparative productivity would fall if the plant size contracted to that of GB. However, only in shipbuilding is this scale advantage significant to NI. Northern Ireland also has larger plants in aerospace and textiles but the GB data suggests that this leads to diseconomies of scale, and having smaller plants would benefit comparative productivity. Overall, one can conclude that the potential gains from economies of scale are not large. Even if Northern Ireland manufacturing plants had the same median size as GB this data suggests that nine-tenths of the productivity gap would remain.

Some additional evidence on the unimportance of scale economies in NI is indicated by an analysis of previously unpublished Census data (supplied to the authors for private research purposes by the Department of Economic Development (NI)). This data relates to how productivity varies according to firm size but enterprise size may be used as a proxy for factory size subject to the qualification that some of the larger firms may represent several establishments.

Table 6.12

Relative factory size and comparative productivity

	Median factory size (employment, 1986)		Comparative productivity, 1985 (GB=100)	
	NI	GB	Actual	Implied
All manufacturing	191	267	80	82
Extraction and preparation				
of metalliferrous ores	18	436	98	..
Extraction of minerals nes.,				
manuf. of mineral products	42	236	93	..
Glass	127	407	90*	101
Refractory and ceramics	139	363	91*	97
Chemicals & man-made fibres	289	494	96	101
Metal goods nes.	30	101	88	90
Mechanical engineering	152	248	102	106
Office equipment & data process.	23	605	44	50
Electrical, electronic eng.	396	531	78	79
Motor vehicle parts	914	439	92*	86
Shipbuilding	5093	1452	50*	36
Aerospace	5613	1670	101*	112
Instrument engineering	251	183	81	80
Food, drink, tobacco	266	383	103	112
Drink only	261	327	76*	84
Tobacco only	966	2305	78*	..
Textiles	265	236	83	83
Leather	153	330	87	..
Footwear and clothing	185	139	88	87
Shirts, men's underwear				
and nightwear only	339	162	72*	70
Timber and furniture	37	72	82	84
Paper, printing and publishing	106	209	83	90
Processing of rubber, plastic	173	238	96	98
Other manufacturing	12	57	91	..

* In 1984 (shirts etc. in 1983).
nes. Not elsewhere specified.
The implied comparative productivities are calculated according to the expected productivity if the NI industry has the same median plant size as its counterpart in GB and the same size-productivity relationship as that GB industry.

Sources: Census of Production and the NIERC employment database.

If firm size greater than 20 employees is examined then four industries which are suggestive of positive scale economies emerge; mineral products, food, drink and tobacco, clothing and footwear and paper etc. Three industries suggest diseconomies; the combination of branches of engineering (metal goods, motor vehicles, transport and instrument engineering), chemicals and man-made fibres, and other manufacturing. In the remaining industries neither economies nor diseconomies can be clearly detected. The position of all manufacturing is also ambiguous. Nevertheless, it is consistent with the conclusion that the actual productivity gains to scale are not very great whether in NI or GB (international studies of comparative productivity have also failed to find comparative plant size a statistically significant explanatory variable; Smith, Hitchens and Davies, 1982; Davies and Caves, 1983, 1987).

Northern Ireland, therefore, has generally smaller factories than GB but the available data suggests that the productivity foregone as a result is only a small part of the total productivity gap. Indeed, in those industries where NI has larger plants the average productivity lag behind GB is still significant.

Conclusions

The official statistics do not suggest that the factors examined are able to explain much of the productivity gap remaining after the structural effect is allowed for. There is some evidence that NI has lower productivity in spite of having several apparent "advantages" over GB; a higher investment rate, a larger proportion of ownership in foreign hands, and factories which are in several important industries no smaller than their mainland counterparts and may even be larger. This is suggestive of the possibility that NI has a lower labour productivity because of a comparatively poor quality of labour and management. We investigate this issue in the next chapter.

Notes

1. Using the data in Table 6.3 as a basis it is possible to calculate NI's comparative net output per head adjusted for transport costs in 1979. In 1979 net output represented 31.8 per cent of gross output in NI and 40.4 per cent of gross output in GB (both inclusive of transport costs). Using the PEIDA estimates for transport costs as a per cent of gross output yields adjusted net output ratios of 27.6 per cent and 37.8 per cent. NI's net output per head becomes 7540 x 27.6/31.8=£6544, and GB's net output per head becomes 9620 x 37.8/40.4=£9001. Thus NI's comparative net output sinks from being 78 per cent of GB's level to only 73 per cent.

2. Our analysis of the impact on productivity of NI's differential transport costs is _ex post_ rather than _ex ante_ (the contrast between these two forms of analysis is considered in Tyler, Moore and Rhodes (1988). We have asked by how much they lower the value-added of the existing population of industries but there is

also the possibility that because of those costs certain high productivity industries have not been able to develop in NI.

3. Tyler, Moore and Rhodes (1988) criticise this type of comparison as failing to allow for regional differences in load factors (with loading held constant they show that NI prices were only 6 per cent higher than those in England and Wales in 1985).

4. With more detailed information one would be able to say to what extent the MNEs in Northern Ireland are structurally biased towards lower productivity activities and the extent to which MNEs with plants in NI and GB reserve their simplest and hence lower value-added products to their NI operations. (Such a bias would be consistent with the evidence that MNEs or multi-regional firms make their least skill- and technology intensive products in the regions/countries furthest from the corporate headquarters and its support services; Harris, 1987). In Chapter 7 we review the evidence as to whether the NI labour force is less skilled than that of GB.

5. Net of disposals (i.e. sales of machines and vehicles to the second hand market), but not exclusive of depreciation. The depletion of the NI utilised capital stock because of plant closures is not allowed for. Figures for net capital expenditure should therefore be regarded as approximate only.

6. An estimate of Gross Domestic Fixed Capital Formation (GDFCF) in NI is given by the Policy Planning and Research Unit (described in Beckett (1987)) as an "enhancement" of the ACOP measure (it includes capital in pre-production units). When GDFCF per employee (the latter measured by the Census of Employment) in NI is compared to GB (National Income and Expenditure) the Northern Irish level is 109.6 per cent of the GB level on average during the period 1961-74 and 153 per cent that of the GB level during 1975-82 period. The latter superiority is very much greater than that derived from the Census data (NI 105 per cent of the GB level during 1975-82). We conclude therefore that the Census measure is a low estimate of the NI investment superiority relative to GB.
   This conclusion remains robust even when one can make allowance for leasing in both NI and GB (the Census excludes those capital assets used by the manufacturing sector but not owned by it). In 1975, the first year for which the CSO has reliable data on leased assets, leased capital represented 5.2 per cent of the total GDFCF (inclusive of leasing) in manufacturing and only 2.8 per cent of NI total GDFCF. By 1982 the proportions had increased to 16 per cent and 11.5 per cent respectively. This implies that a comparison of GDFCF per head inclusive of leasing will show NI in a less good light. Nevertheless, even with this adjustment NI investment still sustains a comfortable advantage; 138.5 per cent of the GB level on average during 1975-82, this compares to the unadjusted average of 153 per cent.

7. It was possible to adjust the Census investment totals for

1983, 1984 and 1985 to include the total spending on land and buildings by the Scottish and Welsh Development Agencies and the English Industrial Estates Corporation (Regional Trends, 1983, 1984, 1985, 1986, 1987, 1988) and by the Northern Ireland Agencies (Statement of Expenditure on Factory Building minus former Commission Projects and Miscellaneous Expenditure; The Northern Ireland Appropriation Accounts). Since the rate of spending was very much higher in NI and GB this adjustment enhances the superiority of NI investment relative to GB; the NI level as a percentage of GB on average during 1983-85 was 112.6 per cent without government factories and 116.2 per cent when they are included (Census net capital expenditure figures used).

8. Figures for the level of net capital expenditure per head in NI MNEs as a percentage of the level of the UK owned in NI were: 1979, 204; 1981, 272; 1983, 284; 1984, 161; 1985, 165. The average investment per head in all of the foreign owned plants in NI is greater than that of the MNEs in GB in each of the years 1979, 1981, 1983, 1984 and 1985 (102, 143, 162, 115 and 105 per cent respectively). In spite of this, as Table 6.6 (a) shows, NI MNEs generally had lower levels of productivity than their counterparts in the rest of the UK.

9. The naive specification of an equation relating NI's comparative productivity level (as a percentage of GB) to NI's comparative median plant size is only significant at results. The correlation coefficient on NI comparative median plant size is only significant at the 5 per cent level for food, drink and tobacco, and for paper etc. at the 10 per cent level.

7 Does Northern Ireland have a lower quality of labour force and management?

"National progress is the sum of individual industry, energy and uprightness as national decay is of individual idleness, selfishness and vice".

Samuel Smiles

Comparative quality of management in NI

The question of the comparative quality of NI's management has been raised by, amongst others, Isles and Cuthbert (1957), Wilson (1964) and Chambers (1979) but little quantitative work has been undertaken. Detailed comparisons of the UK with Germany and other "best practise" economies seem to have centred upon the inferior standards of education and training in Britain (Prais, 1981b; Prais and Wagner, 1983; National Economic Development Commission and Manpower Services Commission, 1984; Daly, Hitchens and Wagner, 1985; Steedman and Wagner, 1987; Steedman, 1988; Sanderson, 1988). With reference to NI, Isles and Cuthbert (1957) suggest that management might be too insular, Wilson (1964) forecast that lack of good managers would inhibit the development of incoming plants in the 1960s. Particular management deficiencies recognised include a lack of innovation (The 1970-75 Development Plan, 1969) and marketing (Chambers, 1979). The Osola Report (1983) pointed to a shortfall in R and D spending (NI firms devoted to R and D less than 70 per cent of the proportion of turnover spent in GB; New Scientist, 1987, August).

While such problems may be more severe in NI it has been asserted that in the UK also managers are poorly trained, rewarded and motivated (Handy Report, 1987). It has proved impossible to give precise quantification of the effect of these deficiencies and therefore to say by how much the UK productivity shortfall relative to American and other European economies can be attributed to that source (Dunning, 1970; Davies and Caves, 1983 and 1987, are amongst some of the attempts).

Table 7.1
Occupational structure of the labour force in NI
and GB in 1981 (as a % of total employment)

	NI	GB
Professional (e.g. accountancy, marketing)	2.3	3.9
Scientists, engineers, and technologists	2.8	5.7
Management	4.3	6.6
Clerical	8.6	11.2
Sales	2.4	2.4
Semi-skilled and unskilled manual*	47.3	36.8
Tool-makers, Metal fitters, electricians	8.4	8.6
Foremen and supervisors	5.1	5.6
Others	18.8	19.1

* All of occupational Orders 11, 12 and 13 minus the tool-makers, metal fitters and electricians and the foremen and supervisors (these groups being regarded as "skilled").

Source: 1981 Census of Population.

Unfortunately the official statistics do not allow us to add much to this debate. What we can say is that NI has a lower proportion of managers in the work-force than GB. Table 7.1 illustrates the relative sizes of various occupations as defined in the 1981 Census of Population. It shows that 6.6 per cent of the total employment of GB manufacturing is engaged in managerial occupations compared with only 4.3 per cent of NI employment.
It is also possible to contrast occupational structures in 20 individual industries (not shown here) and of these NI has a larger proportion of managers in only two cases; metal manufacture and mineral products. Whilst these differences say nothing of the relative needs of NI and GB for such management personnel what they do indicate is that NI is a region not richly endowed with management resources but, as Table 7.1 shows, it is one enriched with a high proportion of manual workers. The figures say nothing about the comparative quality of NI managers, but the small pool together with with the probable difficulty in attracting well qualified outsiders into NI is suggestive of a productivity depressing characteristic. This dependency upon persons whose experience is almost always restricted to NI can be illustrated by comparing the number of NI residents who were born in GB and

abroad with the experience of the Republic of Ireland (there are
two reasons why comparisons with the Republic of Ireland (ROI) are
especially interesting: first, one is controlling for a similar
peripheral location within the British Isles and Western Europe;
second, as Chapter 19 will show, recent productivity growth in the
Republic of Ireland has exceeded that of NI and GB.)

Table 7.2
Numbers of residents Northern Ireland and Republic of Ireland
(ROI) with birth places outside of Ireland[a]

(thousands, and % of total population)

	1971 Census		1981 Census	
	NI	ROI	NI	ROI
	No(%)	No(%)	No(%)	No(%)
Birth Place:				
Great Britain[b]	56.6(3.7)	84.0(2.8)	54.1(3.5)	146.4(4.3)
Rest of world	15.0(1.0)	27.1(0.9)	16.3(1.1)	45.4(1.3)

Note: [a] and [b] refer to Appendix E.3.

Sources: Statistical Abstract (Ireland) 1982-85, NI Economic
Council (1986a).

   It is notable (see Table 7.2) that the number of persons of GB
origin in the ROI grew markedly during the 1970's whereas in NI
their number fell. The Labour Force Survey shows that the annual
in-flows into the Northern Irish work-force of persons from other
UK Regions are much smaller (in proportional terms) than those for
any other UK Region. Thus NI is failing to attract its "fair
share" of persons from England, Scotland and Wales and moreover it
might be argued that those who do come to NI may on average be
substandard because employers in NI are unable or unwilling to
create a premium over and above the salaries being offered for
comparable jobs on the "mainland" which is sufficiently large to
compensate for the perception that NI is a highly unattractive
place to live in. It is striking too that NI's Jewish community
is proportionally smaller than that in either GB or ROI and has
been declining dramatically since 1971 (the importance of Jews in
wealth creation in Britain and the United States is illustrated by
Rubinstein (1981) and Majewski (1988)); other entrepreneurial
ethnic groups may also be under-represented.
   It was noted in Chapter 6 that foreign owned plants in Northern
Ireland had substantially better productivity than those owned by
UK companies. Further research is required to determine to what
extent the MNEs in NI are employing people from outside NI and
how this affects their productivity and whether the imposition of
foreign management systems can sometimes raise local managers to a
level closer to international standards. Hitchens and O'Farrell's
(1988b; O'Farrell and Hitchens, 1988a) findings on the performance

of small companies in the Shannon Development Company Area (SFDCo)
illustrates that the MNEs are of benefit not only in themselves
but also as suppliers of foreign nationals and better trained
indigenous entrepreneurs.[12]

Skills of workers other than management

A number of indicators have traditionally been employed to show
differences in   skill levels (Rostas, 1948; and Davies and Caves,
1983, 1987). For example a work-force might be considered less
skilled the higher the percentage of females, manual workers and
part-timers which are engaged (there may, of course, be some
individual female and part-time workers who are highly skilled,
but it is in an average sense that the generalisation is made;
Rostas, 1948, Caves and Davies, 1983).

Table 7.3
Composition of total employment, 1983

% of males in total

	NI	GB
Metal manufacturing	80	90
Non-metallic mineral products	88	82
Chemicals	82	71
Man-made fibres	95	88
Metal goods NES	85	77
Mechanical engineering	90	84
Office equipment and data processing	71	75
Electrical, electronic engineering	54	68
Motor vehicles	75	89
Other transport equipment	91	90
Instrument engineering	61	68
Food, drink, and tobacco	67	59
Textiles	51	51
Leather etc.	65	60
Clothing	15	26
Timber and furniture	88	80
Paper, printing and publishing	65	67
Rubber and plastic	80	72
Other manufacturing	50	52
All manufacturing	65	71

Note: data for the extractive industry are not shown because this
industry is of negligible size in NI.

Source: Census of Production.

   NI in fact does have a lower proportion of male workers (65 per
cent of all manufacturing compared to 71 per cent in GB, see Table
7.3) than GB though this difference would entirely disappear if

NI had the same industrial structure as GB; the greater weight of female employment in NI reflects the importance of the textiles and clothing industries. When the nineteen industries are considered separately Northern Ireland has a greater proportion of male workers in more than half (10). A perverse relationship is observed as regards part-timers of which NI has proportionately fewer (4.5 per cent compared to 7.9 per cent in 1978).

The 1981 Census of Population occupational breakdown of employment provides a further means of comparing the two labour forces. Table 7.1 showed that NI has a shortfall in the employment of professionals and scientists, engineers and technologists. Such groups would tend to be highly qualified in terms of university, polytechnic, technical and professional qualifications. Taking these groups separately, 2.3 per cent of NI manufacturing employment is of professionals. In only two of the 20 individual industries which can be compared (not shown) does NI have more professionals: office equipment and data processing machinery, and other manufacturing. GB has more than twice the NI proportion in two industries; man-made fibres and instrument engineering.

NI has fewer scientists etc. in all of the 20 industries while in eight industries the GB proportion is more than double that of the comparable industry in NI; metal ores, metal manufacturing, extraction of minerals, office machinery and data processing equipment, electrical and electronic engineering, textiles, timber and furniture. From a productivity standpoint these deficiencies are indicative of NI having a lack of complex high-technology high value-added products whilst NI specialises in simple and low skill product lines which produce low value-added per head (NI has a weak tendency to have its worst comparative productivity performance in those industries which have high levels of value-added in GB; see Chapter 4). We can therefore say that NI is clearly less well skilled from the point of view of the numbers of highly qualified persons in the work-force.

It is possible to draw a less strong conclusion from an analysis of relative sizes of the employed skilled manual (for the sake of comparison defined as tool-makers, fitters and electricians) and foremen occupations. In all manufacturing there is virtually no difference in the proportion of skilled manuals; 8.4 per cent compared with 8.6 per cent in GB (Table 7.1). Northern Ireland also has a similar proportion of foremen and supervisors; 5.1 per cent compared to 5.6 per cent in GB.

These findings receive some confirmation from an alternative data source; the Labour Force Survey. This gives data on the proportions of the work-force (in all sectors) holding various qualifications.

Table 7.4 shows NI is under-qualified with respect to degrees and A-Levels but not in terms of completed apprenticeships, the qualification most relevant to the level of vocational skills in the manual work-force. Whilst the larger number of apprentice-trained workers in NI might suggest a higher level of skill in NI there may be qualitative deficiencies. Given the narrower range of industries in NI the training for apprenticeships in NI may be inferior to that in GB in quality, relevance and type. The on-the-job training received by the manual work-force may also suffer from the restricted experience of most in-company training instructors in NI.

Table 7.4
Educational qualifications of
the manufacturing labour force, 1981
(% who have achieved each of these as
their highest qualification)

	NI	UK
Degree or equivalent	1.6	3.3
Other higher education	2.7	5.4
Apprenticeship (completed)	21.6	19.5
Apprenticeship (uncompleted)	3.2	3.3
A-Level or equivalent	2.3	2.7
O-Level or equivalent	4.5	7.7
CSE below Grade 1	2.7	4.0
None	50.7	43.1
Other (includes not stated & unknown)	10.8	11.1

Source: Gudgin and Healy (1990).

The statistics conceal the oft-cited fact that the NI educational system produces more high achievers than GB (though also more very poor ones), because many (most?) high achievers leave NI without entering the labour force (emigrating either before they enter third level education or after they have obtained a degree from one of the NI universities; Osborne, Cormack, Miller and Williamson, 1987; Kearney, 1989).
No firm conclusions can be drawn from the official statistical sources about the comparative skills of manual workers except to say that foremen, fitters, tool-makers and electricians are roughly as well represented as in GB. What cannot be tested is how appropriately well qualified they are in comparison with GB.

Strikes and absences

A study by Black (1987) has compared strike-proneness between NI and GB. Based on the official statistics which exclude political strikes and stoppages, he compares working days lost per 1000 employees engaged in both industry and services in NI and the UK between 1956-84. The raw data shows the strike rate at 10 per cent lower in NI without correcting for differences in industrial structure. After taking structural differences into account, especially allowing for the two most strike-prone industries coal mining and iron and steel making which are not represented in NI, he shows that NI has a substantially higher rate of stoppages (30 per cent greater on average for the period 1966 to 1984)[3]. Black concentrated upon an aggregate comparison for the whole NI economy, the details for manufacturing alone are shown in Tables 7.5 and 7.6.

Table 7.5
Northern Ireland's strike rate compared to United Kingdom
(NI as a % of the UK level, days lost per 1000 employees)

	Average 1962-80
Orders of 1958 or 1968 SIC	
All engineering, VI-XII	141
Textiles, leather, clothing & footwear, XIII-XV	242
Combination of above, VI-XV	87
Combination of above, adjusted by UK indust. structure	147

Note: Industries defined by 1958 SIC for the years 1962-69 and by 1968 SIC thereafter. Data for all manufacturing (Orders III-XIX) not available.

Sources: Employment Gazette, Monthly Digests of Statistics, NI Annual Abstract of Statistics, NI Digest of Statistics, and Regional Trends.

Table 7.5 shows the available data on long run comparisons of strike rates. Unfortunately data for all NI manufacturing is not available before 1980 and comparisons with UK are restricted to the engineering and the textiles and clothing industries alone, although, they represent about 70 per cent of NI employment in these years. The Table illustrates a paradox, while separately the engineering sector and textiles and clothing sectors have a higher strike record than comparable GB sectors, when they are combined the NI strike rate is behind that for GB. The explanation for this difference is entirely one of industrial structure; textiles and clothing have in absolute terms a low strike rate (relative to engineering) irrespective of location but are more important sectors in NI than GB. If the NI structure is imposed upon the UK data then NI is shown to be 47 per cent more strike-prone in these industries in the years 1962-80.

Table 7.6 gives greater detail for the 1980-85 period and shows that NI still has a better average strike record on average than UK. However this optimistic conclusion is qualified by the relatively high rates experienced in textiles and clothing and other manufacturing (dominated by food, drink and tobacco). NI's strike record relative to the UK is improved by the low rates in metals, motor vehicles and shipbuilding plus aircraft.

78

Table 7.6
Comparison of strike rates in Northern Ireland and
United Kingdom, 1980-85

	Days lost per 1000 Employees, NI as % of UK						
	1980	1981	1982	1983	1984	1985	1980-85 average
Metal manufacturing & metal goods nes.	0	0	0	8	0	0	7
Engineering, instrument, mechanical, electrical	26	120	18	22	355	37	96
Motor vehicles	51*	52*	59	3	5	0	17
Aircraft, shipbuilding	51*	52*	43	87	1	20	38
Textiles, clothing	127	23	52	412	112	475	201
Other manufacturing	89	24	229	177	87	175	130
All manufacturing	12	54	74	74	57	112	64

All manufacturing (structurally adjusted):

	1980	1981	1982	1983	1984	1985	1980-85 average
	36	50	93	94	61	98	72

Notes: Industries defined according to SIC 1968 in 1980 and 1981,
and according to SIC 1980 in 1982-1985.

* All vehicle and transport industries combined.

nes. Not elsewhere specified.

Sources: **Employment Gazette** (1986, June) and **NI Annual Abstract of
Statistics** (1986).

   The data on strike rates in NI manufacturing suggest that for
the most recent years the average stoppage rate for all
manufacturing is lower than that for GB which may reflect the
importance of very high unemployment (Black, 1987). Nevertheless,
in some large individual industries NI still has a higher rate
of days lost even in the first half of the 1980s (worrying
evidence on the strike-proneness of NI factories relative to those
in Germany and its effects on productivity is presented in Chapter
15).

Absenteeism

Data on absence from work for reasons other than strikes are less
readily available. A limited survey by the CBI (1987) indicated
little difference between the NI absence rate and the UK average
(Table 7.7).

Table 7.7
Relative rates of absence (% of employees)
Absence for all reasons:

Full-time manuals		Full-time non-manuals		Part-timers	
NI	UK	NI	UK	NI	UK
4.3	4.7	2.9	2.6	4.5	4.3

For sickness only:

Full-time manuals		Full-time Non-manuals		Part-timers	
NI	UK	NI	UK	NI	UK
4.0	4.0	2.3	2.2	na	na

A similar survey conducted in 1985 found that 4.5 per cent of the NI sample had been absent for at least one day in the previous week due to sickness, which was not statistically different from the 4.4 per cent for the UK as a whole (<u>Regional Trends</u>, 1987). The Industrial Society survey of sickness absenteeism (again) in 1985 however, found a much higher rate of 8.5 per cent in NI (4.6 per cent UK) but this was also based on a very small sample (reported in Financial Times, 1987, August 19). If there is reason to retain a suspicion that absenteeism is a more serious problem in NI it would be based on the fact that the general NI population appears to be less healthy than its GB counterpart (medical prescriptions per head are around one-sixth higher than for the UK as a whole, <u>Regional Trends</u>, 1986) and it is not improbable that this would be reflected in more frequent absences from work. During 1977-78/1981-82 NI lost proportionately more days (76 per cent more) through chronic illness (such as physical handicaps and officially recorded illnesses (<u>Regional Trends</u>, 1984).

In both NI and UK the loss of days from such causes is many times that lost in strikes (the link between poorer health and higher absenteeism is complicated by the fact that unemployment is also higher in NI i.e. the poor health of the NI labour force may be concentrated amongst those who are not in employment). Apart from the disadvantage of a relatively unhealthy population NI manufacturing has a structural bias towards higher absenteeism through its greater use of female labour (this is further compounded by a higher fertility rate in NI; see Chapter 15).

Further work is required to test whether NI workers lose more work days and are less highly skilled and/or motivated than their GB counterparts, as well as on the relative quality of local management.

Notes

1. It is a common pattern for developing economies to be especially dependent on industrialists of outside origin during the early phases of industrialisation (e.g. Germany during 1800-50; Kindleberger, 1975).
The absence of a large inflow of GB and other outsiders to study at the two NI universities is one explanation of the under-representation of outsiders in the labour force. Osborne, Cormack, Miller and Williamson (1987) note that while NI is not unusual in having a large out-flow of 18 year olds to study at institutions in other GB regions, what is unique is the negligible counter-flow of English, Scots and Welsh youths into the Province. A large part of NI's net export of higher level students can almost certainly be attributed to the Troubles. A further (and related) reason could be that some young NI people perceive NI society as being excessively parochial and obsessed with its own narrowly defined problems (see Chapter 21). Unfortunately their migration would help to make such a perception more of a reality.

2. A possible indication of the relative insularity of the NI labour force is given when one compares rates of readership of quality national newspapers with the UK mainland. Only 6 per cent of NI adults read one or more daily qualities and only 9 per cent of Sunday quality and this contrasts with 12 per cent and 16 per cent respectively in GB. This disparity may also reflect different levels of education and complications arising from the three major provincial papers which do aspire to a level above a mere local paper. Source: Belfast Telegraph Readership Survey, 1986.

3. This result has been criticised as misleading by the Labour Relations Agency (1988). Whilst there is some force in their argument that one should adjust for other sorts of "structural" divergence between NI and GB (e.g. male/female, skilled/unskilled composition), Black's use of the standard shift share methodology is still an advance on the comparison of unadjusted strike rates.

8 Northern Ireland's performance in international perspective: conclusions to Part 2

"As far as such [manufactured] goods are concerned Northern Ireland is now on a par with middle-range Latin American countries like Argentina or Chile. It is, in effect, an under-developed country kept afloat by subsidies from the UK".

Bob Rowthorn (1987), Beyond the Rhetoric (P. Teague: ed)

Northern Ireland compared to international best practise

Part 2 has compared NI's productivity performance, in terms of levels and trends, with Great Britain, while Chapters 1 and 2 summarised the performance of the UK as a whole relative to other industrial economies. By placing the two sets of results alongside each other one gets a rough indication of how NI is performing relative to the economies which represent international best practise. Such comparisons are of interest in their own right since NI firms not only have to try to be competitive in UK markets but also in international ones and the results presented in this Chapter (especially those relating to Germany) lay a foundation for the matched plant comparison which is reviewed in Part 3.

Table 8.1 links together a comparison of NI with GB, with one of Germany to the UK.

Table 8.1
Comparative productivity levels NI, Britain and Germany, 1985

	WG/UK (UK=100)	NI/UK (UK=100)
Food, drink and tobacco	117	91
Mechanical eng. & metal goods nes.	161	100
Instrument engineering	89	81
Electrical engineering	94	75
Shipbuilding, motor vehicles & other transport	180	51
Textiles, clothing, leather, & footwear	144	84
Paper, printing, publishing	257	79
Timber and furniture	236	85
Glass, pottery, other mineral products	215	95
Chemicals and man-made fibres	146	93
Rubber, plastics, other manufacturing	152	96
All manufacturing	142	76

Note: nes. Not elsewhere specified.

Sources: As in Table 1.5 and Census of Production.

The qualification to Table 1.5 is worth repeating. Since there were inadequate data to complete a finely detailed harmonisation of the two national systems of industrial classification, these results should be considered for their rough orders of magnitude. Nevertheless, it can be seen that by placing the two sets of results together Germany is implied to have a substantial productivity advantage in every comparison with Northern Ireland (the gap is sufficiently large for one to ignore the discrepancy arising from comparing a UK-based comparison with one based on GB).

The NI-Germany shortfall varies from one of 10 per cent in instrument engineering through to the worst case of shipbuilding etc. where productivity levels are implied to be about three-and-a-half times higher in Germany than NI. Manufacturing in Germany would appear to have a productivity level almost twice that of NI. Whilst Chapter 4 noted that NI has made some small gains relative to GB over time these improvements have been swamped by the growing divergence between German and UK productivity between 1950 and 1980. In other words, NI's performance relative to Germany had suffered long run deterioration. This has implications for the trends in NI's output, employment and output per head compared to the OECD economies.

Table 8.2 shows the percentage growth for these indicators of the relative performance of manufacturing in each of the OECD economies.

Table 8.2
NI's growth in output, employment and output
per head compared to the OECD economies
(% change, 1955 to 1987, economies ranked from
fastest productivity growth to lowest)

	Employment	Output	Output per head
Japan	138	1327	499
Belgium	na	164	288**
France	-17	217	281
Austria*	-7	249	276
Italy	35	343	228
Finland*	32	337	232
N.Ireland	-47	75	221
Canada	27	271	193
West Germany	8	208	186
USA	13	214	177
Great Britain	-38	63	162
Luxembourg	-5	101	112

* Austrian data for the period 1956-87 and Finnish data
for 1959-87.
** Belgium output growth during 1960-86.

Sources: International data from OECD indices of output and
employment (Main Economic Indicators: Industrial Production) and
Liesner and The Economist (1985). NI and GB were derived from
Index of Production and Census of Employment (Appendix G notes
some of the general problems of this method of measuring
comparative changes in productivity as well as those which are
specific to NI).

Table 8.2 suggests that Northern Ireland's comparative growth
performance has been mixed. For example, in terms of long run
productivity growth, NI does out-perform four of the OECD's seven
largest economies; Canada, United States, Germany and the UK
(this result is hard to reconcile with our earlier statement that
the NI-Germany productivity was widening over time but Appendix G
presents evidence which suggests that the statistical series used
may exaggerate NI's relative rate of productivity growth).
However, it is notable that NI's reasonably rapid productivity
growth was much more the outcome of employment decline than
output growth. In fact, next to Great Britain, NI is at the
bottom of the league as far as output growth goes and NI's loss of
employment is even worse than that suffered by manufacturing in
the rest of the UK. With the exception of Luxembourg all the OECD
economies shown achieved output growth at least double that of
either NI or GB. Great Britain's productivity performance was
even worse than NI's although it was not much worse than that of
America.

Conclusions

In this statistical study of manufacturing productivity in Northern Ireland over the last seventy years we have used GB productivity experience as a benchmark by which to evaluate NI performance with three objectives in mind. Namely; how does the level of productivity differ in NI compared with that achieved in GB, how do growth rates compare, and, can we indicate hypotheses to explain the differences observed?

NI manufacturing is shown to have a level of productivity about four-fifths that of GB in the first half of the 1980s. This level represents a small improvement on the position in the 1940s and 1910s. Most of the improvement was concentrated in the 1960s and although NI's post-war productivity growth rate has been higher than GB it is nonetheless lower than that of most Continental European economies. The labour productivity level of NI seems to have got stuck at a level significantly lower than GB and this is reminiscent of the persistence of the huge gap still existing between the UK and USA. This is a disappointing conclusion to arrive at after several decades of catch up by the Continental economies and Japan on the American levels of manufacturing productivity and after a period of active industrial development policy in NI; a large outlay of public resources has not been sufficient to raise NI to GB standards (during the 1970s and 1980s public assistance to manufacturing amounted to about £6 billion in constant 1988 prices: Appendix B).

Only a partial indication can be given for why NI's level of productivity is lower than that of GB. Part of the difference (roughly one-quarter in recent years) is attributable to NI having more of those industries which are generally of a low productivity type though this explanation is of decreasing importance (regrettably the "improvement" in NI's structure relative to GB owes more to the decline of the traditional low productivity industries of shipbuilding, textiles and clothing than to the development of a broad range of new productivity industries in, for example, pharmaceuticals, electronic and instrument engineering. It is also a matter of concern that the long term position of some of the high productivity level industries in NI is precarious, notably that of tobacco and man-made fibres and perhaps aerospace). Although there is an adverse effect arising from structure it would be a mistake to think that NI's comparative productivity failure arises because of a dismal performance in only a handful of industries. Instead, lower productivity is experienced across a wide front of industries. There is some weak evidence that NI is especially deficient in those industries which have high absolute levels of productivity.

Of lesser importance, but still not inconsiderable, are the measurable impacts upon value-added of differential energy and transport costs. The smaller average size of factories in NI, and the possibility of a lower stock of capital per employee probably have very little explanatory value. If the impact of structure, transport, energy, economies of scale and capital are taken together, one probably has an explanation for between half and three-fifths of the twenty or so percentage point productivity gap.

This means that there is a very large unexplained residual and it is not clear to what extent the productivity gap reflects product price differences as opposed to physical productivity differences, or compositional differences at the level at which industries are matched and variations in quality. To the extent that the product price and compositional factors are not significant then the quality of labour and management may be important explanations for the failure in physical productivity or the unduly high concentration upon low value-added products. Comparisons of occupational sizes and of paper qualifications produce some results which are favourable to NI and some which are unfavourable. Unfortunately, these statistics may be missing the most crucial aspects of work experience and appropriateness of training. Given that NI's population of "outsiders" is unusually small and the narrow range of industries operating in the Province it seems reasonable to hypothesise that there may be deficiencies in the quality, relevance and type of training received by the NI work-force and management.

It is notable that the key element in most diagnoses of the British disease has been management and labour, their interaction and the general effect of British society and culture on the attitude, experience, motivation, incentives and ability of these groups (Handy, 1987; Crafts, 1988b; Rubinstein, 1988; Sanderson, 1988) and we would also wish to stress the human element in the explanation of NI's manufacturing problems. In fact it is worth giving a preliminary consideration to whether the suggested explanations for the generally low productivity of the UK (Chapter 2) are different from those which apply to the low productivity of NI within the UK (this question is also asked in Chapter 18 where the results of the matched plant comparisons are used as part of a fuller answer).

Capital has been found to be an important explanation of productivity differences between the UK and other economies. Unfortunately, the official statistics do not show conclusively whether NI has less capital than GB, or whether the machinery is older, more prone to breakdown with less efficient feeding devices. However, matched plant comparisons (Hood and Young, 1983; Hitchens and O'Farrell, 1987, 1988a, 1988b) have been strongly suggestive of NI having more capital per worker than GB. More of the machinery may be of a sophisticated nature and breakdowns are not a problem (this would be consistent with the level of capital utilisation being much lower in NI than GB). Whilst it might be presumed that capital is inadequate relative to that in America and Germany it seems much less likely that capital intensity is an explanation for NI's comparatively low productivity relative to the UK.

The UK labour force has been judged to be the least well educated of any major Western economy and it is notable that the NI labour force has more persons with no qualifications than even the GB labour force. NI also appears to be deficient even by the standards of GB when one considers the size of the pool of highly qualified personnel such as manages, scientists and technologists. Even where paper qualifications are comparable (as in the proportion of apprentice trained workers) there is reason to fear that NI may be qualitatively inferior because the range of experience is smaller (NI has a narrower industrial base and this perpetuates itself in the training of each generation of workers, as a peripheral region NI may have an in-built tendency towards insularity and this may have been reinforced by discouragement of immigration arising from the Troubles). We hypothesise that the qualitative deficiencies (including strikes and absenteeism) of the NI labour force are a more extreme case of those operating throughout the UK.

Whilst the UK factory size in the heavy industries tends to be much smaller than that found in either America or Germany, in most industries the difference between NI and GB median plant size is small. Moreover, the limited evidence relating to the relationship between plant size and productivity in NI and GB suggests that even if NI attained GB plant size there would be no great gain to comparative productivity.

Rates of R and D spending in UK firms are lower than those in America, Germany, and Japan. Even by the poor standard represented by the UK average NI is deficient (New Scientist, 1987) and, as Harris (1988) shows, the Northern Irish output of innovations is also comparatively low. This lack of technological orientation in NI manufacturing is consistent with the way the labour force lags GB (and even more so Europe) in standards and experience.

The UK as a whole does not appear to have a structural disadvantage relative to America or Germany. However, whereas the structure of UK industry may be comparable to that of other Western economies, the regional difference between NI and GB is significant. NI's structural disadvantage relative to GB has been decreasing over time but it remains true that NI has "too much" of certain low productivity industries such as textiles, clothing and shipbuilding and "too few" of certain high productivity ones such as parts of mechanical, electrical and instrument engineering and chemicals. NI has only 700 industrial companies of more than twenty employees and so inevitably the range of the industries represented is not as broad as that in GB.

By the standards of Continental Europe (though not the Republic of Ireland) the UK is unusually well endowed with foreign MNEs. Since most of these MNEs originate from economies which have higher productivity levels than the UK it is probable that their UK subsidiaries act as islands of high productivity in the sea of British inefficiency (thereby raising the average level of productivity and perhaps even having favourable demonstration effects upon the indigenous firms (Ackrill, 1988)). In the 1970s NI had a larger proportion of employees in MNEs than GB and even in 1985 the proportions were similar. Therefore, a "lack" of MNEs cannot explain NI's productivity shortfall relative to GB.

Most commentators have focused on a cultural explanation of Britain's relative poor manufacturing performance during the last one hundred years. Given the peculiarities of Irish history it cannot be assumed that the economic impact of "Northern Ireland culture" (whatever that may be) will be identical to that of "British" culture. Nevertheless certain cultural influences which affected industrial performance in GB may have had a similar impact in NI (in the same way that the the post-Independence education of the ROI may have inherited the alleged English anti-industrial bias as a legacy of the 1800-1921 period (O'Farrell, 1986)). While the role of culture as an explanation of manufacturing performance in Ireland is considered in more detail in Chapters 19 and 21 it is important to stress that culture of NI (broadly defined) may have represented more of a handicap to efficient industrial performance than its counterpart in GB (or perhaps even the rest of Ireland). This is for two reasons. First, the limited nature of nineteenth century Irish industrialisation. Second, the indirect results of the violence since 1969. These will now be considered in turn.

Mid-nineteenth century England as a result of its earlier achievement as the first industrial nation may have been too complacent about the rise of industry in the United States, Prussia and elsewhere (Williams, 1896; Johnson, 1972; Crafts, 1988b). Late Victorian and Edwardian Ulster had its undoubted industrial glories, the creation of the world's greatest shipyards and producers of rope, cigarettes and textile machinery, and these stood it stark contrast to the failure of the rest of Ireland to industrialise (Lyons, 1981; Bardon, 1987; News Letter, 1987; O'Malley, 1989). Unfortunately this may have led NI industrialists and workers to draw the conclusion that they were invulnerable to foreign competition. Thus the general unwillingness of the UK to learn from examples of best practise abroad may have been more pronouced in NI with a resultant loss of comparative productivity.

The Troubles have probably assisted the development in NI of certain attitudes which inhibit the achievement of higher productivity levels. An environment of lawlessness may have infected industrial relations (see Chapters 15 and 21) and that the spectacular growth of the public sector in NI and of dependency on revenue transferred from the UK Exchequer (the Subvention) have produced a mentality of dependency (see Chapters 17 and 21 and Appendix B). Whilst the high rates of grant aid to the firms in NI cushion them from the effects of a low level of comparative productivity they may not have the incentive to try to attain GB levels of productivity. Not the least of the cultural costs of the Troubles may be the extent to which they have discouraged in-migration by talented outsiders. Thus if there are any defects with home grown culture (from the productivity point of view) there is little acting to dilute them.

In terms of the amounts of money spent (in proportion to output and employment) government industrial policy since the 1950s has been more vigorous in NI than in GB (see Appendix B). Thus a "lack" of industrial development policy cannot be blamed for the low comparative productivity relative to GB. However, some crude measures would throw doubt on the efficacy of the policy which was practised. For example, in spite of the higher rates of subsidy given, the decline in NI manufacturing employment was greater than in GB during 1951-86. There is also the question of whether the relatively indiscriminate giving of grants in fact inhibits the achievement of higher levels of productivity.

We can therefore consider the extent to which NI is either a more extreme case of the "British Disease", or different in type as well as degree from the rest of the UK. NI does appear to be different in type in so far as (relative to GB) capital and plant size may not be a major problem but industrial structure is. NI's weaknesses in the appliance of technology and the skills and experience of the work-force may be more intense versions of general UK weaknesses. Returning to the contrasts with GB, one might speculate that Northern Ireland's long run economic history and recent political history both act to mark it out in an unfavourable way from the rest of the UK and indeed from the Republic of Ireland. NI's status as a particularly strong case of the British disease is strongly indicated by the evidence which will be considered in Part 3.

The results of this Part have placed emphasis on the deficient quality of the NI labour force (this message will be underlined by the evidence arising from the matched plant comparisons). This is somewhat at variance with the conventional wisdom as to the relative excellence of the local work-force (Department of Commerce, 1982) in terms of the alleged work ethic and relative harmony of industrial relations. Conversely, the available statistics suggest that most of the productivity gap cannot be attributed to those factors, the differential costs arising from transport, energy and the "Troubles", which have traditionally received most attention (Department of Commerce, 1982; Bridges and Birley, 1985). The NI industrial location is not inherently hostile towards the achievement of higher levels of productivity and human factors explain much of the present gap behind GB. Whilst further research is required to ascertain the importance of attitudinal and industrial relations differences between NI and GB, it seems highly probable that the primary locational advantage of NI is not the so called work ethic but the much higher rate of public subsidy received. Unfortunately, it is not clear whether this advantage of a cheaper cost of capital in NI has resulted in higher labour productivity in NI than would otherwise have been the case. There is a strong suspicion that the advantage of the relatively high rate of grant aid has in fact failed to produce higher productivity, rather it has saved the manufacturing firms in NI from suffering some of the consequences of comparatively low productivity (lower profits, lower wages, and lower employment and closure of firms (see Chapter 17)).

Chapter 21 will consider some of the policy recommendations which arise from consideration of both the statistical and matched plant comparisons of productivity.

PART 3

MATCHED PLANT COMPARISONS OF NORTHERN IRELAND WITH WEST GERMANY

"Why the sceptre of industrial progress passes from one nation to another is a question that excites much curiosity: politicians may point to national pride and determination; theologians will point to the Reformation and the doctrine of individual accountability; educationalists will point to advances in scientific knowledge and the diffusion of orderly and purposeful habits of life, and will place emphasis on vocational training".

S. J. Prais (1981), Productivity and Industrial Structure

9 Introduction

"It has been at times a highly successful industrial country".

Mr Adam Butler's description of Northern Ireland to the House of Commons Industry and Trade Committee, June 1982

Introduction

An international comparison of levels of labour productivity such as the one described here is grounded and justified in two fundamental bases. Firstly, since labour costs are a significant component of total costs, differences in labour productivity are a major explanation of the extent of international competitiveness. Then secondly, at the national level, variations in output per employee, and hence output per head of population, are the primary determinants of relative living standards. Thus whilst UK firms (including those in Northern Ireland) may find it possible to be cost competitive and profitable despite relatively low levels of productivity, this is not a desirable state of affairs if its cost is relatively low wage rates and a concentration on simple, low quality products.

Labour productivity is not synonymous with overall economic efficiency. To consider the latter one would require very comprehensive data on all the factors and resources used in production and proportions of their mix, therefore output per worker is not identical with "total" or "multi-factor" productivity which can only be measured if some allowance, at least is made for the input of capital (Matthews, Feinstein and Odling-Smee, 1982; Borooah and Lee, 1989). In this study variation in the level of capital between matched companies is treated as a source of explanation for observed differences in labour productivity (in fact this matched plant technique can go beyond "growth accounting" in that it considers not only the quantity of capital but its quality in terms of characteristics such as: modernity, technological appropriateness, utilisation, ancillary devices and reliability).

Although the international comparison of productivity levels is a relatively young branch of economic research an impressive array of studies has already been conducted (Rostas, 1948; Kravis, 1976; Matthews, 1988; and see also Chapter 1). These have been diverse in their methodology and the level of aggregation of treatment (national, sectoral, industrial, firm or plant). The methodology used here represents a compromise between the "fine-grained" method of the highly detailed case study and the "coarse -grained" method of statistical analysis of large data sets . The matched-pairs method aims to catch some of the subtleties of historical, enviromental, cultural and non-quantifiable economic determinants of relative national (or regional) performance whilst employing a reasonable sample size has use for policy makers of considerable scope for generalisation (Daly, Hitchens and Wagner, 1985; Hitchens and O'Farrell, 1987, 1988a, 1988b; O'Farrell and Hitchens, 1988a, 1988b, 1989a, 1989b).

Justification of comparisons with Germany

Our standard of comparison is the performance of German companies, even though Britain's productivity performance has most often been compared with the United States (Flux, 1933; Rostas, 1948; Frankel, 1957; Paige and Bombach, 1958; Smith, Hitchens and Davies, 1982). As Chapter 1 demonstrates American productivity levels have been two to three times higher than those in the UK throughout most of this Century. Since it is not clear to what extent this reflects the USA's advantages of a larger market and greater natural resources comparisons with Germany (an economy with similar population, resources and industrial structure) may be more instructive. German productivity levels represent a more realistic target for policy makers in the UK. In comparing Northern Ireland to Germany it should be recognised that NI is a relatively low productivity economy even within a UK context (see Part 2).

Nevertheless, even though this study is primarily concerned with the comparative labour productivity of Northern Ireland, it is still relevant to consider how the UK compares to Germany. There are two reasons for this. Firstly, the gap between average UK and German levels of output per head is considerably greater than the gap existing between NI and GB (see Chapters 1 and 4). This implies the second reason for the relevance of comparisons of Germany to the UK as a whole, given that a large proportion of the total productivity gap between NI and Germany is one which is "shared" with the UK as a whole, by extension some of the explanations for the generally low UK productivity are shared by NI. In the course of this Part we will mark out those occasions when NI's performance mirrors the generally poor showing of manufacturing throughout the UK and also pick out cases where NI is exceptionally bad even by the standards of the UK as a whole.

Table 9.1 provides a summary of previous studies of comparative net output per head in Britain and Germany. Comparative productivity calculations based on the Census of Production are included for NI.

Table 9.1
Comparative manufacturing productivity, 1860 to 1986
(levels of net output per head)

	NI/GB (GB=100)	Germany/UK (UK=100)	Germany/UK* (NI=100)
1865-74	na	68	na
1885-94	na	88	na
1905-13	79[a]	118	149
1936	62[b]	104	168
1937	62[c]	120	194
1950	71[d]	71	100
1968	84	135	161
1977	80	152	190
1980	76	151-176	199-232
1985	77	142-155	184-202
1986	79	200	253

Notes: * Calculated by Germany/UK divided by NI/GB. The discrepancy between UK and GB is sufficiently small to be ignored. The range of results presented for 1980 and 1985 illustrates the highest and lowest values implied by different studies.
[a] In 1912.
[b] In 1935.
[c] In 1935.
[d] In 1949.

Sources: Germany/UK: Rostas, 1948; Maizels, 1963; Smith, Hitchens and Davies, 1982; Guinchard, 1984; Ray, 1987; Commission of the European Communities, 1988; Crafts, 1988b; authors' own calculations. NI/GB: Census of Production.

Whilst the precise magnitudes of these UK/German comparisons are subject to uncertainty and there is a lack of consistency between studies based on different methodologies (compare the various results for 1980, 1985 and 1986), it is clear that the historical trend has been for German productivity levels to grow more rapidly than those in Britain including Northern Ireland. (German levels may have surpassed those in the UK during both the 1900s and 1930s Prais (1981a) illustrates that different studies came to various views as to whether this was in fact the case.)

The post-war "economic miracle" enabled Germany to achieve productivity growth rates such that the UK level was clearly surpassed. The level of output of German manufacturing has increased more than threefold since the mid-1950s whereas NI's output is only three quarters higher and that of GB 63 per cent higher (Chapter 8). The long run employment performance of NI has been equally dismal when compared to Germany. While German employment in manufacturing has maintained its 1955 level, NI employment has almost halved and that of GB decreased by over one third. It is important to make clear that the slower output growth in Britain has led to Germany overtaking the UK in the absolute amount of manufacturing output produced, while in the mid-nineteenth Century British output was around four times that of Germany, and although in 1953 Britain still had a size advantage[1], by the 1980s the Germany level of manufacturing output was at least one-third greater (Bairoch, 1982).

There remains the question of whether Germany remains a suitable model for British industrial practise given the recent productivity "miracle" in the UK (Muellbauer, 1986; Boakes, 1988; Crafts, 1988a). Whilst a dramatic improvement in the UK's productivity growth performance is to be welcomed it does not alter the fact that in the second half of the 1980s the productivity gap between Britain and Germany remains sizeable. There is therefore still much to be learnt from German industrial practise . The best way of ensuring that British productivity continues this process of catch up is to learn more about the best practise economies. Unfortunately Northern Ireland, as the region with the lowest productivity within the UK, has even more need to learn from Germany than the rest of the United Kingdom (see Chapter 4 and 8).

Resumé of the explanatory factors which will be considered

Part 1 has already summarised the vast body of literature relating to the possible explanations of Britain's relatively poor productivity performance. It now seems unlikely that this productivity shortfall can be given a simple monocausal explanation. Indeed, a whole range of factors have been indicated as being important such as capital and its level of technology, "add ons to machinery", ancillary devices, machine downtime because of inadequate maintenance and repair services. The quality of human capital has been stressed including the width and depth of training of production managers and general managers, the quality of engineers and the incentives given to them, the lack of formal training amongst British foremen, the inferior scale and scope of the British apprenticeship system, inadequate quantities of civilian research and development and weaknesses in the process of commercial exploitation of innovation. Some stress has also been places on such institutional factors as the reliance on stock market finance as opposed to industrial banking, the strong and socially responsible employers' organisations in Germany, single industrial unions in German factories in contrast to the British craft unions, German social and political attitudes which were more conducive to maintaining a strongly competitive market economy. Despite the fact that the range of possible explanations is legion there is increasing consensus that the deficiencies Britain must most urgently address are those relating to human resources (Prais, 1981a; Olson, 1985; Crafts, 1988a). Even given some improvement since 1979 (e.g. better industrial relations and tighter management) it is not clear to what extent there has been a trend change in the UK's productivity growth which will persist into the 1990s (Boakes, 1988; Crafts, 1988a). Moreover, it remains to be seen whether the present Conservative Administration or any new government in the 1990s can achieve the kind of fundamental upgrading in Britain's system of technical and vocational training which has been required for at least a century. Consideration of those factors which have been found to be important at the UK level has directed the course of our matched plant comparison, as have the types of questions asked by previous matched plant inquiries (these are described in detail in Chapter 10).

Chosen sectors and their characteristics

In our sampling of firms in Northern Ireland we were guided by the fact that NI manufacturing is dominated by four sectors: engineering, textiles , clothing and food, drink and tobacco. The proportion of employees in these four sectors is larger than that in either the UK or Germany and so our sampling (as the next Chapter shows) gave greater weight to these sectors. Whereas engineering accounts for 54 per cent of manufacturing employees in Germany (1985) and 44 per cent in the UK (1986), its share in NI is 30 per cent. On the other hand NI textiles represents a tenth of total NI employment (compared to about 3 per cent in Germany and UK), NI clothing one-seventh (4 per cent in UK and 3 percent in Germany) and food, drink and tobacco one-fifth (9 per cent in UK and 7 per cent in Germany). The miscellaneous industries are of less importance in NI than either UK or Germany.

Since we have already listed the general factors which account for the UK's overall poor productivity performance relative to Germany, it is worthwhile asking whether these individual sectors have any distinguishing characteristics which might mark them out from the "average" in either NI or UK (we also sampled from the miscellaneous trades, that is all activities other than those in the four industries listed above). These distinguishing characteristics helped inform our investigations of the different sectors.

Previous studies have found that German manufacturing as a whole has a capital stock which is superior in both quantity and quality to that of Britain's. However, Prais (1981a) doubted whether the German food industry had more machinery than its counterpart in the UK. At the same time, British food processors had fewer CNCs, less linking of machinery and problems with packaging machines (NEDO, 1985). British kitchen furniture makers were also characterised by relatively few CNC's and linked machines

97

(Steedman and Wagner, 1987). In contrast, parts of British clothing may be distinguished by the relative modernity of their equipment. Whilst Steedman and Wagner (1989) noted the greater use of automatic cutters and overhead systems amongst UK ladies garments manufacturers than in Germany, Britain also had more primitive sewing machines). Thus previous studies would suggest that there is doubt as to the appropriateness of the machinery used by the UK clothing, furniture and food packaging industries.

Median plant sizes in British clothing, textiles, food etc. and miscellaneous (excluding rubber, glass and furniture) are comparable with those in Germany, but British engineering and metals factories are typically only one-half to one-third the size of those in Germany (Prais, 1981a). Small plants in British engineering reflect an inability by British management to handle large plants given an historical tendency for British industrial relations to be especially problematic in process and assembly-line industries (these being dominated by male manual workers and craft unions). Whilst British labour may have been especially unco-operative in the heavy industries there is also some evidence (albeit impressionistic) that British management in some branches of engineering was unusually autocratic (e.g. shipbuilding (Pagnamenta and Overy, 1982) and textile machinery (Rothwell, 198)). Given a tradition of family run firms it has been argued that textiles also suffered from weak management. However, it is possible that the shake up and rationalisation of UK textiles after the 1980's slump led to an influx of managers from other sectors (Financial Times, 1988, April 28). Thus previous investigations have placed a question mark over the quality of labour and management in textiles and certain branches of engineering.

Germany's largest engineering firms are substantially bigger than their British counterparts (compare Rover with Volkswagen, GEC with Siemens or Jaguar with BMW). As in the case of differences in average plant sizes there is uncertainty as to the extent of Britain's loss of economies of scale. Moreover, small firm size may be more a result of corporate failure than the cause of that failure. Whilst it is not clear how UK and German firm sizes compare in the other industries, British textiles companies such as Coats-Viyella and Courtaulds are amongst Europe's largest.

Turning now to NI, not only is the manufacturing base markedly more dependent on textiles, clothing and food etc. than either UK or Germany but structural differences also exist at a finer level of disaggregation. While a later Chapter (21) will consider in detail the extent to which manufacturing in NI is structurally handicapped given likely shifts in demand at the world level, it is worth outlining at this stage the argument that an inappropriate range of industries is a major explanation of poor performance. After this thesis has been outlined we will turn to review the evidence which exists in secondary sources on the performance of individual sectors in NI.

Half of NI's employees in textiles are involved in linen production. To the extent that this has been a sector with heavy output decline throughout the Western world, this suggests that NI manufacturing is structurally handicapped. Similarly it might be said that NI's garment manufacturers are too reliant on low price products vulnerable to competition from the Newly Industrialised Countries; one-third of NI clothing employment is found in shirt-making compared to 7 per cent in Britain and hardly any in Germany (NI Economic Council, 1987). Relative to their counterparts in Great Britain, the NI food, drink and tobacco industries are more heavily dependent on the contracting products of cigarettes and alcohol. Perhaps the most characteristic feature of NI's industrial structure is the heavy dependence (one tenth of employment) on shipbuilding and aerospace. Despite some success in diversifying away from the stagnant market for supertankers orders for the Harland and Wolff shipyard were equivalent to only 4000 man years of work at the start of 1989 (compared to a work-force of 2400 in mid-1989). The successful management-employee buyout of the yard did bring guaranteed orders for up to three years from the Olsen group. Short Brothers appeared to have a more buoyant order book at the start of 1989 (£1 billion; four years work for about 7000 employees). Nevertheless, like Harland's it has been persistently unprofitable which in part derives from its dependency on civilian aviation; 44 per cent of its 1987 turnover, compared to 16 per cent of British Aerospace's and 27 per cent of MBB's (the leading German aircraft-maker). With the exception of some of the Boeing airlines almost every major passenger aircraft since the 1950s has been a loss maker. On the other hand, Shorts' strength may be its missiles which represent 39 per cent of turnover (34 per cent of BAe's and less than a quarter of MBB's). Apart from ships and aircraft, NI engineering may be too dependent on slow-growing areas of heavy engineering such as textile machinery (Mackie's), power station turbines (GEC) and oil-drilling equipment (Hughes Tools and Camco). It is not clear to what extent the health of NI engineering has been boosted by externally controlled plants making motor vehicle components (Ford and General Motors) and consumer electricals (Glen Electric).

There might therefore appear strong grounds for explaining NI's relatively poor manufacturing performance (see Chapters 4 to 8) entirely in terms of NI's structural handicap (Department of Commerce, 1982). One of the most important aims of this piece of research has been to separate the effects of industrial structure from the other explanations of poor performance in NI (e.g. machinery, innovation and quality of labour and management) through designing our sample so that each NI firm was matched with a German firm which was making a similar product line.

We have already seen how plant size economies of scale have been investigated at the UK level and so a rough comparison of German and NI plant sizes is possible (by linking the results of the Anglo-German comparisons with those outlined in Chapter 6[3]). The only major sectors where NI would appear to have a serious size disadvantage relative to the Germans are mechanical and electrical engineering and rubber processing. NI clothing, food, drink and tobacco factories are if anything bigger than their German counterparts and Harland and Wolff and Shorts are several times greater in size than the German medians. As the following Chapter will make clear the sample was designed with special care to ensure that NI suffered no disadvantage through a lack of potential economies of scale.

A lack of indigenous talent in design has been held to inhibit the recovery of NI linen; the industry finds it more difficult than its Italian counterpart to develop linen garments (IDB, 1985). This study investigates design efforts not only in textiles but in each of the sectors. Kurt Salmon (1988) criticises the reliance of NI clothing firms on standardised products with long-runs. Trends in the international retail market suggest that buyers will demand more flexibility from suppliers. NI clothing may also have special problems in its recruitment of labour (because wages are so low) and keeping turnover rates down (Labour Relations Agency, 1988). This study investigated comparative absenteeism, turnover and strikes in NI and Germany. NI clothing may also be dangerously over-dependent on a single customer. In this case Marks and Spencer, orders for which may employ 40 per cent of the 17,700 workers in NI garments industries (NI Economic Council, 1987). Whilst M & S could be seen as a benign influence prodding NI firms in the direction of greater quality it does leave NI vulnerable to any shift in M & S 's buying strategy, for example, an end to its "buy British" policy (Financial Times, 1989, January 31). This study investigated the structure of firm ownership in NI and Germany, compared the number of recent changes in ownership and the incidence of lame ducks.

This Chapter has given a brief overview of the literature on the characteristics of individual manufacturing sectors in the UK. The purpose was to highlight some of the factors which it would be worthwhile for a matched plant comparison such as the present one to investigate. Turning specifically to the case of Northern Ireland it was shown that the industrial structure of the Province still shows the legacy of its Edwardian and late Victorian apogee when Ulster (and more specifically the Lagan Valley) was the world's greatest producer of such commodities as ships, cigarettes and textile machinery as well as a dominant player in the markets for shirts, linen and a number of brands of drinks (Bardon, 1981; Kennedy and Ollerenshaw, 1985) . One of the aims of this matched plants study is to show to what extent, and for what reasons NI's position weakened in these traditional industries. Previous studies suggest that we should focus attention on such factors as design, market strategies and ownership types. Apart from selecting sample firms from the major types of heavy engineering, clothing, textiles and food, drink and tobacco in the Province, the study is also concerned to test NI's comparative performance in other industries where NI does not have as large a representation. Apart from the factors already mentioned, the statistical consideration of NI's comparative productivity outlined in Part 2 was used as a basis to suggest the kinds of explanatory variables which should be investigated.

Notes

1. In 1913 Germany had a superiority relative to the British volume of manufacturing output of about one-tenth.

2. It may be that the primary cause of the British productivity miracle has been the recognition that the American ,Continental and Japanese economies have higher standards which Britain needs to copy.

3. By using the median size data of Prais (1981a) for Germany, and that presented in Chapter 6 for NI. This comparison is approximate given that Prais' data relates to 1970-73 whereas the authors' calculations apply to 1986.

10 Design of the inquiry

" O wad some Pow'r the giftie gie us
To see oursels as others see us!

It as frae monie a blunder free us
An' foolish notion".

$$\text{Robert Burns (1785), } \underline{\text{To a Louse}}$$

Introduction

At the outset it was decided to cover as wide a cross section of
manufacturing in Northern Ireland as time and resources permitted.
At the same time the sample was to cover a significant proportion
of the total number of manufacturing employees within the
Province. Those initial decisions necessarily restricted analysis
to relatively small numbers of firms sampled within each
industrial sector and to a preponderance of medium sized or large
firms. However, with that decision made great care was taken to
ensure that the German counterparts to the Northern Irish sample
were closely matched by product and (if possible) by size of
plant. We will first describe the sample and then evaluate to what
extent it provides a biased representation of NI manufacturing as
a whole.

The sample

Table 10.1 shows the number of factories sampled by sector in Northern Ireland and West Germany (hereafter usually referred to as Germany or sometimes in tables as WG) and the number of different products matched.

Table 10.1
Number of plants visited and products matched by sector

	Northern Ireland	Germany	Matched product groups
Engineering	12	10	10
Food, drink and tobacco	5	4	4
Textiles	6	5	4
Clothing	16	12	8
Miscellaneous	6	8	6
Total	45	39	32

Forty-five plants in Northern Ireland were compared to 39 in Germany involving 32 different product groups (the 45 plants in NI represented 41 different firms, i.e. four of the NI companies in the sample were represented by two different factories). Whilst in most instances a single Northern Irish plant was matched with a single plant in Germany within the same product category, in twelve cases multiple matches were made, for example in a number of cases in the clothing sector. Those additional cases were required to improve the reliability of the productivity measurement.

Table 10.2 examines further characteristics of the plants matched. Part A of the table shows that almost equal numbers of firms were sampled in each of the large, medium and small firm size categories. Part B shows that on average firm size was a little smaller in the German sample in all sectors except engineering. In those cases where the matched plant size was not of the same order of magnitude the relevant activity or department was closely matched by size. Total employment sampled accounted for 12.4 per cent of all employment engaged in manufacturing in Northern Ireland in 1987 (or 16.1 per cent if one includes all the plants of the multi-plant firms within our sample).

Table 10.2
Part A: Distribution of plants by size (%)

	Northern Ireland	Germany
Large (500+ employees)	22	20
Medium (100-499 employees)	49	53
Small (under 100 employees)	29	27
	100	100

Table 10.2
Part B: Average size of plant by sector (number of employees)

	Northern Ireland	Germany
Engineering	471	693
Food, drink and tobacco	690	440
Textiles	306	246
Clothing	311	204
Miscellaneous	198	161
All	385	361

Table 10.3 illustrates how the distribution of employment within the sample differs from the sectoral breakdown for all manufacturing in Germany and Northern Ireland.

Table 10.3
Comparison of sample and population
(% of employment)

	NI sample		NI all manufacturing		WG sample		WG all manufact.
	1982	1987	1982	1987	1982	1987	1987
Engineering	32	20	34	32	40	38	53
Food etc.	27	19	20	21	11	15	7
Textiles	11	15	12	12	18	15	3
Clothing	24	36	16	18	25	22	3
Miscellaneous	7	10	18	18	6	10	35
All*	100	100	100	100	100	100	100

* Because of rounding the sum of the sectoral percentages may not equal 100.

Sources: Census of Employment (NI), and Statistisches Bundesamt (1988).

The sectoral distribution of employment within the sample in NI is reasonably close to that of the population of firms in 1982 (food etc. and clothing are over-represented within the sample and miscellaneous trades are under-represented). Employment change within the NI sample causes engineering to be substantially under-represented in 1987 and clothing to be substantially over-represented. Turning to the German sample of firms, it can be seen that their distribution of employment under-represents engineering and over-represents the other sectors, that is, given our priority to match NI firms with comparable producers in Germany, the German sample has been skewed towards the NI distribution of employment between the sectors (i.e. large food etc., textiles and clothing sectors). The next section examines whether there are any biases in the sample we used. Sampling techniques are then described in a following section.

Representativeness of the sample

The total population of firms in NI is relatively small (about 700 employing more than twenty persons) and as a result in many cases the firms sampled were the sole representatives of a given activity in NI. For nine products in engineering we visited the only producer in NI and the same was true for one product in textiles, three in food and four in miscellaneous. In addition, we visited a textiles firm which dominated the NI production of one good and our sample included most of the producers of three types of ladies garments and one type of menswear. In other words coverage was either complete for 21 individual product lines or negligibly different from 100 per cent.

Whilst for these individual products the question of representativeness and bias cannot arise given complete coverage within the product line, the question still arises as to whether these 21 products were themselves representative of NI manufacturing as a whole?

Comparison of our sample with the population suggests that the sample is, if anything biased towards the better performers in NI. This is partly because larger plants are over represented in the sample (almost four fifths of factories visited had more than 100 employees compared to only 6.1 per cent of all manufacturing plants in NI in 1986; Business Monitor, 1986). To the extent that positive economies of scale can be realised this over-representation of the largest factories will have introduced a positive bias into the measurement of NI's performance. The sample also has a strong representation of the largest firms in NI: four out of the ten largest manufacturing companies and 11 out of the 25 largest employers. In other words our sample tells us something not only about those NI firms which are the sole representatives of certain activities in NI but it also includes many of the largest companies in NI some of which have often been regarded as the best which NI has to offer by way of industrial practise. Apart from over-representing larger plants, the sample also includes an over-representation of plants under external control (both in terms of the number of plants controlled by GB and foreign companies and the numbers of employees represented, this is considered in more detail in Chapter 16). To the extent that these plants out-perform their NI owned counterparts then in this respect the sample has bias in favour of NI. Since an earlier set of comparisons (Hitchens and O'Farrell, 1987, 1988a, 1988b; O'Farrell and Hitchens, 1988a) has considered in detail the problems of small, indigenous companies in NI (discussed in Chapter 20) this piece of research was directed towards the larger firms in NI and those which are externally controlled. If there are any biases in the sample they are ones in favour of NI's performance.

Sampling techniques

The sample was selected using the IDB Trade Directory to choose NI plants with special emphasis given to products which have a large weight in the total sales of NI manufacturing. Managing directors were approached by telephone between early 1987 and the summer of 1988. They were geographically spread throughout the Province.

Having selected both a product and target range of plant size, companies were then matched randomly within that size range in both Germany and Northern Ireland. Typically, there was only a single firm within Northern Ireland making a given product whereas in Germany a choice was available. Half of the German managing directors agreed to co-operate following the initial contacts and 91 per cent of managing directors in Northern Ireland. Interviews took place in all parts of West Germany (including West Berlin) and in one instance it was necessary to travel to Austria to match a significant Northern Irish trade with the subsidiary of a German company.

Two methods were employed to select the German counterpart firms. Where the NI companies knew of a competitor in Germany an attempt was made in the first instance to match the NI factory with that firm. If no competitor was recognised, or if permission was refused to visit the competing German company, then the following German trade directories were used to randomly select a firm operating within the appropriate product group.

BDI (Bundesverband der deutschen Industrie) ed(1986) Die deutsche Industrie, Schloss Mindelburg, Gemeinschaftsverlag.

Verband deutscher Adressbuchverleger ed(1987) Wer liefert was? Hamburg.

Seibt-Verlag ed(1984) Bezugsquellennachweis fur den Einkauf, Munchen.

When matching with Germany attention was given not only to principal products manufactured but to the entire product range and to plant size. Plant visits within Germany were grouped together according to their regional location: West Berlin, southern Germany, and northern Germany (each of these areas represented about one-third of the German sample). Such grouping not only reduced travel costs and time expended but enabled the inclusion of plants operating under various policy regimes (e.g. the Berlin plants, like their NI counterparts, received capital grants). If there were doubts as to matching on either products or plant size these were resolved by phone calls and/or the request for company brochures. In a small number of cases difficulties in finding a satisfactory match in Germany required that more than one company formed the match with NI.

Almost all the visits were conducted by two of the authors. Each

interview lasted about half a day, usually with the managing
director or plant manager.

Matching

Eighty-seven plants spread across a wide range of industries were
visited and of these it was possible to match eighty-four.
Thirty-two product groups were included, e.g. drinks of various
kinds, cans, carpets, cloths, ladies' and men's garments of
various sorts, electrical apparatus, two types of vehicles, and
precision engineering. Occasionally when a product could not be
matched the capability to produce a given product was the deciding
criterion, for example in engineering. Given the generally higher
quality standards of German products it was not always straight
forward to match "like with like". Indeed in a number of cases
(clothing in particular) German firms had shut down their
production of certain product lines (e.g. mass produced shirts)
many years earlier.

In a number of cases the NI products were of an equivalent
standard, for example in parts of engineering and in the food,
drink and tobacco sectors, but in a number of other industries NI
products were said to be of poor standard even at the price for
which they were charged (see Chapter 11). Those product
deficiencies are considered in more detail below. Difficulties in
matching products and criticisms made of those products are
indicative of the more highly trained work-force in Germany (see
Chapter 14). Before showing the results of this matched plant
comparison we review of earlier uses of this technique of economic
research.

Previous matched plant comparisons

Visits by British industrialists and trade unionists to American
and German factories have a long history. A group from the
Lancashire cotton industry visited the US in 1902 (Shadwell,
1906). Further Anglo-American comparisons in the textile industry
were made during the Second World War (Plate, 1944) and some
German factories were visited after the end of the War (Barnett,
1986). The Anglo-American Council on Productivity provided the
first comparative study across a broad front of industries
involving over sixty sectors (Hutton, 1953). In more recent years
the National Economic Development Council has continued
international comparisons of factory performance as a means to
inspire British workers and managers to higher standards (Gauge
and Tool SWP, 1981).

The rigorous and academic development of the technique of
matched plant comparisons was achieved by the National Institute
of Economic and Social Research. In the first exercise of its kind
Daly, Hitchens and Wagner (1985) compared over thirty British and
German engineering component manufacturers (e.g. screws, nuts,
coil springs, drill bits and hydraulic valves). In subsequent
studies ten German kitchen furniture makers were matched with a

similar number in the UK and 10 German ladies' garments manufacturers with an equal number in Britain (Steedman and Wagner, 1987, 1989).

In each of these National Institute studies the German companies had an impressive productivity superiority relative to the British counterparts. This advantage varied from 63 per cent higher for engineering productivity, to a range of 40-100 per cent higher in clothing, nition of clothing, and to 130 per cent higher in kitchen cabinet panels. It should be stressed that all these measures are of physical productivity (i.e. springs, or panels, or skirts per operator). This determined the factors which could be considered as explanations of productivity differences. Some of the general explanations which we have outlined above for the higher productivity in German industry (see Chapter 2), such as the size of firms, differences in the system of industrial finance, and variations in the extent of R and D, were not considered by these studies. By contrast, the focus was largely restricted to shop-floor related factors; age of machinery, use of CNCs, manning levels, breakdowns, relative importance of planned and emergency maintenance, the skills of operators and of foremen and supervisors.

A fairly consistent picture emerged as to the importance of capital in explaining Anglo-German productivity differences. Whilst the Germans did not necessarily have younger machinery (in engineering components average ages were similar), they did have the advantage of more CNCs and more appropriate machinery (automatic feeding and linking). In one sector, clothing , there were curious imbalances in the British machine stock with old lock-stitching machines working alongside machinery which was more highly automated than that in Germany (Steedman and Wagner, 1989). German manning levels were consistently lower (and in kitchen furniture this could explain almost all of the productivity difference observed). Breakdowns were of negligible significance in Germany but downtime was frequent in Britain. The UK companies were often not capable of fixing their own machines and so had to rely on their suppliers (usually Italian, German, Japanese or American). Planned maintenance and regular cleaning of machinery was common in Germany but practically unheard of in the UK.

A major reason for the better maintenance of machinery in Germany was the preponderance of skilled persons amongst the operators. "Skilled" being defined as those who had passed through the two/three year German apprenticeship system (the excellence of the German technical and vocational educational system was considered above as a general explanation for better productivity in Germany). As Table 10.4 shows, the British companies rely on the semi- and unskilled.

Most British foremen were only time-served whereas the German Meister is required to pass written and practical examinations . As a result the Meister could prepare, set and repair machinery, draw up and realise production plans whereas his British counterpart was largely restricted to supervising line balance. Steedman and Wagner (1989) also considered the relative qualifications of management and discovered that German clothing

managers were much more likely to have higher level
qualifications.

Table 10.4
Percentages of shop-floor workers
with formal qualifications

	UK	Germany
Engineering components	25	50
Kitchen cabinets	10	90
Ladies' garments	0	80

Sources: Daly, Hitchens and Wagner (1985); Steedman and Wagner
(1987, 1989).

The National Institute studies therefore suggest that Britain
has a considerable productivity problem at the shop-floor level
which cannot be solved simply by purchasing more modern machinery
given that the UK work-force is inadequately trained to operate
and maintain the existing machine stock. Whilst these studies
proved that British workers produce fewer units of output than
their German counterparts they gave less attention to the extent
to which, product for product, British goods are of lower quality,
reliability or technical up-to-dateness than their German
counterparts. There is reason to expect that the value component
to the Anglo-German productivity gap may in some cases be at least
as significant as the physical component when (see Chapter 2) the
width and depth of experience of German managers is higher than
that in Britain and their commitment to R and D is greater. In
our matched plant comparison we consider not only those factors
reviewed by the National Institute but also some of those relevant
to product quality.
The following Chapter compares the employment, exports, capacity
utilisation, productivity performance and research and development
inputs of the two samples of companies.

11 Indicators of company performance

"The Germans make everything difficult, both for themselves and for everyone else".

Goethe

Introduction

Employment growth, exports, and capacity utilisation are considered as indicators of the comparative success of firms in NI and Germany. Using these performance indicators as a background this Chapter will compare the productivity (physical output and value-added per employee) and research and development inputs used by the two sets of companies.

Employment

Comparative employment growth rates for each of the sectors were calculated for the five year period 1982-87. The results are summarised in Table 11.1. (In certain cases the performance of one firm has a substantial impact on employment change within an entire sector taken as an unweighted average of the individual companies, where this is so the results are shown in parentheses for that sector excluding the single firm.)

Table 11.1
Comparative employment growth rates by sectors

	Percentage change 1982-87		Percentage of companies contracting		Sample size*	
	NI	WG	NI	WG	NI	WG
Engineering	-52	- 8	67	33	12	9
Food, etc.	(-18)-46	32 (0)	80	0	5	4
Textiles	6	-21 (14)	50	20	6	5
Clothing	19	-14 (6)	31	40	16	10
Miscellaneous	(-12) 16	45 (4)	33	0	6	6
All	(-16)-22	- 3	49	24	45	34

* Employment data was not disclosed in every case. Hence the difference between the sample size here and that in early tables.

Overall, half the NI companies contracted over the period compared to one-quarter of their German counterparts. This led to a 22 percent decline in NI employment at those factories compared with a three per cent decline in employment in Germany (the NI performance improves to a 16 per cent fall when the two extreme observations which are noted below are excluded). At a sectoral level employment in engineering suffered the greatest fall in NI followed by food, drink and tobacco, whilst firms in the remaining three sectors achieved positive employment growth rates on average. Comparative employment change was poorer in NI companies than their German counterparts in engineering, food, drink and tobacco and miscellaneous trades (in the last case whether one includes or excludes one extreme observation in both NI and Germany) but in clothing and textiles NI firms achieved a superior performance. This comparatively poor German performance in textiles is largely the responsibility of a single firm and when this case is removed the performance of the remaining German firms is better than that of their NI counterparts. The German performance in clothing remains inferior even when one exceptional firm is removed from the calculation of the NI average.

Table 11.2 illustrates how the performance of firms in the sample compares to the actual employment change of all manufacturing and the sectors in both Northern Ireland and Germany. In both NI and Germany the decline in employment of the whole sample is worse than the actual decline for all manufacturing (albeit the difference in the case of Germany is marginal, and most of the difference between the performance of the sample and the population in NI is attributable to two extreme observations). The average employment performance of the NI sample was recalculated by giving each sector a weight equal to its actual representation in all manufacturing. The impact of the differential structure of the sample was found to be comparatively small (an employment change of 2-4 per cent points) and of uncertain direction (negative if all observations are included and positive if the two extreme ones were excluded).

Table 11.2
Employment change 1982-87 sample compared to population

	NI Sample	NI Population	WG Sample	WG Population
Engineering	-52	-16	-8	3
Food, etc.	(-18)-46	- 9	(0) 32	-6
Textiles	6	-13	(14)-21	-15
Clothing	19	1	(6)-14	-19
Miscellaneous	(-12) 16	-13	(4) 45	-6
All	(-16)-22	-11	-3	-2

Note: Numbers in parentheses show average values when a single extreme observation is excluded.

Sources for population data: Census of Employment (NI), SOEC (1987) and Statistisches Bundesamt (1988).

Turning to the performance of individual sectors, in engineering and food etc. the sample in NI under-performs the population. This situation is reversed in the remaining three sectors. The German sample in food, miscellaneous and clothing outpaced the population. In engineering the sample performs worse than the population and in textiles the result depends on whether one includes one extreme observation.

Capacity utilisation

The differential performance of the sectors was reflected in the comparative rates of capacity utilisation. Whilst on average NI plants had a utilisation rate fifteen percentage points lower than that of their German counterparts, the worst NI utilisation rates in comparison to Germany were in the engineering, food, drink and tobacco and miscellaneous sectors. In clothing and textiles, however, NI plants operated at a capacity utilisation comparable with that of their German counterparts (comparative rates of capacity utilisation are considered in more detail in Chapter 12 and especially Table 12.6).

Exports: quantity and destinations

Table 11.3 shows the pattern of export performance. Overall companies exported a quarter of their output. Unfortunately, there is no recent statistical data relating to what proportion of the output of all manufacturing in NI is exported but for the sake of comparison it can be noted that only 13 per cent of manufacturing sales were to non-UK markets in 1977 (Department of Commerce, 1981). If NI's aggregate trade performance remained roughly constant during the following ten years then this would imply that the sample of NI firms was outperforming the population in terms of its propensity to export. Nevertheless, the NI export performance is less impressive than it seems given that over one quarter of those exports (i.e. 7 per cent of sales) were to the Republic of Ireland which was the sole export destination for about one-fifth of companies. A further third of the Northern Irish companies had significant sales to continental Europe and North America and the remaining companies sold to the Far East. By contrast German export sales were more heavily weighted (in 70 per cent of cases) towards the wealthier Continental European markets. (The percentage of output exported by the German sample firms are broadly similar to those given by the official statistics: all manufacturing exports were 30 per cent of turnover in 1985, engineering exports were 41 per cent, textiles 27 per cent and clothing 18 per cent; Statistische Bundesamt, 1986. A more up-to-date estimate is that German mechanical engineering exports amount to 60 per cent of sales while supplying 30 per cent of the entire European Community market for machinery and plant; Financial Times, 1989, March 21.) A small number of the German companies also sold to the Far East. The export success of the sample of German companies was achieved in spite of the appreciation of the <u>Deutsche Mark</u> against most currencies during this period (Financial Times, 1989, April 7). This testifies to the ability of German products to compete on quality rather than price (product quality is considered later in this Chapter).

Table 11.3
Comparative export* performance

	Exports* as a % of sales		% of firms exporting	
	NI	WG	NI	WG
Engineering	40(27)	38	100(42)	88
Food etc.	32(24)	4	100(60)	67
Textiles	43	38	100	100
Clothing	1	18	30	100
Miscellaneous	23	18	25	67
All	25(18)	24	72(50)	90
Number of companies	36	31		

* Defined to include sales to the Republic of Ireland but not sales from NI to Great Britain (where trade within Ireland was significant, NI exports exclusive of those to the Republic are shown in parentheses).

The conclusion that the NI firms were primarily orientated towards softer markets was confirmed by the answers given to the question as to how many competitor firms were recognised by the companies surveyed. On average the NI firms claimed they had nine competitors within the UK and the same number overseas. The

Germans recognised a similar number of competitors from within Germany (10) but 18 outside of Germany. The fact that they had twice as many competitors abroad is suggestive that the Germans were operating in more difficult markets.

Comparative physical productivity: method of measurement

Table 11.4
Methods of productivity measurement

	Total number of matchings	Type of output and employment measure
Engineering	6	3 Whole principal product output and all employees
		1 Sample activity output and operators
		2 Sample activity output and matched labour time by production workers
Food etc.	5	1 Whole principal product output and all employees
		2 Whole principal activity output and all production workers
		2 Sample activity output and operators
Textiles	5	4 Whole principal product output and all employees
		1 Sample activity output and operators
Clothing	16	10 Whole principal product output and all employees
		5 Principal activity and matched production workers
		1 A major product line and matched labour time by production workers
Miscellaneous	7	3 Whole principal product output and all employees
		1 Sample activity and all production workers
		3 Sample activity and matched labour time by production workers
All manufacturing	39	

In comparing productivity preference was given to matching the actual output achieved of principal products, over as long a period as possible, e.g. a year, month, or week. Fifty per cent of our individual reported measures were based on this approach.

Where principal products could not be measured, principal activities (those involving significant numbers of employees) were compared and these included: output achieved from sets of machines over extended periods; packaging time; items assembled; and, in three cases, the time required to manufacture a specified item was used to compare productivity. These different measures were summarised in Table 11.4 for each sector. A total of thirty-nine measurements are made as the basis of the summary productivity calculations for each of the five sectors. The Table also shows that in most cases the denominator of the measure is total employment in the plant. In four cases output per production worker was the preferred measure (this occurred when there was a marked difference between the size of the marketing and sales department in either NI or Germany). In four matched engineering trades no single summary measure was calculated. In contrast, in some cases it was possible to match the output per head of one firm (in either NI or Germany) with that of more than one firm in the other country.

Comparative physical productivity: the productivity gap

Table 11.5 shows comparative productivity for each sector (taken as the unweighted average of the productivities of the individual firms compared).

Table 11.5
WG physical productivity as % of NI, 1987-88

	(NI=100)	Number of pairs
Engineering	248	6
Food, drink, tobacco	190	5
Textiles	145	5
Clothing	133	16
Miscellaneous	175	7
Total number of matchings		39

This Table shows that average German comparative productivity in the matched trades lies between 33 per cent and 148 per cent above the NI level. From the NI point of view, the better performers are the clothing and textiles sectors, whilst a comparatively poor performance is returned by companies sampled in the food etc. and miscellaneous trades. With an average productivity level only 40 per cent of the matched German counterparts, engineering in NI is the worst performer in relative terms.

Whilst Chapter 1 demonstrated that there is some doubt as to the precise magnitude of the UK's productivity shortfall relative to Germany, it is possible to demonstrate the consistency between our results and those of previous considerations of international productivity differences. Table 11.6 illustrates Germany's sectoral comparative productivity in 1985 as measured by two techniques: purchasing power parities (Commission of the European

Communities, 1988), and, secondly, weighted comparisons of physical outputs up-dated using indices of output and employment (Smith, Hitchens and Davies, 1982).

Whilst comparisons between Tables 11.5 and 11.6 should only be made with caution (apart from possible difference of industrial classification, the sample results in Table 11.6 differ from those of the statistical studies because they relate to physical output of number of units as opposed to value-added/net output, and in 1987-88 rather than 1985), a number of points can be made. The sample of German engineering firms achieved physical productivity levels 248 per cent of those in Northern Ireland and this appears to be better than the statistical comparative productivity in mechanical and electrical engineering, whilst at the same time being worse than the statistical superiority of German productivity in ships, aircraft and vehicles. German physical productivity in textiles and clothing is at the lower end of the range suggested by the statistical comparisons (the comparatively good performance by our sample of textiles firms in NI is not surprising given that some of them were involved in the production of carpets which is a line where British physical productivity may be comparable to that of Germany (SOEC, 1987b). In miscellaneous trades (embracing glass etc., paper etc., timber and furniture and chemicals and man-made fibres) the sample of German firms had a physical productivity advantage of three-quarters relative to the level in NI. Again this lies at the favourable end of the range indicated by the Census of Production data. Given the large scope for structural differences (between the sample in the miscellaneous trades and the overall composition of the sector in NI and Germany) it is probably not surprising that there is a divergence between our measure of physical productivity and the results of the various statistical studies.

A more notable contrast may be that between the physical productivity in food etc. (German level 190 per cent of NI) and the statistical results: between 92 per cent and 129 per cent. Whilst this could imply that the matched sample of firms was based on those activities where NI's performance was relatively weak, it should also be noted that statistical comparisons of net output in food etc. are prone to unreliability (e.g. difficulties arise when making allowance for differential excise payments on cigarettes and alcohol). In any case two out of the five sample comparisons of food etc. productivity fall within the range suggested by the official statistics. In the other three measures German productivity is about double that of NI or even higher, a possible explanation for this is that these measures were based on efficiency at the packaging stage and this may be an area where the UK food industry is peculiarly weak, especially in terms of machine feeding devices and factory organisation (Prais, 1981a; NEDO, 1985).

Turning now to a more detailed consideration of the distribution of NI firms according to their comparative productivity performance, two NI firms achieved levels of physical output per head which were clearly higher than those in their German counterparts. At a further eight NI firms productivity levels were indistinguishable from those of their German counterparts (i.e. within a margin of plus or minus 10 per cent of German levels). Thus in 26 per cent of all matchings (i.e. 39) the NI firm had a performance either better than or equal to the German counterpart. Ten other matchings where distributed at the bottom end of the distribution of NI performance relative to Germany with productivity levels of less than half those in Germany. In the remaining 19 matchings (i.e. 49 percent of cases) NI productivity levels were between half and 90 percent of those of the matched counterpart.

Table 11.6
WG value-added per head as % of NI and the UK, 1985

	WG/UK (UK=100)	NI/UK (NI=100)	WG/NI (NI=100)
Mechanical engineering[a]	161-230*	101	161-228
Electrical, electronic	94-154*	75	125-205
Ships, aircraft, vehicles	180-261*	51	353-512
Textiles, leather, and clothing	120-144*	84	143-171
Food, drink, tobacco	84-117*	91	92-129
Glass, pottery, and building products	178-215*	95	187-226
Paper, printing and publishing	177-257*	79	224-325
Timber and furniture	236	85	278

Notes: *: two sources were used to estimate the WG/UK productivity; Smith, Hitchens and Davies (1982) which was updated using the technique described in Chapter 1 (Table 1.5) and the Commission of the European Communities (1988). In the first three industries Smith, Hitchens and Davies (1982) estimate of the German productivity superiority was the larger and in the remainder the Commission of the European Communities (1988) provided the higher estimate (except in timber and furniture were Smith, Hitchens and Davies provided the only estimate).
[a]   Includes metal goods in Smith et al, and is defined as industrial and agricultural machinery by Commission of the European Communities.

Product quality

The measurement of physical productivity as described above makes no allowance for product quality variability. Hence while every attempt was made to match each NI activity with a similar level of quality in Germany, it was often difficult to find German companies which were still operating at NI quality standards. In fact in forty-eight per cent of the matchings a higher quality product was produced in Germany but in only 7 per cent of comparisons did NI quality exceed that of Germany (three cases in the textiles and clothing trades). That higher German quality is often reflected in a greater value-added achieved by the counterpart German company. An attempt was therefore made to partition the higher comparative value-added per head achieved by the German companies between that which could be accounted for by a higher physical productivity and that which was the consequence of a greater quality produced by the company. The method simply compares the ratio of value-added (at the 1987 average market exchange rate of 2.94 Dm/£) between the matched plants with their comparative physical productivities (where the firms supplied data on turnover this was adjusted to value-added using the ratio between net output and gross output for the appropriate industry given in the official statistics). After accounting for the greater value-added per head consequent upon a higher physical productivity in Germany, the unexplained residual of Germany's value-added per head superiority is assumed to reflect variations in other factors including product quality. The results are shown in Table 11.7.

Table 11.7
Importance of differences in product quality

	Percentage of cases where Germany quality greater	Total cases	Per cent of German productivity advantage attributable to*:	
			Physical output	Quality
Engineering	50	10	40	60
Food, drink etc.	0	5	100	0
Textiles	50	6	48	52
Clothing	57	16	53	47
Miscellaneous	60	5	62	38
Total cases	48	42	61	39

* The partition of the value-added gap between quality and physical productivity is based upon a total of 22 matched pairs where it was possible to compare both value-added and physical productivity. Given this smaller sample size the results are not directly comparable with those in Table 11.5.

On average two-fifths of the value-added productivity gap between NI and Germany is attributable to quality differences as measured in this way. Whilst measurement problems imply that the magnitudes shown should be regarded as more indicative than precise, the analysis does serve to highlight the importance of factors other than physical productivity in the determination of relative net output per head. (In order to analyse the sensitivity of the results to the level of the Deutsche Mark/Pound exchange rate chosen, the partition between physical productivity and quality was re-estimated for the whole sample using a high and low extreme for the exchange rate. Firstly, 3.79 Dm/£ which was the average rate for 1984 and the highest value of the Pound during

1982-87, and, secondly a hypothetical rate of 2.5 Dm/£. Using these rates the contribution of product quality was respectively, 21 per cent and 48 per cent of the total difference in levels of value-added per head).

Set beside the estimates are the percentages of cases where German product quality exceeded that of the NI matched comparison[1] according to the assessment of managers in Germany and NI. Some examples of particular cases were as follows.

In engineering in four out of the five cases where NI quality was criticised the NI firm was the sole representative of a given industrial activity within the Province. In three of those cases the German counterpart was recommended as a competitor and a good match by the NI firm. This is one reason for giving some attention to the details of these cases. Another reason is that all five NI firms were heavily dependent on subsidisation. Indeed, in some of these cases (perhaps all of them) the firms would not have remained in existence but for continual injections of public funds. In some cases poor quality in NI was not simply a case of a low quality good at a low price but in at least two cases the goods being producing were actually shoddy (i.e. poor workmanship and NI prices were insufficiently cheap to compensate for this).

Engineering quality: example 1

At one NI firm the company chose to make for the bottom half of the market of its German counterpart. The matched German firm competed on design and research and development. It developed expensive top of the range products about which their customers were said to talk for half an hour whilst dismissing lower range products within five minutes. The technical quality of the German company's production was such that one large client had told them that they required only one-fifth of the maintenance personnel it required to service a comparable British made product.

Engineering quality: example 2

The NI firm had entered into a collaborative project with the German counterpart. We were told in NI that "much bad language was exchanged because of the different methods of manufacture. In NI we would be manufacturing for application whereas the Germans manufacture for perfection. They are a race considering themselves infallible in the Teutonic way". The German counterpart claimed "We gave them simple components but the manufacturing was not according to the drawings. They did not get it right. In simple terms the hole was not in the right place. Because it was not made to measure it could not be used". The result was that when the NI and German companies made separate halves of the one machine the two would not match together. The Germans attributed the problems in NI to the limited range of work experience and the shortness of the apprenticeships. It was of note that similar collaborative manufacture with companies in the Netherlands, France, Japan and England had not encountered such difficulties.

Engineering quality: example 3

Similar problems of lack of precision in engineering standards were detected in another engineering firm where calibration equipment was recently installed to correct the micrometers in use which were known to be a "couple of thou out".

The product of this company sampled was used by two German firms in the sample. With reference to the NI machine one said "a Belgian machine has double the output per hour, is more precise and is more technologically up-to-date". The other German customer said "they use technology which is twenty to thirty years out of date". Moreover, a NI user of the NI machine stated that they had won a productivity advantage because their European competitors had bought more of the NI machines than they themselves had. Their competitors therefore suffered proportionately more breakdowns, problems with repairs and delivery of spare parts. The manufacturer responsible for these products was aware of the need to raise quality and had posted notices around the factory exhorting better standards of workmanship. Moreover, they paid to send some shop floor workers to a Continental trade fair. The effect of seeing the standards of competitors was described as salutory.

Engineering quality: example 4 and 5

In two further cases where German quality exceeded that of N I the NI companies were operating in a low price/low quality market. A German manager described one of the products as "rough" but "sufficient for its use". In contrast, the German counterpart had left this market behind by successfully competing in markets dependent on specialised and designed products.

Quality in food etc. and textiles

Product quality of the firms sampled in the food, drink and tobacco sector was more nearly comparable in Northern Ireland with Germany. In textiles while two Northern Irish plants sold higher quality or better designed products than their German counterparts, at two others the German factory held an edge in quality. One German company had increased its competitive advantage by tailoring output more closely to the market by supplying products designed for individual requirements. The owner of that company had worked in Northern Ireland and considered the Northern Irish philosophy to be one geared to the producer rather than the customer. At another NI company the product was again aimed at a lower segment of the market than that of its German counterpart; "We have no inspection or quality control but are cheap", we were told by the manager.

Quality in the clothing sector

The quality of German garments was superior to the output of the

NI clothing factories. With only one exception the NI companies were manufacturing to lower design, quality or fabric standards. The greater emphasis on quality in Germany was not surprising given that German labour costs are at least double those in NI, as any German garment manufacturer who attempted to competing on price and physical productivity alone would have been forced out of existence under pressure from the Eastern Bloc economies and competition from the Newly Industrialised Countries would have been forced out of existence some years ago. When shown shirts from a number of NI firms within the sample one German manager made the following judgment "Shirt A is poorly made, shirt B has an unacceptable collar and is poorly packaged".

Quality in the miscellaneous trades

In three cases in the miscellaneous trades sector the NI output demonstrated problems of workmanship. At one company problems arising from an inconsistency in standards were due to an incorrect calibration of machines. The operator "had never been trained to get it right, he just pushed it through". Samples taken from another company were considered of poor quality by the manager of the German counterpart because the plastic was too thick. To use thinner plastic would have required more skill than was available in NI. One German miscellaneous trades firm had used some supplies bought from NI and manager said that he had complained to the NI supplier about its quality. This had no effect and now they buy from Italy where "a better product is produced at a better price".

Quality, value-added and reject rates

Germany's crushing quality advantage told when we compared the value-added of pairs of firms. In only two cases out of the 22 possible pair-wise comparisons did Germany fail to achieve a higher level of value-added per head than NI. Five German firms (23 per cent)had levels of value-added per head more than four times those achieved in their matched counterparts. A further eight (36 per cent) German firms had levels of value-added per head between two and four times greater than that in NI. The remaining seven German firms (32 per cent) had a value-added productivity advantage of between 50 per cent and 100 per cent.

We considered a further dimension of product quality by comparing reject rates (both those internal to the factory and from the customer or retailer).

Table 11.8 shows that NI has a slightly better performance in textiles and miscellaneous trades but performed slightly worse in engineering. However, in clothing NI's reject rate was more than double that of its German rivals. A later section will consider to what extent this reflected the comparative skills and training of operators in the two countries.

Table 11.8
Reject rates (combination of internal and external)

	NI % (Number of firms)	WG % (Number of firms)
Engineering	2.3 (4)	1.8 (2)
Food etc.	na	na
Textiles	0.7 (3)	1.9 (2)
Clothing	5.7 (9)	2.2 (5)
Miscellaneous	2.9 (2)	3.8 (2)

Design and research and development

The number of plants which undertook design or R and D was
compared and, where possible, the intensity of design or R and D
in terms of the numbers of persons working in those departments as
a proportion of the total employment in the firms concerned.
Seventy-two per cent of plants visited in NI undertook design or
research and development compared with all companies in the German
sample.   In NI the shortfall was concentrated in the engineering
and miscellaneous trades. The intensity of R and D and design
could be measured in the engineering and clothing trades. In
engineering in NI there was one research and development or design
employee for every 39 persons engaged in the factory whereas the
comparable ratio in Germany was only one to twelve.   Similarly in
the clothing sector the ratio in NI was one researcher or designer
for every 182 employees compared to one for every 62 employees in
Germany. These comparisons somewhat exaggerates the intensity of
design and R and D inputs   within Northern Ireland since they
include designers and researchers employed by the firms but based
outside of NI (usually in London). For every design and R and D
person based in NI there were 328 employees. In the food sector
numbers of persons employed in design and research and development
were not significantly different between the two countries.
   As an example of attitudes to design, one NI engineering company
stated that price was the most important factor affecting
competition and after that design was important but they had no
competitive edge on design and they had fallen behind. The German
attitude was quite different "we have a graduate engineer who
visits customers and advises them on the product and also on
development. Very many products are designed for our customers,
that is the main advantage we have in competition". Another pair
of engineering companies illustrated the same divergence between
NI and German thinking. The NI company said "we tend to make for
the bottom end of the market" whilst the German company felt that
their competitive advantage rested entirely on design and research
and development whereas on the basis of price alone they would be
uncompetitive.
   In another pair of engineering plants the Northern Ireland
attitude to development and design was to make low priced

products. In Germany they said that since 1982 they had vacated the mass market for one which was specialised and design orientated. It was notable that the German engineering firms could exploit agglomeration economies which simply do not exist within the much smaller range of industries in Northern Ireland. For example, a mechanical engineering firm drew on the expertise of excellent electrical engineering firms in Germany in order to add electronic controls to their products. The NI counterpart was trying to do the same but it was co-operating with a company (also included in our sample) whose speciality was electrical hardware rather than software. A further NI company showed us some innovatory ideas for future products. Unfortunately its research and development was a rather <u>ad hoc</u> affair arising from the part-time activities of one man. The company had however improved its product range by producing under licence an American product.

In the miscellaneous trades in NI the product range of one company had been allowed to drift down market because of the conservative attitudes of a long established family based management. Following take over, the new manager had attempted to improve the presentation of the product and had "taken a chance with a Birmingham packaging designer" to modernise the range. Nevertheless, even these efforts were insignificant as compared to the German counterpart which engaged a university professor as chief designer and in addition employed qualified full-time designers.

Problems occurred in a NI clothing company attempting to raise the quality standards at their factory. In that instance they had to abandon the standard minute piece work system in order to attain quality standards and reduce their internal reject rate from catastrophic levels (they stabilised at 17 per cent). The German counterpart managed to work on a piece work system. One NI clothing manufacturer emphasised that little designer clothing is produced there. Another company undertaking such designer style clothing in Northern Ireland emphasised that design teams should be based in fashion centres where they can see innovation in styles and hence it was difficult to design from NI. Thus it may have been rational for a number of clothing companies in the sample to employ designers based either in London or elsewhere in England rather than in NI.

Further evidence of the low priority given to the development of products in NI is indicated by the proportion of firms which chose price competition as the leading aspect of competition between firms in their market. Sixty-four per cent of NI companies chose price compared with 36 per cent German firms. The proportion of firms in Northern Ireland that indicated price competitiveness to be the most important aspect of competition was higher in all sectors compared. Similarly 58 per cent of German companies chose quality as the most important aspect of competition compared with 36 per cent of their NI counterparts. Again the shortfall is important in all sectors with the exception of food etc. in relation both to quality and price.

The varying sophistication of NI and German products was indicated by the different export markets served. Whereas we have noted a similar proportion of output is exported by both Northern Ireland and German sample companies, the major destination for export of about 20 per cent of companies in NI is the relatively "soft" market of the Republic of Ireland (the dependency on the Republic's market was especially notable in engineering although one NI supplier complained that the Southern Irish were nationalistic in their purchasing and tended to have bad debts). Half the remaining NI companies export to Western Europe and the rest to USA, Canada and Japan. In contrast 70 per cent of German companies which exported, did so to Western European destinations.

Product range

One important characteristic of product development is product range and we estimated the number of different product brands which were made by firms in each pair of cases in the engineering, food and miscellaneous trades sectors. We found that in 47 per cent of pairs the German company had a wider range and in 76 per cent of pairs of cases the German company had a range either greater than or equal to that of their NI counterparts. Range of products is also important with regard to productivity where diversity limits the length of production run, imposes costs in terms of change over time, variety of stocks etc., thereby affecting specialisation and physical productivity performance. Clearly it is not the case that German companies are specialising on a narrower range in these three sectors and thereby achieving a potential productivity advantage relative to NI. (With one notable exception in engineering where an NI firm made 100 product lines compared to only four at its German counterpart. One consequence of the phenomenal range at the NI firm was that a very large number of different spare parts were stored, not only for the existing range of products but for all types made since the 1950s. The effectiveness of this commendable provision for after sales service was somewhat weakened by the fact that some sets of spares were delivered late.) Although not directly quantified the impression was that in the textiles and clothing trades no less wide a product range was manufactured by German counterpart firms. Overall, one can say that NI's productivity performance relative to Germany was not disadvantaged by a wider product range.

R and D and product development: summary

There is ample evidence to show that the UK as a whole has problems of poor product quality and inadequate quantity and quality of research and development. For example, the falling share of Britain in world trade in manufactured goods is more rapid than can be explained by price factors alone (Schott and Pick, 1984). Quality, design, technology, reliability, delivery and service have been identified as factors which have played a key role in Britain's relatively poor trade performance (NEDO, 1979, 1983). By outperforming the UK on these non-price dimensions of competition German manufacturers have been able to sell their goods at a higher price per unit of output (e.g. in engineering and clothing; Saunders, 1978; Rossini, 1988). Moreover, detailed sectoral studies suggest that Germany has been able to move into up market segments of expanding consumer demand whereas the British producers which remain at the bottom end are increasingly vulnerable to price competition from imports from the Newly Industrialised Countries (Parkinson, 1984; Steedman and Wagner, 1987). Unfortunately there is little or no official data which allows for an analysis of the trading performance of NI manufacturing separately. However measures of the input of R and D in NI and its productivity (innovations per unit of output) and suggest that even by the second-rate British standards (the UK being a poor performer within the OECD) NI's performance has been inferior (New Scientist, 1987; Harris, 1988).

Conclusions and the managers assessment

This Chapter has shown that the comparative performance of the NI sample of firms (which, it should be noted represents at least one in eight of all manufacturing employees in the Province) is dismal on almost every front. Employment decline has exceeded that of Germany, margins of excess capacity are sometimes large and exports are directed towards relatively easy markets. These characteristics are interlinked and stem from the fundamental uncompetitiveness (both in terms of price and non-price characteristics) of the NI firms which have comparatively low levels of physical output per head combined with a reliance on low quality goods.

The rest of this report will investigate the reasons for the generally higher productivity in Germany including differences in physical assets; premises and plant and machinery and their contribution to physical productivity differences. Attention will also be given to the quality of the labour force, manning levels, strikes, attitudes, turnover and other labour characteristics. However before considering possible explanations it is worth examining the companies' own assessment of their comparative productivity performance and its explanations.

The managers in NI were asked whether they considered their productivity in Northern Ireland was lower than that of Great Britain, and whether there was a productivity gap between Northern Ireland and West Germany. In comparison with GB 25 per cent of the managers sampled thought that productivity was lower in NI, 55 per cent thought it was equivalent with NI and 20 per cent thought that NI productivity was superior to that of GB. Those assessments were spread evenly between sectors. When asked whether there was a productivity shortfall in comparison with Germany 72 per cent of respondents thought there was, whilst 17 per cent considered productivity at their plant equal that of Gemany and 11 per cent thought that their productivity superior to that of Germany.

The companies seem to have been reasonably accurate in their self-assessment relative to Germany (when physical productivity levels are compared almost one-quarter of sample firms in NI achieved productivity levels either indistinguishable from those in Germany or at least 90 per cent of those in Germany). However, the claim by four-fifths of the companies that their productivity levels were at least as good as those in the rest of the UK is more doubtful. Chapter 4 shows that Northern Irish productivity levels are generally 15-20 per cent lower than those in Great Britain. If the Northern Irish managers have interpreted "productivity" to mean only physical productivity their self-assessment would imply that whilst NI has relatively good physical productivity, value-added per head is depressed because simpler and cheaper products are being made there.

Respondents in NI were then asked for their assessment of the source of the productivity failure.

Table 11.9
NI assessment of reason for shortfall relative to Germany

Percentage of respondents in NI*

Product related:
higher rate of output	19
variety and batch size	11
	(30)

Machinery related:
better technology	11
better machinery	
and handling systems	6
capacity utilisation	6
set up and machine downtimes	5
	(28)

Labour related:
manning levels	
and labour restrictions	36
management and organisation	6
	(42)
	(100)

Valid responses: 36

* Where managers cited more than one explanation they were asked to weight these in importance.

It can be seen from Table 11.9 that 30 per cent believed that output factors were important in determining the productivity difference relative to Germany. We have already shown that there was no evidence to indicate the variety of products was narrower in Germany or that product lines were more specialised. This would suggest that the 11 per cent which stressed variety and batch size were wrong. However, the rate of output was found to be higher in Germany (this is considered in Chapter 13 in relationship to machine manning rates). Whilst it might be claimed that running speeds are exogenously determined by external demand conditions it is debatable whether this is in fact the case. To the extent that both the NI and German firms are selling to international markets then their rate of output will be determined by the competitiveness of their products (principally in terms of quality). Thus what appears to be an external constraint on the performance of the firm is in fact determined by its ability to make internationally competitive products.

Of the remaining factors, 28 per cent of companies cited Germany's machinery related advantages while a majority of companies cited labour differences arising from manning levels and restrictive practises. A minority of 6 per cent of companies expected management or organisational advantages to explain Germany's superiority.

Over two-fifths of the respondents stressed human explanations for NI's productivity shortfall (i.e. labour and management) and the remainder product-related and machinery-related factors. This result is broadly in line with that of Pratten's summary of the causes of the Anglo-German productivity differential in his survey of international companies (Pratten, 1976). He attributed about half of the gap to economic causes (rate of output and length of production runs, plant and machinery, product mix, capacity utilisation and availability of labour) and about half to behavioural causes (incidence of strikes and major restrictive practises, manning and efficiency).

It is of interest that this assessment of the reasons for NI's productivity shortfall is reflected in the managers' assessment of the explanations of recent productivity growth. Before analysing this we show the percentage of firms in the two countries that achieved productivity growth during 1982-87.

Table 11.10
Percentage of firms reporting productivity growth, 1982-87

	NI	WG
Engineering	100	80
Food etc.	100	100
Textiles	100	50
Clothing	78	67
Miscellaneous	80	100
All	90	77
Observations	30	26

Most companies in both samples achieved productivity growth though rather fewer in Germany (77 per cent) than in NI (90 per cent). NI's somewhat better productivity performance is not entirely surprising given that UK productivity increase since 1981 has been generally better than that of Germany (see Chapter 1). However, it should be stressed that in both NI and Britain the productivity shortfall relative to Germany was so large by the end of the 1970s that any progress since then has narrowed the gap only slightly.

Table 11.11 outlines the reasons given for the productivity improvement in NI. The most important conclusion to be drawn is that most of the productivity gains were achieved through a better use of people while mechanisation and other factors were less important.

Table 11.11
Sources of productivity growth in NI companies

Percentage of companies

Improvements in human resources:	
better management	19
better manning, work organisation and training	37
	(56)
Capital related:	
Improved technology	10
Modern equipment	27
	(37)
Other factors (economies of scale and improved capacity utilisation)	7
	(100)

Examples of the sources of NI productivity growth included the following: a change in handling systems, improved working practises, better production control, higher quality materials, use of job cards, more rigid control of manning levels, better organisation of movement of materials within the factory.

This stress on human resources rather than fixed assets was in marked contrast to the balance of the factors held to be responsible for recent German productivity growth. Only a minority of Germans (31 per cent) attributed their growth to reduction in manning and reorganisation. This may indicate that the Germans were already highly efficient in this respect and therefore had less scope than the NI firms for improvement in this department. The majority of German firms (69 per cent) stressed improved technology and machinery.

When all these results are taken together they are strongly suggestive of labour (and management) related factors being more important explanations of NI's productivity shortfall than capital. The next Chapter considers the role of capital in the explanation of the productivity differences.

Notes

1. The data on the left hand side of this Table is ordinal whereas that on the right hand side is cardinal and one should not therefore expect the two halves of the Table to mirror each other. Furthermore, the sample sizes used were different but in each case the maximum possible number of pair wise comparisons were made.

12 The quantity and quality of machinery and equipment

"In some respects Germany may boast superiority to Britain in her means for manufactures. The arts of design and their application ... are more successfully wrought and worked; chemical knowledge is more advanced than with us... mechanical improvements have made rapid strides, and have served to open a wide field for the characteristic development of the German intelligence; which if not specifically distinguished for invention and discovery, seems particularly fitted to laborious and thoughtful application".

John Browning (1840) Report on the Prussian Commercial Union, addressed to Lord Palmerston, Secretary of State for Foreign Affairs

Age of machinery

We first consider one of the most obvious characteristics of the capital stock which has relevance to comparative productivity, namely its average age in the two countries (see Chapter 2 and Prais, 1986).

Table 12.1 compares the average percentage of numbers of machines normally used in production which were under five years old in each sector. Also shown is the percentage of cases where NI machinery was either younger or equivalent in age to that of its German counterpart.

Table 12.1
Comparisons of capital stock

	Comparative age of machinery, unweighted % of machines under five years		% of cases where NI machine-age equal to or younger than WG counterpart
	NI	WG	
Engineering	17	39	36
Miscellaneous	31	57	50
Food, drink etc.	30	56	40
Textiles	26	28	67
Clothing	66	57	64
All manufacturing	33	48	52

Note: Number of pair-wise comparisons were; engineering 11; miscellaneous 6; food etc. 5; textiles 6; clothing 14; all manufacturing 42.

This Table shows that overall NI is at disadvantage as a consequence of a slightly older stock of machinery; 33 per cent younger than five years as compared with 48 per cent at the German plants. The gap was widest in engineering, food and the miscellaneous trades whereas in textiles NI is at no disadvantage on this measure (old machines were typical of factories in both NI and Germany). It was notable that the average age of machinery in NI clothing plants was younger than that in Germany. Whilst these comparisons generally suggest a younger capital stock in Germany, when comparisons are made on a case by case basis in 52 per cent of cases NI companies were found to have machinery as young or younger than Germany. This different method of comparing the vintage of machinery indicates that in the clothing, textiles and miscellaneous sectors NI companies were at no disadvantage as a consequence of machine age. Significantly, previous studies which have considered the average age of the machine stock in UK manufacturing have also failed to detect a disadvantage relative to either Germany or the USA (Rostas, 1948; Anglo-American Council on Productivity, 1950; Bacon, 1974; Prais, 1986).

Level of technology

In addition to the age of machinery, the technical sophistication of that machinery also influences productivity. Attention was focused on the use of not only computer numerically controlled machine tools (CNCs) but other computerised and advanced equipment. For example, whilst the incidence of CNCs alone in engineering indicated a technological advantage to NI (one CNC available for every 35 employees in NI compared to one for every

41 employees in Germany), the more refined quantitative and qualitative measure suggests that German engineering enjoys a higher level of technology. Table 12.2 (a) shows that while overall the level of technology found at the NI plants was similar to that in Germany, on a sectoral basis, NI was ahead in the clothing and textiles sectors but behind in the engineering, food and miscellaneous sectors. The importance of technology can be illustrated by consideration of detailed cases.

One German engineering company was using CAD/CNC machinery to develop a high quality product whereas the matched firm in NI was still using NC machinery to manufacture a lower quality product. The early adoption of a specialised machine enabled another German engineering company to undertake subcontract work on behalf of its matched NI counterpart. In the case of a further matched pair, the German company had more cutting and turning centres. The German firm had 45 computerised machining centres compared to only one in Northern Ireland (which was liable to be out of action for several hours per week as the operator came late in the morning). A German firm in the miscellaneous trades had used automatic or computerised machines to replace labour to a greater extent than its NI counterpart (for example; through a night-time ghost shift, using double headed machines and by bringing together a number of steps in the production sequence). The situation in food etc. can be summarised by saying that packaging and bottling were more highly automated in Germany.

Table 12.2
Comparative levels of technology and the extent of
its adaptation to the specific circumstances of the firm

| | (a)Level of technology | | (b)Machine adaptation/customisation | |
	NI more advanced	WG more advanced	NI greater	WG greater
	(% of pairs)	(% of pairs)	(% of pairs)	(% of pairs)
Engineering	18	46	8	27
Miscellaneous	0	67	0	83
Food, etc.	20	60	20	80
Textiles	17	16	10	40
Clothing	64	15	26	14
All manufacturing	31	36	15	38

Note: Number of pairs considered; engineering 11; miscellaneous 6; food 5; textiles 6; clothing 14; and all 42.

In the clothing sector the German companies concentrated on greater skill intensive inputs mainly by attainment of better design and quality, while their NI counterparts employed more computerised equipment to manufacture long runs of middle quality garments.

It was not always clear whether the level of technology used in NI was appropriate to the task in hand. For example, an automatic folding machine was purchased with grants, but subsequently operators could not be trained to use it though attempts to do so improved work methods and productivity. Two NI companies used automatic overhead systems and computerised cutters whereas their German counterparts did not. It was notable that the entire balance of investment in the NI and German clothing firms was different. The NI firms were still using relatively primitive lock-stitching machines yet at the same time they made large outlays on computerised, dedicated machinery (which the Germans considered too rigid and inflexible). In one case three computerised loose stitch machines were used to only 40 per cent capacity whereas the matched German counterpart needed only one. The proprietor of the NI firm justified his decision to have spare machines on grounds of breakdowns. His German counterpart did not have such difficulties. One NI manager said of two other firms of which he had experience "A and B have excessive equipment which involves a loss of versatility arising from de-skilling".

Turning to the appropriateness of NI machinery in other sectors, a grant aided and expensive paint finishing and rust proofing machine lay idle in one NI engineering firm, where the management preferred to use more labour intensive techniques. At another engineering company a CNC saw was purchased with generous grant aid but had never been used. Similarly the sole representative in the Province of a certain miscellaneous trade, used only one-third of its six advanced machines (and these were overmanned). The production manager at the German counterpart firm was told by a representative of a French machine tool firm that Ireland had become one of his most successful export markets. In a further matching in miscellaneous trades the German manager knew that his NI counterpart had three times as many of a particular sort of advanced machine. This did not concern him "our first word is not the modern machine but the economical way to produce".

The adaptation and customising of machinery in Germany

Table 12.2 (b) summarised the extent to which the firms have adapted and customised their machines to their own specific production circumstances. German companies were found to be at an advantage in 38 per cent of cases principally through machine adaptation, machine feeding devices, robotic transport machines and machine linking equipment, while in Northern Ireland those companies which adapted machinery to a better advantage were mainly found in clothing. These together with the use of multistage machines exemplified the gains to production methods from co-operation with the equipment suppliers. Significantly, only two NI firms in our whole sample worked with their machinery suppliers compared with 40 per cent of those in West Germany. Co-operation was especially strong in the engineering, food and miscellaneous trades. Much of the incentive to design such specialised machines arises from the proximity to, and strength of, local machine tool manufacture[1] allied to a strong representation of engineering knowledge and skills in the factories visited, and the need to conserve high cost labour. While working with local machine tool producers was common among the German firms sampled it should be emphasised that many developed machine "add ons" and undertook alterations "in house" with their own engineers.

Payback periods and capital grants

The German firms use less stringent financial criteria in their decisions as to whether to purchase a machine. The following Table shows that on average the German companies sought a payback period of four years compared to three years in NI (net of grants received). It should be emphasised, however, that German managers used payback as a guide but not a rule. If equipment was thought to be needed on technical grounds it would be bought. In NI we were frequently told that investment had to be justified by a payback rule.

Table 12.3
Payback periods
(number of years)

	NI	WG
Engineering	3.5	4.3
Miscellaneous	1.7	6.0
Food, etc.	2.4	4.3
Textiles	4.0	5.8
Clothing	2.8	2.3
All manufacturing	3.0	4.0

Only in the clothing sector was the average payback period shorter in Germany though the assessment of the importance of the difference in payback periods must be modified by the incidence of grants (i.e. the NI firms applied payback rules to their own net expenditure after grants, and the time taken to payback gross expenditure would be longer).

Table 12.4 shows that the total grants for machine purchases received in NI ranged between 30 per cent and 47 per cent. In Germany nine companies located in West Berlin received grants of between 10 and 25 per cent on capital. When one adjusts for grants in both Northern Ireland and Germany then NI would have a longer payback on gross expenditure in three of the sectors (engineering, textiles and clothing). In a later section of this report we will consider the extent to which the relatively high rate of grant aid in NI has acted as a subsidy to corporate profitability. By so doing the grants may have reinforced a situation of "market failure" the management of the NI firms do not have the incentive

133

to make the changes necessary to achieve higher productivity since they are already profitable enough.

Table 12.4
Rate of grant support for capital in NI
(unweighted average)

Engineering	44
Miscellaneous	40
Food, drink and tobacco	30
Textiles	47
Clothing	44

National origin of machinery

The importance to the German companies of a strong local machinery industry (for opportunities for design modification, repairs and lessening of downtime) is indicated by analysis of the national origin of the main types of machines used. Fifty-six percent of the German companies bought mainly German machines (compared with 35 per cent of the NI companies which tended to make "off the peg" purchases from the German suppliers). The German firms were slightly less dependent upon American or Japanese equipment than their NI counterparts (25 per cent of firms compared to 31 per cent of NI firms which bought mainly from these areas). The precarious position of the British machinery industry noted by Daly and Jones (1980) and Prais (1981a) was indicated by the fact that only 14 percent of the NI companies bought machines from either the Province or Great Britain (and only 9 per cent of the German firms sampled purchased from the UK). At one NI company it was said "we make a lot of machines ourselves, the only problem is that seventy percent are over 10 years old and they breakdown all the time".

Interestingly, two companies in the sample which bought Northern Ireland machines (one in NI and one in Germany) were equally distressed as a result of their purchases. In the case of the NI purchaser, the judgment was that the machines were so unreliable that 50 per cent capital grants were a necessary compensation for the resultant loss to productivity. The German comments were equally severe. "The quality of new machines is poor. Some use technology which is 20-30 years behind. The old machines are perfect but from an economic point of view are hopeless. Prices are high and they have delivery problems. The new machines are so poor that they have sent a fitter from Ireland who has been working here permanently for a few years to put them right. He was here so long that he fell in love and married a German". Despite having four specialised fitters from NI present at the time of the interview that company still had to send out for additional assistance from a local engineering company. In Germany one man could do the job of all of them because the NI mechanics are so narrowly trained that they do not understand the whole machine. They had to send to Austria to get a job done there which none of the NI fitters was capable of. Another German critic compared the machine from the NI manufacturer with a Belgian equivalent. The

Belgian machine was said to have double the output per hour, take a higher load, and to be more precise and up-to-date.

Maintenance of machinery

Forty-five per cent of the NI sample stated the maintenance of machinery presented a serious problem either because of frequent breakdowns or because of difficulties in repairing those breakdowns (either internally or with outside engineers). In contrast, only eight per cent of the German firms had similar problems. For example, one NI company complained "we have teething problems and have to fly people in from Germany" and another said "if we have serious difficulties we have to go to Switzerland". A German company in the same sector said "we try to buy machines that can be serviced here so there is no loss of production time".

In one pair of companies in the engineering sector the NI firm suffered 15 per cent breakdowns in some weeks, whilst its matched German counterpart was not only more up to date in technology and appropriateness of machinery and in engineering but also practised planned maintenance and had minimal breakdowns. In the miscellaneous sector one NI company described their problems as "dramatic... have to call over the Germans" and in another case in that sector down time was running at 10-12 per cent. A more mechanised German plant described their problems as "insignificant". In food production no special problem were reported, albeit one factory reported one of its machines frequently jammed (the Germans had similar problems). In textiles one NI factory had a particularly antique machine stock. "Firefighting" was constantly needed and the cost of breakdowns was 10 per cent lower production. In the clothing sector NI problems were generally greater than those of Germany especially with regard to advanced computerised equipment (in some cases specialists had to be flown into NI).

The relative incidence of breakdowns was indicative of the extent to which planned maintenance was conducted, whereas nearly half of the German companies did this, less than one-fifth of the NI companies did so. These measures exclude the routine cleaning of machines in Germany and some of the German sample cleaned their machines _every_ day (Daly, Hitchens and Wagner, 1985). Moreover, the standards of maintenance given in NI and Germany differed and complaints about this were frequent in NI. One German company which was familiar with NI maintenance and engineering said "they do not know their machines as well as the Germans do". One NI observation was "we have trouble with the computerised part of the finishing machines". Another said "our problem is an electronic weakness, we have problems of technical control". A NI clothing firm said "we are not able to service our machines well, the maintenance staff are not well skilled, they can get the machines going but cannot tune them sufficiently". This resulted in poorer product quality. Another company had given up on attempting to service its machinery with semi-skilled workers and was adding to its maintenance department. As another manager put it "letting our maintenance man deal with the machinery would be like letting a plumber loose on a nuclear power station". A German manager, who had actually worked for some time in the NI firm with which we matched his company, claimed there was "an inability on the part of their [i.e. NI] maintenance labour force to keep the machines running properly because of poor management, and poor maintenance affects quality". One NI clothing firm was reduced to 40 per cent capacity on three of its newest machines because "we have problems servicing them". Machine breakdowns reduced the productivity of a NI firm in miscellaneous trades by 10-12 per cent compared to only 7 percent at its German counterpart. A further NI miscellaneous firm was dependent on bringing over engineers from Germany whereas the matched counterpart could cope with problems in house.

Difficulties with maintenance in NI were not a consequence of having too few maintenance engineers. As the following Table makes clear, the NI companies had more than their German counterparts.

Table 12.5
Comparative size of the maintenance labour force
Number of maintenance workers as a proportion of all employees

	NI	WG	NI/WG
Engineering	1 to 31	1 to 59	1.90
Miscellaneous	1 to 10	1 to 29	2.90
Food, drink, tob.	1 to 6	1 to 8	1.30
Textiles	1 to 10	1 to 26	2.60
Clothing	1 to 75	1 to 115	1.50

Total number of matched pairs 32

The implication would seem to be that these workers in NI are less skilled or knowledgeable than their German counterparts, and that this function is considerably overmanned (comparable problems have been evidences in branches of GB manufacturing; in the mid-1970s breakdowns in the British car industry took twice as long to repair as those in Continental factories despite the presence of 60 percent more maintenance personnel; CPRS, 1975). Whilst frequent breakdowns and inadequate maintenance may be part of a general UK problem (Prais, 1981a; Daly, Hitchens and Wagner, 1985) it does seem bizarre that they such a large maintenance work-force should be required in NI given the extent to which machinery is operating below full capacity.

Capacity utilisation

The utilisation of machinery was found to be generally lower in Northern Ireland. Once again, the question arises as to whether NI's difficulties were mainly the result of external demand factors. Given that firms matched were making similar product types it could be argued that potentially they faced similar world markets. Lower utilisation in NI might then follow from the tendency for its products to be of lower quality and hence more restricted in their access to export markets (we have already shown that the trade performance of the NI sample was relatively poor for export markets other than the Irish Republic).

Table 12.6 shows that average capacity utilisation was 75 per cent in NI compared to 90 per cent in Germany. Since this was defined as the extent to which actual output was less than the maximum which could theoretically have been obtained from the resources present within the factory, NI's comparatively low utilisation rate was the result of poor utilisation of machinery compounded by overmanning (see the next Chapter). Lowest rates of utilisation were found in the engineering, miscellaneous and food trades, whilst the differential between NI and Germany narrowed (or disappeared) in clothing and textiles.

Table 12.6
Comparative capacity utilisation (%)

	Northern Ireland	Germany
Engineering	69	89
Miscellaneous	63	85
Food, drink and tobacco	93	100
Textiles	85	85
Clothing	80	95
All manufacturing	75	90

Number of observations 43

Premises: layout and cleanliness

Before considering the part played by management and labour in NI's comparative productivity performance we consider one further factor related to the physical assets of the companies, their premises. Twenty-five per cent of the NI sample and 44 per cent of the German sample occupied premises which were old and not entirely suitable for their present use. For example, in some cases production took place on different levels or in different buildings which set a constraint on improvements in work organisation and work flow. Nevertheless, few firms in either country were prepared to make an issue of the standard of their premises (Fothergill and Guy (1989) found that premises were not a significant factor in explaining the closure of branch plants in NI during the 1980s). In one case there was an ironic contrast between the NI firm and its matched counterpart. The German firm had run out of factory space to meet all the demand for its product. It had therefore converted part of its carpark into the site for a new factory block. The NI firm faced such a slump in the demand for its products that it was able to lock employees' cars in redundant factory sheds. One factory in NI had been bombed and one in Germany had to be rebuilt after a fire.

Perhaps the most significant difference between the two samples was that the German plants were, irrespective of age or suitability, generally cleaner, tidier and better organised than their NI counterparts. There was a wide variability in orderliness in NI. At best they approached German standards and at worst a visible negative impact on productivity could be perceived. The German store rooms were especially methodical. At one NI plant the managing director had appreciated the problem. He had drawn yellow lines on the factory floor to guide the positioning of goods inward and outward. Unfortunately, during our visit, the storeman was randomly unloading goods in all places. There were many instances in NI where the shop floor was itself untidy and unswept and where reception areas were maintained without consideration for the interests or impressions of customers and visitors.

Machinery: conclusion

The role of machinery in explaining NI's productivity performance is very complex. This is because whilst NI does not appear disadvantaged in terms of either the age or up-to-dateness of its equipment, the machinery in Germany does appear to be more appropriate to the task in hand. One reason why this was so was that the German companies were willing to co-operate with their machine tool suppliers (most of these were also German). The machinery in NI was much more liable to be out of action as a result of breakdowns. Both the inappropriateness of the machinery and the incidence of down time in NI raise questions as to the technical awareness and ability of the NI management and labour force at all levels. As a result of a very high rate of grant aid NI had acquired a machine stock which was in some respects younger and more advanced than that in Germany but NI still did not know how to use it effectively. Poor capital productivity was caused by some of the labour force characteristics which will be described in Chapters 14 and 15 but first it is necessary to consider the extent to which the machine stock in NI was overmanned relative to Germany.

Notes

1. The kind of vigorous interaction between machine supplier and user evidenced today in Germany was present in NI during the high point of development in the textiles machinery and linen industry in the late nineteenth century. One observer of the Belfast textile machinery industry in 1874 commented that the engineering firms were "visited almost daily by spinners, who thus were able to see the progress being made in the execution of their orders, and to point out their exact requirements and the defects of previous machines" (quoted in O'Malley, 1989). Unfortunately the progressive decline of these industries since 1900 has limited the scope for the realisation such external economies in NI.

13 Overmanning in Northern Ireland

"There is nothing wrong with the use of illustrative examples, provided that the generalisations which they decorate or illuminate are soundly drawn from a representative sample of the universe under discussion...".

Charles P Kindleberger (1975), "Germany's Overtaking of England 1806-1914", Part II, Weltwirtschaftliches Archiv, pp. 477-504

Introduction

This Chapter is two broad parts. First, the manning levels of NI and Germany on similar or identical machines or processes are analysed. Second, it is reported whether the managers considered their plant was overmanned in general.

Machine manning levels

In 17 pairs of cases it was possible to match exactly the number of persons operating equivalent systems of machines. The best NI comparative manning rate was 70 per cent of that in Germany whereas the worst NI rate was almost three and third times higher. On average NI manning was 80 per cent greater than that in Germany i.e. 10 Germans could look after 10 machines whereas 18 NI employees would be required to do the same job. Individual examples included a German engineering firm where one man

supervised three CNCs. His NI counterpart could only operate two.
In the miscellaneous trades two men operated a <u>Boucherie</u> machine
in NI whereas this machine would be controlled by a single German.
Similarly, in textiles one man operated a single machine in NI,
while in Germany two would be operated together. In Food etc.
there were two cases where bottling/filling lines in NI were more
heavily manned and one where Germany had more operatives. Finally,
in the clothing industry the observation was made that two persons
manned a computerised cutting machine in NI whilst the Germans
would have used this machinery to save one man.

The reasons for the generally lower manning in Germany were as
follows; in twelve cases additional ancillary equipment was worked
in Germany (these add ons were inexpensive), in two (13 per cent)
cases the Germans arranged their machinery better, and in nine
cases (60 per cent) the NI operation was simply overmanned (the
reason why the sum of these is greater than 17 is that in some
cases more than one explanation could be given).

Output levels

In 12 of the cases where manning was compared the rate of output
through the machines in Germany was higher than that in NI, while
in the remaining 5 cases running speed and throughput was similar
to that in NI.

Whilst in principle a higher rate of output in Germany could
have entirely macroeconomic explanations, i.e. a higher level and
rate of growth of aggregate demand (Pratten, 1976), it is doubtful
if this was the major explanation of the differences between NI
and Germany. The introduction to this article stressed the reasons
for thinking such demand side factors unlikely explanations for
Britain's poor post-war productivity performance (Crafts, 1988a).
The firms sampled tended to stress internal (supply side)
explanations of machine running speed as opposed to external
demand conditions. In any case, Northern Irish aggregate demand
(as measured by regional GDP) was probably growing at least as
rapidly as that in Germany during 1982-87.

In six of those twelve cases the German company benefited from
the collaboration with machinery suppliers. These benefits
included: better feeding and off-loading devices, machine systems
whereby a single machine was adapted to undertake more than one
stage of production, in one instance the use of a larger machine
than that of its NI counterpart, and in two cases machine "add
ons" enabled the operator to get more from the machine in question
(output was more consistent during the course of the day). In one
of those instances the device was known by its NI counterpart but
could not be justified on their strict one year payback criterion
(the German firm undertook the investment on engineering grounds
and used an eight year payback criterion).

In the remaining six cases the greater German output was a
consequence of using more advanced or more up to date equipment
(this more up to date equipment did not necessarily require any
less manning). In two instances the equipment in question was

computerised for bottling etc. while in four cases advanced
computerised linking was incorporated.

Table 13.1
Number of detailed observations of matched processes
by sector

Engineering	2
Miscellaneous	4
Food etc.	5
Textiles	4
Clothing	2
Total	17

General overmanning

In addition to considering manning rates on matched machine
systems and the extent to which machine stock is fully utilised,
it is also worth considering to what extent the plants were
overmanned in a global sense, i.e. under optimal conditions what
would be the largest cut in manpower which could be achieved
whilst leaving output at its present level (and without changing
the machine stock)?

No German company visited believed they were overmanned in any
department. In NI 59 per cent of companies said that they were
overmanned in some department (given existing machinery and
equipment).

Table 13.2
Percentage of NI companies reporting overmanning

Engineering	70
Miscellaneous	33
Food etc.	40
Textiles	50
Clothing	67
All manufacturing	59

It might be objected that the phenomenon of general overmanning
lacks an economic rational. If it exists firms are foregoing an
opportunity to enhance their profits by reducing the wages bill.
However in practise there were a number of constraints on the
firms in NI which made a measure of general overmanning
"rational". In a later section we will show that the comparatively
high rate of absenteeism in NI clothing obliged the firms to carry
extra labour so as to cover for absent colleagues. Given the
predominantly unskilled nature of the operatives in all the
sectors in NI, indirect functions (maintenance and quality
control) had to receive a higher representation than in the
counterpart German plants where an operative was largely capable

of doing his own machine maintenance and product quality inspection.

Finally, as a later section will make clear, most of the NI companies were already reasonably profitable and so they lacked the incentive to remove all of their general overmanning. This would suggest that general overmanning in NI was part of a state of market failure (i.e. profit signals were not signalling those changes which would be in the long-run interest of the NI economy).

The NI companies were able to be profitable in spite of overmanning partly because of the relatively low level of labour costs as compared to those in Germany (less than half) and through selling to markets (e.g. NI and the Republic of Ireland) which are probably subject to fewer competitive pressures (we have already seen that the NI firms generally recognised a smaller number of foreign competitors). The market failure may have been aggravated by the very generous rate of state grant assistance given to these firms (see below) to the extent that this allowed NI management to go for the easy option and avoid tackling chronic overmanning. In this context it is instructive to draw a contrast with Great Britain where the very severe 1979-81 recession was accompanied by signals from the Thatcher Administration that it would not underwrite inefficiency in the manufacturing sector through devaluing Sterling, or inflating the economy or by increasing industrial and regional assistance. Manufacturing in GB responded to these signals by removing the overmanning which had accumulated during the 1960s-70s (Crafts, 1988a). Higher rates of grant aid have shielded NI from such shocks. We now turn to some of the individual cases of overmanning in NI.

One engineering firm had too many "chiefs" and capacity utilisation had slumped to 50 per cent. In three other cases in engineering their had been a lack of adjustment in the numbers employed relative to a very rapid down-turn in demand for the good produced. Despite a shedding of over one-third of employment during the last five years many shop-floor workers were still visibly idle during our visit. At a principal department in one of the companies 26 out of 30 men were inactive (we were assured that there was no formal tea break). We also noticed that there were dartboards on the walls of some workshops (this was observed in another engineering company which reported gross overmanning). In this factory one third of the large CNCs were in operation, machine utilisation was only 40 per cent though utilisation of manpower was said to be "50 to 70 per cent on average".

Similarly in another company a count indicated that between one-third and one-half of employees were apparently idle. This company hoped to receive a substantial IDB grant so as to modernise and re-equip (which would result in a fifth fewer employees). At a third firm machine utilisation was below two-thirds on the advanced CNC machines and in the preceding two years employment had fallen by one-third. No adjustment for an imbalance between employment and output was possible at another factory which was overmanned by 27 per cent. In this case the workers were in effect operating under self-imposed limits on their output (see the consideration of work attitudes in Chapter 15). The production manager of another engineering firm (trained at an American subsidiary) considered the shop floor had 15 per cent excess manpower. Progress would be made by improving organisation and work methods. Another engineering firm was looking forward to a flexibility deal with the unions which would improve the direct/indirect ratio from one-to-one to one-to-zero point seven. This reduction would require further training (of a low grade nature) to broaden skills (to handle material, operate fork lift trucks as well as machines).

In the miscellaneous trades the NI manager of one externally controlled company was familiar with two German counterpart firms. He thought that differences between NI and German productivity could largely be explained by a combination of overmanning in NI along with insufficient job flexibility and overly generous relaxation allowances. In addition, the workers were inclined to take their own unofficial tea breaks. Another miscellaneous trades company in NI had achieved 15 per cent productivity growth through retraining the semi-skilled to have wider job flexibility. It was anticipated that more such gains could be achieved. Moreover, they had been able to reduce the number of unskilled direct workers in material handling.

There were three food companies reporting overmanning. In two of these cases employment had yet to adjust to severe falls in demand. In one case the preparation stage was 50-60 per cent overmanned and one set of machinery could have been operated with four fewer persons. Two other machine sets were overmanned by 10 per cent and 20 per cent respectively. At another company the bottling line was said to be overmanned.

Three textiles firms admitted to overmanning. A poor factory layout was blamed in one case though it was felt that there was further overmanning over and above this. The manager made the revealing comment "when the grants were cut we got rid of employees without changing output". Finishing was overmanned in a further firm and in a third case overmanning was said to be the consequence of the factory being in decline.

Finally, seven clothing firms reported general overmanning. Consultants advised one company that they were 8 per cent overmanned (mainly in indirects). "Finish" at another company (now bankrupt) was said to be overmanned by 50 per cent. One part of the plant was said to be "in flux". A high level of absenteeism and poor job flexibility was the key source of overmanning at a third firm. "While the right person would work at 100 per cent her substitute would work at 75 per cent and when absenteeism rose to 17 per cent there was a problem of finding any substitutes at all". He reported their work study standards were loose. Similar problems were reported by the managing director of another firm where poor training and absenteeism were said to be the source of overmanning. At another company work study techniques had measured 20-25 per cent overmanning arising from the use of the same standard minute values as set in the 1950s. The managing director expected union opposition to any moves towards a reduction since manning agreements explained at least half of that overmanning.

143

Yet another company thought it could produce its current output with a third fewer workers. Quality control was excessively large in another firm which was a function of the preponderance of trainees on the shop floor and an internal reject rate which had been as high as 50-60 per cent.

Overmanning in the indirects

In indirects we include all employees other than production operatives directly involved in production. Whilst in principle one might expect the presence of some indirects to enhance value-added (researchers, designers, and managers) it is worth investigating whether the NI plants were carrying an undue proportion of the "unproductive" indirect employees (clerical, canteen, stores, warehouse, transporting, packing). Admittedly our data combines both sorts of indirect workers but it is still of use given that the number of researchers, designers and managers is likely to be small relative to the total employment of indirects (and we have already seen that researchers and designers are comparatively less well represented in NI). Thus the following Table shows the percentage of matched pairs where NI had a higher proportion of indirects in total employment than did Germany.

Table 13.3
Size of indirect employment
(Percentage of matched pairs where NI had the higher
proportion of indirect workers)

Engineering	80
Miscellaneous	50
Food etc.	25
Textiles	75
Clothing	86
All manufacturing	68
Number of pairs	22

These results are strongly suggestive of NI having a problem of over manning amongst indirect workers.

Overmanning: conclusions

On matched machines or processes the NI firms used 80 per cent more operatives than their German counterparts. Over half the NI firms reported that they were overmanned in at least one department of the plant. Evidence suggested that the NI plants tended to have too many indirect workers. One reason why manning rates were lower in Germany related to the quality (experience and training) of the German employees and employers. The next Chapter will examine the relative qualifications and skills of management and labour in NI.

14 Management and labour force qualifications and training

"Train up a child in the way he should go: and when he is old, he will not depart from it".

Proverbs Chapter 22, Verse 6, The King James Version of The Bible

Higher qualifications

We examined the number of higher level qualifications at the matched plants expressed as the percentage of employees with a university level qualification, and the percentage having either a technical qualification (an HND in NI) or a degree. The results are shown in Table 14.1.

Table 14.1
Higher level qualifications (% of total employment)

	NI	WG
Degrees and technical qualifications together	2.3	11.0
Degrees only	1.0	4.7

(Number of matched pairs: 24)

Table 14.1 shows the average percentage frequency of the qualifications for all the pairs of companies where comparison was possible and it can be seen that higher level qualifications were about five times more common in Germany. Results for the individual sectors are not shown because in some cases only a small number of comparisons were available. However, it can be noted that in every sector the frequency of degrees and technical qualifications combined was much higher in Germany and the same held true for the incidence of degrees separately.

Sixteen per cent of the firms in NI but only 8 per cent in Germany employed no persons with technical qualifications or higher and those factories in Germany would typically by individuals who had themselves an apprenticeship or <u>Meister</u> qualification. Exactly two-thirds of plants visited in each country employed at least one person with a degree but as has already been noted the intensity of technical, vocational and university qualifications at the plants was several times higher in Germany than in Northern Ireland.

It should be stressed that part of what we are observing is a general British problem; the under-representation of higher qualifications in the UK labour force relative to that in almost every other major industrial economy (Prais, 1981b; Prais, 1989). However, it is worrying that whereas Prais (1981b) noted a slight superiority in the rate of graduate qualifications in German manufacturing relative to that in Britain, this sample suggests that Germany has more than four times more than NI pro rata. The implication is that NI is under qualified even by the standards of Great Britain (see Chapter 7).

The literature relating to the importance of higher level qualifications as a means of realising performance gains has focused not only on the quantitative gap existing between Britain and Germany but also a qualitative dimension. For example, it has been argued that the structure and content of a German engineering degree gives it greater relevance to practical business problems than does its British counterpart (Prais, 1989). It has also been noted that the types of qualifications held by German managers are more appropriate than those found in UK firms (i.e. engineering and scientific degrees are more prevalent than accountancy qualifications, MBAs or non-vocational university degrees; Lawrence, 1980; Handy, 1987). To the extent that he has better technological training, the German manager may be superior to his British counterpart in terms of his commitment to continuous upgrading of product quality and to changes in capital equipment and labour force training which are required.

In two sectors, engineering and clothing, it was possible to systematically check the type and appropriateness of higher qualifications. These will now be described in detail for illustrative purposes. In the remaining and rather more heterogeneous sectors German plant managers/managing directors tended to have engineering or technical qualifications whereas the Northern Irish were more frequently holders of commercial and non-vocational qualifications. Thus there was evidence that Northern Ireland suffered from a shortfall of those qualifications most relevant from the point of view of production.

Qualifications of engineering managing directors

There was a startling difference between the qualifications of the managers in Northern Ireland and Germany. Thus nine of the ten German directors had an engineering degree and one of them also a PhD in engineering. In four out of the dozen visits in NI the highest technical qualification was an HND. Only two of the NI managers had degrees and in neither case were these in engineering or science (British engineering companies may tend to reserve their top positions for non-engineers (Sorge and Warner, 1980)). Their companies did employ graduate engineers at a lower level. Four of the NI plants employed no technical qualifications above the level of craftsmen.

Whilst the frequency of technical qualifications in Germany may seem remarkable it is not unrepresentative of the industry as a whole. In 1987 8.2 per cent of all employees in German metal working plants were graduate engineers. Two-thirds of the degrees were from polytechnics and one third from universities. Whilst most of the German graduates work in the traditional fields like Research and Development and construction, one-third of them have positions in management, administration and marketing. Even in small plants of less than fifty employees graduate engineers represent 10 per cent of employment (Verband Deutscher Maschinen- und Anlagenbau, 1988).

Germany surpasses the UK in terms of the annual output of graduate engineers. Passes at the Doctoral level are 50 per cent higher, and the numbers at the MSc, Bachelor and technician level are more than twice those of Britain (Prais, 1989). Three-quarters of German graduate engineers subsequently enter industry whereas the proportion in Britain is probably lower. Apart from a quantitative difference between the two countries, German engineering degrees may be of a superior quality and more relevant to production requirements (Sorge and Warner, 1980). Moreover, half of the graduates from German polytechnics have previously passed an apprenticeship (Kaiser, 1981). Thus they are more familiar with the problems and language of the shop-floor and do not need intermediaries and "translators". They also understand the effects of investment on products and production processes. The higher technical competence of German managers gives them a greater awareness of the importance of computer based systems and an improved ability to use them (Financial Times, 1989, January 20). Prais (1989) suggests a qualitative superiority in Germany given that the average first degree lasts more than six years which is more than double that in Britain. Even the "polytechnic" course in Germany has an average duration longer than the basic degree in the UK.

Returning now to consideration of the matched plants, the superior know-how and skill of managers and labour in one German company allowed it to diversify away from fabrication of standardised products to ones which were customised whereas its NI counterpart was concerned with traditional fabrication only. The fruit of its large investment in design was that the German plant was able to maintain its employment whereas the NI factory suffered a one-third job loss during 1982-87. A graduate engineer was employed by one German firm to liase with customers on product design and development. This ability to customise their product represented their competitive edge and half of their products were described as "new". In contrast, at their NI counterpart we were told "nobody in the factory has any qualifications" and no new products were introduced recently. At another pair of companies the German factory had six technical or business qualified persons at the top whereas the NI counterpart again engaged persons with "no qualifications".

Qualifications of clothing managing directors

Eighty per cent of managers in the German plants had started their career with a three year apprenticeship. This route to management is well accepted in the German clothing industry (used by two-thirds of all managers in the industry (Klinke and Becker, 1987)) and in some cases is supplemented by two years of full-time schooling to the technician level (six of the plant managers in our sample). Two of the German managing directors had studied at a polytechnic for four years in order to attain a degree in clothing.

Most of the NI managers had moved from other industries and used work study courses to gain acquaintance with work processes in clothing. Only two had taken the apprenticeship route. Two others had gone to university and achieved general business studies qualifications, one had achieved a doctorate in science. Thus the incidence of university level qualifications amongst the NI managers was higher than that amongst their counterparts in the German firms (although when other staff are included the total frequency of degrees was still higher in the German clothing firms). However, on average the NI managers were still less appropriately qualified than those in Germany. The involvement of NI managers overlooking the shop-floor and production planning was much less than in German plants. German plant managers often combined the positions of plant director, production planner and plant manager. They usually knew the background and type of skills of the workers on the shop-floor; they were familiar with the sequence of production and were able to improve the plant layout so as to facilitate frequent changes of style. In NI these tasks of the German managers were usually split between specialists. So it was not uncommon to find twice as many managerial and supervisory personnel in NI plants than in their German counterparts.

Qualifications of textiles managing directors

When personnel with university degrees were compared in the two countries, Germany had a ten-fold advantage. In one matched comparison the NI manager was a craft-trained engineer whereas his

German counterpart was a graduate engineer. In another there was an accountant in NI but a graduate engineer in Germany. Only one of the companies in NI had an engineering graduate as manager. A managing director at a factory west of the Bann said that he could not persuade his senior personnel to go to training courses in Belfast in their own time. Moreover, the narrow range of industries within the Province was said to limit the possibility for attracting skilled or trained persons into NI from the outside. This is an example of the well known principle of external diseconomy.

Supervisors and middle management

We examined the importance of the supervisory and middle management functions with special reference to the engineering and clothing trades. Briefer comments will also be made about textiles, food etc. and miscellaneous.

(a) Engineering

About half of the supervisors in NI had passed an apprenticeship, while the other half had been promoted from the shop-floor without any further technical training, in Germany all the supervisors were apprentice trained and some had achieved the Meister level. The Meister has at least two years experience after his apprenticeship and undertakes two to three years of part- or full-time schooling (950 hours) which are completed by extensive practical, oral and written examinations. This training includes aspects of both administration and production control and so provides him with technical and organisational skills. Such skills are particularly valuable in smoothing out production problems when processes have to be changed, such as during the introduction of new technologies and products (Prais and Wagner, 1988).

German engineering companies made extensive use of Meister such that in one plant there was one Meister for every eight production workers and in another one to 25. These Meister eased the adoption of higher value-added products and reorganised and re-equipped entire workshops. The high competence and flexibility of their middle management and the work-force allowed these companies to find and utilise market niches, to develop products in co-operation with their customers and also to design and implement unique machinery. If retraining was required it was taken for granted and did not cause any labour disputes. The other German plants also employed Meister. In spring making (an apparently simple product) four Meister and five graduate engineers were employed out of a total of one hundred mainly skilled workers. The responsibilities of the Meister were largely innovative: to test new metals, develop better machinery and production methods, co-operate with customers so as to customise products. This had to be done in addition to their supervisory duties. Apart from these tasks, Meister were found to be responsible for planning work for CNC machines, guaranteeing work delivery schedules, small repairs, adjusting and adapting machinery which had been bought off the shelf, improving work methods and organising production flows. However, any comparison of productivity achievement must be seen in the context of the generally higher level of skills in Germany. The importance of Meister with their highly developed organisation skills has also been demonstrated in a matched plant comparison of the kitchen furniture industry (Steedman and Wagner, 1987).

All the supervisors in NI had been promoted from the shop floor without any further technical training while all the supervisors in Germany were apprentice trained and some were trained to the Meister level. The Meister has at least two years experience after an apprenticeship and then undergoes two/three years of part- or full-time schooling (950 hours) which are completed by practical, oral and written examinations. This training includes aspects of both administration and production control and so provides them with both technical and managerial skills. Such skills are particularly valuable in smoothing out production problems (Prais and Wagner, 1988). Two of the larger German Engineers made extensive use of Meister such that in one plant there was one Meister for every eight production workers, and in the other one to 25. These Meister had eased the adoption of higher value-added products and in one case reorganised and re-equipped entire workshops. The high competence and flexibility of their manpower allowed the managers of these companies to find (and utilise) market niches, to develop products in co-operation with their customers and also to design and implement unique machinery. If retraining was required it was taken for granted and did not cause labour disputes.

All the other German plants also employed Meister. Even in spring making (an apparently simple product), four Meister and five graduate engineers were employed out of a total of one hundred mainly skilled workers in order to test new metals, develop better machinery and production methods, co-operate with customers to customise products, over and above their supervisory tasks. The extent of technically skilled amongst our sample was not unrepresentative of the industry in Germany. The Ingenieur-Erhebung survey 42 per cent of employment in metal working and found that 14.8 per cent of all employees were Meister, technician or draftsmen. Apart from some of the tasks already outlined, Meister would have responsibility to plan work for the CNC machines, co-ordinate production, guarantee delivery schedules and distribute work. The importance of the Meister is stressed in a matched plant comparison of the kitchen furniture industry (Steedman and Wagner, 1987).

In Northern Ireland both the supervisors (foremen) and production (line) managers were generally without any formal technical training. This was associated with frequent difficulties in meeting delivery deadlines or in keeping the CNCs in operation. In some cases it was difficult to organise the mainly semi-skilled workers and maintain a smooth running of production. One NI company was sufficiently familiar with their German counterparts to say that that their NI supervisors were good at the "social side" of the job but not at solving technical problems. They

151

resisted change and were said to be insufficiently well trained. At another NI firm supervision and work study were both primitive. As a result they did not know how much operative labour they needed to accomplish certain tasks.

(b) Clothing

Once again, all the German supervisors had at least been apprentice trained (three years) whereas all their NI counterparts had been promoted from the shop floor (with the exception of one supervisor with a Clothing Board Certificate, CAPITB). The Northern Irish supervisors had responsibility for work distribution, identification of faulty work, training and line balance. This is a much narrower domain than that controlled by the German supervisor (who also supervised work methods, cost control and delivery dates). Unfortunately, even within their comparatively small range of responsibilities the Northern Irish were sometimes ineffective, on the day of the interview one supervisor had placed the wrong parts on the line which imbalanced output and interrupted the production flow. While working methods, such as how to handle and sew a garment most efficiently, had a high priority in German plants, in few NI plants had these been given much attention by managers and supervisors. One of these plants had gained a 25 per cent productivity improvement as a result.

(c) Textiles

Once again there was a substantial representation of Meister and technicians in Germany that was not paralleled in NI. These were responsible for running single departments, decisions on production schedules, changes in set-ups and sharing in investment decisions as well as supervising the on-the-job training of semi- or unskilled workers. The NI technicians were more exclusively directed towards maintenance. The German rate of qualifications at the middle layer of plant management was four times that of the NI plants.

(d) Food

Most German departments were managed by a Meister overlooking semi-skilled workers who organised the work flow and improved productivity. Typically, there was a Meister for every 20-40 workers. By contrast, the NI plants were using foremen who were at most time-served and more probably promoted from the shop-floor without qualification. They recognised that certain problems arose as a result. One NI firm had difficulties in training its semi-skilled workers, another considered it had bad working practises and a third had used consultants to try to improve work organisation. In the last case it was claimed that manpower reductions of 20-40 percent had been achieved across different departments without any loss of output.

152

(e) Miscellaneous

The broad pattern was similar to that found in the other sectors. Compared to their German counterparts the NI supervisors were largely untrained and the NI companies paid a price for this in terms of a number of opportunities for greater efficiency which were foregone.

Shop-floor skills

Having compared the quality of management and supervision in the two countries, this section will examine the skills of the shop-floor labour force. Table 14.2 illustrates the percentages of employees with apprentice training.

Table 14.2
Percentage of the shop-floor labour force with a skill

	Percent of pairs where WG has a higher proportion of skilled workers	Averages of percentage skilled	
		WG	NI
Engineering	80	68	36
Miscellaneous	71	22	14
Food, drink, tob.	80	23	8
Textiles	100	29	6
Clothing	100	48	4
All manufacturing	88	42	14

Note: Number of pair-wise comparisons considered were; engineering 10; miscellaneous 7; food etc. 5; textiles 5; clothing 15; all 42. In engineering the 10 pair-wise comparisons involved 12 companies in Northern Ireland.

On average three times as many skilled persons were employed in Germany as in Northern Ireland. In thirty percent of pairs the German proportion was at least three times that of NI and in fifteen percent of cases there were no apprentice trained personnel in NI. Overall, in just over four-fifths of the comparisons the German plants had more skilled workers. In both countries engineering was found to be the most skill-intensive industry. Northern Ireland came closest to the German proportion of skilled workers in the miscellaneous trades.

These figures reflect the much higher acceptance of the importance of training by the Germans. The in-company trainers used by the German firms had themselves followed the two or three year apprenticeship vocational training course which includes one or two days a week release from work for vocational schooling.

This so-called dual system follows a national syllabus terminating with intermediate and final written and practical examinations. Most of the Germans who leave school at sixteen enter the dual system with the result that in the early 1980s three fifths of the labour force were qualified to apprentice level or better and this proportion is increasing. In Britain, only a third of the labour force achieves this standard (Prais, 1981a, 1981b).

The two most skill intensive sectors in Germany, engineering and clothing were once again given special attention.

(a) Skills in engineering

This sector emerges as the most skill intensive in most countries and this finding confirms that of other matched plant comparisons (Daly, Hitchens and Wagner, 1985; Steedman and Wagner, 1987; Steedman and Wagner, 1989) and the implication that the proportion of the German labour force skilled is twice that of NI is supported by a similar result as regards engineering component workers in Britain and Germany (Daly, Hitchens and Wagner, 1985). Although we attempted to match the apprentices trained in Germany with the numbers passing City and Guilds examinations in NI, it was found that NI managers generally had only imprecise knowledge of the qualifications held by their labour force.

The NI plants ranged widely in the extent to which their employees were skilled. Thus one plant had 90 percent skilled but three employed only semi- and unskilled. By contrast, between 40 per cent and 90 per cent of shop-floor workers in the German plants were skilled. There were only two pair-wise comparisons where NI employed a higher proportion of skilled than the German counterpart and in one of these cases the extra skilled labour seemed superfluous (i.e. the Germans used semi-skilled workers and yet were able to produce a more complex product with four times the productivity level of an overmanned NI factory). In a branch plant of a GB company we were told that even relative to GB this factory was biased towards the simplest fabrication tasks.

As with the findings for managers and supervisors, these results are entirely consistent with the generally much better output (both quantitative and qualitative) relative to the UK of the German vocational and technical education system. The closest British comparison with the three and half year apprenticeship in electrical and mechanical engineering are the City and Guilds Part II courses, each recognised nation-wide. Since the German annual output of mechanical and electrical engineering craftsmen is three times that of Britain, and total employment in these trades is about one-quarter higher in Germany than Britain, it follows that the proportion receiving skills qualifications in Germany is just over double that of Britain (Prais and Wagner, 1983).

We were told that the main advantage of having a skilled labour force was that shop-floor workers became flexible enough to handle complex machinery, computers and higher product quality. Whereas the highly skilled German work force maintained close to full utilisation of their CNC machines, two NI companies complained that these machines could not be run at their expected levels of utilisation. One company reported that its workers failed to calibrate their tools properly. In general the Germans stressed that all their operators were familiar with the workings of their machinery and could read technical drawings, at one German factory technical drawings were stuck on the wall.

The German companies were further distinguished from those in NI by the fact that they were moving towards higher value-added production whereas the NI companies (as we have already shown) tended to concentrate on less advanced products. The skills of the German labour force were said to be essential to the introduction of sophisticated and customer-designed products as has been noted elsewhere (Zedler, 1988).

(b) Skills in clothing

Only four percent of NI shop-floor workers had achieved a City and Guilds clothing craft certificate at either stages I, or II or III. These qualifications correspond to the three levels of the German apprenticeship in clothing (Steedman and Wagner, 1989). The proportion of skilled workers in Germany was 48 per cent which was twelve times that of NI (this mirrors the fact that the annual output of stage I trainees is eleven times higher in Germany than in Britain, and the difference as regards stages II and III is even larger at thirteen to one (Steedman and Wagner, 1989). The differing degree of skills in the two labour forces was revealed by the range of tasks for which operators were proficient. The Germans were capable of four to six different operations at high speed. In contrast the NI machinists with only six to thirteen weeks of training could manage only two operations at full efficiency. De-skilling had been caused in the NI clothing firms by the application of automatic machinery which had led in some cases to training periods being as little as one or two days. Long runs allowed this direction to be taken in NI while in Germany although such methods existed 10-15 years ago they were subsequently scrapped and changed to small batch sizes in response to competition and market change. The implications of skills for productivity were as follows:

Change over time Batch sizes were smaller in Germany (on average one-fifth those of our NI sample) which reflected the generally shorter runs of given garment styles in Germany. By concentrating on short runs which can be delivered at short notice to the retailer the Germans are able to charge a premium and hence enhance their value-added relative to the Northern Irish firms which concentrate on standardise long runs (Kurt Salmon, 1988). The German companies were much more adept at achieving quick change-overs between garment styles and could sometimes do this within a few days whereas the NI firms required much longer to adjust fully to a new line. Given their very rapid speed of response, the German firms could adjust more quickly to shifts in domestic demand than plants selling to Germany from abroad. Thus to some extent the German industry was able to retain competitiveness with the low wage Newly Industrialised Countries.

155

The NI garment manufacturers which were competing mainly on price (Kurt Salmon, 1988) had no such advantage. In several cases the German companies stressed that they were "responsive to the market". "We see ourselves as being retailers whereas in NI they think of themselves as producers". Indeed the matched counterpart to the German firm which said this was in decline partly because of general weak demand but also because its market share had slipped. The NI company recognised that it needed to introduce "ingenuity in design and colour" and asked the interviewer if he had any suggestions!

Quality German value-added was further enhanced by the fact that the highly trained operators could recognise faults at an early stage in the production of the garment so that repairs could be effected. Thus the German supervisors unlike their NI counterparts were largely free from responsibility for quality control (in an earlier study of the clothing industry the ratio of quality controllers to machinists in Germany was only one-third that of Britain) and could take on tasks which were undertaken by managers in NI including managing the production lines and ensuring delivery schedules were met.

One NI company was handicapped by being in a situation where 27 percent of the shop-floor were trainees but the trainers were comparatively inexperienced. "There is no way they can train satisfactorily" the production manager said. The result was a disastrous internal reject rate of 50-60 per cent. This company was bankrupt and is currently being kept alive by large injections of IDB "equity". During the rescue operation reject rates had stabilised at about 20 per cent. Overall, reject rates in clothing in NI were more than twice as high as those in Germany (for consideration of reject rates see above).

Line balancing and absenteeism Another advantage of a skilled labour force arises in the context of balancing for absenteeism. As garments are made in sequence of machining tasks the production process will be very sensitive to whether anyone is missing or to individuals who cannot work at the projected speed. The more specialised and less skilled labour force in NI was less able to replace absent colleagues and unfortunately absenteeism (considered in more detail below) was higher in NI than Germany, 11 per cent versus 6 per cent (excluding maternity leave). One NI company had attributed a 7 per cent productivity loss to an absenteeism rate of 16 per cent. The consequence of the much higher absenteeism in NI was that the plants there had to carry spare (substitute) operators plus extra machinery so as to compensate for the effects on production of absenteeism. Absenteeism in NI created its greatest havoc within those factories using computerised overhead transportation systems where the whole system could be paralysed by the weakest work station.

(c) Skills in textiles

The share of skilled workers in textiles is relatively low in NI whereas it is in the middle range in Germany. In proportional terms about five times as many skilled persons were employed in Germany as in NI. Although in both countries the operators and chargehands were semi-skilled, the Germans had much longer periods of in-company training (up to two years). One NI company commended the local people for good attitudes to work but still found them hard to train (some could not read).

Apart from having fewer skilled workers than Germany, the NI plants demonstrated a different distribution of skills. Most of the NI skilled men were concentrated in maintenance departments (which were twice as large as those in Germany) whereas in Germany skills were used in production too. In addition the skilled production supervisors in Germany had an important part to play in enhancing the productivity compared with the unskilled counterparts in NI. This was achieved by repairing breakdowns, better production organisation and better on-the-job training of skilled operators.

All the German plants trained apprentices according to a three-and-a-half year schedule. In the plants visited 3-10 per cent of the shop floor labour force were apprentices trained on the production floor plus one day a week of training instruction in a vocational school. In NI the apprentices were only found in maintenance departments.

(d) Skills in food

Whilst this industry is comparatively unskilled in both countries, the German representation of skills remains four times higher than that of NI. As in the case of textiles most of the NI apprentice trained workers were concentrated in maintenance departments whereas the Germans also had skilled shop-floor workers and supervisors. For example, in the case of food preparation the German shop floor workers were largely apprentice-trained and only the operators of the can filling lines were semi-skilled. The Germans felt that preparing and heating quality food required highly skilled workers.

(e) Skills in miscellaneous

In both countries these trades are comparatively unskilled. In terms of the proportions of shop-floor labour skilled it is the sector where Germany has the narrowest advantage relative to NI. However, the semi-skilled operators in Germany are still more flexible than their NI counterparts in terms of the number of kinds of machines they can work with. As in the other sectors, the German operators are supervised by skilled Meister and they are largely responsible for their own quality control. The NI operators who have little or no formal training were most comparable with the semi-skilled Gastarbeiter (i.e. Turkish, Greek and other migrant workers in Germany).

A number of NI companies recognised deficiencies arising from the untrained state of their labour. Two companies blamed a lack of training for poor work attitudes and others pointed to rough handling leading to rejects (4 per cent in one company). Some of the NI companies had already realised productivity gains through improving the quality of the shop-floor labour force. One had introduced more flexibility and training when it moved to a new site and as a result it produced the same output as before but with only two thirds of the previous manpower. In another NI firm improved work practises and better use of machinery led to a productivity growth of 15 per cent (and in another case similar measures achieved 60 per cent higher output per head).

Management and labour force qualifications and training: conclusions

This Chapter has reviewed the relative qualifications and training of the entire hierarchy of employment in the two sets of factories (i.e. from managers, down through foremen, technicians, supervisors, craftsmen down to semi-skilled and unskilled operatives). At every level formal qualifications are under-represented in NI relative to Germany. The implications for productivity were traced and these were gloomy. Not only did NI's quality control suffer on given products but the narrow width of experience by management and labour led to the entire range of products being biased towards simpler ones with a low technology content (see also Chapter 11). Given that the UK's system of technical and vocational education has been found wanting when compared with that of almost every other major industrial country (Campaign for Work, 1988; Steedman, 1988; Finegold and Soskice, 1988; Prais, 1989) NI's difficulties are not surprising. What is surprising is how the characteristics of our sample (which includes almost half of the 25 largest manufacturing companies in NI) contrast with the conventional wisdom as to the excellency of the NI labour force (Department of Commerce, 1982; Pathfinder, 1987). And, as the following Chapter will show, not only are the NI workers comparatively unskilled but the much vaunted "NI work ethic" is very well disguised!

15 Other labour force characteristics

"Ireland is in a state of social decomposition".

Benjamin Disraeli, House of Commons, July 2 1849

Introduction

This Chapter considers labour force characteristics other than those of education and training: absenteeism, turnover, strikes and labour force attitudes. Given that there is evidence that work attitudes in NI have been affected by the continous political violence since 1969, it was felt most appropriate to consider the effects of the Troubles in this Chapter.

Absenteeism

Table 15.1 shows absenteeism is on average slightly worse in the plants in NI. However, when one considers individual sectors NI is better than Germany in every case except clothing.

Where rates of absenteeism were high in Germany these were predominantly associated with factories employing large numbers of semi-skilled persons, frequently <u>Gastarbeiter</u> (i.e. Turkish, Greek, Yugoslavian or other immigrant labourers). This was a more important determinant of high absenteeism than the employing of female labour (for example, German absenteeism in clothing was not relatively high though this figure excludes maternity leave). When absenteeism rates for Germany are recalculated so as to exclude the Gastarbeiter plants then average absenteeism falls to 5 per cent and is only 4 per cent in both engineering and miscellaneous (adjusted figures cannot be calculated for textiles and food given that all the companies sampled employed large numbers of Gastarbeiter).

Table 15.1
Absenteeism

	NI better, % of pairs	Average % of days lost	
		NI	WG
Engineering	88	4	6(4)
Miscellaneous	71	4	6(4)
Food etc.	60	4	7
Textiles	83	5	7
Clothing	10	11*	6*
All	47	7	6(5)

* Excludes maternity leave which is much lower in Germany[1]. Figures in parentheses excludes the plants employing mainly Gastarbeiter.

Problems with immigrant labour were frequently commented on by German managers "we are please to say that we don't have any foreign workers except Austrians and although absenteeism is high at 6 per cent, it is normal amongst the Germans" (their NI counterpart regarded a ten per cent absenteeism rate as normal). The association of German absenteeism problems with the Gastarbeiter is of interest because it indicates that low skills (which are related to low rates of pay) are major causes of absenteeism. This of obvious relevance to the case of NI.

Of particular note in NI were peculiarly high rates of absence in the clothing sector: 20-25 per cent was not uncommon. One manager admitted that absenteeism reduced productivity by 10 per cent and perhaps by more when one allowed for the lower efficiency of the substitutes for the absent operator. One company in desperation introduced a policy of home visits and succeeded in reducing the rate closer to a tolerable ten per cent.

Although the generally lower absenteeism in NI in the sectors other than clothing might be expected to enhance comparative productivity, the differences between Northern Ireland and Germany are not great and insufficient to redress much of the disadvantage arising from the other factors considered above.

Labour turnover

Turnover was defined as the annual number of persons entering or leaving the permanent employment of a firm expressed as a percentage of the total employment of that firm. Firms with high rates of turnover may not be able to retain employees long enough for those workers to become fully proficient in certain tasks (i.e. the more often a task is performed, the more efficiently it is done, but if the employee leaves before these economies through doing are exhausted then the firm foregoes a potential benefit).

Table 15.2
Labour turnover

	NI better, % of pairs	% of total employment	
		NI	WG
Engineering	60	7	10 (6)
Miscellaneous	83	3	5 (4)
Food etc.	33	5	2
Textiles	50	5	9
Clothing	7	20	10
All manufacturing	38	11	8 (7)

Notes: Number of pairs 34. Results in parentheses exclude those plants employing largely <u>Gastarbeiter</u>.

On average NI reported worse turnover but this is entirely accounted for by the labour force in clothing and food. In all other sectors turnover is lower in NI (they average 4.4 per cent compared to 6.9 per cent in Germany). However, in engineering and miscellaneous all or most of the difference between Germany and NI disappears if one excludes those plants employing <u>Gastarbeiter</u> (results shown in parentheses). It is important to stress the association between relatively high absenteeism and an unskilled work-force because it suggests that one of the longer term rewards from increasing training would be lower rates of absenteeism (ironically, it is precisely the fear that workers would leave the firms once they had been trained up with highly marketable skills which may be holding back private companies in GB and NI from investing more in upgrading skills).

Strikes and disruptions

Strikes and other disruptions to working time are not only important in their own right because of the resultant loss of output but also as indicators of the general climate of industrial relations. Factories where strikes are common are also likely to be characterised by such problems as overmanning, inflexible use of existing labour and resistance to investment in process innovation.

The results shown in Table 15.3 are in contrast to Germany where strikes were conspicuous by their complete absence. Several German managers said "if there was a strike we'd close the factory and walk out". Forty-three per cent of NI plants had experienced at least one disruption during the last three years (there were also some political strikes over and above these stoppages).

Table 15.3
Incidence of strikes and disruptions in NI*
(% of cases during previous 3 years)

Engineering	56
Miscellaneous	50
Food etc.	40
Textiles	33
Clothing	36
All	43

* None of the German plants had experienced any form of stoppage during the previous 3 years. Stoppages were defined so as to exclude political strikes and very short breaks in normal work, of less than 30 minutes.

The highest incidence was in the engineering and miscellaneous trades and least amongst the female labour force employed in clothing and in textiles. It was notable that almost none of the disruption in NI was concerned with pay (although two companies had trouble every year because of wages), but rather the reasons for disruption included: flexibility agreements, introduction of piecework or new methods or new machinery, tea breaks and discipline of workers. Fifteen per cent of companies experienced strikes once a year or once every two years or "frequently" (one manager at a foreign owned plant complained that his employees had been on a permanent go-slow since they started production in NI in 1968).

The fact that the NI strike rate was higher than in Germany is not surprising given that the much greater degree of industrial harmony in Germany relative to the UK is well established (during 1982-86 the UK strike rate in all production industries, that is mining, construction and transport as well as manufacturing, was seven and half times that of Germany, and, while NI's strike intensity in manufacturing during the same period was only about 70 per cent of GB, this would still imply an incidence of strikes in NI five times greater than that in Germany; see Chapter 7 and Department of Employment, 1988). It would be interesting to know whether the incidence of strikes observed here (over two out of every five plants) was higher than that in Great Britain. Black (1987) demonstrated that the incidence of strikes in NI manufacturing was 10 per cent higher than that in GB (when industrial structure was allowed for). Chapter 7 showed that in some industries (textiles, clothing and food, drink and tobacco) NI had a much higher average strike rate during 1980-85.

The frequent incidence of strikes in NI was part of a wider problem of work attitudes and this is described below. Before turning to attitudes it is appropriate to consider the impact of the political violence in NI on the firms.

Impact of the Troubles

The Troubles had little direct impact on the firms. One Belfast firm had been bombed in 1987 and a firm in Tyrone noted that one of its employees had been shot on the premises in the 1970s. A former managing director at that Tyrone plant had been advised by the police to carry a gun with him during the 1970s. Most previous studies of the economic consequences of the Troubles have used shift share statistical techniques to assess the impact on output and employment in manufacturing and the other broad sectors of the aggregate economy (New Ireland Forum, 1983; Canning, Moore and Rhodes, 1987). Whilst the available statistical data is limited it is probable that the direct impact on NI manufacturing (e.g. factories bombed) has so far been limited.[2]

Nevertheless, the political situation had some subtle effects. A firm in west Belfast complained that it was difficult to get workers to travel in for the night shift. We have already seen how on a number of occasions engineers had to be flown into the Province. Two engineering companies made the interesting remark that Japanese and German mechanics were prepared to come but the English were more scared. Of the fifty or so plant managers and production managers interviewed in NI only five originated from outside Northern Ireland (one chairman from continental Europe, 2 plant managers from England, one production manager from the Republic of Ireland and one chief engineer from Scotland). It is highly probable that this relatively low representation of "outsiders" reflects the image that NI has of a strife-torn location in which it was unpleasant to work (to the extent that this has narrowed the range of experience within NI productivity performance has suffered (see Chapter 7). Significantly the percentage of "outsiders" in this sample of managers is much lower than that measured in a much larger survey on NI management made 20 years ago (Bates and Bell, 1971). There was even some evidence that perceptions arising from the Troubles reduced the mobility of managers within NI: two firms in the north west of the Province complained that people would not come from Belfast.

Four firms in Derry and the north west claimed their workers were particularly obstructive. The probable explanation was that they largely recruited from housing estates dominated by the IRA (in one case the criticism of the work force may have reflected a sectarian prejudice on the part of the manager, but it should be noted that the other three complaints came from someone from England, from the Republic and from Continental Europe). One of these plants was under foreign ownership and the manager felt that the group would hold back production at the NI factory until there was greater political stability. In the meantime grants were accepted as a compensation for low productivity in NI. At the same time there were other firms operating in Counties Tyrone and Derry which were satisfied with their work forces (in these cases the plants tended to be sited in rural areas). In most other cases it was not possible to pick up a direct link between the Troubles and work attitudes though twenty years of violence may have caused a growth in general contempt for authority. It was also notable that in eight plants (in Belfast and Counties Down and Antrim) there were very extensive displays of "loyalist" emblems within the factory (no equivalent nationalist displays were seen in any factory visited). Management did not feel these displays a problem despite their questionable legality and the possibility of harmful impact on some foreign markets (especially America). In two plants there had been short stoppages as part of the unionist campaign against the Anglo-Irish Agreement. Whilst we did not question managers as to whether the composition of their labour force reflected the sectarian composition of their recruitment catchment area (however that might be defined) two companies volunteered that they had a "fair" mix amongst their workers. They also claimed that relationships within the factory were good. Taking the sample as a whole, poor productivity and its attendant problems were as clearly evidenced in the mainly protestant work forces as in the mainly catholic ones.

Work attitudes

Table 15.4 shows that 24 per cent of German plants and 31 percent of NI plant managers complained of poor worker attitudes.

Table 15.4
Poor attitudes to work (% of companies reporting attitudes).

	NI	WG
Engineering	20	30
Miscellaneous	80	60
Food, drink and tobacco	0	25
Textiles	33	60
Clothing	27	0
All manufacturing	31	24

In Germany the complaints were largely associated with those plants employing semi-skilled Gastarbeiter. This is reflected in the sectoral composition of the complaints but not in comparatively poor productivity performance. Moreover, there remained a qualitative difference between worker attitudes in the two countries. No German firm, in contrast to NI, described them as "very bad", "difficult", and including "a resistance to train".

One reason why Germany has fewer and less severe problems, and why they are concentrated amongst the Gastarbeiter plants is because the work-force is better educated and trained. More persons achieve secondary level educational certificates than their UK counterparts (Prais and Wagner, 1985) and more complete apprenticeship training courses (Prais, 1981b). In contrast the NI labour force is less educated and less skilled. Indeed a number of producers trained little and emphasised the advantages of deskilling investment.

In NI a number of remarkable comments were made. At one Derry factory the labour force linked their daily output direct to their pay and when they had produced their self imposed limit they stopped (productivity was under half that in Germany). The manager of that plant regretted the decision to locate production in NI because he felt the workers were only concerned with "what's in it for me". Another manager in the same sector described his workers as "greedy". In the miscellaneous trade in central Belfast one manager spoke of recruiting from the "sludge" (i.e. a ghetto area of the city). A more general problem was the clannishness of the workers, if one employee was disciplined they would gang together. As a result a number of companies adopted a policy of recruiting from a widespread geographic area. Otherwise, as one company reported, there was a danger that local workers would continue their social life during time on the shop-floor.

In the clothing and textiles sectors problems of illiteracy were encountered and an inability to read had made training very difficult. One company said that poor education had led to obstructive attitudes and that NI people did not live up to their reputation for a work ethic: "many are ready to lead a strike and have a mind bending attitude on the part of some people". A bankrupt clothing firm sampled reported labour turnover and absenteeism rates of twenty-five percent and claimed the employees were "reluctant to work, lazy and late". Workers at another firm had a mentality of "we were allowed to do that before" with the result that they blocked improvements in work methods. In that instance the managing director was scared to even walk on the shop-floor lest this start rumours and another disruption. In the miscellaneous trades one firm reported trouble every week including three hours lost the day before the interview because girls on the night shift felt cold.

In contrast to the other sectors the managers of NI food firms did not report attitudinal problems (only one firm said there was "occasional" difficulties). This may be related to the location of those food plants. In general rural work forces were reported to be co-operative and satisfactory: "the attitude of our work force is good: commendable". In two cases in clothing the intensity of effort of stitchers in NI was measured to be higher than in Germany.

It is not possible to give a complete explanation for why work attitudes should have been generally better in Germany but comparisons of Britain with Germany suggest a range of social, political, cultural and institutional factors play a part in Germany's superior performance (see Chapter 2). For example: single industrial unions in each plant, co-determination between representatives of the employees and employers, political consensus around the social market economy, memories of desperate economic conditions in the 1940s, and relatively authoritarian social attitudes (Lawrence, 1980; Prais, 1981a; Johnson, 1984). Suffice to say that any improvement in NI would require very wide sweeping changes especially since the Troubles and their effects on attitudes may have introduced a further negative element which is not observed in Great Britain.

It should be stressed that management in NI may carry some of the responsibility for the poor attitudes of their labour forces.

For example one NI manager described his labour force in terms which would be considered as rascist if used by a manager in GB of black people[3] and at another firm the managing director was described as autocratic and secretive with the result that morale amongst middle management and shop floor workers was low.

Further investigation of the poor worker attitudes described in this section would need to take into account management style. For example, a number of plausible reasons can be suggested as to why NI management might be more autocratic and less able to work with its work-force than their German counterparts. Lawrence (1980) argues that the Germans (both management and labour) see themselves as belonging to a meritocratic society where hard work gets its fair reward. It is probable that a much higher proportion of German shop-floor workers perceive themselves as "middle class" than their NI counterparts, thus managers and workers in Germany may find it easier to believe that they have common interests. Indeed many of the managers in our German sample had risen from the shop-floor. Furthermore in Chapter 9 we noted that textiles and heavy engineering in Britain have been characterised as having second rate and autocratic family based management. Unfortunately these sectors are relatively heavily represented in NI.

Labour force characteristics: conclusions

NI has a mixed record in absenteeism and is generally better than Germany in turnover (except in clothing). The most alarming findings relate to strikes and work attitudes both of which are very serious problems.

Notes

1. The German net reproduction rate in the 1980s was 0.64 (Statistisches Bundesamt, 1988).

2. Unfortunately there are at the time of writing a number of indications that the IRA is going to intensify its campaign against industrial targets (News Letter 1989, March 29). The repeated disruption to the Belfast-Dublin rail link (from December 1988 onwards) is one example where employment in manufacturing is threatened as are the recent bombings of parts of the premises of Shorts. Given the escalation in violence during the last four years (and memories of the period during the 1970s when businessmen were murdered and kidnapped) it would be highly rational for managers in NI to hold back on the expansion of investment in human capital, organisation and physical plant until they could have more confidence in the longer term political situation. Thus whilst the direct damage done by the Troubles may so far be negligible the fear of possible violence in the future is one factor depressing the "animal spirits" of investors in NI and hence an obstacle to economic improvement. In making comparisons with Germany one would ideally wish to make some

allowance for the impact on the confidence of German managers of the Red Army Faction's periodic assassinations of prominent German industrialists and financiers.

3. The same managing director talked about rather sinister ways of gaining greater control over his work-force. For example, he liked to get husbands and wives working together in the same factory (this technique was also employed by nineteenth century factory managers (Marx, 1976)).

16 Characteristics of the firms relevant to productivity

"... by comparison with Britain's more advanced regions, Ulster's achievements were still modest".

Description of NI manufacturing in the 1870s, J. Othick, in L. Kennedy and P. Ollerenshaw (eds)(1985), An Economic History of Ulster 1830-1939

This Chapter examines some of the characteristics of the sample firms which may be relevant to their comparative productivity performance. These factors are: the ownership and institutional type of firm; their age; and nationality of their control. While it is possible to use economic theory to identify a range of possible effects on productivity, it is not always possible to predict whether any given characteristic of the firms would, ceteris paribus, have a net effect which is positive or negative.

Ownership type

It has been argued that branch plants are less likely to produce high value-added products to the extent that certain value enhancing activities, such as research and development, tend to be concentrated around the group headquarters (Harris, 1987). We therefore compared the numbers of "free standing" plants in the two countries (i.e. those which were not part of a larger corporate group). Perhaps unexpectedly NI emerged at no disadvantage in this respect and indeed 46 per cent of the NI plants were free standing as compared to only 30 per cent in Germany. Of course such independence would be a disadvantage if the alternative was membership of a larger group with access to larger capital resources.

We therefore compared the numbers of public companies (i.e. those quoted on stock markets) as an indicator of potential to draw on external capital. In this respect NI again emerged ahead of Germany (46 per cent, compared to 30 per cent). This finding is not surprising given that the aversion of German industry to use of the stock market is well known (Prais, 1981a). The German reliance on industrial banks has several significant consequences. German firms are under less pressure to report high profits and hence good dividends and this is reflected in our findings. Whilst the German firms sampled were generally reticent about disclosing their profitability, where NI and Germany could be compared in matched pairs the NI profitability was usually at least as good as Germany and sometimes better. A later section will consider whether this demonstrates market failure in NI, i.e. firms in NI were as profitable as those in Germany despite having a performance which in several respects was less desirable from a social point of view. Suffice to say at this stage that the greater representation in NI of public limited companies may lead to less emphasis on investments which will only pay off in the longer term (such as research and development).

Apart from considering the present ownership structure of the firms it also of interest to examine their recent history in terms of ownership. One German company in the miscellaneous trades had been subject to a management buy-out and one engineering firm was taken over by another group. In the latter case, the firm had been owned and managed by one family for around a century and its performance was becoming increasingly lack-lustre. This type of phenomenon, take over after a prolonged period of poor performance, was more common in NI where there were three such take overs (one in miscellaneous trades of a company which had been in family control for two hundred years, and two successive take overs of a single firm in engineering). Additionally, two clothing firms were bankrupt at the time of our visit and were the subject of Industrial Development Board(IDB)-financed rescue operations and subsequently one of these rescue operations failed (similarly, one engineering firm has been engaged in protracted negotiations with the IDB in order to obtain a very large grant so as to facilitate sale to an external company, otherwise the company will close). Another bankrupt company, in engineering, had been the subject of a management buy-out (some public money had been necessary to make this deal sufficiently attractive to the manager). In a further case in engineering, a plant had been saved from closure by a workers buy-out but morale was still very bad and there was obvious disunity amongst the key personnel managing the plant. One NI food firm was involved in frequent changes in ownership (North American to Republic of Ireland, and then Irish to French). In this case the take overs probably reflected the perception that the product (which in this case was of first class standard) would be more profitable if given better marketing and brand management. Thus one could say that the organisational background in NI was more unsettled than that in Germany and this would have a harmful effect on productivity (e.g. reluctance to make long run investment decisions, a souring of industrial relations). At the same time, the greater frequency of take overs and state financed "rescue" bids in NI is symptomatic of the poor health of NI manufacturing (since the time of the interviews two of the NI factories visited have ceased operations).

We have already noted that there were cases in both Germany and NI where a family firm got into difficulties and was then taken over by a wider group (family firm being defined as one where ownership and control are largely concentrated in the same family). It is an argument familiar from the economic history of Victorian England that when the founder of a company dies his son may lack the entrepreneurial thrust and ability of the father (Kindleberger, 1975; Wiener, 1981). More generally, it is argued that the long run performance of family firms suffers to the extent that they exclude outside managerial talent. Six family owned firms could be identified in our sample in NI (that is 15 per cent of the total). If there were managerial difficulties one would expect these to be evidenced in the older family firms and two of the three NI firms managed with a third or fourth generation descendant of the founder (i.e. the company had been founded during the late Victorian era) had been chronically unprofitable. At the same time it should be stressed that the other third or fourth generation family firm in NI was reasonably profitable and had one of the best comparative productivity performances of any company in our sample (albeit that company announced in 1990 job reductions equivalent to one-sixth of its employment). This suggests that the links between family ownership and performance are complex. Moreover, a large proportion (11 out of 37) of the sample in Germany were identified as family firms and, with the exception already noted of one engineering company passing out of family control, their performance seemed excellent. Admittedly, most of these firms had been established since the War so they were probably still managed by the original founder. However, it was notable that in textiles there were two firms dating from the first half of the nineteenth century and there was no evidence that these firms were suffering from family ownership (the next section will consider age of firm as an explanatory variable in its own right). Perhaps the comparatively poor performance of some of the NI family firms is more indicative of a general weakness in the quality of NI management than a deficiency in family firms per se.

Age

The relationship between the age of a company and its rate of growth of employment or sales is a subject of some controversy in the literature (Storey, 1982). However, it seems plausible to suggest that to a certain extent productivity will be positively associated with the age of a company. For example, the well established company can move along the learning curve for production processes which have been in use for a long time (Hill, 1985). Thus, if identical products or processes are matched one might expect the older producer to have a higher productivity. Apart from this gain the older company is more likely to introduce high value-added goods to the extent that improvement in product quality, design, complexity or technology is cumulative (i.e. it depends not only on today's research and development but the entire history of research in the company). At the same time there is also the danger that as a company gets older (and probably larger) it sinks into lethargy, becomes risk adverse and X-inefficiency[1] increases. Thus it seems reasonable to predict that beyond a certain age productivity increases less rapidly than it would otherwise have done so. Alfred Marshall (1919) argued that although like the trees in the forest some old firms grow to be very tall, they all eventually fall down and die (admittedly the greater development of public companies since 1900 may somewhat have lengthened the longevity of old firms). Whilst it is therefore unclear whether age is a good or a bad thing from the point of view of productivity we include the following results from our survey.

Table 16.1
Age of companies* by date of foundation

	NI	WG
Nineteenth Century	7	4
1900-1939	4	9
Post Second World War	13	4
Total observations	24	17

* Where the plant visited was part of a wider group we considered the year when that plant started operation.

NI has proportionately more of both the very young and the very old firms. Given the theoretical arguments which we have already outlined this may be a bad thing if it means that NI had more of those companies which are too young to have exhausted all the learning effects, and yet also more of those companies which are suffering the problems of old age if not senility. Such an hypothesis is extremely speculative and it is not clear to what extent German firms in general are more middle aged than those in NI.

Nationality of ownership

Previous statistical studies have shown that foreign owned firms in Britain and in NI generally out perform their indigenous counterparts in productivity terms (Pratten, 1976; Dunning, 1985; and Chapter 6). It is less clear what role non-German subsidiaries play in the aggregate performance of manufacturing in Germany but suffice to say that our sample included only two (one Danish and one American). By contrast five of the plants sampled in NI were under non-British control and represented over one-sixth of the total employment of our sample. Most of the 2200 employees in these foreign subsidiaries were in American owned plants. Since the US has historically been the exemplar of international best practice in terms of labour productivity (Chapter 1) it might be expected that inclusion of these American plants should impart a positive bias into the comparative performance of our sample in NI. Overall, the proportion of the NI sample under foreign control was broadly representative of manufacturing as a whole (though perhaps slightly higher in the sample). A further 5185 employees were represented by firms controlled from GB. Thus subsidiaries of GB firms were somewhat over-represented in our sample (two-fifths of total employment) as compared to the population as a whole (about 28 percent; NIERC Employment Database and the Census of Production (1986)). To the extent that indigenously owned NI companies have especially poor comparative productivity (Gudgin, Hart, Fagg, Keegan and D'Arcy, 1989) then our sampling has introduced a bias in NI's favour by under-representing these firms relative to externally controlled ones. Unfortunately our results would suggest that some foreign owned companies in NI fail to achieve the productivity levels of their counterpart plants in the country of origin of the company. One Continental European branch plant was unhappy about a productivity level in NI which was only two-thirds that at home. Nevertheless, they decided to stay in NI and take continual grant payments as a form of compensation for the comparatively poor performance of the subsidiary.

Employment of Gastarbeiter in Germany

Six of the German firms (i.e. 15 per cent) were largely dependent on Gastarbeiter for their shop floor employment. In 1972 immigrant workers represented 15 per cent of German employment in manufacturing (Paque, 1988) but this proportion has since declined to 10 per cent (Statistisches Bundesamt, 1988). Employment of immigrants varies by sector and when account is taken of the sectors from which the sample is drawn it can be shown that Gastarbeiter represent 10.8 per cent of total employment in the cross section of sample companies, and is therefore representative to the incidence of foreign workers engaged in German industry.

Conclusions

This Chapter has reviewed some of the characteristics of the firms (ownership type, method of financing, age, country of origin) to determine whether there was any structural bias in our sample either for or against NI. There were some particularly poor performers in the NI sample which were either family firms, or of nineteenth century origin but there were firms of a similar type

172

in Germany which were excellent performers. Compared to Germany there were more American companies in the NI sample (probably a bias in NI's favour).

Notes

1. The term X-inefficiency was coined by Leibenstein (1966) to describe economic inefficiency caused by reasons other than straight forward allocative inefficiency. For example, a firm could have efficient factor proportions (capital/labour) and yet still lie within its production possibility frontier because of general slackness of management and labour.

17 Growth, market failure and policy failure

"The hand of authority was seen in everything and in every place... and as it always happens in this kind of officious univeral interference, what began in odious power ended always, I may say without exception, in comptemptible imbecility".

Edmund Burke (1795) Thoughts and Details on Scarcity.

Prospects for future growth

Firms were asked to state what the main constraints on their growth would be. The results are summarised in the Table 17.1. It can be seen that demand was of roughly equal importance in the two areas whilst quality and design was twice as important a constraint in NI as in Germany. Poor quality may ultimately be more significant as a constraint than the 30 per cent citation would suggest because in some cases the NI firm was facing a declining demand precisely because it was operating in a down market or inferior quality market. For example, one NI engineering firm continued to make a product line which has suffered a world-wide fall in consumption by two-thirds since 1973 whereas its German counterpart had diversified. Similarly a NI producer in food concentrated on traditional brands and by contrast, its German competitor had built-up a relatively strong position because of the introduction of new products, packaging and greater concentration on up market brands. The question then arises as to why this position is allowed to continue, i.e. why does market competition not remove the relatively weak performers in NI and so raise the average performance of industry there? Or put another way, is there a lack of incentive to raise productivity and product performance in NI. After all as we have seen nearly three-quarters of NI managers interviewed recognised that productivity in Germany is higher in their own industry. We now consider the answer to this question in terms of the possibility of market failure.

Table 17.1
Main constraint on growth*
(% of firms)

	NI	WG
Demand	42	40
Lack of price competitiveness	2	0
Lack of quality/design competitiveness	30	15
Other**	27	45
Total number of firms responding	28	9

Notes: * Where a firm named two types of constraint these were each given a weight of one half relative to the total of all the named constraints.
** Other includes: marketing, premises, finance, labour supply, labour costs, transport and logistics.

Market failure

Market failure is the description of a position where the market signals (i.e. corporate profits) give management in NI insufficient incentive to make the changes necessary to achieve higher product quality and hence enhanced productivity. Despite their comparatively poor productivity (described above), their under-utilisation of capacity and machinery and unco-operative work forces only one-fifth of the plants visited in NI were unprofitable. Profit rates were provided in 16 cases and these averaged 8.4 per cent on sales (pre-tax). The best profit rates were in food (12 per cent), engineering (10.8 per cent) and miscellaneous (9.4 per cent) whilst the lowest rates were observed in textiles (6.9 per cent) and clothing (6.1 per cent). Given that most of the NI firms were already profitable it was privately rational for the management to continue to make relatively cheap, simple and inferior quality products using low wage shop-floor labour without much input of either design or research and development. There would be large social gains if the entire labour force was trained up to something more nearly approaching German standards but most of this gain would be taken out in the form of higher wages (not only in terms of take home pay but also through a better "social wage"[1]) rather than an increase in profitability. We have already noted that the greater importance of publicly quoted companies in NI (and indeed Britain as a whole)

175

relative to Germany makes NI more sensitive to profit signals and where profitability could be compared within the sample NI was generally as good as Germany. Hence the market fails to provide the signals for NI firms to improve their product design, technology, and quality and to increase training. By implication public policy is required to shift incentives in the right direction (a similar argument can be made for the UK as a whole (Crafts, 1988a)).

It might be argued that policy makers should make no such changes given that they will be risky and previous attempts to introduce complex products into NI (e.g. De Lorean, Lear Fan, man-made fibres) were sometimes expensive failures. Moreover, it might be claimed that NI has a comparative advantage in labour intensive, cheap and simple products and therefore NI should continue to concentrate on these lines. The weakness of this argument is its lack of dynamic consideration. NI may be profitable today making the present product lines but there is no guarantee the same will be true in ten years time given increased competition from low wage Newly Industrialised Countries (NICs). In other words, if NI does not achieve the ability to compete with Germany in its high quality, high technology and high price markets then the long run consequence of competition on price with NICs may be living standards closer to those of Latin America rather than those of Continental Europe. We have already noted that in certain cases matching of NI to Germany was difficult given that a particular product line was no longer made in Germany (e.g. certain types of engineering, clothing and textiles products) and this was indicative of NI being locked into a position of a low wage, low quality producer. To the extent that policy is concerned with long run employment and wealth creation incentives should be given to break out of this mould. Unfortunately, the conventional forms of industrial assistance may have exacerbated the market failure.

Policy failure: the subsidisation of inefficiency

We have already indicated that four-fifths of the NI firms had a reasonable level of profitability in spite of an undistinguished record in terms of comparative productivity. The fact that NI labour costs were under 50 per cent those of Germany provides part of the explanation for the paradoxical relationship between productivity and profitability. The other major explanation is the very large implicit subsidy to profits provided by grant aid to industry in NI. The following Table considers Selective Financial Assistance.

Table 17.2
Selective financial assistance (SFA) to sample companies in NI

	Total 1981-87 £ million (1987 prices)	Total 1981-87 £ per employee	SFA in one year as % of sales
Engineering	16.1 (21.4)	2651 (3561)	3.6
Textiles	22.1	11961	3.1
Food etc.	6.5 (21.0)	3024 (9738)	1.3
Clothing	20.0	3935	3.5
Miscellaneous	8.8 (9.5)	8018 (8666)	1.3
All manufacturing	73.5 (94.0)	4526 (5790)	2.6

Note: Values in parentheses include additionally estimates for standard capital grants were these could be made. Unfortunately the published data for these grants is less useful than that for SFA. This is because many companies lease their capital from separate financial firms. In such cases the purchases are recorded to the financial firm rather than the NI firm which uses the machine. As a result the values in parentheses do not represent the full amount received in terms of both standard capital grants and SFA together. They should be treated therefore as minimum estimates.

Sources: SFA data from British Business 10 October 1986, 3 February 1987, 8 May 1987, 7 August 1987, and 27 November 1987 and earlier editions.

SFA payments averaged about 3 per cent of turnover in a given year. Whilst this may not seem too much it should be stressed that value-added is itself only about 30 per cent of turnover. Hence selective assistance averages one-tenth of value-added. Moreover, whilst it was not possible to obtain complete information on the amount of capital grant received by the firms, standard capital grants averaged about three-fifths of total SFA for NI manufacturing during 1981-87 (Appropriation Accounts (NI)). Thus by implication SFA and capital grants combined might amount to about one-sixth of the value-added of our sample firms. For ten companies within our sample it was possible to match data on profits with that for SFA (both as a per cent of sales). Profits averaged 7.3 per cent whereas SFA averaged 5.2 per cent. That is, even without considering capital grants let alone subsidised buildings, training, marketing, and research and development, grant aid is "explaining" most of the profitability of the NI companies. Whilst it might be objected that a sample of ten companies is too small to be meaningful it should be noted that total state assistance to industry in NI is about one-fifth of manufacturing GDP (this remains so even when Harland and Wolff and Shorts are excluded; Appendix B).
This very high rate of state support to industrial profits[2]

makes the market failure worse. Without the grants some firms with very low productivity levels would be driven out of business, hence raising the average performance of manufacturing in NI. Other firms would adapt to the harsher environment by achieving gains in their performance. We have argued elsewhere that the comparatively lavish rates of state assistance in NI is at the very least a permissive cause of NI's comparatively low productivity within the UK (Appendix B). The divergence between rates of support in NI and GB is not justified by any measurable difference in transport costs. This was confirmed by those firms in our sample which stated their differential transport costs (less than 2 per cent of sales) and in no case did a NI company name transport as a major constraint on growth. In contrast two West Berlin manufacturers did regard peripherality relative to the Federal Republic as important. The German firms in Berlin did receive capital grants but the rate of assistance was only one-half/one-third that in NI and as a result the impact on profits was much smaller.

Conclusions

The most important conclusion to be drawn from this Chapter is the recognition of the paradox that NI firms can still be profitable in spite of low productivity. Unfortunately this does not mean that the present situation is desirable from a policy makers point of view given that in this position of market failure management in NI is being quite rational in its failure to make those changes (increased labour training, more research and development and higher product quality) which are necessary for long run growth. Past policy has made this position worse given that very high rates of grant aid have cushioned profits and so denied NI managers the incentive to change. This is an important conclusion and we would recommend further research in this area.

Notes

1. The common currency comparisons made by the Swedish Employers' Federation (Ray, 1987) and the Dresdner Bank (quoted in Economist, 1989, March 3) show German manufacturing labour costs to be double those of the UK (the superiority relative to those in NI would be even larger). Ray (1987) shows that most of the difference between German and British hourly labour costs is the result of higher social charges in Germany; better provision against unemployment and sickness. In might be noted en passant that it is ironic that labour would be the main beneficiary of higher productivity given that organised labour in Britain has traditionally seen higher productivity as a destroyer of jobs and a "bad thing". German labour seems to have recognised that this is not in fact the case and this is probably one explanation for the much better work attitudes there.

2. Admittedly grant aid could also be viewed as a subsidy to wages. Some may leak into wages which are higher relative to GB than NI's comparative productivity performance would justify (Appendix A). However, whether one views the grants as raising profits, or wages, or as lowering product prices in NI (there was one example in our sample where a foreign purchaser demanded that the NI plant cut its prices since it knew about the grants the plant was receiving) the practical result is the same. Constraints on management in NI are relaxed and they are enabled to make softer decisions.

18 The comparative productivity of a sample of matched manufacturing plants: conclusions to Part 3

"The industrially more developed country presents to the less developed country a picture of the latter's future".

Karl Marx (1867), <u>Capital, Volume I</u>

Whilst Caves (1968) described the historical record of the UK's manufacturing performance relative to Germany as, "this dark fable, bardic with years of telling", the evidence presented in Part 3 suggests that the NI chapter of this tale is peculiar in its gloom because NI has lower productivity than any other UK region (Chapter 4 and Appendix D). Before we draw out these points it is worth recounting what results were favourable from the point of view of Northern Ireland.

Positive aspects of Northern Ireland's performance

Almost one quarter of the NI firms (10 companies) reported physical productivity levels indistinguishable from their matched counterparts in Germany. The proportion of NI sales going to export markets was comparable with Germany, and the Republic of Ireland had developed as an important destination for sales (especially in engineering). Two NI companies had advantages in product quality through superior knowledge as compared to Germany in working a particular material (one further NI company had a product quality superior to its matched counterpart). In two sectors, clothing and textiles, the NI sample employment change was at least as good as that in Germany. NI firms in general were not handicapped by having machinery which was older than that used by their German counterparts and in a majority of matched comparisons the NI machinery had technology which was at least as modern. This edge in terms of advanced machinery was especially notable in clothing.

Managers in rural areas of NI said they were satisfied with their work forces' attitudes. In two cases in clothing the actual intensity of effort by operatives appeared to be even greater than that of their German counterparts. With the exception of clothing, average absenteeism and turnover rates for the sectors were similar to those in Germany.

Neither differential transport costs nor direct damage arising from the Troubles indicates that the NI location was inherently detrimental to performance. No NI firm mentioned energy costs as a problem. NI premises were on average no less modern or inappropriate than those in Germany. Four-fifths of the firms visited in NI were profitable and in some cases their rate of profit was higher than that of their German counterparts.

These points taken by themselves might indicate a situation with which policy makers could be broadly satisfied. However, there was also overwhelming evidence that NI's performance was far from satisfactory.

Negative aspects of Northern Ireland's performance

Seventy-six per cent of the firms matched with Germany recorded lower levels of physical productivity and all but two German firms had higher levels of value-added per employee. Of the ten matched comparisons where NI productivity was either better than that in Germany or indistinguishable from the German level none were in engineering. This suggests a division where NI has a comparative disadvantage in sectors which are of the high-skill and high-technology type and a comparative advantage in sectors where skills and research and development inputs are relatively unimportant: food processing, textiles and clothing (this would be consistent with the UK as a whole; Midland Bank Review, 1986). Even in those cases where NI's comparative performance was strong this was often due to some exceptional problems with the matched German counterpart; firms which were above average within the distribution of performance in NI had been matched with firms at the bottom end of the spectrum of performance in Germany. Thus in two of the ten cases NI's productivity equality or superiority was largely a consequence of being matched with a particularly poor German company. A further three cases of comparable productivity occurred in activities which were marginal to German manufacturing in the sense that the whole activity could barely be profitable at German wage rates. In two further cases NI's relatively good physical productivity performance was accounted for by a concentration on simpler, more standardised products (the Germans in these cases sacrificed physical output to gain higher quality). One German firm was undermined by its reliance on _Gastarbeiter_.

The superiority in German levels of physical output per head on average ranged from one of 33 per cent higher in clothing up to 148 per cent higher in engineering (i.e. the average German engineering employee produced between double and three times as many physical units as his NI counterpart).

In every sector average German value-added per head was double or more that of NI. Previous comparisons of German value-added with that of the UK as a whole suggest that German levels are between 50 and 100 per cent higher than those in Britain (Chapter 1; Smith, Hitchens and Davies, 1982; Ray, 1987). This would imply that NI's comparative performance is worse than that of the rest of the UK (not a surprising conclusion given that NI labour productivity has been shown in Part 2 to be 15-20 per cent lower than that in Great Britain).

That there was a productivity shortfall relative to Germany was recognised by roughly three-quarters of the NI managers interviewed. In addition to higher physical productivity the Germans also had an edge in terms of the quality of products (superior to NI in 58 per cent of cases). As a result of this most of the NI firms reported that they were operating in markets where price was the key determinant of competitiveness. The inferior products produced by NI was reflected by the destinations of their exports, almost one quarter of these went to the relatively "soft" Republic of Ireland market. By contrast the Germans sold most exports within the more demanding Continental European market. Employment in the NI sample collapsed during 1982-87 (falling by around one-fifth) whereas it was roughly stable in Germany (3 per cent decline, all manufacturing employment declined by 11 per cent in NI and 2 per cent in Germany according to the official statistics).

Whilst in most respects NI had an equality or superiority in its machine stock, this advantage remained unfulfilled. In the first instance some of the advanced technology in NI was simply inappropriate to the given production processes. Even where it was appropriate part of the NI machine stock was out of use. This partly reflected generally low capacity utilisation and partly problems with breakdowns. The Germans more frequently adapted machinery to their own requirements and they made a better use of known technology and they were prepared to co-operate with machine tool suppliers in so doing. Disruption of production by machine breakdowns were rare in Germany.

NI's difficulties in realising the full potential of its machine stock were compounded by the dirt, untidiness and disorder of the factories (these were problems conspicuous by their absence in Germany). Irrespective of any difference in the characteristics of the machine stock in the two countries, the level of capital productivity in NI was also comparatively low and this was related to certain qualitative weaknesses in the work force which we will now describe.

Poor labour productivity in NI in part derived from overmanning. When machine processes were closely matched it was found that the NI firms required 1.8 men for every one engaged in Germany. Furthermore, there was strong evidence that most NI companies were overmanned in terms of the number of indirect employees (cases of overmanning in Britain were noted by Pratten (1976) and Prais (1981a).

At every level of the hierarchy (managers, technicians, supervisors, maintenance, craftsmen and semi-skilled) NI was outclassed in terms of the quality, quantity, width and intensity of skills, training and practical experience. German employees were four times more likely to have higher technical or university qualifications. This was reflected in the fact that most German managers had vocational degrees (this was not the case in NI). The intensity of R and D effort (measured by R and D employees as a percentage of employment in engineering and clothing) was three times greater in Germany. Twenty-eight per cent of plants in NI undertook no R and D at all whereas all the German companies did. The NI firms reported neither the inclination nor the ability to co-operate with either their suppliers or their customers to adapt and customise their machinery or their final products.

On the shop-floor all the German _Meister_ had extensive formal training whereas the NI supervisors were merely time served or without any qualification. The operatives they led were mostly semi-skilled or unskilled while the representation of formal skills was much higher in Germany.

Our results testify to serious consequences of the lack of skills in NI. For example, in some cases NI was making products which Germany had abandoned ten years ago, while in spite of their relative simplicity, the NI product reject rates were sometimes very high (over 10 per cent in some clothing firms).

Unlike their German counterparts, the NI operatives usually did not understand their machines and as a result could not set machines or undertake simple repairs when breakdowns occurred. Relative to their German counterparts the NI maintenance departments were grossly overmanned yet in spite of this the NI firms were still more likely to have to call in engineers from Great Britain or Germany or Japan.

Absenteeism and labour turnover were problematic in NI clothing but the record was better in the other sectors. Thirty-one per cent of the NI firms complained about labour force attitudes to work. This rate of complaint was much higher than that recorded for other regions in the British Isles in previous matched plant comparisons (Hitchens and O'Farrell, 1987; Hitchens and O'Farrell, 1988a, 1988b). The only German plants to complain were those employing mainly _Gastarbeiter_. In this report the labour force in NI had more in common with the unskilled workers in Germany though even the _Gastarbeiter_ plants were able to achieve higher productivity than NI counterparts.

About one in five of the NI plants visited were unprofitable. Some of these companies were chronic lame ducks and were in continuous receipt of assistance from the development agencies. As for the companies which were in profit, the evidence would suggest that at least half of their profits would disappear if grants were removed. Thus public policy would appear to have reinforced market failure, i.e. the firms in NI lacked the incentive to train more, to invest more in R and D, and to aim for

183

higher quality products, because they were already profitable enough (Chapter 21 considers the policy recommendations which follow from these results).

The worst case of the "British Disease"?

In Chapter 8 we noted that it is worth asking to what extent the reasons for low productivity in NI are the same as those which explain the general shortfall of the UK relative to Germany. Comparisons of capital stock suggest that machines in the UK are not any older but are less likely to be advanced, e.g. computerised (Rostas, 1948; Bacon, 1974; Daly, Hitchens and Wagner, 1985; Steedman and Wagner, 1987). By contrast many in the sample of NI firms had levels of technology which were equal to those in Germany. At the same time the NI firms did evidence the general UK problem of poor feeding devices, and other ancillary machinery including a lack of development of known technology and inattention to maintenance and frequent breakdowns (CPRS, 1975; Pratten, 1976; Prais, 1981a; Daly, Hitchens and Wagner, 1985).

The shortfall in NI skills at every level is paralleled in the UK but there is the implication that NI's position is even worse than the rest of the UK. For example, whereas Prais (1981b) suggests that the percentage of manufacturing employees with degrees (or equivalent) was only slightly lower in Britain than Germany, we found that the Germans had four times as many (per employee) as NI. At the same time, the under-qualification of maintenance men and foremen in NI is part of a general British problem (Prais 1981b; Prais and Wagner, 1988). Unfortunately, the problems facing supervisors in NI may be more taxing than in other UK regions because the percentage of the labour force with no formal qualifications is higher and the extent of adverse work attitudes is greater.

UK manufacturing as a whole has a relatively low rate of R and D effort but NI is the worst region within UK in terms of both the input of resources to R and D and the resultant output of innovation (New Scientist, 1987; Harris, 1988).

Most commentators on Anglo-German comparative productivity have agreed that social, cultural and institutional factors have played a major role in enabling German productivity levels to catch up with Britain and then overtake (Pratten, 1976; Caves and Krause, 1980; Wiener, 1981). Some of these explanations rely on different patterns of industrialisation in the nineteenth century (e.g. Britain's reliance on markets in the Empire, the political dominance of the English aristocracy, a division between manufacturers and the City of London, the development of industrial banking in Germany; Glyn and Harrison, 1980; Prais, 1981a; Wiener, 1981; Barnett, 1987). Others are of more recent origin (the development of a social consensus in Germany after the Second World War in contrast to the "institutional schlerosis" which afflicted employers, trade unions and the civil service in Britain (Olson, 1985).

Most of these ideas are at a fairly high level of generalisation and they are not amenable to empirical testing. Moreover, it is not clear how far ideas developed with English culture and institutions in mind are appropriate to Northern Ireland. Nevertheless, two peculiarities of the NI experience are worth highlighting: the limited nature of nineteenth century Irish industrialisation and the impact of the troubles. The industrialisation of the north east of Ulster in the nineteenth century was in contrast to the much slower progress in the rest of Ireland (Daly, 1981; Kennedy, Giblin and McHugh, 1988). This achievement in Ulster perhaps created the perception that the quality of local labour and management was uniquely high and this attitude may have persisted in the form of complacency as to NI's ability to compete on world markets. This view should be modified because whilst late Victorian and Edwardian Ulster had its undoubted industrial triumphs, little recognition was then given to NI's structural weaknesses and the fact that some industries had only developed because of immigrant entrepreneurs (Lee, 1973).

The possibility that NI has rested on its laurels is made more probable to the extent that one of the results of the troubles has been to make NI more inward looking. For example the percentage of the population which has been born outside of the Province is lower than that for the Republic or Great Britain. It is therefore highly probable that NI has fewer of those people (e.g. Americans or Germans) who have had experience of living or working in a high productivity economy (see Chapters 1, 7 and 15), and the proportion of English, Scots and Welsh is also relatively low. Furthermore migrants into the Province may be of relatively low calibre. The perceptions created by the Troubles mean there is less competition for equivalent positions to Great Britain although the same salary is offered. The other respect in which the troubles have contributed to NI's poor performance in manufacturing is through the damage done to attitudes relating to respect for authority. Matched plant comparisons within the UK and the island of Ireland (Hitchens and O'Farrell, 1987, 1988a, 1988b; O'Farrell and Hitchens, 1988a) suggest that NI is unique in the extent to which poor work attitudes are reported. The location of the factories which claim to have the worst problems is strongly suggestive that industrial militancy is related to political instability and violence.

One might summarise this consideration of the causes of comparatively low productivity in NI by saying that in some respects NI is the worst case of the "British Disease". For example, the incidence of machine breakdowns and the lack of training at all levels. However, there is also evidence that in some ways NI is unique. Labour force attitudes are peculiarly poor and a link with the troubles is suggested.

Given all this, perhaps the most important question to arise is whether these results are representative of NI manufacturing as a whole? Could it be that this dismal tale is simply the result of the selection of an unrepresentative sample of NI companies? In fact this is extremely unlikely. Our results for NI's comparative productivity are generally not out of line with those implied by the official statistics. The sample of NI companies selected in fact over-represents foreign and GB owned plants. These plants might be expected to achieve higher productivity than the locally-owned firms in NI (Pratten, 1976; and Chapter 6) and to this extent the sample is biased in NI's favour. Previous studies have suggested that the small, indigenously owned firms in NI are outperformed by their counterparts in Wales, Scotland, South East England and the Republic of Ireland (Hitchens and O'Farrell, 1987, 1988a, 1988b; O'Farrell and Hitchens, 1988a) for reasons such as inadequate recognition of external quality standards, under-utilised and inappropriate capital equipment and poor labour force training. One of our most important findings is that the same problems emerge amongst the larger firms and also in those owned by GB or foreign firms when compared with Germany. The fact that some of these larger firms do manage to sell on international markets does not guarantee them a clean bill of health for the evidence suggests that the NI exports in this sample are concentrated on easier markets.

PART 4

THE COMPARATIVE PRODUCTIVITY OF NORTHERN IRELAND AND THE REPUBLIC OF IRELAND

"Ireland is a country in which the probable never happens and the impossible always does".

J.P. Mahaffy (1839-1919)

19 Levels of output per head in the Republic of Ireland compared to Northern Ireland

"The Irish from different parts of that kingdom are very different. One might think on so small an island an Irishman must be an Irishman: yet it is not so: they are different in their aptitude to, and in their love of labour".

St. John De Crevecoeur (1792) <u>Letters from an American Farmer</u>

Introduction

A number of similarities between Northern Ireland and the Republic of Ireland make it interesting to set the comparative productivity performance of Republic of Ireland (ROI) alongside that of Northern Ireland.

In both parts of Ireland relatively high transport costs (Business and Finance, 1989, April 6) and energy tariffs have been stressed as likely explanations of relative productivity and competitiveness performance. Fisher (1987) shows that electricity prices in 1986 were between 11 and 40 per cent higher than the UK average. However, the position as compared to West Germany was mixed (between 89 and 122 per cent of German levels). In the discussions relating to the Delors Report on European Monetary Union the Governor of the Central Bank of Ireland indicated his fear that the completion of the EC Internal Market could substantially de-industrialise ROI unless the reliability and cost of its transport links to the core of the European market were improved (quoted in Financial Times, 1988, December 12). However, the importance of transport costs has been disputed both as an explanation of the lack of industrialisation in the nineteenth century and the present difficulties of manufacturing in both NI and ROI (Daly, 1981; Hitchens and O'Farrell, 1987).

Whilst the tangible impact of peripherality has been disputed there would be more agreement that Ireland is remote from the centres of idea-, taste- and design-formation within Western Europe. Such peripherality would handicap NI and ROI manufacturing in their attempt to produce high quality products. While persistent out-migration from both NI and the ROI has been perceived as part of the cumulative process of relative economic decline (Kennedy, 1973) some attention has also been focused on the extent to which reverse migratory flows (either of Irish people living overseas returning to Ireland, or of GB persons or other "outsiders" coming to work, live or study in Ireland) could counteract this peripherality in terms of ideas (Commission on Emigration, 1954; Osborne, Cormack, and Miller, 1987).

Apart from sharing similar perceived problems both NI and the ROI have pursued active industrial development strategies. Indeed the rates of assistance to manufacturing industry have probably been higher than those of any other peripheral region within the British Isles (see Appendix B). When subsidies as a percentage of value-added are considered, out of ten EEC members only Italy and Greece gave larger subsidies to manufacturing than ROI during 1981-86 (data for Spain and Portugal was not available to the EC Survey of State Aid 1989 (Financial Times, 1989, November 20)).

Policy makers in NI and the ROI turned to the promotion of inward investment in the late 1950s as the best way to achieve employment growth in manufacturing. While this policy was not without its success the world recession from 1974 onwards conincided with increasing disillusionment with use of inward investment as the primary instrument of economic development (Telesis, 1982; Teague, 1987). Doubts were raised as to the extent to which the benefits from inward investment equalled the social opportunity cost of the incentives used to attract such external capital (the low rates of corporate profit tax in the ROI and the generous capital grants and discretionary assistance in NI). Apart from unease about the cost of subsidising inward investment the viability of the strategy has been undermined by a decrease in the supply of internationally mobile capital (largely as a result of the declining competitiveness of the USA and hence of its international firms) and increasing competition for that inward investment. Ironically the ROI's agencies (principally the IDA) now have to compete with agencies in NI, Scotland, Wales, Spain, Belgium and elsewhere which were themselves set up to imitate the perceived success of the ROI.

While such similarities between NI and ROI are one reason why consideration of their comparative productivities are interesting, the differences between the two areas provide another reason for comparing their productivity record. A later section will outline these but first productivity levels in NI and ROI are compared.

190

Comparisons of the productivity performances of NI and ROI

Table 19.1 compares NI and GB manufacturing productivity growth with that of the ROI.

Table 19.1
Manufacturing productivity growth
(% compound growth rates)

	NI	ROI	GB
1951-73	4.5	3.6*	2.9
1973-79	1.0	4.4	0.6
1980-86	4.1	9.3	5.4

* Includes mining and quarrying.

In spite of the small differences in the systems of industrial classification, it is probably correct to argue that in the 1950s and 1960s NI had more rapid growth than the ROI which in turn was superior to GB. What is strikingly different is the paths taken by the two economies between the two OPEC "oil shocks"; NI productivity growth decelerates dramatically whereas that of the ROI accelerates. Even in the present British "productivity miracle" rates of growth seriously lag those of the ROI (though it is possible that the ROI growth is being distorted by the transfer pricing by the foreign owned companies within the Republic, the extent of any such distortions is considered below). Given that the ROI productivity growth has exceeded that of NI (and hence GB) the implication is that the ROI levels of productivity have converged towards those in GB and NI.

Historical comparisons of NI and ROI productivity

Table 19.2 illustrates the historical development of comparative productivity levels in NI and ROI during the entire period for which Census data are available (i.e. since the 1920s).

The most significant conclusion to be drawn from Table 19.2 is that all manufacturing in ROI has sustained a very strong improvement in its comparative productivity performance since 1973. During 1963, 1968 and 1973 ROI and NI net outputs per head in all manufacturing were broadly similar. However, by 1984 ROI had moved so far ahead that average NI productivity levels were barely three-fifths those in the Republic. The very high ROI comparative productivities recorded for the years prior to the Second World War may be misleading. The total size of the manufacturing sector was much smaller than that of the 1980s and a higher weight was given to the high productivity beer and tobacco industries which represented about one-quarter of manufacturing net output but only 7 per cent of employment. Remove the brewing, malting and tobacco industries from the Republic's aggregate output and employment figures in 1926, 1931 and 1936 and about half of the productivity advantage of ROI relative to NI disappears. The Irish protectionism of the 1930s "Economic War"

191

could explain some of the remaining difference in nominal net output's per head. Irish tariffs were higher than those in the UK (79-84 per cent compared to 51 per cent on a weighted comparison for 1937 (Haughton, 1987)) and if the Irish rate of effective protection was also higher this would have made it possible for Irish firms to inflate the selling price of goods sold to the home market.

Table 19.2
ROI's net output per head relative to NI (market exchange rates)
Selected industries
(NI=100)

	1926	1931	1936	1963	1968	1973	1980	1984
All manufacturing	149	166	166	101	102	108	131	159
Food, dr.& tobacco	122	192	..	79	73	80	108	114
Chemicals	130	98	..	50	59	76	318	265
All engineering	102	109	107	93	113	129	151	193
Textiles	95	109	122	110	122	120	104	117
Clothing & foot.	102	128	135	114	120	135	101	101

.. Not available.

Notes on sources: This comparison of Census of Production data faced three major technical problems; the early Censuses in NI and the ROI were not synchronised, there are some definitional differences for which adjustments cannot be made, and, thirdly, the ROI Census includes all firms employing more than three persons whereas the NI Census is based on only those establishments employing more than nineteen persons. These problems and the necessary data adjustments are described in Appendix E.3.

The reasons for ROI's catch up with NI during the post-War period and subsequent overtaking can be summarised as two-fold; shifts in the structure of industries towards those which are generally of a higher productivity type and, secondly, comparatively rapid productivity growth within individual industries. By the early 1980s ROI had acquired an industrial structure which had a very favourable impact on comparative productivity levels relative to NI (and indeed GB, as is shown below). The growth of individual industries which contributed most to ROI's improvement in aggregate comparative productivity were those of chemicals, electrical and electronic engineering and office equipment and data processing machinery. Thus, whereas prior to the late 1960s ROI chemicals had productivity levels only half those in NI, by 1984 ROI output per head was around three times that in NI. In electrical and electronic engineering (not shown separately in the Table) ROI comparative productivity increased from about 90 per cent of the NI level to between two and three times the level there. By the 1980s ROI had also achieved a substantial superiority in instrument engineering and other transport (not shown separately in the Table). (Whilst the latter is not a comparison of like with like, since Shorts and Harland and Wolff are compared to a diverse range of firms in the Republic, there are now a substantial number of aerospace component manufacturers in the Republic which should provide a reasonable match for part of the NI industry.) Long run ROI performance in the more traditional "metal-bashing" mechanical engineering and metal goods not elsewhere specified was more variable. In textiles, clothing, mineral products, timber etc. and paper etc. ROI's comparative performance was relatively stable. It is notable that ROI was achieving higher productivity than NI in the textiles and clothing, i.e. ROI success was not restricted to the higher technology industries (albeit during the late 1970s NI was catching up on ROI in clothing).

Historical comparison of ROI and UK productivity

Table 19.3 illustrates the historical development of comparative productivity levels in the United Kingdom as a whole and the ROI since the 1920s.

Table 19.3
ROI's net output per head relative to the UK
(market exchange rates)
Selected industries
(UK=100)

	1926	1931	1936	1963	1968	1973	1980	1984
All manufacturing	103	108	109	79	87	99	104	127
Food, dr.& tobacco	108	114	116	74	80	94	92	106
Chemicals	66	74	63	70	100	106	169	213
Mechanical eng.	84	90	82	67	97	94	83	96
Electrical,								
& electronic eng.	84	90	82	77	94	99	133	211
Textiles	70	79	84	85	95	102	102	105
Clothing & footwear	74	81	88	81	85	103	81	85

Notes on sources: Censuses of Industrial Production for the UK and the ROI. See also notes to Table 19.2 (and Appendix E.3).

In summarising the ROI's performance relative to the UK as a whole one could repeat most of what has been said about trends in ROI/NI comparative performance. As regards all manufacturing, the ROI had a small lead relative to the UK prior to the Second World War but when brewing, malting and tobacco are excluded from RoI then its comparative performance falls to 80-90 per cent of the UK level (and this still includes any boost given to value-added by the relatively high tariffs). The later figure is similar to ROI's comparative productivities in the 1960s. ROI overtook the UK after 1973 and by 1984 had established a productivity lead of around one-quarter.
    The individual industries most responsible for this improvement were once again Chemicals and electricals etc. In most other industries Irish productivity levels were stuck below those of

Britain though there was a slow improvement in ROI's comparative performance in textiles.

Detailed comparison of productivity levels in the 1980s

Table 19.4 shows ROI comparative productivity after having adjusted the ROI data by removal of the firms employing less than twenty persons so as to provide a fair comparison with the size range used by the UK Censuses (this harmonisation of the statistical sources is not possible for years before 1980 and is the source of small discrepancies between Tables 19.2 and 19.3, and Table 19.4 subsequent Tables).

ROI has consistently lower productivity levels than both NI and UK in mineral extraction, man-made fibres, motor vehicles, and timber and furniture. However ROI has consistently higher productivity levels in chemicals, office machinery etc., instrument engineering, food and textiles.

Whilst in principle comparisons of Northern Ireland with the Republic of Ireland should be based on Northern Ireland factory gate prices relative to those in the Republic, in practise the lack of intra-UK data means that any price comparison has to be one of ROI to the average of the whole of the UK. Adjustment for product price differences could follow one of three methodologies; exchange rates, purchasing power parities and physical quantities. Table 19.4 compared ROI, NI and UK values using the average annual market value of the pound sterling-IR pound exchange rate. The theoretical justification for this method includes the so called law of one price, i.e. in the long run internationally tradeable goods tend towards parity in their common currency price. Unfortunately, market exchange rates spend long periods away from their Purchasing Power Parity level. Moreover, the law of one price is at best only applicable to tradeable goods and their is evidence that the traditional and indigenous sectors within NI and ROI are heavily dependent on the local market and that in both cases their prices are higher than in GB (Hitchens and O'Farrell, 1987, 1988a, 1988b; O'Farrell and Hitchens, 1988a).

Comparisons based on exchange rate therefore have to be regarded as a simplification, albeit a simplification which is sometimes necessary. Exchange rate based comparisons are likely to most reliable in the traded goods sectors (e.g. some parts of food, drink and tobacco, engineering and chemicals) and less so in those sectors producing mainly for the Irish market (some parts of food, timber and furniture, building products, paper etc.).

Table 19.4
ROI's comparative productivity level 1980, 1984, and 1985
(net output per employee engaged, exchange rates)

	ROI/NI (NI=100)			ROI/UK (UK=100)		
	1980	1984	1985	1980	1984	1985
Metal manufacturing	104	107	87	86	78	83
Mineral extraction	56	73	77	52	50	93
Mineral products	86	109	116	96	104	111
Chemicals [a]	327	280	237	175	224	220
Man-made fibres [b]	74	78	65	89	91	75
Metal goods nes.[c]	117	107	110	103	97	100
Mechanical eng.[c]	97	106	99	84	100	100
Office mach. etc.	378	367	461	149	229	242
Electrical etc.	148	174	178	98	147	134
Motor vehicles	95	85	64	64	72	55
Other transport	152	125	214	84	89	94
Instrument engin.	128	222	228	125	189	185
Food	107	141	]	101	118	129
Drink & tobacco	130	108	]135	80	93	104
Textiles	104	119	121	102	107	102
Leather	112	90	123	106	79	109
Foot. & clothing	101	100	101	81	85	87
Timber & furniture	99	82	93	80	71	78
Paper, printing, etc.	102	109	107	83	84	84
Rubber and plastics	74	123	112	86	109	104
Other manufacturing	145	110	120	125	98	106
All manufacturing	136	171	184	108	137	141

Notes: Using exchange rates of IR £0.885 (1980), 0.814 (1984),
and 0.824 (1985) to one pound sterling.
[a]: ROI/UK based on the NACE European industrial classification
industries numbers 251-8. The ROI/NI result is derived from the
ROI/UK for NACE 251-8 linked to an NI/UK comparison for NACE 25
(NACE 259 is not disclosed separately for NI).
[b]: ROI/UK based on NACE 259-260. The ROI/NI result is derived
from the ROI/UK for 259-260 linked to an NI/UK comparison for NACE
260 (NACE 259 is not disclosed separately for NI).
[c]: The ROI data was adjusted so as to conform to the British
1980 SIC (NACE 315/SIC 3205 Boilers etc. was moved from ROI Group
31 to Group 32). This facilitated comparison with the Groups in
NI.

Sources: Censuses of Industrial Production for the UK and ROI.

The inadequacies of market exchange rates as indicators of
relative prices have caused the collection of extensive data sets
comparing prices for hundreds of matched products in different
countries. The two main sets of PPPs are those associated with the
Craves et al and the United Nations (International Comparisons
Project, 1973, 1977, 1982) and those with SOEC (1983, 1988).
Unfortunately, since this data has been collected for the purpose

of making comparisons of national income per head rather than
levels of product prices, the prices compared are those for final
expenditure. Thus the published PPP for a given good in the UK
and ROI will include the effects of differential indirect taxes
between the two countries. The ideal would be the PPP-standard
for factory gate prices in the two countries (the SOEC data used
to compare prices in 1985 excluded indirect taxes). The published
PPP further fall short of this ideal because they include the
effects of differential retail margins and because they give
weight to products consumed within the country (the pattern of
national consumption of a category of good may differ from that of
national production of that same product category to the extent
that imports are important). Nevertheless, a number of
international productivity level comparisons (Roy, 1982; Ray,
1987; Roy, 1987) have used final expenditure PPPs whilst
recognising the approximate nature of the resultant calculations
(see Chapter 1).
Apart from the possible lack of consistency with factory gate
prices there is the additional problem of obtaining a reasonable
match between the PPPs for given products and the net output per
data for given sectors. In the first instance one must attempt to
allocate individual product PPPs to the appropriate industry
within the SIC or NACE classification (e.g. the PPP for bread,
cakes and biscuits to the bread and flour Industry). Then, in
cases where more than one PPP applies to a given industry these
should be weighted together so as to create a single PPP for the
industry. Ideally the weighed industrial PPP would give each
product PPP a weight equivalent to the share of that product in
the total net output of the industry. Since, the level of detail
as to the output of individual products is limited in both the UK
and ROI the weighting procedure is sometimes imprecise (weighting
by UK and ROI weights will mean that for any given industry there
are two PPPs: one appropriate to the UK production weights and one
appropriate to the ROI production weights). The more broadly
defined an industry is (i.e. the higher the degree of aggregation)
the greater the number of individual product PPPs that will fall
within its boundaries and hence the increased probability that the
average level of product prices is accurately represented. Thus
the individual industry comparative productivities using PPPs
shown in Table 19.5 should be regarded as having a greater margin
of error than the PPP based estimate for manufacturing as a whole.

An alternative methodology based on physical quantities of
output might appear to be superior to either the use of exchange
rates or PPPs as a means to overcoming product price differences
between ROI, NI and UK. This matches homogeneous physical products
in the two countries and then aggregates these by the factory
gate prices applying in both (for example, in a UK/USA comparison
tonnes of cement and tonnes of steel would be added together first
according to their prices in pounds sterling, and then in dollars:
Smith, Hitchens and Davies, 1982). The constraint on this method
is limited by the extent of published data on physical output.
Moreover, across a wide range of industries products are not

homogeneous and international variations in quality substantial. Thus, it has not so far been possible to apply this method to the comparison of the Republic's productivity.

Table 19.5
ROI's comparative productivity using PPPs, 1985
(net output per employee engaged)

	ROI/UK (UK=100) Exchange rate	ROI/UK (UK=100) PPP
Metal manufacture	83	91
Mineral extraction	93	..
Mineral products	111	..
Chemicals [a]	220	169
Man-made fibres [b]	75	..
Metal Goods nes.[c]	100	93
Mechanical engineering [c]	100	77
Office mach. data processing	242	243
Electric, electronic engin.	134	130
Motor vehicles	55	53
Other transport	94	92
Instrument engineering	185	178
Food	129	116
Drink & tobacco	104	80
Textiles	102	114
Leather	96	..
Footwear & clothing	87	81
Timber & furniture	78	70
Paper, printing, publishing	84	70
Rubber and plastic	104	121
Other manufacturing	106	110
All manufacturing	141	130

Notes: .. SOEC data inadequate to construct a PPP for this sector. Where the value of the PPP differed according to whether ROI or UK output weights were employed a mean was used.
[a] ROI/UK based on NACE 251-8. The ROI/NI result is derived from the ROI/UK for NACE 251-8 linked to an NI/UK comparison for NACE 25 (NACE 259 is not available for NI).
[b] ROI/UK based on NACE 259-260. The ROI/NI result is derived from the ROI/UK for 259-260 linked to an NI/UK comparison for NACE 260 (NACE 259 is not available for NI).
[c] The ROI data was adjusted so as to conform to the British 1980 SIC (NACE 315/SIC 3205 Boilers etc. was moved from ROI Group 31 to Group 32). This facilitated comparison with the Groups in NI.

Sources: SOEC (1988) and as in Table 19.4.

The performance of ROI owned and foreign owned firms in the Republic

The comparatively high level of productivity in RoI is largely due to the externally owned sector. This is shown in Table 19.6 where foreign owned firms in the Republic are compared with multinationally controlled ones in the UK and ROI domestically owned firms are compared to their British counterparts. In almost every case the foreign owned firms in ROI out-perform their counterparts in the UK. However, with the exception of food industry indigenously owned firms achieve productivity levels only around three-quarters of the UK level.

The multinational enterprises in ROI are pulling up the aggregate productivity level. They do this by obtaining productivity levels which are on average more than double those of the indigenously controlled plants in ROI.

Table 19.7 shows that the UK and German controlled plants sited in Ireland have relatively small productivity superiorities over the indigeous plants. However, the USA owned plants (which represent about half of all the employment in foreign plants) have a massive productivity advantage; their average level of output per head is more than three-and-half times that of the ROI owned plants. This result is interesting because it indicates that transfer pricing may be most prevalent in American subsidiaries (this subject is considered in more detail below). A further interesting result en passant is that the ROI's own multinationals in UK production locations. These do comparatively badly and fail to achieve the productivity level of the British owned plants in the UK.

(please see the following page for Table 19.6)

Table 19.7
Productivity of foreign owned plants in the ROI
as a percentage of
domestically owned plants, 1984

(Net output per employee engaged, domestic=100)

UK owned	143	(100)
German owned	122	(159)
Other EC owned	134	(121)
USA owned	359	(154)
All foreign owned	249	(146)
ROI owned	100	(95)

Note: Values in parentheses show the comparative productivity for the equivalent nationality of plant in the UK relative to average for domestically owned plants in UK manufacturing.

Sources: Censuses of Industrial Production for the UK and ROI.

198

Table 19.6
ROI's comparative productivity by nationality of firm
Net output per employee engaged (UK=100)
(ROI productivity as a % of the level
attained in the comparable ownership type in the UK)

	All	non-ROI	ROI	Non-ROI owned as % total employment
Metals	80	109	69	18
Extraction of non-metallic ores	50	..	..	..
Manufacture of non-metallic mineral products	104	149	78	22
Chemicals and man-made fibres	210	227	93	68
Metal goods nes.	93	88	78	25
Mechanical eng.	104	93	82	53
Office machinery, and data process.	229	205	89	97
Electric. eng.	147	132	81	81
Motor vehicles	72	100	62	22
Other transport equipment	89	92	82	14
Instrument eng.	189	169	72	96
Food	118	135[a]	102[a]	16
Drink, tobacco	93	120[a]	64[a]	46
Textiles	107	96	90	44
Leather	79	54[b]	76[b]	41[b]
Footwear and clothing	85	55[c]	85[c]	34[c]
Timber & furniture	71	63	64	7
Paper, printing, and publishing	84	77	82	11
Rubber and plastics	109	97	103	62
Other manufacturing	98	84	117	61
All manufacturing	137	145	86	39

Note: .. Data disaggregated by ownership type not available.
[a] Both ownership types in ROI compared to the UK aggregate for all Food, drink and tobacco (no disaggregation by country of ownership available for UK).
[b] ROI data combines of Leather and footwear.
[c] ROI data excludes Footwear .

Sources: Censuses of Industrial Production for the UK and ROI.

Estimation of the extent of   intra-company " Transfer Pricing"

None of these considerations of the impact of the externally
controlled sector on the Republic's comparative productivity allow
one to judge to what extent the general ROI productivity
superiority relative to Britain is a "real" phenomenon as opposed
to a financial one, i.e. caused by the manipulation by foreign
controlled companies of their profits within Ireland in order to
extract the maximum benefit from the Republic's relatively liberal
regime of corporate taxation. In this section we adopt two
methodologies which afford rough indications of the maximum extent
of intra-company "transfer pricing" by the foreign owned
subsidiaries in ROI. While these methods are relatively crude it
is significant that both indicate that even on the most generous
assumptions transfer pricing can only explain a small minority of
the ROI's productivity advantage.

(1.) Using net output/gross output ratios The first method focuses
on comparison of the ratio of net output to gross output in the
ROI and UK. Since transfer pricing involves the inflation of
value-added of the international firms either by increasing the
selling price of outputs of the ROI subsidiary or by decreasing
the buying price of inputs it will, ceteris paribus, be indicated
by the net output/gross output ratio being higher than it would
otherwise have been. However, when net output/gross output ratios
in the ROI are compared to those in UK there is apparently little
evidence of transfer pricing. In both 1980 and 1985 the ratios for
all manufacturing were lower in ROI which was the opposite of the
expected result if transfer pricing was occurring (37 per cent
compared to 41.8 per cent in the UK in 1980 and 38.8 per cent
compared to 41.6 per cent in the UK in 1985). In 1980 most
individual finely disaggregated industries in ROI (34 out of 66)
also had lower net output/gross output ratios than their UK
counterparts. Whilst in 1985 a majority of ROI industries had
higher net output/gross output ratios than their counterparts this
advantage was still slight (in 36 industries out of 70). In any
case, a range of other factors also influence the net output/gross
output with the result that its value as an indicator of transfer
pricing may be limited.
    The data used is still insufficiently disaggregated to ensure
that the industries being compared are sufficiently similar in
structure to ensure net output/gross output ratios do not differ
for reasons other than transfer pricing (e.g. differences in the
types of products and activities represented). To the extent that
the ROI manufacturing tends to concentrate on simple fabrication
as opposed to the product development of high value-added goods
then it might be anticipated that on an industry by industry basis
the ROI will show a systematic tendency to have a lower net
output/gross output ratio than the UK. The ratio's usefulness
further diminished by distortions arising from differences between
the extent of vertical integration in the ROI and the UK. For
example, a highly integrated motor vehicle manufacturer might

smelt its own steel, make its own components and then produce some of the furnishing and electricals for the cars. This firm would thus extract value-added at each of these stages of production whereas if it had bought in the steel, the components, the seats and the lamps then the value-added would have been attributed to the firms supplying these inputs. Hence the distribution of value-added across industries would have been very different. Whilst it is not clear to what extent vertical integration in the Republic differs from that in the UK it is at least plausible to suggest that the much larger absolute size of industry in the UK (allied to the existence of a number of large engineering firms) makes it likely that it will be more important in the UK. This is a further reason why use of the net output/gross output ratio as an indicator transfer pricing fails the <u>ceteris paribus</u> condition.

Despite these qualifications on the use of the ratio it may still be notable that the ROI has a very much higher net output/gross output ratio in three industries where production is dominated by foreign owned branch-plants: chemicals for industrial and agricultural use, pharmaceuticals, and miscellaneous foods. As an experiment the net output of these industries was recalculated to show how much lower it would have been in 1985 if the net output/gross output ratio had been that ruling in the counterpart industry in the UK rather than that actually applying to the ROI industry. IR£265 million of net output would be "lost" under these conditions. Since ROI all manufacturing net output in 1985 was about IR£5,200 million the implication of this measure is that 5 per cent of this was contributed by transfer pricing. In other words instead of having a level of net output per head of 141 per cent that of the UK, the ROI productivity level without transfer pricing would sink to 134 per cent. This implies that whilst transfer pricing is a not insignificant factor when explaining ROI's productivity superiority most of the gap is caused by other factors.

One problem which arises is that of the relationship between this finding that transfer pricing inflates ROI net output by 5 per cent and our earlier calculation that ROI manufacturing product prices were on average 9 percent greater than those in the UK (in common currency terms). More specifically, does this imply ROI's "real" level of productivity is inflated by 14 per cent through financial factors (i.e. 9 plus 5) or is the 5 per cent arising from transfer pricing entirely included within the 9 per cent effect arising from the higher prices of ROI goods? In practise the effect of transfer pricing arising from higher product selling prices should be captured by the calculation based on PPPs. However, the PPPs will fail to allow for the extent to which transfer pricing results from the prices of inputs being lower than what they would otherwise have been. Thus a straight forward addition of the effects of higher ROI prices to those of transfer pricing is likely to exaggerate the "financial" contribution to higher productivity to the extent that there is double counting. At the same time, merely to use the PPPs would be to underestimate that financial contribution. Given all this, on the basis of these calculations, the actual superiority of ROI net output per head (exclusive of that generated by higher product prices and/or transfer pricing) relative to that in the UK was between 22 per cent and 29 per cent in 1985. Even this range of estimates should not be regarded as definitive given that our estimate of transfer pricing depends critically on the assumption that there is enough structural similarity between the ROI and UK chemicals, pharmaceuticals and miscellaneous foods industries for one to neglect other influences on the net output/gross output ratio. Given that we are uncertain as to the validity of this assumption it is worthwhile pursuing an alternative method for measuring the impact of transfer pricing.

(2.) Using comparative profit rates The method is based on the following assumptions. First, the incentive to transfer price is assumed to be greatest for American owned companies. This is because the tax systems of non-American countries heavily penalise any company attempting to repatriate the profits it had made through transfer pricing to its Irish subsidiary (admittedly this would not effect the incentive to transfer price if the company wished to keep profits enhanced thereby within the Republic but, given the extent of profit repatriation from ROI, we assume that this motivation is not significant). Whilst American companies would also be heavily taxed if they attempted to repatriate into America the inflated profits of their Irish subsidiaries, given the generally larger scale of their global operations than, say, the German firms operating in ROI they will have more opportunities to recycle those profits to their operations in some third country. (A complication is that the US Revenue Service limits the extent of transfer pricing between America and Ireland by monitoring the divergence between intra-company profit rates in the two locations. If it judges an ROI subsidiary to be making an unacceptably high profit rate then this is reduced by the imposition of a compulsory royalty payment by that subsidiary to the US parent which can then be taxed.)

If the incentive to transfer price is effectively limited to some American subsidiaries this implies that the sectors where it will have greatest impact are; chemicals (NACE 25 and 26); and electrical and electronic engineering, computers etc., and instrument engineering (NACE 34,33 and 37). We therefore consider transfer pricing only in relation to these sectors (limitations on the available data did not allow us to include NACE 417-418, 423 miscellaneous foods within the scope to this method which is unfortunate given that an American soft drinks manufacturer dominates this industry). Differences between companies sales and gross output were assumed to be negligible.

The maximum possible extent of transfer pricing is indicated by the degree to which ROI subsidiaries have higher profit rates than their American parents (that is when allowance is made for differences in costs between the two countries). The IDA Survey (sample of firms employing more than 29 persons representing 65 per cent of the population's employment) suggests that foreign owned chemicals plants in ROI earned profits of 29 per cent of sales in 1984 compared to 18 per cent for their parent companies (the pre-tax average of the 20 most important foreign companies in this industry which are located in ROI).

Thus the ROI plants had excess profits equivalent to 11 per cent of sales. Unfortunately, there is no readily available data which would allow one to determine how much of this 11 per cent is the result of differences in fuel and material inputs, interest charges and the absence of charges for certain higher order services (e.g. management, research and development, designing, marketing) provided by the American headquarters of the companies to the ROI subsidiaries (whilst some international companies may charge their subsidiaries fees for these services the level of these may be set in such a way as to reallocate profits to the least tax location i.e. they become part of the process of transfer pricing). In principal these differences in inputs should be picked up by the ratio of materials, fuels and industrial services to gross output. This ratio is by definition equal to one minus the net output/gross output ratio and so is prey to all the difficulties of interpretation already discussed.

However, it is possible to estimate the extent to which Irish profitability is boosted by lower labour costs. Using ILO (1987) and Ray (1987) total labour costs were estimated as 8.9 per cent of ROI gross output in chemicals but 15.5 per cent in America. In other words, of the excess of 11 per cent, 6.6 per cent could be accounted for by lower wages, salaries and social charges in ROI. This therefore leaves 4.4 per cent of American subsidiary gross output/sales as unexplained and this was assumed to reflect transfer pricing. This was equivalent to IR£39.8 million out of a total net output of IR£906.5 million and therefore ROI chemicals' net output without transfer pricing is estimated to be 95.6 per cent of the unadjusted level in 1984.

This method can be repeated for the electrical and electronic etc. industries (NACE 33, 34 and 37). In this case the ROI excess profit rate was 28.9 per cent minus 14 per cent, that is 14.9 per cent of sales. Lower labour costs in Ireland amounted to 13.1 per cent of gross output which leaves 1.8 per cent of gross output as the maximum possible extent of transfer pricing. This is equivalent to IR£41.8 million out of a total net output of IR£1261.1 million and therefore ROI's electrical and electronic etc. industries net output per head is estimated as 96.7 per cent of the unadjusted level in 1984.

When these two sectoral estimates are combined one has an estimate of the total impact of transfer pricing on manufacturing value-added in the Republic. This is equivalent to IR£81.6 million out of a total net output of IR£4980.4 million in the firms of 20 or more employees and therefore ROI's manufacturing net output per head is estimated as 98.4 per cent of the unadjusted level in 1984. In other words, this method suggests that the total impact of transfer pricing is much smaller than was estimated by the net output/gross output ratios used in the previous section. Unfortunately these two results are not strictly comparable given that in each case a different set of industries are considered. In method (1) chemicals for industrial and agricultural use, pharmaceuticals and miscellaneous foods, but in this method (i.e. (2)) all chemicals and all the electrical, electronic and instrument engineering industries. In each case the industries considered were those which according to the chosen indicator displayed the greatest apparent evidence of transfer pricing. Whilst some doubt therefore remains as to the precise size of the impact of transfer pricing, whichever measured is used it is not a major explanation of the relatively high productivity in ROI.

One could summarise this section on the Republic's comparative productivity by saying that it appears to be a much happier tale than that told about NI in Part 2 (or indeed the story told by the comparisons between Northern Ireland and Germany which are described in Part 3). Current ROI net output per head levels are substantially higher than those in NI or than the average for the whole UK (this remains true even when one allows for differential product pricing and scope for transfer pricing). However, it should also be noted that the responsibility for this comparatively high level of productivity rests primarily with foreign owned firms in a limited number of industrial sectors. The productivity performance of indigenously owned ROI firms remains undistinguished either by the standards of Northern Ireland or Great Britain. The following section investigates whether the differential performance of manufacturing in NI and ROI can be explained by differences between their histories of industrial development.

History of industrial development in NI and ROI: its impact on present performance

The next section will include a detailed consideration of those factors on which commentators have focused as explanations of ROI's performance in manufacturing. By contrast this section will give a broad overview of the differences between the industrial development process in NI and ROI in order to indicate how variations in the productivity today could in part be a legacy from past processes (the terms NI and ROI will be used anachronistically to apply to the areas prior to Partition which are equivalent to the modern jurisdictions).

ROI's disadvantages as a late industrialising economy

Perhaps the most marked contrast is that whereas NI to some extent shared in the so called Industrial Revolution the rest of Ireland failed to industrialise during the nineteenth century. Thus, at the start of the First World War 35 per cent of employment in NI was in industry as compared to only 13 per cent in the ROI (Kennedy, Giblin and McHugh, 1988). While the total industrial output of Ireland in 1907 (as measured by the Industrial Census) put its level of industrialisation approximately on par with Denmark (Daly, 1981) the vast majority of that industry was concentrated in the North and especially along the Lagan valley.

While comparison of late Victorian and Edwardian NI with GB

industrial regions and especially continental Europe and the USA would have indicated the limited extent and diversity of industrialisation, the success of NI was thrown into stark relief by the experience of ROI during 1800-1921. Arguably what happened in ROI was not so much a failure to industrialise as a case of de-industrialisation. The development of the NI textiles and especially linen industries coincided with a massive decline in the domestic textiles industry in ROI (Daly, 1981). Outside of NI total employment in manufacturing shrank during the nineteenth century with the result that by 1914 Ireland was one of the few European economies whose industrial labour force was smaller than that of sixty years earlier (Daly, 1981).

The causes of this de-industrialisation have been sharply disputed but their results are clear (Haughton, 1987). At partition ROI inherited an industrial base which was negligible both by comparison with NI and other small European economies. Thus the growth of ROI manufacturing since independence has been from a very low base which begs the question whether one legacy of this has been a continued handicap on ROI manufacturing performance?

O'Malley (1985a, 1989) stresses the disadvantages of ROI's position as a "late starter" in the industrialisation process. Particular emphasis is placed upon the barriers to entry which ROI owned firms would face if they tried to enter those markets characterised by significant economies of scale or capital investment or external economies, and heavy requirements for R and D and advertising and marketing expenditure. Incumbent firms (say, American, German or Japanese) by virtue of their long established position within such markets enjoy cost and profit advantage relative to the potential ROI entrants. In the absence of some intervention in the market by the state (e.g. by subsidising those costs which represent the barriers to entry) ROI will be excluded from international markets and industrial development will be restricted to those sectors where economies of scale are comparatively unimportant and the home market is in some way sheltered from international competition.

Whilst the requirement for high levels of capital investment has been perceived as a barrier to entry, it is by no means clear that manufacturing in the ROI has been handicapped historically by a shortage of capital. Whereas in the past commentators in the ROI may have attributed the lack of an industrial revolution to a scarcity of investment funds it is now generally agreed that there was no shortage of capital in nineteenth century ROI (Daly, 1981; Kennedy, Giblin, and McHugh, 1988). Outside of Ulster there was little demand for such capital with the result of Irish savings were invested instead in railways, roads and British Government stocks. In his analysis of ROI output and productivity growth since Independence Kennedy (1971) could discern no obvious association between those industries which had rapid growth rates of capital input and those which had large increases in labour productivity during the 1920s-1960s. Geary and Dempsey (1979) attributed about three-quarters of ROI manufacturing growth between the late 1960s and the mid-1970s to total factor productivity (i.e. they could not explain more than a quarter of growth by increases in the volume of the labour or capital input). The investment rate in ROI manufacturing has risen during the post-War period (from 16.5 per cent of value-added during 1949-61 to 27.4 per cent during 1973-84; Kennedy, Giblin, and McHugh, 1988). Geary and Henry (1983) take such results as being strongly indicative of a waste of capital in ROI manufacturing. In other words, ROI may have had too much capital rather than too little. At the same time, just as we have indicated in Chapter 12 the questionable quality of the capital stock in NI, so commentators have doubted the quality of the machinery stock in ROI factories (e.g. because of too great a dependence on machinery of British origin capital in ROI plants was held to be relatively outdated by the Sectoral Development Committee (1985)).

Apart from levels of investment, economies of scale have been identified as a critical barrier to entry. Kennedy, Giblin and McHugh (1988) note the relatively small size of factory units in ROI. Our own calculations suggest that the median factory size in ROI manufacturing was 153-6 employees in 1985 (based on 1985 Census, the range of results arises from the small number of units which are not classified by size) which is significantly lower than NI (191 in 1986) or GB (267 in 1986). However, as in the case of NI (Chapter 6) it is by no means clear how large the foregone potential economies of scale are. Kennedy, Giblin and McHugh (1988) point to how the ROI dairy industry (which includes 8 out of the 20 largest indigenously owned firms) rationalised its number of plants in the 1970s and 1980s but was still making low value-added products at the end of this process.

O'Malley's thesis (1985a, 1989) is that the crucial handicap to ROI's competitiveness in international markets is a lack of economies of scale at the level of the firm. He notes that of the 100 largest indigenous firms in ROI, 85 per cent of sales and 77 per cent of employment lies within the food, drink, tobacco, paper and mineral product sectors, i.e. substantially non-traded goods which lack appreciable technology inputs. However ROI's difficulties cannot be entirely attributed to the small size of the home market because Telesis (1982) noted that while Belgium had least 14 indigenous engineering firms employing more than 1000 persons and Denmark 17, the ROI had only one. Whereas the ROI had only 3 industrial companies placed within the Financial Times ranking of Europe's top 500 companies by market capitalisation, Switzerland with only one-and-a-half times the ROI's population had almost six times as many. It is however worth adding that as in the case of Britain (see Chapter 2) a dearth of large firms may be as much symptom of relative economic decline as its cause.

The better performance of other small European economies such as Denmark, Finland, Sweden, and Austria suggest they have overcome the alleged disadvantages of being a late starter by building up a corps of world class firms which have retained a competitive advantage within those industries which O'Malley characterises as having major barriers to entry. This could imply either that these economies had a more effective industrial intervention strategies than ROI, or that specialisation by an entrant within complex factor product markets can nullify at least some of the advantages of the incumbent behind his barriers (Telesis, 1982). It should also be noted that the status of being a late starter brings benefits as well as costs. Examination of the economic history of Britain and NI suggests that an early start to the industrialisation can be a mixed blessing and one which ROI which was perhaps fortunate to avoid.

NI's disadvantages as an early industrialising economy

Despite being the first industrial nation late nineteenth century Britain was still overhauled by the late starters of that era; the USA and Germany (Bairoch, 1982; Crafts, 1988b). Any barriers to entry against the rising American and German firms were more than counterbalanced by the cost handicap imposed on British firms by virtue of being first in the field (Matthews, Feinstein and Odling-Smee, 1982). Britain inherited from the first industrial revolution outdated technology (e.g. in textiles spinning and metals smelting) and cramped physical infrastructure (e.g. the narrower railway loading gauge). Given the sunk costs of existing plant and equipment and the principal of bygones be bygones it was privately rational for British firms to continue using such capital even though it did not embody least cost techniques (Flood and McCloskey, 1981). A market failure occurred in the sense that while it would have been socially desirable to replace such capital there was inadequate market incentive for entrepreneurs to do this. Presumably the major industries in NI, such as linen and shipbuilding were also characterised by such market failure.

The harmful legacy of being the first industrialised economy also included the fact that as compared to Germany and the USA late Victorian and Edwardian Britain was endowed with a comparatively disadvantageous range of industries (Crafts, 1988b). The so called staple industries of British manufacturing such as cotton, iron and shipbuilding were characterised by less scope for technological advance than in the chemical and electromechanical industries and by low income elasticities of world demand as compared to those facing the products of the new industries of the late nineteenth century. This might beg the question why the UK had failed to imitate Germany in developing a strong electrical engineering sector prior to 1914 or why Britain could not emulate the success of the early motor vehicle industry in the USA. The answer may lie again with a divergence between private and social gains. As late as the First World War (and in some cases even later than that) British capital continued to earn profit rates in the traditional heavy industries which it found acceptable. While British products may have become increasingly uncompetitive on price and quality within the markets of Europe and North America (Williams, 1896; Pavitt, 1982), India and the African Colonies continued to provide a relatively soft market. Even if British entrepreneurs had faced incentives to compete within the types of industries which were increasingly dominated by the Germans and Americans it has been argued that imperfections within the UK capital market such as alleged reluctance to provide long term loans to industry would have hamstrung attempts to make the necessary investment in new plant and machinery (Kennedy, 1987).

If the UK economy as a whole inherited a weak structure as result of its status as an early industrialiser, then the problem was concentrated within the coalfield based industrial areas of Scotland, Wales and North West and North East England (Lee, 1986). Despite its lack of local coal deposits manufacturing in NI shared these structural problems. The 1907 the Census recorded that 80 per cent of output lay within the food and drink, textiles and clothing and shipbuilding and heavy engineering sectors as well as about 70 per cent of employment (Daly, 1981). Indeed, partly by virtue of the small absolute size of the modern manufacturing sector in NI (about 150,000 employees at the start of the First World War) the range of industries found there may have been even narrower than that located in Central Scotland, South Wales, Lancashire or Tyneside. Even as late as the 1960s manufacturing in NI still displayed the least sectoral diversity of any region within the UK (Harris, 1987).

The structural weaknesses of UK manufacturing were laid bare during the inter-war period in terms of the persistent heavy unemployment in the northern industrial regions. NI's peculiarly vulnerable industrial structure was evidenced by its longstanding position as the UK region with the highest unemployment rate (Johnson, 1985). Although, as Chapter 5 demonstrated, the extent of NI's structural disadvantage has diminished since the Second World War as a result of the relative and absolute decline of the clothing, textiles and shipbuilding industries, the pre-1914 history of NI manufacturing continues to case a shadow over economic development today in the sense that not only is physical capital inherited from the past but so may be ideas which are no longer appropriate.

As a result of being early starters Britain and NI were handicapped by physical capital and infrastructure which by the standards of international best practise were suboptimal. However, the most serious and long-lasting cost of being the first industrial nation may have been the way in which this experience shaped social, political and industrial attitudes and institutions. In contrast to Germany, America, Italy, France, Russia or Japan or any of the other late starters of the nineteenth century British (and hence NI) industrialisation was peculiar in that involved a predominately unskilled labour force organised in craft unions, led by managers who had little or no formal training, was financed predominantly by firms themselves without accessing external investment funds, and involved minimal government intervention or control. The success of this formula during the eighteenth and early nineteenth century encouraged the complacent assumption that there was no need for Britain to copy German technical schooling or industrial banking or American managerial practises. While the economic difficulties of the inter-war did encourage some critical analysis of the institutional inheritance from the nineteenth century (e.g. Keynes' The End of Laissez-faire (1925) and The Macmillan Report (1931)) victories in two world wars served to further disguise the

208

extent to which British manufacturing was becoming increasing uncompetitive relative to Germany (Barnett, 1986).

The matched plant comparisons between NI and Germany (described in Part 3) indicated the damage still being done by two particular inheritances from the past: an inadequate industrial training system and divisive industrial relations. These will now be examined in greater depth.

Like the rest of the UK, NI has traditionally relied upon a decentralised, employer-based voluntary apprenticeship and training scheme. Given that technical and vocational education has significant external benefits it is unlikely that the market alone will deliver the socially optimal quality of training. Hence the theoretical justification for some form of government intervention in the market either through compulsion (the legal requirements placed upon German employers) or through the state financed education of sixteen to eighteen year olds (Japan and the USA) (see Chapter 2; Finegold and Soskice, 1988). Unfortunately Britain's success during the first industrial revolution has encouraged complacency about a system which is no longer appropriate to an era of accelerating technical change.

The comparatively poor NI industrial relations and manning rates reported in Chapters 13 and 15 were unsurprising given the considerable evidence that these are deep-seated problems throughout British manufacturing (Pratten, 1976; Pratten and Atkinson, 1976; Davies and Caves, 1987; Crafts, 1988a, 1988b). While over the long run labour relations in America and Germany have been far from perfectly harmonious it seems clear that by the start of the 1980s UK labour productivity levels had been depressed below what would otherwise have been possible if British managers had been willing or able to achieve manning levels comparable to competitors and to adopt new technology and working practises at a rate comparable to other industrial economies (Prais, 1981a). The roots of Britain's industrial relations problems have been variously traced to the relatively slow speed of industrialisation in the early nineteenth century, entrenched restrictive practises, or the variety of craft unions which promoted inter-union strife or cultural and political factors leading to authoritarianism on the part of British managers. To the extent that the industrial structure of NI is still relatively dependent on the industries of the first industrial revolution it is possible that disharmonious industrial relations pose a greater friction to labour productivity improvement than they do in GB.

NI and ROI compared: an early starter versus a late starter

The literature on ROI and UK industrial development up to 1914 therefore stresses two apparently contradictory themes. On the one hand the lack of an established industrial base in ROI is said to have constrained the subsequent development of locally owned manufacturing firms such that they faced insurmountable barriers to entry in all sectors where either economies of scale or technology were significant. However, on the other hand, NI can be held to have shared in the general UK problem that the physical,

social and human capital inherited from the first industrial
revolution was largely inappropriate to the requirements of
successful competition with America, Germany and other newly
industrialised nations. While ROI has faced some difficulties as a
result of its failure to industrialise during the nineteenth
century, it has been able to capitalise upon the fact that unlike
NI it represents one large greenfield site as far as industrial
development goes. The foreign owned firms locating in ROI may have
found the lack of established management and labour practises
especially pleasing. In other words human capital in ROI was more
malleable than its counterpart in NI and GB. In contrast, NI's
inheritance from the past was a mixed blessing including, as it
did, a disadvantageous industrial structure, a voluntary training
system and divisive industrial relations.

   The gap between the experience of ROI and NI may not be as wide
as it seems because, despite the lack of indigenous industrial
development in ROI, the common administration of Ireland and
Britain during 1800-1921 implies that ROI may also have developed
at least some of those attitudes and institutions which were to
the detriment of productivity growth. O'Farrell (1986) suggests
that the educational system post-1921 retained the anti-industry
bias allegedly found in the English system from which it had been
copied (Wiener, 1981; Barnett, 1986). Thus, while in terms of
literacy rates the performance of the ROI educational system in
the nineteenth century was relatively strong as compared to other
European countries, the legacy of an anglicised educational
system was a mixed blessing. In terms of participation in
secondary level education the ROI has kept broadly in line with
the UK since Partition and in recent years has overtaken the UK at
both the secondary and tertiary levels (whether UK standards were
themselves adequate is discussed in Chapter 2). In 1987 almost
two-thirds of the population aged 16 to 18 were participating in
full-time schooling compared to only two-fifths in the UK (and 55
per cent in Germany, 75 per cent in France and about 90 per cent
in the USA, Japan and Sweden (Financial Times, 1989, November 29;
Sweeney, 1989). There were a total of nearly 4,000 undergraduate
engineering students in ROI universities in 1987 (Sweeney, 1989).
This would imply that the ROI's annual output of engineers at the
bachelor degree level is considerably higher than the UK's on a
pro rata basis (Prais, 1989). Public policy became more focused on
the need to increase educational output (especially at the
tertiary level) following the OECD and Department of Education
report Investment in Education (1965). Unfortunately ROI retained
the British bias against technical education and thus the
Vocational Education Act of the 1930s had little real impact
(Kennedy, Giblin and McHugh, 1988). Kennedy, Giblin and McHugh
(1988) note that the long run growth performance of the ROI
economy has been strikingly similar to that of the UK and they
postulate that ROI shared with Britain and social and political
conservatism which made it impossible to achieve the fundamental
changes necessary in order to promote more rapid economic growth.
One common element in both the ROI and the UK has been the
dominance within the policy making administration of the treasury

(Barrington, 1975). Nevertheless, as an independent nation since 1921 the ROI has at least in principle had greater freedom to look to alternative models of economic development whereas NI has remained tied to the UK. As a result the ROI has had a longer history of conscious attempts by the state to operate an industrial development policy.

Early state intervention

Just as the recent performance of manufacturing in NI and ROI reflects in part the various legacies from earlier periods of industrialisation so the success or otherwise of contemporary industrial policy depends in part on the experience accumulated over the years by policy makers.

The imposition of tariffs by the _Fianna Fail_ government in ROI in 1932 marked a new departure in state policy towards manufacturing since the first decade of independence had seen a continuity of nineteenth century _laissez faire_ (i.e. a combination of low taxes, minimal government spending and free trade designed to promote prosperity through agricultural exports). It is unclear to what extent this policy was motivated by infant industry considerations and such developmental theories as those developed by Alexander Hamilton and Friedrich List in nineteenth century America and Germany. The short term priorities of Anglo-Irish diplomacy and the political desire to prop-up ROI agriculture may have been more important (though one of the founding fathers of Irish republicanism, Arthur Griffith, had consciously modelled his recommendation of tariff autonomy on the policies of List and the De Valera administration did make efforts to concentrate industrial ownership in ROI hands; Control of Manufactures Act 1932-4). Nevertheless, at least in terms of nominal rates of tariff the level of protection for ROI industry was relatively high as compared to that given to British (and hence NI) firms during the 1930s (Ryan, 1948/49)[1]. Nor was the policy of protection without apparent success (Blackwell and O'Malley, 1984) since the number of employees in the manufacturing sector increased from 61,000 during the 1931 Census of Production, to 100,500 in 1938, and 140,300 in 1951.[2]

In terms of both financial and intellectual resources the Stormont administration in NI was ill-equipped to face the challenge of mass unemployment in the 1920s and 1930s. In any case NI had little option but to keep in step with the rest of the UK during this pre-Keynesian, pre-regional policy period (Johnson, 1985). The 1932 and 1937 New Industry (Development) Acts offered assistance in terms of rents, rates, cheap loans and free sites. Shorts Brothers decision to relocate from Kent to Belfast represented some light in an otherwise pessimistic picture but it is unclear to what extent their decision was a result of public policy. Thus whereas ROI manufacturing grew rapidly (albeit from a very small base) during the inter-war period, NI in the face of continuous decline in the linen and shipbuilding trades at best managed to stabilise aggregate manufacturing output and employment at levels comparable to those before the First World War with some limited diversification of product range such as a switch from textiles machinery towards heaters, fans and electrical motors (54 firms with a total employment of 6,000 had taken advantage of the provisions of the 1932 and 1937 Acts by the mid-1950s).

Differences during the era of strong outward orientated policies

In spite of their very different industrial histories up to that point it was striking that at the end of 1950s both NI and ROI chose to adopt a so called outward orientated industrial policy with the intention that inward investment by GB and international firms should become the mainspring of development.

In NI the change was associated with stronger regional policy throughout the UK (Canning, Moore and Rhodes, 1987). Inter-regional mobility of firms within the UK was promoted by both carrots (capital and discretionary grants with the highest rates of assistance being given to the Special Development Areas of Scotland, Wales and North England) and sticks (restricted licence to expand industrial premises within South East England). While improvements in NI's comparative industrial efficiency were not explicitly stated amongst the goals of industrial and regional policy during the 1960s and early 1970s Chapter 2 and Appendix G note that NI productivity growth exceeded that of GB in the years before 1973.

Whereas the UK had substantially abandoned tariff protection for industry at the end of the Second World War, in ROI the move towards an inward investment strategy from 1958 onwards coincided with the return to more or less free trade (the intellectual catalyst was T.K. Whitaker's _Economic Development_ (1958) which was itself a reaction to the perceived stagnancy of the ROI economy during the 1950s when the gains from protection appeared to have been exhausted). It should also be stressed that the ROI offered international firms a different package of incentives than those applying to NI and the GB regions. Most significantly, firms locating in the ROI were guaranteed complete exemption from tax on that part of profit attributable to exports (under pressure from the European Commission this provision was replaced in 1981 by a 10 per cent corporate tax rate applying to all manufacturing until at least the year 2000). Apart from using different incentives the experience of NI and ROI diverged in terms of the sectors from which their inward investors were drawn. This was to have important consequences after 1973.

Inward investment after 1973: the Troubles, world recession and disillusionment

In the period since 1973 the industrial development experiences of NI and the ROI have once again diverged and the proximate cause of this has been the differential performance of the externally owned sector in the two economies. Employment in the externally owned firms established in NI before 1973 shrank by 55,800 during 1973-86 whereas the comparable firms in ROI lost only 28,600 (Gudgin, Hart, Fagg, Keegan and D'Arcy, 1989). However, the

externally owned sector in ROI registered net employment growth
during 1973-86 as a result of 43,100 jobs generated by new inward
moving firms. In contrast inward investment during this period
created only 6,900 jobs in NI (Gudgin, Hart, Fagg, Keegan, and
D'Arcy, 1989). Compared with the ROI, NI underperformed on two
counts; first, the collapse of employment in those firms during
the boom in inward investment of the 1960s and, second, a failure
to maintain a continual inflow of new firms. The reasons of NI's
comparatively poor performance can be expected to have
implications for the explanation of NI's productivity shortfall
relative to both GB and ROI.

The role of the Troubles assessed   The Troubles present themselves
as the perhaps the single most obvious cause of the inability of
NI to attract substantial inward investment after 1973 (New
Ireland Forum, 1983). Various estimates have been made on the
basis of a shift-share methodology which allows for both
industrial structure and differential performance relative to the
other assisted areas of the UK of the total impact of the
Troubles, i.e. the combined effect of jobs lost in existing firms
and discouragement to inward investment (Moore, Rhodes, and Tyler,
1977; Fothergill and Gudgin, 1982; Moore, Rhodes and Canning,
1987; Gudgin, Hart, Fagg, Keegan, and D'Arcy, 1989). These suggest
that the total number of jobs foregone lies in the range
15,000-25,000 (Moore, Rhodes and Canning's estimate of 40,000 lost
is the only one which falls outside of this range).
    The question as to the size of the economic impact of the
Troubles can only be answered if one has in mind a counterfactual,
i.e. what would otherwise have happened if the Troubles had not
occurred. Clearly, it cannot be demonstrated what the correct
counterfactual is but the shift-share measures have tended to
assume that in the absence of the Troubles NI's employment growth
would have continued to maintain that relationship with growth in
the other UK Special Development Areas which had held up to 1973.
Thus the   difference between employment growth (adjusted for
structure) in NI and Wales-Scotland-North England in fact
underestimates the impact of the Troubles alone to the extent that
some of their impact was being compensated for by the higher level
of grant aid to industry in NI (Gudgin, Hart, Fagg, Keegan and
D'Arcy, 1989). In other words, the available measures do not
measure the gross impact of the Troubles. What one has is an
estimate of their employment cost net of the positive impact of
more generous levels of subsidisation[3].
    A further limitation on these measures is that they cannot
distinguish between employment loss in existing firms and that
derived from discouraged inward investment. Gudgin et al (1989)
trace how NI received a declining proportion of total inward
investment in the UK peripheral regions (i.e. a declining share of
a total which was itself declining). It seems plausible to trace
some of this to the Troubles especially given the sharp fall in
NI's investment share which coincided with the worst period of
violence (1971-75). However, whilst the Troubles may have a
quantitative impact on inward investment relative to ROI it is

much less clear whether they would have had a qualitative impact (Hitchens and Birnie, 1989b). This question is given weight by the fact that inward investment into NI has generally been of a lower quality in the sense of being less durable than that investment into ROI during both 1960-73 and since 1973. There is no obvious mechanism by which the Troubles could have affected the sectoral type of inward investment into NI except, perhaps, the possibility that only the highest risk projects which had been turned down by development agencies everywhere else would be forced to come to NI. Thus one may have to look to other causes as to why NI has failed to develop a bloc of high technology industries comparable to the pharmaceuticals or micro-electronics sectors in ROI and Scotland. The available evidence is strongly indicative of NI's crucial supply side difficulties lying with the quality of local management and labour (e.g. the externally owned branch-plants in NI have been characterised by standardised products with intensive inputs of capital and semi-skilled labour (Hood and Young, 1983; Teague, 1987)). Such problems could explain why even before the Troubles began NI attracted a mix of international and GB firms which were subsequently to prove less durable than those which moved into ROI at the same time (e.g. man-made fibres rather than computer components)[4]. Not only has the performance of the GB/foreign owned sector itself been disputed but it has so far failed to provide much of a stimulus to the indigenously owned firms within the Province. The level of linkages between the external and indigenous sectors remains disappointingly low (NI Economic Council, 1986b) and management and labour practises in the locally owned sector fail to attain UK best practise (Hitchens and O'Farrell, 1987, 1988a, 1988b).

Dissatisfaction with the foreign owned sector in ROI   While ROI was more than able to keep pace with the decline in the existing stock of its multinational firms by attracting a continual inflow of new externally owned companies, dissatisfaction has been expressed as to their performance. Doubt has focused on the extent of their contribution to the ROI economy and on the cost and effectiveness of the present incentives package.

O'Malley (1985b) observed that whereas NI industry in the 1980s may have been too specialised, ROI manufacturing (foreign and indigenous) had yet to entrench itself within any significant market niches. This might in part derive from the allegedly backward level of product and process innovation in the multinationals which had been established in ROI (Blackwell and O'Malley, 1984). Telesis (1982) noted that few of the electronics plants in the ROI constituted stand alone production locations (i.e. the R and D and design functions were more likely to be based in Los Angeles or Tokyo than the ROI). The Sectoral Development Committee (1985) reported that in the ROI electronics industry qualified engineers as a proportion of total employment were half as well represented as in equivalent Scottish plants and only one-third as well represented as in the USA. Thus, to some extent Cooper and Whelan's (1973) gloomy prediction has been verified. The ROI makes some advanced products but largely fails to use indigenous ROI scientific or technological expertise in the process. The European Management Forum (1981) reported that per head of population Germany had 25 per cent more R and D engineers and scientists than the ROI and whereas 95 per cent of the German technologists were directly involved with manufacturing only 76 per cent of those in the ROI were. The ROI devotes only 0.8 per cent of GNP to R and D which is much lower than the share in UK let alone either Japan or Germany (New Scientist, 1987). A similar inadequacy in the ROI's research efforts is reflected in the figures for R and D in manufacturing alone. While the Sectoral Development Committee (1985) reported that R and D spending in 1982 in the bulk of ROI manufacturing (excluding the small metals, vehicles and a few miscellaneous manufacturing sectors) summed to IR£36 million which represented 0.6 per cent of sales, in the UK R and D conducted within the premises of manufacturing firms was equivalent to about 2 per cent of gross output in 1985 (British Business, 1988, 5 February, p28). The foreign owned firms in the ROI did devote a higher proportion of their resources to R and D than the indigenous (1.1 per cent of sales as compared to 0.4 per cent) but their effort still appeared disappointing from an international perspective (Sectoral Development Committee, 1985).

The other major criticism of the branch-plants contained in Telesis (1982) was that they had low levels of linkage into the ROI economy. O'Farrell and Loughlin (1980) had earlier demonstrated low rates of local sourcing. Management weaknesses within the indigenous sector of ROI manufacturing were recognised during the 1960s as the tariff protection was dismantled and it is not clear to what extent the presence of multinationals within the ROI has provided favourable demonstration effects in terms of the upgrading of management (in a recent survey half of the large ROI firms sampled either spent nothing on management development or did not know how much resources they devoted to this subject; Advisory Committee on Management Training, 1989).

In spite of these problems, the externally owned sector in the ROI has undoubtedly made a major contribution to the improvement in average comparative productivity performance. By virtue of British firms established during the pre-1921 period and externally owned firms which arrived during the protectionist era, a significant externally owned sector has been a long standing feature in ROI. However, its positive contribution to aggregate productivity performance has been increasing over time given compositional changes within the externally owned sector. For example whereas the share of employment represented by British owned branch-plants has declined, that of American owned has increased; the 14,760 employees in USA owned plants represented 6.7 per cent of manufacturing employment in 1973, but in 1986 there were 37,788 employees in US plants which was 18.3 per cent of the total (Ruane, 1987). As we have already seen the American plants in ROI attain productivity levels about three times higher than those in the domestically owned ROI plants.

Despite the high levels of value-added per head achieved in the ROI, this reliance upon "production platforms" (Kennedy, Giblin and McHugh, 1988) would pose a threat to the long term viability of the manufacturing sector if ROI failed to maintain a continual inflow of new firms bringing in newer products to compensate for the increasing obsolescence of the product range of the existing stock of multinational plants. However, at least for the moment the ROI's inward investment strategy is still yielding handsome dividends in terms of rate of manufacturing output growth which are significantly higher than those of either GB or NI. Baker (1988) demonstrates that the rapid growth of ROI manufacturing is mainly attributable to the modern or foreign owned sector (i.e. Industry Groups 33, 34, 37, and 418-423 of the NACE European industrial classification: pharmaceuticals, data processing equipment, electrical and electronic engineering, instrument engineering, and miscellaneous foods) which achieved average output growth of 11.9 per cent p.a. during 1980-87 as compared to 4.7 per cent p.a. in the other "traditional" sectors of manufacturing.

The question does however arise as to what extent ROI can continue to outcompete alternative Western European investment locations in the intensifying battle for mobile American, Japanese and Pacific Rim capital (Blackwell and O'Malley, 1984). Such has been the success of the IDA in the past (Gudgin, Hart, Fagg, Keegan and D'Arcy, 1989) that it seems most probable that ROI's share of the total will decline. How far this matters will depend on what happens to the total cake of internationally mobile investment which in turn will be determined by the state of health of the world economy and the East Asian and American reaction to the completion of the EC Internal Market. There is also some doubt as to whether ROI can and should continue to subsidise at such a high rate (Appendix B) which generates large increases in output with little or no net gain to employment. Ruane (1987) argues that despite IDA protestations to the contrary the incentive package has produced a bias to capital in ROI manufacturing. A "handout mentality" may also have developed and the degree of commitment of foreign firms to the ROI location is low.

Nevertheless, in spite of all these qualifications it is necessary to conclude that compared to NI the recent manufacturing performance of the ROI has been far superior (Rowthorn and Wayne, 1988). While doubts can be raised as to level of technology within the externally owned factories in the ROI, the ROI does at least have a significant production presence within such growing industries as computer components and pharmaceuticals. There is at least the possibility therefore of spin-offs in terms of indigenous development within these sectors (though this may require policy interventions). Hitchens and O'Farrell (1988a) noted that entrepreneurs of foreign origin were heavily represented amongst the most successful firms in their sample of small firms in the Shannon area of the ROI. These non-ROI entrepreneurs had come to ROI with a multinational firm. With a smaller base of multinationals and a lesser likelihood that these firms will bring in outside managers, there is less scope for such development in NI.

The role of the past in explaining present productivity performance

The comparative development of manufacturing in NI and ROI has been outlined in order to extract hints as to how the past may be influencing present differences in efficiency and performance.
Compared to the ROI, NI was an early starter in the industrialising process. Although this has meant that NI, unlike the ROI, has a range of medium sized indigenous firms (mainly in the engineering, clothing and textiles, food, drink and tobacco sectors) which are well established in either GB or international markets the heritage of nineteenth century staple industries, and a "British" industrial training and labour relations system constituted a very mixed blessing from the point of view of achieving productivity gains.
As an independent state the ROI has been able to pursue an active industrial policy from the 1930s onwards. How far ROI derives a benefit from this additional experience is debatable since most commentators have focused on the extent to which ROI policy imitated the incoherence and "short-termism" of Britain (Kennedy, Giblin, and McHugh, 1988). However, compared to NI the ROI did have a much greater degree of policy autonomy (hence the profit tax incentive; Gudgin, Hart, Fagg, Keegan and D'Arcy, 1989) and more scope to be open to American and Continental attitudes and practises as opposed to those originating from GB. Given that, as Chapter 1 shows, Britain's comparative productivity performance has been deteriorating throughout most of the period since the Partition of Ireland ROI's manufacturing efficiency had the potential to benefit from such openness to influences coming from beyond the British Isles[5].
While the Troubles may constitute the most obvious reason for the comparatively poor output and employment performance of NI since the early 1970s, serious conceptual and technical difficulties attach to any attempt to estimate the scale of their economic effect. When consideration is narrowed to the impact of the Troubles on comparative productivity then it may be neither possible nor desirable to disentangle this impact from that of deep-seated supply side problems within NI.

Notes

1. To adequately test the assertion that a higher rate of protection in the ROI relative to the UK allowed ROI prices (and hence value-added) to be inflated one would have to compare not only nominal rates of protection but also effective rates, i.e. to what extent were tariffs on material inputs imported into the ROI depressing the value-added of manufacturing?

2. For a discussion of the reliability of the Census of Industrial Production as an indicator of the growth of manufacturing during

the inter-War period see Kennedy, Giblin and McHugh (1988).

3. It should be noted that it was probably the Troubles themselves which were instrumental in creating the political climate in which the levels of subsidisation could grow to such levels. In other words Westminister has regarded NI as a special case. Thus the true counterfactual to NI's present performance, given the Troubles and the existing high levels of grants, is what NI's would have been if there had been no Troubles and the levels of state assistance had been tied much more closely to those allowed in Scotland, Wales and the other UK peripheral regions.

4. As to the impact of the Troubles on the existing body of firms one should allow for the possibility that they have interacted with (and perhaps aggravated) certain supply side problems such as poor work attitudes (see Chapter 15).

5. Whether the ROI was in fact more open to such non-British influences on economic development than NI is uncertain. On the one hand the ROI's neutrality during the Second World War (in contrast to NI) may have left ROI relatively isolated for a time and had the immediate effect of widening the economic gap between NI and the ROI, but on the other hand the ROI (rather than NI) has been the major heir of whatever benefits (e.g. direct investment, a foreign market) flow from the large, self-consciously Irish community in the USA.

It is of critical importance to ascertain to what extent the dominant ideology in the ROI since 1921 (i.e. Irish nationalism) has been friendly to outside ideas and influences which would promote higher productivity. Kennedy, Giblin and McHugh (1988) note the prevalence prior to 1921 of the belief that once the ROI had one its independence then the economy would automatically develop. Such a mentality was linked to the view point that the crucial cause of Ireland's failure to industrialise during the nineteenth century was the colonial link with England (Lyons, 1981) and may not have been conducive to careful consideration of the best strategy for long term economic growth and it is arguable that it has had persistent ill effects. Keating (1989) argues that it has been inherent in the nature of Irish nationalism since the 1880s with its alleged anti-industry, anti-urban and anti-material bias to downgrade the priority given to economic development. Thus American, German and other foreign economic influences would be resisted to the extent that they were perceived as threats to the ROI's Catholic spirituality and Gaelic culture. At the same time a line could be traced through nationalism from Griffith to De Valera in the 1930s which stressed autonomous economic development as the necessary counterpart to political independence from Britain (Lyons, 1981).

Interestingly, it has also been argued that Britain (and presumably NI) suffers from an anti-industrial spirit (Wiener, 1981). The arguments that politics and culture have promoted insularity in the ROI could probably be applied all the more strongly in NI where the nationalist and unionist ideologies have been all the more absorbed in the constitutional question to the probable expense of consideration of strategies for economic development (see Chapter 21).

20 Performance of the small firm sector in Britain and Ireland

"The people of England and Ireland admit as little of being compared together and differ as widely in their circumstances as the peasantry of Norway do from the struggling hordes of Kamschatka".

Thomas Chalmers (1832), Political Economy

Introduction

Reasons of data availability limited the comparative productivity analysis of Part 2 to only those firms employing more than 19 persons. Whilst the relative productivity performance of the small firms employing less than 20 persons would be of interest, the Census of Production in Great Britain and Northern Ireland does not collect data for these firms (the Census in the Republic of Ireland does consider establishments with three or more employees). However, the comparative employment growth performance of small firms in Northern Ireland and the Republic of Ireland has been the subject of previous statistical inquiry and this will be reviewed in the first part of this chapter. The primary purpose will be consider whether there is evidence of a competitiveness problem in the small firm sector.

In Part 3 our matched plant comparison was largely restricted to the medium- and larger-sized firms in Northern Ireland. This was partly to ensure that the firms considered were those which would be operating in international markets (and hence in competition with companies from Germany). The performance of the small firms sector in Northern Ireland and the Republic of Ireland has already been considered through a set of matched plant studies and these will be reviewed in the second part of this chapter. It is of interest to ask whether some of the issues of concern relating to the performance of the larger firms in Northern Ireland also apply to the smaller ones.

Performance of small firms in Ireland: statistical studies

Although the small firm sector sector represents only a small minority of total employment in manufacturing (22 per cent in GB and 21-24 per cent in Northern Ireland according to the data source used (Enderwick, Gudgin and Hitchens, 1989)) it has received a disproportionate attention from policy makers (Birch, 1979; Fothergill and Gudgin, 1979; Department of Trade and Industry, 1981; Gudgin, 1984). Whilst these policy efforts are held to be justified by the alleged contribution of small firms to employment generation it is notable that the process of small firms growth (as opposed to start ups) has been subjected to comparatively little academic research (Mason and Harrison, 1985). This lack of information as to the growth performance of existing firms is regrettable since policy makers in peripheral areas have all too readily assumed that the key problem for their areas is a lack of "enterprise" which should be compensated for be generous assistance for new firms formation (Pathfinder, 1987).

Table 20.1
Components of employment change* in small firms 1973-86
(firms of less than 50 employees).

	NI	ROI	Leicestershire
Number of employees 1973	17.5	53.3	20.3
Lost by 1986 through closures	-10.6 (-61%)	-25.5(-48%)	-8.5(-42%)
Net growth in firms which survived 1973-86	3.1 (+18%)	4.2(+ 8%)	10.0(+49%)
Start ups since 1973	17.0 (+97%)	29.6(+56%)	19.9(+98%)
Total employment change	9.5 (+54%)	8.3(+16%)	21.4(+105%)

* All employment figures in thousands and components of change expressed as a percentage of the base year employment.

Sources: Gudgin, Hart, Fagg, Keegan and D'Arcy (1989); Enderwick, Gudgin, and Hitchens (1990).

A recent study by Gudgin, Hart, Fagg, Keegan and D'Arcy (1989) has illustrated some contrasts between the performance of small firms (defined in this case as those employing less than 50 persons) in Northern Ireland, the Republic of Ireland and Leicestershire (this East Midlands region is of special interest since it represents a fast growing, non-assisted region located close to the core of the UK economy). What is striking is the extent to which the small firms sector in Leicestershire, where employment more than doubled during 1973-86, outperformed that in either part of Ireland. The responsibility for this better performance in Leicestershire did not lie with new firm formation rates since 1973, the employment gain arising from start ups during 1973-86 was no better than that of Northern Ireland (albeit the employment generated in ROI start ups lagged the other two areas). What is notable is that both NI and ROI surviving small firms demonstrated poor rates of growth throughout the period 1973-86 and this was compounded in NI by a relatively high rate of closure of firms established before 1973. In other words small firms in Leicestershire performed much better than their Irish counterparts in terms of growth and survival. Small firms' policy in Ireland has traditionally emphasised the importance of raising the rate of new firm formation in Ireland. This policy appears to have been successful in NI at least in the sense that the percentage increase in employment arising from start ups equalled that in Leicestershire. Unfortunately, NI's achievement in this respect was undermined by poor employment growth performance of established small firms, a subject which has received less attention from policy makers. The crucial issue for the development agencies is to identify the inhibitions on the growth of existing firms in Northern Ireland and the Republic. The next section will review a set of matched plant comparisons which have indicated a serious competitiveness problem in the small firms sector in Ireland.

Matched plant comparisons of small firms' performance in Ireland and Great Britain

About 110 firms in Northern Ireland and the Shannon ("Mid-West") and Dublin areas of the ROI were matched with over 140 firms in three Great Britain regions: South Wales, Scotland and East Anglia (Hitchens and O'Farrell, 1987, 1988a, 1988b; and O'Farrell and Hitchens, 1988a, 1989a, 1989b). These studies had the aim of elucidating whether any locational disadvantages hindering the performance of small firms in these parts of the British Isles, or whether there were any other regional constraints on the growth of small firms.
Previous theories of small firms growth were limited by their insufficient emphasis on production problems. They implicitly assumed that any firm was capable of turning out a product of the design, quality and price the market demanded (O'Farrell and Hitchens, 1987). In contrast, the matched plant methodology developed by Hitchens and O'Farrell explicitly examines the production process. It also combines considerable attention to

detail with broader generality (O'Farrell and Hitchens, 1988b).

Firms were closely matched according to the product made, age of foundation and employment size. Data were collected on: performance, markets served, number of competitors, product details, the age (and type) of machinery, cost of premises, labour force quality and management characteristics. The types of products considered (including engineering, food, furniture, clothing and such miscellaneous items as electronic components, printing, cosmetics and toys) were those which could potentially be exported from the region. Thus the firms under review were not in principle restricted by the rate of growth of regional demand.

When the six published studies are brought together a number of major findings emerge which have implications for the consideration of RoI and NI competitiveness relative to Great Britain.

(a) Constraints on growth

Northern Ireland emerged as the region with the worst employment decline during the period 1982-87. The ROI Mid-West performance was much more respectable (being superior, for example, to that of a matched sample of Scottish firms). Employment growth in the Dublin firms was broadly comparable to that in the Mid-West.

Whereas English and Welsh firms most often named labour supply as a constraint on growth, the Irish companies were more concerned by cost competitiveness. In addition almost half of the NI firms felt demand to be a constraint.

(b) Markets served

Both the NI and ROI (Mid-West) firms were significantly more dependent on local markets (within 40 miles of the factory) (the Dublin firms did, however, have a comparatively high rate of exports). Whilst their transport costs to main GB markets were higher, the differential relative to the Welsh, Scottish and English firms was equivalent to less than 2 per cent of the value of sales. In fact no region considered transport costs a constraint on growth though firms in every region found it difficult to liase with customers (e.g., in engineering to amend the drawings of components). Irish and Scottish companies regretted their remoteness from skilled service agents (for CNC machines). Marketing methods were primitive in all the regions.

By restricting themselves the the local market the Irish firms may have been trying to minimise the extent of competitive pressure on themselves. What is certain is that the firms in both NI and the Mid-West were aware of a much smaller number of competitors operating in their markets.

(c) Quality and price competitiveness

By asking the managers to quote prices for the products of competitor firms and provide an assessment of quality, Hitchens and O'Farrell were able to trace systematic differences between the price and non-price competitiveness of Irish and Great Britain firms (Hitchens and O'Farrell, 1987, 1988a, 1988b; and O'Farrell and Hitchens, 1988a, 1989a, 1989b).

On engineering components and garments both NI and the Mid-West were uncompetitive on price and by implication the ROI companies were less price competitive than their NI counterparts. However, the ROI quality performance was apparently much better since 72 per cent of Scottish managers judged the ROI product satisfactory (which was slightly lower than the evaluation of Scottish products by ROI: 87 per cent were satisfactory) whereas only 15 per cent of the NI products shown to Welsh proprietors were judged acceptable (in the other direction 90 per cent of Welsh products were regarded as satisfactory by NI managers). Northern Ireland's appalling performance on quality was confirmed when both Welsh and NI products were shown to proprietors in London who came to a similar conclusion (without being told which goods were from NI and which from South Wales). The quality of the clothing products of the Dublin firms was comparatively high but the sample of Dublin firms (like the sample in the Mid-West) was not competitive on price with GB.

(d) Design

Some of the Irish deficiencies related to a low commitment to design. Where designing was done in the Republic this tended to be associated with firms which were managed by immigrants to Ireland from Continental Europe or were clothing companies located in the Dublin area.

(e) Quality of the inputs

This emerged as a special problem for ROI where there were problems from indigenous suppliers. The evidence suggested that ROI companies found it difficult to do simple tasks well: packaging, brochures, bottles, dyeing and chipboard.

(f) Premises

Only three companies from all the areas considered reported these as a growth constraint. The English companies had the highest rents (prices per foot were 10-20 per cent lower in Scotland, Wales and Dublin), while the NI and Mid-West had the locational advantage of very cheap factories (rents were respectively, 33 per cent and 71 per cent of those in the South East).

(g) Machinery and equipment

When the modernity of machinery was considered NI and the Mid-West emerged as the regions having the most up-to-date equipment. England and Wales had on average the oldest machinery and Scotland occupied an intermediary position with machinery younger than that in England and Wales but still of a less recent vintage than that in Ireland.

This rank order according to modernity was not accidental but reflected the rate of assistance in these regions. Thus the Irish and Scottish firms had access to selective assistance at very generous rates. In contrast, two-thirds of the Welsh firms received capital grants which were at a lower rate. Finally, the English firms received no grants at all.

It was also significant that the engineering companies in Ireland and Scotland had many more computer numerically-controlled machine tools than their counterparts in either Wales or England.

(h) Labour and management

Whereas the small firms in NI and the Mid-West could not claim that their performance was being hindered by a lack of up-to-date equipment, the comparison of their labour and management characteristics is less optimistic in its results.

Companies in NI generally paid lower wages than firms in any other region. However, wage levels in the Mid-West were about 30 per cent above those in any of the mainland regions. When this result is taken in conjunction with measured levels of value-added per employee which were at best equal to those in Great Britain (both the wage and productivity comparisons being based on the average annual pound sterling/IR pound exchange rate) then the lack of price competitiveness of the Mid-West firms is unsurprising.

In general it was not possible to trace links between managers' occupational background and the performance of the companies. What did emerge very clearly in the context of the Mid-West sample was the value of having experience of productivity, management and product quality standards which were external to Ireland. Thus most of the rapidly growing firms in the Mid-West area of the Republic were either managed by Central Europeans who had migrated to ROI, or by Irish people who had worked abroad and/or in some of the externally-controlled firms operating in that area. It is significant that the NI sample showed no such representation of foreigners or persons previously employed in multinationals.

The quantity of training in Irish firms was not lacking in a quantitative sense, indeed, the number of trainees per employee was about double that in the GB regions. Unfortunately, the comments of managers suggested that some of that training was deficient in a qualitative sense. NI and Mid-West workers could not attain English standards in terms of either tolerance or finish. The firms in NI also had their own unique handicap in that

225

31 per cent of NI proprietors reported that work attitudes were a serious obstruction to improved performance. The issue of poor attitudes did not even arise in any of the other regions.

Conclusions

The first part of this Chapter demonstrated that both NI and RoI have been shown to have a relatively slow rate of growth in their small firm sector. It might be hypothesised that this problem reflects the relatively poor productivity and competitiveness described in Part 2 and 3 of this book with special reference to the larger firms (and also those under external control). In order to prove whether this was in fact the case, it was necessary to refer to a previous set of matched plant comparisons which reviewed the performance of small firms in NI, the Shannon and Dublin areas of ROI, two assisted regions of GB (Scotland and South Wales) and Southern England as one non-assisted region of GB.

What is striking about the findings of these matched studies is the way they overturn much of the previous thinking about the explanation of the relative performance of manufacturing in NI (Hitchens and O'Farrell, 1987). The perceived conventional wisdom includes the following: the small home market restricts growth potential, communications to distant export markets handicap sales, NI people are infected by a branch-plant mentality along with conservatism and an inferiority complex relative to their counterparts in GB, premises are cramped and the machinery antique, and, finally, the development agencies are too cumbersome in their methods and so it is difficult to get a grant. Fortunately, so the story goes, whilst labouring under all these difficulties the Northern Ireland employee is able to redeem himself by his work ethic, attention to product quality and willingness to co-operate with management in constructive industrial relations.

The evidence reviewed in the rest of this book must place this received wisdom in considerable doubt and it is striking to what extent the findings of the small firms' matched comparisons parallel those outlined in Parts 2 and 3 of this book. Thus, just as the statistical comparisons were able to infer, the performance of small and indigenously-owned firms in the Republic of Ireland is undistinguished by the standards of Great Britain. For both the smaller and larger firms in NI essentially the same story can be told. Levels of value-added per employee are relatively low. Employment growth has been worse than that in any of the other regions and there is an undue dependence upon the local market which cannot be explained by differential transport costs alone. Product quality is not equivalent to that of the companies on the mainland and yet NI goods are also relatively over-priced. This comparatively poor performance co-exists with factories which are well endowed with relatively large quantities of advanced machinery and the NI companies were blessed with premises which only a third as costly as those in England. Whilst the quantity of training in the NI companies appeared satisfactory, NI managers were aware that they could not expect certain things from their workers which would be taken for granted in England. Finally, given that the measured profitability of the NI companies was at least as high as that of the firms in the mainland regions, the small firms sector is also characterised by market failure. That is, managers do not have the incentive to raise NI standards of product quality and skills given that their firms are already sufficiently profitable (partly because of the effects of the grant payments).

Since the question of what policy changes should be made to enhance competitiveness is considered in depth in the final Chapter, it is only necessary to give a brief outline of possible policy emphasises as regards the small firms' sector in Ireland.

The fact that the NI, Mid-West and Dublin firms remained uncompetitive in spite of no lack of modern equipment suggests the traditional policies of giving heavy subsidies to capital do not yield commensurate gains in terms of enhanced performance. Both the UK and RoI are presently moving towards greater selectivity in the giving of regional and industrial assistance but it is unclear what criteria will be used to choose which firms will be grant aided (and which will be left to fend for themselves). The results of the small firms' comparisons suggest that the development agencies should target their subsidies on the improvement of management training and labour force experience. Unfortunately, initiatives to up grade skills or standards of product quality will only be as successful if those who administer them are themselves fully conversant with external standards. NI's problem may be precisely that it has too few people who are aware of such standards. The experience of the Mid-West suggests the importance to all of Ireland of attracting inward movement by highly talented outsiders.

21 Improving productivity: obstacles, policy issues, and recommendations

"Where no counsel is, the people fall: but in multitude of counsellors there is safety".

Proverbs, Chapter 11, Verse 14, the King James Version of the Bible

Introduction

This final Chapter summarises the major obstacles to productivity improvement and at the same time evaluates the extent to which these obstacles could potentially be overcome. The principal aim is to look into the future so as to consider how NI in the medium and long-term might narrow its productivity gap relative to GB. The persistence of this substantial productivity shortfall throughout the last 70 years is indicative of deep-seated difficulties and the need for strong medicines to counter the widespread sources of productivity failure. The following handicaps on the performance of manufacturing in Ireland will be considered: the weakness of world demand for those products which are strongly represented in the industrial structure of Ireland, the likely impact of the completion of the European Community (EC) single market after 1992, the role of the Troubles, and the impact of the cultures of NI and the ROI as an obstacle to increases in industrial efficiency. We will then consider what policies would be most effective in overcoming these constraints on productivity gains. We show the direction in which we believe policy should move but detailed consideration of specific policy instruments is left to those who have specialist expertise. Since the bulk of the primary evidence presented in this book relates to NI we give future policy there the most attention. At the same time, there were a number of cases where it was reasonable to draw inferences for policy in the ROI even though we were much more dependent in those cases on secondary sources of information. However, before considering the constraints on productivity growth and the appropriate policy responses it is worth reiterating why the level of output per head in manufacturing is of such importance.

Why manufacturing and productivity matter

One conviction has been fundamental to all the research on which this book is based and that is the belief that improvements in manufacturing productivity are essential to any properly conceived strategy for economic development in either part of Ireland. If it is accepted that the proper goal for government economic policy makers in NI or the ROI is to establish the preconditions for long run, sustainable improvements in employment and living standards then a commitment to higher productivity follows inexorably. Kravis (1976) in his summary of investigations of international productivity differences states the two reasons why this is so. Not only do measurements of productivity differences identify one component of variations in international competitiveness and hence of employment generation but, secondly, they enable the commentator to indicate the contributions of the different economic sectors to those gaps present between the material living standards enjoyed in one country and those in another.

Table 21.1
Comparative GDP per capita of NI and ROI
(at factor cost, as a % of the UK average)

	ROI/UK (UK=100)	NI/UK (UK=100)	NI/ROI (ROI=100)
1926	54.8	60.1	110
1947	49.0	70.8	144
1960	50.5	67.6	134
1973	60.3	72.7	121
1985	68.0(63.9)	78.2(73.5)	115

Note: All UK figures include the Continental Shelf except 1985 when North Sea oil revenues made a significant contribution to UK GDP (the result shown in parentheses are NI/UK and ROI/UK when oil revenues are included in the UK figure). The ROI/UK comparison in 1985 is based on OECD PPPs but the pound sterling and IR£ are taken on a par for all earlier years.

Source: Kennedy, Giblin and McHugh (1988) except NI/UK in 1985 (Regional Trends, 1989).

Manufacturing productivity and living standards: the case of NI

Table 21.1 shows that NI's longstanding manufacturing productivity shortfall has been paralleled by a substantial gap in living standards between NI and GB throughout the period since Partition. Significantly, any progress to narrow the living standards gap has been both slow and intermittent and this is suggestive of a similar lack of progress in removing the manufacturing productivity gap (see Chapter 4). At the same time, while GDP per capita in NI has remained lower than the UK average, NI has maintained higher levels of GDP per head than the ROI despite the fact that since 1973 levels of manufacturing output per head have fallen progressively behind those in the ROI. The explanation for the continued higher living standards in NI can to some extent be attributed to the dramatic increase since the late 1960s in the level of the fiscal subvention from London to Belfast such that by the mid-1980s public expenditure within the Province was 1.5 billion higher than the tax revenue raised from NI (Rowthorn and Wayne, 1988; Hitchens and Birnie, 1989b). In other words, during the 1970s and 1980s through the rapid growth in public sector spending and employment NI was enabled to enjoy a level of living standards higher than that in the ROI but which was not warranted[1] given the enormous implicit balance of payments deficit which was developing relative to GB (Rhodes, 1986; Hitchens and Birnie, 1989b; Teague, 1989).

In the absence of this continued subsidisation by taxpayers in GB, NI would be forced to try to close this "trade gap" by means of a massive deflation which would cause levels of GDP per head to fall below those in the ROI and perhaps further (Rowthorn and Wayne, 1988). It is notable that in spite of being denied the advantage of access to GB taxpayers money the ROI has steadily narrowed the gap between output per head in the North and the South[2] since the strong set back to comparative GDP per capita imposed by the Second World War. While the marked increase in NI public spending in 1970s may have maintained relative living standards in the short run, it has failed to establish the preconditions for long run self-sustained growth in the private sector and as a result the ROI has continued to catch up on NI in terms of GDP per head. One of those preconditions is a much greater measure of competitiveness in the manufacturing sector and the tradeable goods and services sector generally.

Manufacturing productivity and living standards: the case of the ROI

Table 21.1 shows that comparative GDP per head in the ROI fell during 1926-47 (largely as result of the impact of the Second World War; Kennedy, Giblin and McHugh, 1988) and remained stagnant relative to the UK throughout the 1950s (perhaps an indication of the progressive exhaustion of the benefits of the protectionist strategy pursued since the 1930s (see Chapter 19)). Since 1960 and the beginnings of the inward investment based strategy of development the gap relative to both the UK and NI has been narrowing (especially when one takes out the perhaps temporary boost to UK GDP arising from North Sea oil revenues in the 1980s). This might suggest a favourable picture where advances in the ROI's comparative manufacturing productivity have gone hand in hand with growth in relative GDP per head.

Such optimism should be qualified by recognition of the growing divergence between the levels of GDP and GNP in the ROI, i.e. as a result of international factor payments the value of output within the ROI is no longer a reliable indicator of the level of national welfare. Mainly because of outflows of profits from the MNEs in the ROI as well as repayments on international debt by the mid-1980s the level of GNP per capita was 10 per cent lower than GDP (NESC, 1989). Even if the GDP figures are taken at face value, the relatively rapid economic growth during recent decades has only been sufficient to restore the ROI's GDP to a level relative to that of the UK not very much higher than achieved immediately prior to independence (in 1913 GDP per capita in the 26 Counties which were to form the Irish Free State has been estimated as 61 per cent of that in the UK (Bairoch and Levy-Leboyer, 1981))[3]. Moreover, this comparatively slow progress appears disappointing given that the level of output per head in manufacturing in the 1980s was substantially higher than that in the UK.

A number of factors provide the immediate explanations of ROI's comparatively poor living standards in spite of the impressive productivity performance of manufacturing. In the first instance, even the very rapid progress in the ROI's employment and output between the late 1950s and early 1970s was still insufficient to achieve that level of industrialisation which other countries achieved at a comparable historical stage of their developmental process. Moreover, the growth of manufacturing employment has not been high enough to guarantee something approaching full employment. The 200,000 manufacturing employees in the late 1980s represented about 20 per cent of the employed labour force. This proportion was similar to that in GB and slightly higher than that in NI. Nevertheless, given the chronically poor performance of manufacturing in both GB and NI (i.e. de-industrialisation) neither constitute proper standards of comparison. Consideration of more successful manufacturing nations (e.g. Japan and West Germany) or other late starters to the industrialisation process indicate that the ROI might have expected to have increased the share of manufacturing in total employment to 35-40 per cent by the late 1980s. This would suggest that the ROI should have had as its target a manufacturing employment of about 400,000 instead of 200,000[4].

Not only is the ROI manufacturing sector small but the converse of this is that other sectors with low levels of comparative productivity are "too large". While agriculture represents about 3 per cent of UK employment its share in the ROI is about 15 per cent. Ferris (1989) estimates that GDP per employee in farming in the ROI was 79 per cent of that in GB.

The living standard of the ROI in the mid- and late 1980s are further depressed by the very high levels of unemployment (227,000 in 1986). In fact, just as in NI, at the end of the 1980s the number of those unemployed was larger than those employed in the manufacturing sector. As a result of high unemployment and a relatively small manufacturing sector the proportion of the ROI population which is in employment is unusually small when compared to most other industrial economies; in 1986 only 30 per cent of the population were members of the labour force compared to 43 per cent in the UK, 45 per cent in the USA, 48.2 per cent in Japan, 41.4 per cent in Germany, 37.8 per cent in France, and 45.9 per cent in Canada (HM Treasury, 1989). In short, partly for demographic reasons, too few persons are in work and too few of these are employed on highly productive activities (partly because of the ROI's failure to generate enough internationally competitive manufacturing and tradeable services enterprises). The relationship between manufacturing productivity and living standards in Ireland is therefore more complex than might be at first thought. Nevertheless manufacturing still matters.

Improvements in manufacturing productivity a necessary condition for higher GDP per capita: in NI and the ROI

An increasing dependency on public spending and subvention from GB has only been able to roughly stabilise NI living standards. The gap relative to GB is still substantial and it seems certain that no British government of whatever ideological complexion would allow levels of public spending in the Province to rise to those levels necessary to remove the gap in living standards (spending per head of the population is already substantially higher than in England, Scotland or Wales). By implication the private and tradeable goods and services sectors will have to be the engines of growth in the future. Given that manufacturing is in general the principal source of extra-regional exports (Harris, 1987) for UK regions, and the lack of any substantial evidence that NI's producer services (see below) are capable of filling the gap created by the deficiencies of manufacturing within the Province, then this throws the policy maker back upon an improvement in manufacturing competitiveness as being a necessary condition for higher living standards and (in the long run) employment[5].

Manufacturing also remains central to the economic development agenda for the ROI. The ROI may have more scope for increasing productivity, exports and employment in the services sector (e.g. tourism and banking and finance) but international comparisons (both contemporaneous and historical) strongly indicate that the manufacturing sector is still too small. In other words, the ROI's industrial revolution is still incomplete and it is how the ROI could generate an additional 100,000 or 200,000 jobs in manufacturing which needs urgent attention on the part of policy makers. Part of the answer is likely to involve improvements in manufacturing efficiency and competitiveness especially among indigenous firms (where problems of low productivity, low quality, and high costs may be concentrated with consequent failure to generate rapid employment growth; see Chapters 19 and 20).

Constraints on productivity improvement: introduction

This section will consider four factors which have commonly been considered constraints on the achievement of higher productivity levels and improved manufacturing performance in NI and the ROI and also as obstacles to the general economic development of Ireland: a disadvantageous dependence on products and industries which face weak demand conditions, the probable negative net effect of greater market liberlisation within the EC, the costs arising from the political violence in NI (the Troubles) and the impact of culture in Ireland. The aim will be to not only to outline possible mechanisms whereby these factors could affect industrial efficiency and growth but also (if possible) to evaluate the size of their impact and the extent to which they could be overcome given appropriate policies.

The constraints: the role of demand

It has traditionally been argued that the past performance and future prospects for manufacturing in NI and the ROI has been hindered by a relatively heavy dependence on those industries and product types which are in secular decline throughout the Western, industrial world (perhaps because of reasons of the product life cycle or low cost competition from the NIC (Newly Industrialised Countries): Vernon, 1966; OECD, 1988). The apparent accidents of economic history or geography are used to explain the over-representation in Ireland of such structurally declining industries as textiles, clothing, shipbuilding, basic food processing, cigarettes and spirits (Daly, 1981; Kennedy and Ollerenshaw, 1985). A more sophisticated approach has been to stress the role of barriers to entry (usually large economies of scale) in preventing the development in Ireland (and especially the ROI) of large and medium sized indigenous firms competitive in the "modern industries" (e.g. electrical and mechanical engineering and chemical based) where the elasticities of world demand are typically high and competition from NIC is usually weak (O'Malley, 1989).

In Chapter 5 we traced the impact of industrial structure on NI's comparative productivity and this was shown to be both substantial and negative. However, it was also noted that the size of the structural effect on NI's comparative productivity was decreasing over time as NI's industrial structure became more similar to that of GB. Chapter 19 demonstrated that the ROI's experience has contrasted to that of NI in that the manufacturing sector has been characterised by an over-representation of certain industries with high levels of output per head (e.g. pharmaceuticals, electronic engineering and computer related). It has been this "modern" and almost entirely foreign owned sector within ROI manufacturing which has been largely responsible for the rapid productivity and output growth during recent years (see Chapter 19; Baker, 1988). By contrast, the indigenously owned firms in the ROI include an over-representation (relative to GB) of such low productivity activities as clothing and textiles and their output and productivity growth performance has continued to be poor (see Chapter 19; O' Malley, 1985a, 1989; Baker, 1988). In order to evaluate to what extent a disadvantageous industrial sector will continue to handicap the performance of manufacturing in Ireland the strengths and weaknesses of the portfolio of industries in NI and the ROI is considered given likely trends in demand.

Demand prospects for NI manufacturing

Unless they achieve a greater degree of diversification a large number of activities in NI will almost certainly continue to face adverse world demand conditions. For example, the electrical generation equipment industry will probably continue to be characterised by over-supply throughout Western Europe allied to a very low demand for new power stations in the UK during the 1990s (Financial Times, 1989, January 11). The UK textile machinery industry has suffered a long run decline which has been especially marked since the 1950s as the German, Swiss and Italian machinery producers have increased their market shares (Rothwell, 1982). Unfortunately a substantial revival of textile machinery manufacture is unlikely given that the number of major producers in the European and world market is likely to increase in the near future. Japan has already begun to challenge Germany and the entry of East Asian NIC is probable. Moreover, to the extent that the surviving British firms have concentrated in the less sophisticated segment of the market they may find that this part of the market comes under increased pressure from lower cost producers in East Germany and Czechoslovakia.

Although the future of the UK garments and textiles industry as a whole is questionable the outlook for NI may be especially bleak. There is a higher representation of those lines which are especially sensitive to the effects of NIC competition (NI Economic Council, 1987; Kurt Salmon, 1988) and such competition would be intensified if the Multi-Fibre Agreement is re-negotiated or if entry of the UK into the EMS forces the exchange rate to be maintained at a high level. Another problem for the NI carpets and clothing industry in the 1990s arises from its heavy dependence on a single customer; Marks and Spencer (NI Economic Council, 1987). Whilst the advent of the European Single Market makes it more likely that Marks and Spencer will be able to increase the number of outlets throughout Continental Europe (hence boosting the demand for NI garments and carpets) there remains the danger that it will also adjust its traditional "buy British" marketing and purchasing strategy to the detriment of NI suppliers (by moving up market to higher quality goods with lesser standardisation; Financial Times, 1988, April 28, and September 13, and 1989, January 31; and The Times, 1988, May 9).

Present trends of falling UK consumption of cigarettes and beer will almost certainly continue. The two mainstays of the NI food processing industry (dairies and beef) face two major difficulties in the 1990s. First, income elasticity of demand for their basic products is much less than unity in most industrial economies, and, second, the Commission of the EC is likely to place increasingly severe restriction on both the quantity of output while insisting on higher standards of quality.

Intensifying competition from the NIC casts doubt on the continued survival of even a residual man-made fibres industry in NI (Financial Times, 1988, June 8). At the same time the prospects for the application of new materials to consumer products look good (Roberts, 1990). NI may have some expertise in this area as a result of the ill-fated Lear Fan project.

The success of privatised Harland and Wolff and Shorts will partly depend on the trends in the world market for ships and aircraft in the 1990s. Future growth in Shorts can be expected to be based on one main strength; the supply of components to major manufacturers of airliners. Shorts is a contractor to Boeing which can expect strong demand throughout the next decade as the world's airlines engage in replacement expenditure. Of a more uncertain nature are the prospects for Shorts output of guided missiles. In 1987 their defence work (i.e. almost entirely missiles) represented 44 per cent of the company's turnover as compared to a 39 per cent of output on civilian work (Company Reports). Shorts was thus more dependent on missiles work than either British Aerospace (missiles/civilian 16/34 per cent) or the principal German aerospace concern MBB (27/25 per cent missiles/civilian). While an optimism about missiles' sales might be grounded on the possibility of a diversion within constrained defence budgets from very expensive jet fighters to guided weapons, it is also possible that the reduction in military spending in real terms in the 1990s will be so great that the absolute size of expenditure on guided weapons will fall. The third main factor in Shorts future is its own commuter aircraft programme but this is likely to be of declining importance as the aircraft designs become relatively aged. The Canadian purchasers of Shorts have said that they wish to use Belfast as a production site for a 50-100 seat aircraft. As a private firm Shorts will now have to reckon with the fact that even the best European aerospace firms tend to be out-performed by their US counterparts in terms of profitability (because of less scope for economies of scale).

Whilst there is room for cautious optimism about parts of the aerospace industry the prospects for shipbuilding are more uncertain. Various sources forecast an upturn in world demand for bulk carrying shipping which will start some time before 1992 and continue for the rest of the 1990s. The future of a privatised Harland and Wolff will depend critically on the accuracy of these forecasts and movements in the relative price of material and labour inputs in Europe and the Far East given that there seems to be return to emphasis on bulk tankers (it is not clear to what extent the strategy of the Belfast yard will be compatible with the EC Commission's strategic directive for European yards to vacate the production of low value-added vessels in favour of the Koreans).

Not only is there ambiguity as to the demand prospects for shipbuilding and aerospace but a similar situation may apply to another major employer, the linen industry. Prospects for basic yarn production appear least optimistic given intensifying Italian and Far Eastern competition. Some growth has been forecast in the use of linen as a fashion material (IDB, 1985) but despite this some of NI's largest producers cut-back their employment at the start of the 1990s.

The demand prospects for some parts of the NI engineering industry may be more assured. For example, as long as Ford and General Motors maintain their share of the European car market and that market continues to grow then the demand side prospects are good for the two motor component firms in the Province which are dependent on these American companies although some concern might be generated by the possibility that the Japanese plants now operating in England would expand their sales at the expense of the Americans. It is also worrying that General Motors are planning to concentrate their component sourcing at suppliers which lie withing a 100 mile radius of one of their assembly plants (NESC, 1989).

Demand for electrical and electronic consumer durables and telecommunications products is likely to undergo moderate growth during the 1990s. However, the strongest growth is likely to be concentrated on advanced products such as microwaves and high definition TV which are not so far represented among NI manufacturing activities. In this context the recent decision by the Korean company Daewoo to locate a video-recorder factory in NI is encouraging if it heralds the start of a wave of Far Eastern consumer electronics investment in NI industry (though such optimism would have to be qualified according to the amount which has to be paid in industrial assistance in order to bring such firms to NI and keep them there).

Demand prospects for ROI manufacturing

Turning now to the portfolio of industries in the ROI much of what was said for NI can be repeated. For example, the doubts expressed as to the future demand for carpets, clothing, cigarettes, dairy and beef products also apply to these activities in the ROI (Telesis, 1982; Sectoral Development Committee, 1983a, 1985a; NESC, 1989).

To a much greater degree than NI, the mechanical engineering industry (Sectoral Development Committee, 1983b) in the ROI has been dependent on agricultural machinery. With the exception of specialised products the demand prospects for this sort of machinery are not good. During the 1970s the small scale metal articles industry in the ROI experienced strong growth mainly on the back of domestic demand. Prospects for the 1990s are less favourable given that the advent of the EC single market combined with the introduction of flexible manufacturing technology may give larger scale Continental producers major cost advantages relative to their ROI competitors (NESC, 1989).

The continued existence of the publicly owned steel making industry in the ROI will depend critically on the extent to which EC Commission allows the Dublin government to maintain high levels of subsidies (in 1986 each tonne of finished steel produced in the ROI was subsidised at a rate 70 per cent higher than the EC average (Financial Times, 1987, December 7)).

The demand for pharmaceutical products has experienced very rapid growth during recent decades (Sectoral Development Committee, 1985b; Commission of the European Communities, 1988) but there are uncertainties as to the future. For example, growth in the demand for drugs by American and European public health services may be constrained by government cost cutting exercises. On the other hand, assuming that the public sector procurement of drugs is successfully liberalised as a result of the provisions of the 1992 project, then some multinational pharmaceuticals firms may choose to use the ROI as their production location to service the whole of the EC (whether they do this will depend critically on factors such as the profit tax incentives in the ROI and adequacy of the supply of trained labour). The prospects for the motor components industry in the ROI (2,700 employees; NESC, 1989) is uncertain given the demise of vehicle production in the ROI and the possible centralisation of supplies by Ford and General Motors. The ROI shares with NI an under-representation of those advanced electrical and electronic consumer goods which can expect buoyant demand during the 1990s. However, unlike NI, the ROI does have a well developed computer components industry (Sectoral Development Committee, 1986). If this industry is to continue its previous rapid output growth it will have to switch away from basic production runs (e.g. capacitors) where it is becoming increasing uncompetitive on cost relative to Singapore, the Phillipines, Mexico and other NIC. The outlook remains brighter for the production of those wafer fabrication semiconductor chips which the Japanese NEC and Fuijitsu have chosen to site in the ROI (i.e. the ROI is starting production at an early stage in the product life cycle (Financial Times, 1989, February 2)).

Demand prospects for NI and the ROI: conclusions

One important conclusion to be drawn from this analysis is that from the perspective of demand prospects both NI and the ROI have mixed portfolios. Both NI and the ROI share certain activities which will continue to face the prospect of structural decline throughout the 1990s; textiles, clothing, linen yarn, dairy and beef products, cigarettes and alcohol. In addition the demand side outlook is probably bleak for the electrical generation equipment and textile machinery industries in the north and the motor components and steel industries in the south. The demand for ships, aircraft, man-made fibres and agricultural machinery is also uncertain. Taken together these groups of industries with weak or uncertain demand prospects represent roughly one-half of manufacturing employment in NI and three-tenths in the ROI.

At the same time, the existing industrial structure in NI has the following strengths from the point of view of demand prospects; telephones, application of synthetic materials to manufacturing and car components. The following ROI activities can probably look forward to favourable demand prospects;

micro-electronics, especially very high scale integration electronic components, some telecommunications and pharmaceuticals.

While it is true that in both parts of Ireland the industries which can be identified as having favourable demand prospects are much smaller than those where the demand outlook is more pessimistic, the output and productivity growth in any industry is always the outcome of the interaction of supply side and demand side forces (Marshall, 1919). Thus, an activity characterised as being in structural decline throughout the Western economies may still show considerable growth in individual countries where an appropriate supply side response has been achieved. Part 3 illustrated how German manufacturers were in general adapting much better to declining demand through supply side changes than their matched NI counterparts. The comparison of matched clothing firms provided a good example of this since the Germans had consciously designed product and management strategies to ensure a competitive edge relative to low cost garments coming from the NIC. These strategies included achieving a price premium through being able to provide European retailers with small batches of fashion ware at very short notice. By contrast, the NI clothing managers saw no need to change strategies which had achieved employment growth in the past through reliance upon very long runs of standardised products (the divergence between German and NI management strategies in clothing is explored in more detail in Hitchens, Wagner, and Birnie, 1990) even though this growth had been heavily dependent on large scale investment in inflexible machinery allied to reliance to narrow range of markets (particularly Marks and Spencer). Informed German opinion judged the NI position to be precarious, i.e. unlike its German counterpart much of the NI industry would be unable to survive the probable market trends during the 1990s. The latter part of this Chapter will consider which policies should be adopted in order to strengthen the supply side in NI. However, before doing this we will consider first whether completion of the EC's single market after 1992 will exacerbate Ireland's structural weaknesses, and then the role of the Troubles and culture in Ireland as impediments to the achievement of greater manufacturing efficiency.

The constraints: 1992, centralisation of production and removal of non-tariff barriers

Three main ways can be identified in which it is feared the advent of the EC single market after 1992 will represent a threat to the future development of manufacturing in Ireland, namely; the centralisation of production within the EC, the liberalisation of procurement policies, and the removal of existing non-tariff protection.

Implicit in the calculation of the economies of scale to be gained from the 1992 project (Pratten, 1988) is the assumption that where cost structures make it appropriate, production will be concentrated at a few locations within the EC rather than fragmented across each of the member states (NESC, 1989). Such a trend to centralisation would probably be negative in its net impact on Ireland because the manufacturing base is already small in absolute terms and Ireland has a small percentage share of the output of most commodities in Western Europe. Thus MNEs might be expected to close down their operations in NI and the ROI and expand production in GB, Germany or elsewhere. Possible exceptions exist in the case of soft drink concentrate, and some parts of pharmaceuticals and micro-electronics in the ROI where transnational firms within the EC might find it rational to re-locate production to an already large Irish production base (NESC, 1989). However, both the threats and opportunities of production centralisation may have been exaggerated. Kay (1989) argues that substantial fragmentation of the EC production will persist after 1992 because national markets will continue to be segmented from each other by differing tastes thus some of the small scale branch-plants in Ireland may be able to survive.

A further perceived threat arising from the successful completion of the internal market relates to liberalisation of procurement policies by the governments of the EC. For example, after 1992 the ROI state agencies would not be able to operate a discriminatory "buy Irish" policy as regards the purchase of, for example, clothing, wood and paper products. Similarly, in the north Harland and Wolff and Shorts could in principle face competition from mainland Continental Europe as well as GB in bidding for Ministry of Defence work. Of course, liberalisation of state purchasing policies could bring opportunities as well as threats (NESC, 1989). The internationally owned electronics and telecommunications sector in NI and the ROI should be able to compete for contracts involved in the re-equipping of the German telephone system and other European postal and telephone utilities. However, Kay (1989) once again stresses that we should not exaggerate the impact of 1992 since the relative importance of the manufacturing sectors still subject to national discrimination in procurement policies is small. Moreover, he thinks it politically realistic to be sceptical as to whether the EC Commission will attain complete liberalisation in sectors such as telecommunications, drugs, aerospace and armaments (the ROI government has itself already been accused of flouting EC liberal trading arrangements by placing restrictions on cross-border shopping).

If one accepts that the bulk of NI manufacturing and the indigenously controlled sector in the ROI are failing to maintain competitiveness with their counterparts in GB let alone producers in most of the rest of Western Europe (see Parts 2 and 3, and Chapters 19 and 20) then manufacturing in Ireland may be ill placed to gain from the reduction of non-tariff barriers (NTB) projected to occur after 1992. However, while it may be true that the indigenous sector in Ireland is critically dependent on a sheltered home market (Hitchens and O'Farrell, 1987; O'Malley, 1989) it is not clear whether the reasons for the comparative protection of the Irish market include the types of NTB which can be removed after 1992 i.e. regardless of the efforts of the EC

Commission Irish producers can expect continued protection to arise from their location within a small, peripheral market with easy access to certain raw materials (notably food products). Overall, one might deduce that the increased competitive pressure arising as a result of the single market may be relatively small. A possible exception is the textiles and clothing industry where a relaxation of the Multi-Fibre Agreement (MFA) to allow in more NIC imports would have dire implications for the NI industry (and probably its ROI counterpart; Telesis, 1982; Sectoral Development Committee, 1983a) given that it has so far failed to move as far up-market as German producers (Part 3). Even if the aggregate quote level for East Asian clothing imports into the EC remains at its present level post-1992, the abolition of separate quota limits for each of the EC members is likely to be detrimental to both Britain and Ireland given the concentration in the retailing sector (i.e. post-1992 Britain and Ireland would buy an increased share of the MFA imports into the EC).

As in the case of the projection of likely demand trends, it is important to qualify this discussion of the impact of 1992 with the recognition that what actually happens is as much dependent on Ireland's supply side response as externally determined structural and demand side factors.

The constraints: costs arising from the Troubles

It goes without saying that policy makers throughout Britain and Ireland should aim to end the NI Troubles or at the very least contain and reduce the loss of life resulting from terrorism. This commitment should remain in place even though the extent of the economic benefits which would arise from the success of such a policy are disputed. In both NI and the ROI the direct impact of the Troubles on manufacturing appears to have been small (see Chapters 15 and 19). Nevertheless, the considerable sums of public money expended on security and law and order do certainly entail an opportunity cost in terms of the benefit which would occur if such resources had been applied to industrial development instead (New Ireland Forum, 1983). However, it is doubtful if the money which was spent on security would have been made available to industrial development in the absence of the Troubles. In NI the more likely outcome would have been a lower subvention from the British Exchequer. In the ROI the consequence of lower security spending might well have been more resources for other programmes, lower taxation or a lower level of external borrowing rather than extra funding of the industrial development budget. In any case, it is by no means clear that manufacturing in either NI or the ROI was constrained by an inadequate quantity of public funding (whether the quality of that funding by way of monitoring, hands-on advice and a cost efficient allocation was sufficient is less clear). It is also doubtful whether the direct impact of the Troubles can excuse the weak performance of the externally owned sector in NI given that the Troubles can at most have been only a contributory factor in the high closure rate (Gudgin, Hart, Fagg,

Keegan and D'Arcy, 1989) amongst the external companies established before the early 1970s (the performance of the externally owned sector is considered below together with policy recommendations). Moreover, this disappointing rate of job generation and a high rate of failure continued into the late 1980s (NI Economic Council, 1990). Apart from tracing mechanisms whereby the Troubles might have influenced these trends it might be more to the point to question the appraisal and selection techniques being used by the development agencies (notably IDB) when they were evaluating inward investment.

While the direct impact of the Troubles on NI manufacturing has probably been smaller than that of either the world recession of the 1970s and early 1980s or NI's entrenched supply side weaknesses, there is the worrying possibility that the politics of NI have interacted in a complex way with the economics. Chapters 7 and 17 (and Appendix B) noted that manufacturing in NI has been and continues to be very heavily dependent on public subsidy. To the extent that the seemingly intractable political instability and violence created the perception of NI as a special case, the Troubles were a major permissive factor in the development of such a state of dependency (see Chapter 19). A further indirect cost of the Troubles may be the relatively small population of "outsiders" within NI (see Chapter 7). The reduced flows of in-migration have prevented NI from augmenting its narrow range of indigenous skills with external experience of higher productivity. Moreover, any tendency for NI to be an inward looking society has been reinforced. Despite occasional spill-overs from violence in the Northern six counties, the ROI appears to have retained a reputation for political stability (Allied Irish Bank Review, 1981). Thus, as Chapter 7 noted the ROI has received much more substantial migratory in-flows of people from other higher productivity countries. A further contrast with NI is that the counter-flow of Irish emigrants returning home to the ROI after having worked in America or on the Continent is almost certainly stronger.

Therefore, in NI and even more so in the ROI, the direct costs of the Troubles are not so large that any policy to improve productivity would necessarily require for its success a cessation of the political violence. The latter section of this Chapter will consider some of the industrial policies which could be pursued even in the face of the pessimistic assumption that political progress is unlikely in the immediate future. However, we would strongly suggest that the government in NI should implement closely monitored measures as part of the schooling process in attempt to ameliorate sectarian attitudes. While such policies are desirable in their own right we believe they would also have valuable spill-over effects to economic performance in terms of improving the attitudes of what will be the NI labour force of the future. Before outlining these policies it is necessary to consider a final possible constraint on improvements in productivity; the role of culture in NI and the ROI.

The constraints: role of culture in Ireland

This section will consider six possible ways in which the culture (or perhaps one should say cultures, e.g. north and south, Catholic and Protestant, unionist and nationalist) of Ireland may have impeded the achievement of higher levels of productivity. It should be stressed that consideration of the impact of Irish culture is necessarily a much more conjectural and subjective exercise than consideration of other factors affecting productivity presented in Parts 2 and 3 of this book. Indeed, one recent review of economic policy in the ROI noted that arguments based upon supposed features of the national character are usually "so vaguely specified and so dependent on subjective anecdotal evidence that they are ignored by those undertaking economic analysis" (NESC, 1989). Nevertheless, while we may never be able to quantify the role of culture this does not mean that it should be ignored. Part 1 demonstrated the central role which many commentators have given to British culture (i.e. attitudes, values and institutions) in explaining the long run relative economic decline of the UK. Since manufacturing in NI and the indigenous sector in the ROI have had longstanding productivity shortfalls relative to GB this presents the possibility that culture in Ireland has been inimical to the achievement of higher levels of productivity and improved industrial practise.

1. A trade off between cultural benefits and economic efficiency?

On occasions a society may in effect decide to forgo certain improvements in economic efficiency and living standards in order to preserve certain cultural characteristics which would otherwise be threatened by economic change. For example, at least until recently it appeared that a majority of Canadians placed a higher value on the advantages of retaining some tariff protection against the USA (e.g. "cultural independence") than they did on loss of consumption as a result of the failure to achieve the gains from free trade. Similarly, since independence the ROI educational system has placed special emphasis on teaching the Irish language. Presumably a majority of ROI citizens regard this as a social good. However, the preservation of that part of Ireland's indigenous culture has involved an economic opportunity cost (i.e. the benefits which would have been enjoyed if similar resources had been devoted to teaching German, French, Japanese or other commercially useful languages (Kennedy, Giblin, and McHugh, 1988)). The economist as economist has no right to tell society that it must alter its culture in such a way as to ensure maximum output of economic goods (Galbraith, 1967; Mishan, 1984) but he does have the responsibility to inform society of the economic opportunity cost implied by its cultural decisions. Only then will a democratic society be able to make a wise decision. In any case it is probable that the total cost of the specific measures taken to protect Irish culture is relatively small. In other words, it would appear to be possible to protect some desirable elements of

Ireland's culture whilst at the same time raising productivity.

However, this raises the question whether in some general sense the Irish refuse to make certain changes in their national character because, while these changes might bring economic benefits in train, the social cost of these adjustments are perceived to be too great. For example, it might be argued that if German productivity levels require German social attitudes and institutions then this is too high a price for Ireland to pay. According to such an argument the Irish (north and south) benefit from living in a society which is more "easy going" than that in Germany and more communitarian than America (Barry, 1989). It is certainly true that to the extent the greater authoritarianism of German social attitudes contributed to the horrors of the Nazi period they have represented a very mixed blessing from the point of view of both Germany and Europe (Prais, 1981a). We will later consider whether people in Ireland are prepared to accept a trade off of a higher quality of life (and especially human relationships) for a lower material living standard. It can in any case be questioned whether this trade off is in fact achieved, for example, certain social attitudes may impose a cost in terms of lower economic efficiency and these attitudes may be far from attractive. Thus, the so called easy going nature of Irish society (north and south) may in practise mean a damaging disrespect for the law, property and persons in authority. Strong communitarianism may also degenerate into sectarianism. The next section will consider the adequacy of the work ethic in Ireland.

2. An inadequate work ethic?

At its most unpalatable this argument appears to be a racist denigration of the Irish national characters. However, whatever the truth in these allegations they have certainly been persistent[6]. To summarise these claims, it might be argued both that employees in Ireland put too little effort into their work and that employers expect too a low a standard from their workers. Other things being equal, these attitudes would contribute to comparatively low physical productivity and product quality. The allegations of a poor work ethic in Ireland have often involved the application of the Weber thesis (Weber, 1976) as to the differing degrees of economic motivation between Roman Catholics and Protestants[7]. We will therefore consider first the extent to which the lack of the work ethic is a peculiarly Protestant or Catholic phenomenon before reviewing the evidence as to comparative state of the work ethic in Ireland as a whole.

The comparative productivity results provide little support for a neo-Weberian interpretation of modern comparative economic development in the two parts of Ireland (see Chapters 19 and 20). When the foreign owned sector in the ROI is excluded then manufacturing productivity performance of the mainly Protestant north is broadly similar to that of the predominantly Catholic south. Moreover, the more detailed results of the matched plant inquiries within NI (see Chapter 15) displayed no systematic tendency for attitudes towards work to be any better in Protestant areas as opposed to Catholic ones. What seems more likely is that the rural and small town areas of the north attain much more harmonious and co-operative industrial attitudes than some parts of Belfast and Derry (both Catholic and Protestant). In other words one religious grouping is not exclusively associated with negative work attitudes but such attitudes may be most intense where urban sectarianism has interacted with an unsettled social and educational background[8].

We will now review the evidence for the proposition that in NI in general both Catholic and Protestant have a poorly developed work ethic. Taken together, the results of the matched plant comparison and the small firms studies (see Chapter 15; Hitchens and O'Farrell, 1987, 1988a, 1988b) are strongly indicative that NI is peculiar in the extent to which obstructive and damaging attitudes to the intensity of work, workmanship and productivity improvement are evidenced. The attitudinal effects of the Troubles might be employed as one explanation why NI attitudes are not only worse than those in Germany but also than those in other British Isles regions. Chapter 15 provided supporting evidence for this thesis in that there was an association between the location of factories with acute labour problems and some of the most violent areas of NI. Perhaps significantly, Rottman (1989) argues Belfast has a position as one of the most crime-ridden cities within the British Isles if one accepts the evidence of surveys and other indicators (Craig, 1986). In other words, not only terrorism but the rate of burglaries (when measured by household surveys of victimisation) is higher than in England and Wales (the rates of reported burglaries are comparable but the value of these official statistics may be weakened by differences in (a) public reporting to the police and (b) police reporting practises (Breen and Rottman, 1985)). If the rate of "ordinary" crime is relatively high then this could suggest that parts of NI have a problem of a lack of respect for property and authority which may in part derive from the Troubles since 1969. The comparative strike rate performance of NI industry is also worth pondering (Black, 1987) since on a matched industry-by-industry basis during the 1960s, 1970s and early 1980s NI has often been more strike-prone than GB. Even if this is no longer true in more recent years this may be more the result of the much higher unemployment rate in NI than a better climate of industrial relations (see Chapter 7). While the evidence presented in Parts 2 and 3 contains a few elements of comfort (in sectors other than clothing rates of labour turnover and absenteeism may be comparable to those in Germany and in a few cases in the NI clothing industry the intensity of work effort was higher than in comparable German factories) but overall the traditional emphasis on the NI work ethic (Department of Commerce, 1982) is unsupported.

Unfortunately consideration of the strength of the work ethic in the ROI has to rest on a narrow range of secondary sources of information. Ingham and Ingham (1989) show that the average rate of days lost by strikes in the ROI economy during 1970-87 was almost the same as that of the UK. Further research is required in order to determine whether the ROI has been more or less strike-prone at a matched industry level within manufacturing. Hitchens and O'Farrell (1988b) found that small firms operating in the Shannon area did not evidence the attitudinal problems reported by proprietors of matched small businesses in the north. Perhaps more surprisingly, there was a similar failure to identify negative work attitudes in a sample of small companies which drew their work-forces from some of the most socially deprived parts of Dublin. This begs the question of why conditions which are similar to those in parts of Belfast fail to produce comparable problems of negative work attitudes? (Dublin may have escaped terrorism but Rottman (1989) shows that it shares with Belfast the distinction of relatively high rates of crime against property.) The investigation of work attitudes in the ROI might reward further research because it seems that the managers in Dublin had been successful in containing any difficulties through a combination of selective recruitment and training.

In general we would wish to stress that high quality management can overcome some of the cultural obstacles to the achievement of higher levels of productivity. The performance of the multinational firms in the ROI and (to a lesser extent) the foreign owned companies in NI suggests that any labour attitude problems which may exist in Ireland can be overcome by a mixture of external management and production techniques, superior labour force training and attention to non-Irish productivity and product quality standards. Later sections will outline some policy recommendations for NI which are either designed both to bolster the work ethic and to substitute for any deficiency in it. These include; the use of schooling to promote lesser sectarianism and greater economic awareness, attention to product quality and innovation, improvement in the standards of producer services and the quality of advice given by the public agencies.

The hypothesis then that the Irish national characters are inherently hostile to the achievement of higher productivity and efficiency standards remains unproven. Even if there were some truth in the hypothesis, the available evidence would also suggest that appropriate training of Irish managers and workers could overcome any such problems of cultural attitude. This would imply that improvements in human capital should be given much more attention by policy makers.

3. The Irish are too easily satisfied ?

A number of commentators have noted that, whereas Ireland tends to come near the bottom of the league when levels of economic development are being compared within Western Europe, when perceptions of happiness are compared NI and the ROI are placed at the top of the European league (Fogarty, Ryan and Lee, 1984). This raises the possibility that the reason productivity is low in NI and in the ROI indigenous sector is that the Irish are too easily satisfied. It might be objected that the mainstream of Western economic thought has tended to consider that individuals are their own best judges of their well being. Thus if the Irish think they are happy the economist has no right to intrude into this scene of social tranquility with the notion that Ireland must aspire to German levels of productivity (the Germans emerge at the gloomier end of the European attitude surveys; Fogarty, Ryan and Lee, 1984). However, there are a number of reasons why one is justified in regarding the present situation as unacceptable.

First, while the poll evidence may suggest the Irish are satisfied despite comparatively low levels of productivity, there may be an inconsistency in the sense that the Irish do not accept some of the economic implications of such low productivity. For example approximate wage parity with GB seems to be desired rather than wage rates which closely reflect the relative level of output per head (the possibility that Irish policy makers should restrain wage fixing is considered later in this Chapter). Not only does wage setting seem to be regarded as unconstrained by the productivity level but there is little social or political recognition of the constraints upon small open economies such as NI or the ROI (Kennedy, Giblin and McHugh, 1988). The price paid for continued uncompetitiveness in large parts of the tradeable sectors is a combination of high rates of unemployment and out-migration (and this conclusion follows all the more strongly in the case of both NI and the ROI where population growth is considerably faster than in most of the rest of Western Europe). Thus it can be argued that if the Irish were made aware of the social and economic implications of their failure to achieve higher productivity levels then they would not be so happy.

Some doubt can also be cast on the strength of the state of "happiness" in Ireland. Fogarty, Ryan and Lee (1984) show that in the ROI the least satisfaction is shown by the young, unemployed and the educated. In other words, the groups which are most likely to emigrate. This raises the possibility that over the longer run there might be a selection bias in the surveys of attitudes, i.e. those who remained in Ireland would largely be those who were relatively happy. It is also unclear how the level of unhappiness has varied over time but T.K. Whitaker (<u>Economic Development</u>, 1958) noted that economic stagnation in the 1950s had produced widespread attitudes of despair in the ROI. Thus he regarded accelerated growth of output, employment and living standards not only as being economically desirable but a psychological necessity (Lyons, 1981). It might similarly be argued that as long as mass unemployment, high out-migration and political violence (factors likely to occasion a return to such despair) persist policy makers in NI and the ROI cannot afford to relax into a complacency induced by the apparent evidence that the Irish are generally fairly satisfied.

4. A declining industrial spirit or one which never developed at all?

Perhaps one reason why some Irish people have been satisfied with a sub-standard level of economic achievement is that the modern industrial (or competitive capitalist) spirit has been too poorly developed in Irish culture. To illustrate the importance of the industrial spirit it is necessary to consider the role of culture

246

and social attitudes explaining the relative economic decline of Britain during the last one hundred and forty years (Matthews, Feinstein and Odling-Smee, 1982; Barnett, 1986 and 1987; Crafts, 1988b). Particular, emphasis has been placed on the alleged waning of the "English industrial spirit" (Wiener, 1981). It has been argued that the British establishment perceived that there was indeed a trade off between economic growth and efficiency on the one hand, and an attractive, compassionate and just society on the other. Unlike their counterparts in the USA and Germany they chose the latter[9](Johnson, 1972).

It is not clear how Ireland can be fitted into such a model of the decline of the industrial spirit given that the narrowness of NI's industrialisation during the nineteenth century and the ROI's de-industrialisation during the same period suggest that Ireland may never have developed a modern industrial ethos. Perhaps Ireland is still waiting to acquire a modern, capitalist spirit. What is certain, is that most parts of the ROI and some parts of NI have a much shorter tradition of employment in modern, factory-based industry than GB. Thus a large proportion of workers in factories in the ROI and some parts of NI includes representatives of what is only the first, second or third generation within a family to work in modern manufacturing. This comparatively late movement out of farming into industry might result in an under-developed attention to quality standards and workmanship. Our own work shows evidence. In Chapter 15 we reported that work attitudes in NI tended to be more positive in the rural areas. It should also be noted that most of the economies which had a much later movement of employment off the land than Britain, have now a considerably higher level of manufacturing productivity (e.g. France, Italy and Japan). Whatever the impact of a work-force with rural and farming roots it could be argued that there is a general backwardness in industrial ideas and practises in NI manufacturing and in the indigenous sector in the ROI. Such a backwardness would be associated with the relatively stable long run productivity shortfall relative to GB (itself a laggard in international terms). Thus the management and labour attitudes, ideas and practises prevalent in many Irish firms today might be similar to those found in GB five or more years ago. (The evidence presented in Chapter 12 which showed that by German standards the machine stock in NI was modern and up-to-date implies that the time lag behind GB is more likely to be found amongst the human resources than the physical hardware.)

A poorly developed industrial spirit in Ireland might also be exemplified by attitudes to risk taking. Certainly, the Irish education system (to the extent to which it inherited some of the features of the English approach to schooling) and the frequency of political instability could both have operated against the development of entrepreneurial and risk taking attitudes (O'Farrell, 1986). The statistical evidence of this proposition is however not straightforward. For example, the rate of small firm formation in NI is probably about average by UK standards and the ROI may be above average (O'Farrell, 1986; Gudgin, Hart, Fagg,

Keegan and D'Arcy, 1989). In other words, if new firm start ups are taken as the index of entrepreneurship, the Irish appear to be at least as well endowed with this quality as the inhabitants of GB. Unfortunately, this may be too optimistic a deduction given that the rate of state aid to business start ups in NI and the ROI is considerably higher than in GB. Moreover, as Chapter 20 indicates, firms which are established in Ireland are much less likely to achieve growth of employment and sales than their counterparts in GB. Thus traditional policies for promoting the small firms sector in Ireland may only have succeeded in shifting the consequences of poor entrepreneurship and unambitious management from one of a low rate of start ups to a low rate of growth.

Once again we would stress that this type of cultural constraint can be overcome by improved labour force training which could also compensate for the lack of a long tradition of industrial employment and discipline. If NI and ROI managers and entrepreneurs are culturally inclined to accept low growth product and management strategies because they perceive these as involving low risk then the government and its agencies should respond in several ways. Irish managers should be informed as to how their product strategies and views of future market trends differ from those adopted by companies and managers in those countries which represent industrial best practise (such international comparisons of managerial visions and techniques could be based on further comparative research of the type piloted by Hitchens, Wagner and Birnie (1990)). Such information might persuade Irish managers that continuation of their traditional approaches was in itself a high risk strategy given that the experience of Germany and other economies suggest those approaches cannot guarantee survival.

Government agencies in Ireland should not only inform business managers as to standards of international best practise in terms of value-added and competitiveness but they should provide hands-on help to ensure that some Irish managers can reach these international standards. For example, the development agencies should ensure that their personnel have sufficient competence to advise firms as to product quality, and innovation and use of producer services. Such policies are outlined in more depth in the latter part of this Chapter.

5. A cultural insularity to those ideas which would raise productivity?

Chapters 1 and 2 suggested that part of the explanation for the longstanding relatively poor productivity performance has been a reluctance to accept that other economies have been moving ahead with the result that British managers and workers have been slow to learn from the examples of best industrial practise. Not only may NI and the ROI have absorbed some of this British sense of complacency but there are some factors peculiar to Ireland which have worked to make it even more insular than GB.

The most basic of these is geographical: Ireland's location as an offshore island peripheral to Europe's offshore island (i.e.

GB). Not only does Ireland suffer as a result of the friction of distance but at least in recent decades it has experienced much less ethnic mixing than most other Western European countries. Ireland's longstanding divisions between Protestants and Roman Catholics obscures the ironic fact that the population in both NI and the ROI is in other respects much more homogeneous and certainly more Caucasian than that of most other Western societies (though the example of Japan reminds us that homogeneity does not necessarily prevent economic success). Ireland's own more distant history (e.g. Scots planters in the seventeenth century, Hugenots in the eighteenth and central Europeans after the Second World War) testifies to the disproportionate role which ethnic minorities can play in economic development (Lee, 1968, 1973).

Insularity and low living standards may sometimes be related to each other by a process of cumulative causation. Thus the comparatively low level of GDP per head in Ireland may make it difficult to establish a market there for the most up-to-date and hence expensive products. For example, if Irish clothing consumers lag behind the centres of European fashion this acts as a disincentive to local producers to establish a position at the forefront of styles and design (Chapter 11 showed that NI sample clothing firms devoted a much smaller share of resources to designing than their German counterparts). Just as Irish firms may be following GB practises after a lag of a certain number of years so the tastes of Irish consumers may be several years behind GB (and the gap relative to mainland Europe would be even more substantial).

Both parts of Ireland may have suffered an economic loss as a result of self-absorption in their own peculiar political difficulties and particularly the longstanding disputes about the Union and the Border. This argument will be examined in more depth below but it can be noted here that such self-absorption would have been a further force acting to insulate the ROI and NI from appreciation of trends in the economic development of America, and European best practise economies. On top of any such political reluctance to accept external economic ideas the force of Ireland's Protestant and Catholic religious traditions may have acted to intensify insularity. Ryan expressed the conviction of many Irish people that Ireland should not be allowed to fall into "this mid-Atlantic, cosmopolitan, secular, latter day Sodom and Gomorrah" (Fogarty, Ryan and Lee, 1984).

However, while we can list geography, ethnic homogeneity, nationalist/unionist politics and embattled spiritual traditions as factors acting to isolate Ireland from accepting the need to imitate best industrial practise, there are forces acting in the opposite direction. Since the early eighteenth century and especially since the Famine there has been a tradition of migration from Ireland to the USA. Such a tradition could have made those Irish who stayed in Ireland more receptive to American ideas of industrial practise. In the case of the ROI the post-1921 political imperative to stress independence from Britain may have made the Republic more receptive to ideas coming from other European countries. Thus, it is by no means clear how strong the net tendency to insularity is in either NI or the ROI. What it is probable is that the ROI has managed to maintain more openness given that the political system has not been as monopolised by the constitutional question. The ROI has also benefitted from the conscious cultivation of the link with America and a certain presumption in favour of American and Continental ideas as opposed to those coming from the former colonial ruler. In any case, insularity by itself does not cause relative economic decline. Indeed, as the example of Japan testifies a certain sense of separateness and moral superiority can sometimes accelerate national economic development (Morishima, 1984) albeit the Japanese case also illustrates the dangers of such chauvinism.

6. Distraction of the political and administrative elite?

On the basis of his study of nineteenth century European and North American economic history Rostow (1962) emphasised that a precondition for the take off into self-sustained economic growth was the creation of a political and administrative elite which would make such growth their first priority. It is not clear whether any such elite has yet been formed in Ireland. A case could be made for its development in the ROI since the beginning of the 1960s and the adoption of the inward investment strategy (Lyons, 1981; Irish Times, 1989, March 16; O'Malley, 1989) but the position in NI is much less optimistic (Ulster Business, 1988). To some extent the Border and security questions may have crowded out political and administrative talent (Pringle, 1989) which could otherwise have been devoted to economic issues. Ireland may represent a less severe case of the pattern found in many less developed countries where tribalistic and irredentist politics precluded a rational consideration of economic options and policies (Bauer, 1982). However, it is probable that most politicians, administrators and voters in the ROI during recent years have regarded the Border and the Northern Troubles as at worst an irritating sideshow which should not be allowed to obstruct the serious business of economic development in the South. Even in NI the true situation may be more complex since the effect of the Troubles may have been precisely the opposite of that stated above, i.e. the perception of NI political life as equivalent to Hobbes' state of nature in being "nasty, brutish and short" may have driven NI middle, professional and business classes out of political activities. Thus, if anything the attention paid to economic matters, or at least private self-enrichment, may have been increased.

The cultural constraint: a summary

It is therefore by no means clear to what extent culture in Ireland (north and south) operates as an unambiguously negative factor as regards the attainment of higher levels of industrial efficiency. What the available evidence does suggest is that any such negative influences can be overcome given appropriate policy responses (considered below). The other main conclusion to be drawn is that certain intellectual defences of Ireland's relatively poor record cannot readily be accepted. It is by no means clear that the Irish are in fact accepting their position as a relatively low productivity economy. They certainly show little inclination to accept the implications of such a position (lower wages[10] and/or lower birth rate and/or higher emigration). Nor is it clear that this relatively low level of productivity is part of the price which must be paid to protect certain desirable features of Irish culture.

Policy in NI: improvements in productivity can and should be expected

Given that improvements in productivity are the best way to achieve that increase in competitiveness required in order to reach satisfactory levels of employment and living standards, and given that the constraints on such increases in Ireland are not insurmountable, it is entirely realistic for policy makers to aim for accelerated growth of productivity (especially in the NI owned companies). Here we deal with policy in NI in detail and summarise some conclusions for the ROI at the end.

Our analysis suggests no reason why there should be any productivity difference between manufacturing in Northern Ireland and Great Britain other than that attributable to differential costs arising from the Northern Ireland location. In fact disadvantages of industrial structure and higher energy costs, and the direct impact of political violence explain only a minority of the 20 per cent productivity shortfall of Northern Ireland (Part 2). Whilst Teague (1989) emphasises the peripherality of Northern Ireland it should be noted that differential transport costs are relatively small (see Chapter 6; Hitchens and O'Farrell, 1987, 1988a, 1988b; Wood and PEIDA, 1987). NI firms may have some logistical problems when they try to sell to the markets of southern England but it is improbable that geography is the main reason why their export performance is relatively weak (Hitchens and O'Farrell, 1987, 1988a, 1988b). There is therefore nothing inherent to the Northern Ireland location which makes a much greater degree of competitiveness attainable and this is emphasised by the fact that the other UK peripheral regions (Scotland, Wales and North England) have some of the highest regional productivity levels within the UK (see Appendix D).

In considering how policy could help bring about the necessary productivity improvements we will first consider the externally owned sector and the locally owned companies and then the role of training, small firms' policy, product quality and R and D, producer services, schooling, north-south economic co-operation, the competence of the development agencies and the possibility of wage restraint. Before considering specific policy areas we will outline why there continues to be a strong case for industrial policy in NI, i.e. why the market left to itself will not produce socially desirable outcomes.

The case for industrial policy

A necessary condition of the design of an effective set of industrial policy recommendations is that such a policy is assigned a coherent and intellectually valid goal (NI Economic Council, 1990). In particular policy makers should ask what are the grounds for public intervention in the market. Apart from the traditional micro-economic approach which has identified certain market imperfections (e.g. monopoly, externalities, public goods and incomplete markets) as justifying government intervention, there are further arguments which have been used to justify policy in NI. These relate to the perceived vulnerability of NI as a peripheral region within a Western European economy where production is said to be increasingly organised on a transnational and centralised basis (Cowling, 1989). Moreover, the subsidisation of manufacturing in NI has sometimes been regarded as a device to reduce the relatively high rate of unemployment in NI (according to such a view grant payments to firms are viewed as an alternative to either a regional exchange rate devaluation or reduction in relative wage costs (NI Economic Council, 1990)).

All these approaches have some validity but lack sufficient precision to specify exactly what costs should be subsidised. The failure to ask the question "what are the subsidies for?" may produce a situation where tax payers money is scattered indiscriminately in the pious hope that even if this lacks clear economic rational perhaps a higher social goal is achieved (e.g. keeping inefficient NI workers in employment might at least keep them out of the hands of the paramilitaries). The present system of industrial subsidisation in NI is probably Pareto-inefficient in the sense that an alternative allocation of existing grant resources could make the beneficiaries better off without forcing the tax payer to provide more cash. Policy measures should be designed to alter market signals so as to promote a more rapid upgrading of the quality of the labour force and management. The theoretical justification for such a policy is the contention that a range of market outcomes are possible and hence government policy has the potential of altering the dynamic path of the economy so that the final equilibrium is a high wage, high skill, high technology one as opposed to the current position of low wages, low skills and low technology (Quigley, 1976). Unfortunately, as Chapter 17 demonstrated, the existing structure of public assistance to manufacturing may have the effect of blunting the incentive to move to a more socially desirable equilibrium because firms have been able to maintain profit levels without improving comparative skills and productivity.

The answer to the question "what should be subsidised?" is that skills and experience should be subsidised as opposed to physical capital. The traditional policy of capital subsidises has raised the standards of the capital stock towards those found in Germany without providing a labour force which is sufficiently well trained to adequately use that machinery. Policy makers should be sensitive to the fact that NI manufacturing faces a problem of inadequate external economies. There is not much industry there and that makes it more difficult and costly to establish new industries. Policy measures are therefore required in order to improve management, innovation and producer services within the region as well to ensure the highest possible level of migration into NI of highly skilled outsiders.

Inward investment

The question arises as to how much emphasis should be placed upon externally controlled firms as a means to improvements in competitiveness. In Pathfinder (1987) there is an implicit downgrading of inward investment in favour of indigenous firms (Teague, 1989). However, there is still evidence that multinationals are in general an effective means of transferring knowledge and techniques from areas of high productivity to areas of low productivity (Dunning, 1985).

There is scope for further investigation to see whether this has arisen for external investment in NI. In particular, the types and characteristics of the firms which located in NI could be compared and contrasted with those which moved to other British Isles regions. To what extent were those which came to NI below average in their level of skill and technology-intensity? Hood and Young (1983) evidence a preponderance in NI relative to other regions of the British Isles of low skill, low technology multinational plants and these may have been more vulnerable to closure after 1973 (Teague, 1987). Recent American investment in NI has been characterised by a very disappointing rate of closures and low rates of job attainment even when one excludes the most disastrous failures (NI Economic Council, 1990).

From the policy maker's perspective the key question to ask is what factors led to Northern Ireland attracting an inferior mix of international firms, especially during the 1960s before the onset of the Troubles, and hence what should be done in the 1990s to ensure that higher quality investment is attracted in the future. Whilst it is highly probable that the Troubles have reduced the quantity of inward investment into Northern Ireland (Canning, Moore and Rhodes, 1987; Gudgin, Hart, Fagg, D'Arcy and Keegan, 1989) it is much less obvious that they should effect the quality of that investment (unless it were felt that Northern Ireland was forced to take only the most risky investment projects which the Scottish Development Agency, and IDA etc. had already turned down). A relatively optimistic evaluation of the direct impact of the Troubles (see Chapter 19 and earlier in this Chapter) taken together with the conclusion that the Northern Ireland location is not significantly more costly than that of either Scotland or the Republic, implies that if Northern Ireland can ensure the quality of labour and management are sufficiently high, then there is no reason why Northern Ireland should not compete for the types of investment the Republic and Scotland have been successful with (notably, microelectronics and pharmaceuticals). That an inadequate level of labour force and management training and experience has strong and direct negative impacts on the level of physical productivity, product quality and development and machine maintenance was demonstrated by the results of the matched comparisons (see Chapters 11 and 14). Any deficiencies in Northern Ireland's skill base could be tackled by transferring to training some of grant resources previously allocated to subsidising the capital purchases of incoming plants.

It is worth noting that the rate of closure of branch-plants in Northern Ireland during the 1980s was 50 per cent higher than that of similarly depressed Tyneside and several times greater than that of two non-peripheral regions (Leicestershire or South Hampshire; Fothergill and Guy, 1989). Moreover, the rate of job attainment in IDB-assisted American owned plants during 1982-88 was as low as 8.5 per cent (i.e. of all jobs promoted only 8.5 per cent were actually in existence at the end of the period (NI Economic Council, 1990). This raises the question as to why Northern Ireland attracted inward investment from such a vulnerable selection of externally controlled firms during the 1960s, 1970s and 1980s.

One might ask whether part of the reason was a deficiency in the availability of skills. Development agency interviews with the senior management of the international firms located in NI (as quoted in IDB promotional material) might suggest that these MNEs are very happy with the quality of the NI labour force compared to that in the country of origin of the international firm. Unfortunately such claims are not unique to the MNEs in NI and may have to be regarded with some scepticism. Surveys of foreign owned firms in other assisted areas produce similarly glowing reports where the comparative productivity performances being claimed by MNE executives cannot readily be reconciled with the results of Censuses of Industrial Production. For example, 90 per cent of the MNE micro-electronics plants surveyed in Scotland claimed productivity levels better than or equal to those anywhere within company (PEIDA, Firn, Crichton and Roberts, 1986). Comparable results were found from a survey of foreign owned plants in Wales (in a survey of 114 MNEs in the ROI in the late 1970s 65 per cent reported their productivity was "good" (quoted in O'Malley, 1989)). Whilst the statistical evidence (see Chapter 6) would lead one to expect MNE plants to have higher productivity than domestically owned firms, Census of Production-based data suggests it is unlikely that MNEs in Scotland and Wales generally attain productivity levels equivalent to, say, American, Japanese or German manufacturing. (However, the results shown in Chapter 19 suggest that average MNE performance in the ROI is on par with the US.) The upbeat responses from international managers may also reflect strategic answering (i.e. what is the best way to maintain good relations with the development agency so as to enjoy continued grant payments). Alternatively, if local skills are not thought to be responsible for the poor quality of the externally controlled firms coming into the Province then some doubt might be placed on the development agencies' wisdom in attracting those types of firms into Northern Ireland. Ideally the kind of inward investment which NI should aim to receive includes MNE plants which are stand alone (i.e. not just production platforms). Such plants should have a long-term committment to training up both their labour forces and management. We recommend that public agencies should evaluate the on-the-job training currently being provided by externally controlled firms in NI (and also by the indigenous sector). The social benefits of such training would be greatest if the skills are transferable (rather than specific to the company providing the training). Since the private benefits of such transferable skills are likely to be smaller than the social we suggest that the development agencies internalise this externality by making some of the grant payments to MNEs conditional on the performance of training programmes which would be subjected to outside monitoring.

Indigenous firms

Whilst in theory the multinational firms within Northern Ireland could provide an impetus to the indigenous sector through offering scope for a sub-supply industry previous studies of this sector suggest that the indigenous firms may be incapable of rising to this challenge. When the NI Economic Council (1986b) surveyed foreign and Great Britain owned firms in the Province it discovered that rates of local sourcing were low and Northern Ireland suppliers were perceived as inferior in terms of price and technical sophistication.

The problem which NI policy makers should address is the weakness even by GB standards (and especially the standards of the peripheral areas of GB) of the indigenous sector in NI. An inward investment strategy has so far by itself not been enough to raise levels of efficiency through imitation in the locally owned sector. The root of the problem may be that in a relatively protected and isolated Irish home market, Irish firms can survive for some time without being aware that their price and quality standards are deficient relative to GB and even more so relative to European best practise (though one might expect that the completion of the EC single market will reduce the extent to which the NI and the ROI home markets are sheltered).

While previous commentators have emphasised the structural barriers preventing Irish indigenous industry from breaking into new, higher value-added activities (O'Malley, 1989) we would wish to stress that even within the existing body of locally owned firms performance has been sub-standard. This has been demonstrated by the low rate of linkage with the externally owned sector. The barriers to entry may in some cases be insuperable but there is no good reason why policy makers should accept current levels of price and non-price uncompetitiveness amongst existing indigenous firms. The next section will consider the importance of training as a means to raise competitiveness. Teague (1989) and Cowling (1989) stress the need for European regions to develop networks of indigenous firms inter-linked by the technologies and organisational structures of flexible specialisation (as

exemplified by manufacturing in parts of north Italy and Denmark;
Piore and Sabel, 1984) and the following sections will consider
some types of policy which could assist the achievement of this
goal.

Training

Previous investigations of the relative performance of
manufacturing (Gudgin, Hart, Keegan, Fagg and D'Arcy, 1989; NI
Economic Council, 1990) have deduced that the shortfall in NI's
performance can be attributed in part to deficiencies in human
capital. However, the results of the matched plant comparisons
directly demonstrate the mechanisms whereby the levels of skills,
training and experience in NI are translated into comparatively
low levels of physical productivity and value-added per head.
    While the education system in NI has its undoubted strengths
particularly in terms of educating the elite for university and
then of producing high quality graduates in certain technical
disciplines (e.g. aeronautical engineering and computer science
(New Scientist, 1987)) NI shares in the general British deficiency
as regards providing adequate technical and vocational training
for the bulk of the labour force (Financial Times, 1989, November
29). NI is doubly unfortunate in that it does not necessarily even
benefit from its success at the top end of the ability range
because a large proportion of graduates take up employment in
either GB or further afield (this may be an even greater loss to
NI given the comparative weakness of the flow in the opposite
direction; Osborne, Cormack and Miller, 1989). Consideration of
social benefits would suggest that NI education policy should be
tailored more closely to the needs of those members of the labour
force who are most likely to stay and work in NI. (The use of
schooling to promote positive economic and political development
in NI is considered below.)
    Given the traditional stress by the authorities on the supposed
excellency of the Northern Ireland "work ethic" and the quality of
the local labour force (Department of Commerce, 1982) there might
be some political opposition to any strong policy commitment to
raising technical and vocational education standards there. After
all, to admit that there could be something wrong with the
Northern Ireland labour force could have the short term effect of
discouraging some inward investment. However, to do nothing would
be to perpetuate the present position where Northern Ireland's
share of inward investment may on average be less skill-intensive
and perhaps less durable than that going to either Scotland or the
Republic.
    The large deficiencies in the quality of the shop-floor labour
force in NI are paralleled by the narrowness of width, depth and
appropriateness of the training and experience gained by a
significant proportion of management in NI relative to their
counterparts in Germany (see Part 3 and especially Chapter 14;
Hitchens, Wagner and Birnie, 1990). (This narrowness is likely to
be especially marked in the indigenous sector whereas in the

externally owned sectors there will be the benefits of some
managers who have experience of industry outside NI.) Whereas
Pathfinder (1987) stressed inadequate marketing and corporate
structures as major obstacles to international trading, the
evidence of the matched plant studies (see Part3; Hitchens and
O'Farrell, 1987, 1988a, 1988b) indicates that it is not inadequate
marketing or financing which prevents the world from buying Irish
products but the fact that they are often of poor quality whilst
being too expensive. Once again, this NI problem is paralleled by
a general British failing (Saunders, 1978; NEDO, 1979; Parkinson,
1984) but the existence of a productivity gap between NI and GB is
indicative that the difficulties in NI are even more intense.
Detailed comparisons of management and product strategies in NI
and Germany have also suggested that some managers in NI are
deficient in foresight, i.e. the Germans have adopted strategies
which are more likely to enable their companies to survive
probable medium-term changes in demand and market structures
(Hitchens, Wagner and Birnie, 1990). (A parallel British problem
has been identified by Campbell, Sorge and Warner, 1990.) By
implication the focus on managerial upgrading should be shifted
towards making the Northern Irish aware of external quality and
productivity standards and of facilitating their own improvement
in these respects. In particular, research and policy responses
should concentrate on the extent to which R and D, product quality
and product and management strategies in NI differ from those
found in exemplars of industrial best practise (Hitchens, Wagner
and Birnie, 1990).

Enterprise and small firms growth

One of the Pathfinder (1987) taskforces was given the objective of
correcting a supposed deficiency in enterprise in Northern
Ireland. Such policy emphasis implies that the rate of new firm
start ups was less than the average for Great Britain but there is
some doubt as to whether this is in fact true (Gudgin, Hart, Fagg,
Keegan, and D'Arcy, 1989). There is at least the possibility that
Northern Ireland really suffers from too many start ups. That is,
a very generous rate of grant aid supports poor quality
entrepreneurialism which would otherwise not be viable. The grants
raise the birth rate of firms but their subsequent growth remains
poor (Hitchens and O'Farrell, 1987, 1988a, 1988b). Perhaps NI
should imitate the policy response recommended in the ROI; grants
should be given on a two-tier basis with a lower rate of automatic
assistance being supplemented in those cases where a firm had
demonstrated an ability to grow (Kennedy and Healy, 1985). In any
case, even if start ups were fewer in Northern Ireland than Great
Britain the situation might still be more complex than Pathfinder
implied. A comparatively low rate of new firm formation in NI
manufacturing could be a rational response by the labour force to
market signals (such as well paid, secure employment in the public
sector) rather than a demonstration of a cultural disinclination
to entrepreneurship. Such market failure would require government

action to review and if necessary change the structure of incentives. Grant aid to the indigenous sector in NI should be more tightly linked to the attainment of performance targets in terms of such variables as physical productivity, product quality and management and labour force training. A Centre for Inter-Firm comparisons should be created so as to monitor such indicators of comparative performance (Hitchens and O'Farrell, 1988a). The success of such a Centre will depend critically on the extent to which its financial and constitutional arrangements enable it to maintain full independence from government agencies in NI.

Product quality and product development

Teague (1989) stresses the relevance to NI of such examples of regional manufacturing development as Massachusetts USA (science-based growth) and northern Italy (flexible specialisation). Unfortunately, NI has revealed comparative weaknesses in terms of both the inputs into the production of high quality, innovative goods and the output of such products (see Chapter 11; New Scientist, 1987; Harris, 1988). While some of the deficiency in terms of rates of R and D, design input and output of innovations could be attributed to NI's dependence on branch-plants, there is also reason to stress the comparatively low quality of management and labour (see Chapters 7 and 14). Indeed, the evidence presented in Chapter 11 and elsewhere (Hitchens and O'Farrell, 1987, 1988a and 1988b) suggests that NI falls short on product quality even when the machinery used is similar or better than that used elsewhere.

Producer services

The weaknesses in NI's product quality and product development performance may be related to the characteristics of the producer services (both in-house and bought-in) used by manufacturers (e.g. banking and finance, accountancy, management consultancy, computer services, designing and marketing). There are strong indications that the producer services sector is unusually small. In 1986 private services accounted for only 27.5 per cent of total employment in NI compared to 40.2 per cent in the UK as a whole (Census of Employment). Per head of the population the output of finance and business services was only 54 per cent that of the UK in 1984 (Rowthorn and Wayne, 1988). If producer services in NI are deficient in either quantity, quality or price then this would represent additional external diseconomies for manufacturing industry. Carefully directed subsidisation may be necessary in order to reduce this obstacle to industrial expansion. Before such policies are implemented further research is required to elucidate to what extent such services in NI have a higher supply price and lower quality than comparable services in Germany. One might also wish to evaluate the quality of the business information received by NI managers through their networks and whether the development agencies have successfully filled any gaps in such information.

Schools, economic awareness, sectarianism and fair employment

That the style and content of schooling has contributed to Britain's relative economic decline has become an all too familiar litany (Chapter 2). However, changes in schooling may be required to fulfil an even more critical role in the case of NI. This is because in spite of certain broad similarities with schools in GB, the NI education system has its own peculiar characteristics.

Selective secondary level education has more or less remained intact in NI. The academic excellence of some of the grammar schools in NI alongside the weakness of the secondary modern and technical sectors has contributed to the situation where NI produces highly qualified emigrants but a comparatively underqualified local labour force (see Chapter 7). One is tempted to note the apparent irony that NI may have required comprehensive secondary education more than most parts of the UK but was almost the only major region to escape its introduction during the 1970s. However, the German case where a tripartite secondary system also operates (Prais, 1981a) suggests that the NI problem is not selection per se but the failure of the secondary modern and technical schools to achieve social prestige comparable to the grammar schools or to attain high enough standards of technical and vocational education. Technical and secondary schools throughout the UK failed to reach the standards set by their German counterparts but these schools in NI have had the added difficulty of dealing with pupils from those areas which have been most unsettled by violence (hence, perhaps, the localised problems of acutely damaging work attitudes in some parts of NI; see Chapter 15). There would therefore be a case for shifting some of the allocation of public funding away from the NI grammar schools and towards the technical and secondary schools. If the City Technology Colleges (CTCs) prove to be a success in GB then the local education authorities should regard it as priority to obtain local business support to create several CTCs in Belfast and Derry. The academic achievements of the NI schooling have often been regarded with pride but if comparison is made with Germany or Japan rather than England and Wales, then this pride needs to be qualified. The work of Prais and others suggests the enormity of the task if the output of the public education system is to reach international best practise. The average technical and secondary school-leaver especially in mathematics should be raised to the average for sixteen year old grammar school pupils and ideally that standard would be achieved at the age of fifteen (Prais and Wagner, 1985; The Independent, 1990, February 8). While detailed recommendations might best be left to educationalists, it is not clear whether the National Curriculum and inter-disciplinary pay differentials for teachers reflect these priorities.

As compared to GB, schooling in NI takes place against an even more precarious economic background. This gives added importance to the NI Department of Education's (DENI) economic awareness teaching initiative. We recommend that NI school children be told how dependent their economy is on subsidy from outsiders (i.e. the Subvention from GB). They should also be encouraged to think critically about certain aspects of received wisdom, e.g. that the NI economy has something to learn from the ROI, whether there is a strong work ethic, and that this is no more evidenced among Protestants than Catholics. One might hope that a growing recognition of the difficult economic situation facing NI would have some effect in diluting sectarianism by focusing on the economic problems which are shared by all the people of NI.

DENI has recognised that sectarian attitudes represent a unique problem for schools in NI and has instituted Education for Mutual Understanding (EMU) because "education has a significant contribution to make in dispelling prejudices and improving relationships" (Education for Mutual Understanding, 1988, Northern Ireland Council for Educational Development). We recommend research in order to establish a base-line against which EMU's success can be evaluated (i.e. the present extent and intensity of sectarian prejudices should be measured). EMU could be adapted in such a way so as to yield economic as well as political benefits. For example, pupils could be encouraged to think about the nature of the NI polity, economy, society and culture within an international perspective. Such open-mindedness might best be facilitated if the teachers charged with special responsibility for EMU were not of NI origin. Our own findings on the location of especially poor work attitudes suggest that EMU might have its greatest pay-off if resources are concentrated on schools in Belfast and Derry (i.e. where sectarian prejudice may be most marked).

While the issue of fair employment is too complex to be discussed in full here (Rowthorn and Wayne, 1988; Wilson, 1989), it can be noted that employment discrimination is likely to be related to sectarian attitudes in the work-place and the development of destructive attitudes towards work. A consideration of the possible negative and positive impacts on productivity of fair employment regulations should inform consideration of the appropriate government policies.

Turning first to potential negative effects, the opportunity cost of compliance with the legislation will include the use of management time which might otherwise have been devoted to other aspects of labour relations and productivity. If the implementation of the legislation promotes greater sectarian suspicion and division on the shop-floor this would also represent a negative effect on productivity. Thirdly, the performance of firms could also suffer if they felt obliged to hire a worker for fair employment reasons who was less appropriately qualified than an alternative recruit.

At the same time, certain potentially positive effects can also be noted. If the recruitment and promotional practises within a firm are seen to be fair this could promote greater job satisfaction amongst those workers who previously felt disriminated against by that firm. Firms with links to the US might be able to head off disinvestment or boycott campaigns if they could demonstrate to American politicians a commitment to fair employment (e.g. Shorts (Financial Times, 1990, February 7)). Thirdly, to the extent that the Roman Catholic school sector within NI has had a longstanding bias towards arts subjects as opposed to the sciences (Osborne, 1985), this might be reduced if Catholics perceived that technical and science based jobs within NI were as open to them as, say, teaching and the law. Given the need of the NI manufacturing labour force for more highly qualified managers, technicians and engineers (see Chapters 7 and 14) such a change would bring economic benefits quite apart from its political consequences.

North-south economic co-operation

The weakness of the indigenous sector in both parts of Ireland limit the gains which might be expected from increased economic co-operation across the Border. It is true that there are occasions when economies of scale would justify treating the island of Ireland as a single economic unit (New Ireland Forum, 1983) but these are unlikely to be large enough to make a critical difference to economic performance on either side of the Border (indeed such co-operation would probably have more political than economic significance). Thus the development agencies would have to be careful lest partnership between firms in Northern Ireland and the Republic of Ireland was a case of the blind leading the blind.

This is not to say that Northern Ireland has nothing to learn from the Republic of Ireland given the differences in sectoral comparative productivity levels reported in Chapter 19 (especially when foreign controlled firms are considered). For example, it might be worth imitating the way in which the Southern development agencies have been able to ride industrial development on the back of growth in tourism (craft shops). Industry in the Republic has benefited from the demand stimulated by the network of "Irish" shops in the USA. It might to possible to set up something similar for Northern Ireland (perhaps funded by the International Fund for Ireland). We would also stress that there is no reason why firms in both the north and the south should not treat the whole island as a single home market. Indeed one of the more encouraging findings from the matched plant comparison (see Chapter 11) was the extent to which some engineering firms in NI had achieved a growth in sales through exporting to the Republic (Black (1977) predicted that the development of more diversified manufacturing sectors in NI and the ROI through MNE investment would lead to an increase in the extent of north-south trade integration).

Competence and effectiveness of the development agencies

Chapter 17 outlined the evidence for the worrying possibility that previous grant assistance to manufacturing in NI has worked towards making performance worse rather than better. In the future the agencies should ensure that grants are used as springboards to greater efficiency rather than cushions against the failure of NI firms to achieve levels of productivity and competitiveness comparable to other peripheral regions within the UK. It follows from this that the demands on the competence of the agencies will become even heavier. We recommend that IDB, LEDU and other public agencies should ensure that they have sufficient expertise to scrutinise requests for grant aided purchases of new technology. They should ensure that capital purchases are appropriate and that the firms have sufficient human capital to work such machinery to its full potential. Ideally, the agencies would use a combination of in-house talent (perhaps top class industrial managers in Europe and America should be given considerable cash incentives to accept posts in the NI agencies and Hong Kong might also provide a source of future NI entrepreneurs (Financial Times, 1989, August 10)) and bought-in talent (IDB and LEDU should be prepared to pay a premium to use London and international offices of consultancy firms as opposed to relying exclusively on Belfast-based consultants). Greater use should be made of outside consultancy in order to make the evaluation of grant applications more rigorous. (Recent appraisal practise by the IDB may have included an excessively optimistic bias, i.e. selective assistance payments consistently failed to realise the promised job creation (NI Economic Council, 1990). Indeed, two firms within our sample of matched comparisons received grant payments of more than 500,000 from the IDB on the basis of promised expansion of sales and employment. In both cases within two years of the grant-aided investment employment had fallen. This suggests that both the firms and the IDB made mistakes when evaluating future demand prospects.)

The political masters (and paymasters) of the IDB and LEDU should recognise that employment generation (whether in terms of the cost per job promoted or actually realised) should not be the exclusive measure of the contribution of the agencies to industrial development. Improvements in competitiveness and value-added should be given priority over short-term employment targets because in the long run without such improvements NI manufacturing is doomed to repeat its previous dismal performance in terms of employment creation.

Policy: wages constraint and competitiveness

Whilst we have so far emphasised improvements in value-added per head as a means to greater competitiveness, a policy of wage cuts (Gibson, 1981) or at least of constraining local wage inflation to the rate of productivity improvement within the Province (Borooah, 1987) perhaps accompanied by some alterations to the structure of tax and benefit incentives in NI (Gibson, 1989), could be used to improve cost competitiveness. Such suggestions see the quest for wage parity (whether between different industries or regions) as being a major cause of structural and regional unemployment in the UK (Meade, 1982).

However, recent reviews of policy in NI (Pathfinder, 1987; Teague, 1989) have failed to consider this option which may reflect doubts as to the practicality of a policy which would have to overcome the entrenched expectations of NI employees that they should have something approaching parity with pay levels in Great Britain (Black, 1987; Harris, 1989). Even if the policy could be implemented its long term impact is unpredictable given that it would give highly skilled members of the Northern Irish labour force an incentive to migrate to Great Britain. The pool of highly qualified personnel in Northern Ireland is already proportionately smaller than in Great Britain (Chapter 7 and 15) and pay cuts would reinforce the perception amongst talented outsiders that Northern Ireland was an unpleasant place to work and live in (because of the political Troubles).

Perhaps an even more serious objection is the fact that low wages in Northern Ireland would reinforce the market signal to firms to specialise in low skill, simple products of poor quality. That is, a state of market failure would persist in which it remained profitable for NI firms to stay in those markets which most Western economies have now vacated in favour of the low wage NIC and they would receive no incentive to increase their input of training or research and development (Crafts, 1988a) towards (say) the levels of the West Germans (Prais, 1981a, 1988b; Patel and Pavitt, 1987). Nevertheless, it is possible to imagine some theoretically optimal combination of relative wage constraint in NI together with subsidies to employers (and perhaps also in some cases to the employees) which would increase their incentive both to increase the number of their employees and the training they are given.

What is certain is, as Borooah (1987) argues, that any policies for improving productivity and competitiveness can only be built on the basis of a much greater understanding of the present productivity shortfall. The authors feel that such a determination of the respective importance of capital, labour and management can only be achieved through the methodology of matched plant comparisons (Daly, Hitchens and Wagner, 1985) as described and used in Part 3 of this book. It should also be stressed that while restraint on wages should be regarded as a second best, policy makers should not rule it out as a policy option to fall back on if attempts to raise productivity fail. Policy makers should remind labour and management in Ireland that the consequences of a failure to narrow the productivity gap with Western Europe will either be a fall in relative living standards or a rise in relative unemployment (or both).

Policy in the ROI

These recommendations are necessarily more tentative that those presented earlier for NI. In the case of the ROI we are much more dependent on secondary sources in our attempt to explain the productivity gap and hence make recommendations for public policy. O'Malley (1989) has convincingly stated the case for an activist industrial policy in the ROI and Cowling's (1989) argument in terms of the need to counteract the impact of transnationalism, centripetalism and short-termism is also especially relevant to the ROI given its heavy dependence on an externally controlled sector.

One problem for policy makers is that the aggregate data for the ROI masks the underlying dualism within the manufacturing sector. Thus consideration of average levels of output growth and productivity allows the very good performance of the foreign owned sector to obscure the much weaker position of the indigenous firms (see Chapters 19 and 20). Nevertheless, one can deduce with confidence that the performance of the indigenous sector has been relatively weak. This is because the Commission on Industrial Organisation (early 1960s) and Commission on Industrial Progress (CIP, 1973) concluded that there were severe weaknesses the management of Irish owned firms. The employment performance of that sector since the early 1970s gives little ground for believing there has been substantial improvment (NESC, 1989; O'Malley, 1989). The productivity comparisons in Chapter 19 suggested that the indigenous sector in the ROI had broadly the same productivity levels of manufacturing in NI. Indeed, the available evidence suggests the ROI owned firms share some of the major problems which beset their counterparts in the north (e.g. low productivity, poor product quality, inferior quality of management and labour force (O'Farrell and Hitchens, 1988a, 1989a, 1989b)) and it is not clear whether the traditional excuses (e.g. energy and transport costs) are sufficient to explain the extent of the gap between the ROI and GB.

Locally owned firms in the ROI should aim to attain at least the productivity standards of counterparts in GB and special reference should be given to the much higher productivity levels achieved by firms in the other peripheral areas of the British Isles. At the same time they should be aware that it is by no means clear that GB standards are themselves satisfactory given the scale of the deficiency in British performance relative to international best practise.

During the 1980s the traditional emphasis on external investment as the main engine of growth in manufacturing was weakened (Telesis, 1982; Fitzpatrick and Kelly, 1985; Sectoral Development Committee, 1985a; O'Malley, 1989). Despite this, even allowing for the problems noted in Chapter 19 (e.g. the cost of incentives, the prevalence of production platforms, uncertainties arising from the product life cycle), the ROI's experience of inward investment has been a much happier one than that of NI. Since the start of the 1960s the ROI has continued to attract a breadth of inward investment which has been sufficient to raise average productivity levels. It might be objected that the rate of productivity growth in the MNE sector in the ROI has if anything been too rapid, i.e. gains to output have been achieved without increasing employment, but it is doubtful if a trade off of less productivity for more employment could have been achieved in practise. Indeed, slower productivity growth might have been translated into a more rapid decline of employment given the loss of competitiveness (O'Malley, 1989). While the level of linkages to the local economy remains disappointing the greater number of foreign owned firms in the ROI provides its indigenous sector with a wider range of role models and greater scope for start ups arising from entrepreneurs leaving employment in the externally owned sector (O'Farrell and Hitchens, 1988a, 1989a, 1989b).

Just as in NI the development of an indigenous sub-supply industry to the MNEs has so far been disappointing (O'Farrell and O'Loughlin, 1980; Sectoral Development Committee, 1986). However, O'Farrell and Hitchens (1988a) found that non-Irish firms in the Shannon area of the Republic were making some use of local suppliers there even though these were on average less price competitive compared with counterpart firms in Scotland and South East England (perhaps the multinationals were willing to trade-off higher prices for the greater convenience of a nearby supplier). While Teague (1989) described the beneficial linkages between multinationals and local firms primarily in terms of demand, O'Farrell and Hitchens (1988a) noted the positive impact of inward investment may be wider than this. The foreign owned firms in Shannon brought talented outsiders into the Republic some of whom subsequently left these plants to set up their own small businesses. Some ROI employees of the foreign owned plants also became entrepreneurs. In both cases experience of working in the multinational firm provided demonstration effects through superior standards of training, work methods, product quality and labour and management practise which may have improved the subsequent performance of the small firms.

Policy makers in the ROI may be less bound by a misconception that labour force standards are already excellent but the ROI shares with NI the problem that any industrial training system is only as good as the trainers who run it. Thus the first priority should be to raise the quality of in-company training instructors. There are also indications that a quick pay off would be derived from encouraging the movement into Ireland of outside technicians and supervisors who had wide experience of superior standards of industrial practise. Our own interviews with West German managers indicated that the work of some clothing factories in East Germany, Poland and Yugoslavia has been raised to something approaching West German quality standards as a result of placing West German technicians in those plants.

Like the IDB and LEDU in the north, the IDA and other development agencies in the ROI are most likely to gain value for money from their grant expenditure if those who scrutinise the grant applications are trained to the highest possible level. Emphasis should be given to not only financial and accountancy skills but also the technical expertise of the IDA managers so that they can adequately vet the machinery purchases of their clients. It is notable that the IDA has already in place a significant commitment to staff development (some of its managers are already taking MBAs (McHugh, 1989)).

Small firms policy in the ROI has traditionally focused on the need to raise the level of new firm formation. When comparison is made with GB this policy appears to have been a major success given that the rate of formation is now considerably higher than the UK average (O'Farrell, 1986; Gudgin, Hart, Fagg, Keegan and

D'Arcy, 1989). Unfortunately, as in NI the comparative growth performance of ROI small firms appears disappointing (O'Farrell and Hitchens, 1988a, 1989, 1989b). In order to combat these problems Kennedy and Healy (1985) recommended a much more hands-on, proactive and selective approach by the agencies in the ROI. Such commitments reinforce the need to ensure the highest possible levels of management training and experience amongst the personnel of the development agencies.

In the ROI the gap between the level of wages and those in the UK has also narrowed substantially (Ray, 1987; O'Malley, 1989) though it is unclear to what extent wage bargaining in the ROI is linked to that in the UK (a deliberate attempt to gain parity and the role of migration in creating characteristics of a common labour market are possible mechanisms; Ruane, 1980). A further complication is that at least in principle the ROI has the ability unlike NI to depreciate its exchange rate relative to GB. Whether any such nominal depreciation of the IR would lead to a sustained improvement in cost competitiveness depends on how one thinks the ROI wage bargainers would react to an increase in import prices[11]. It should however be stressed that given the existence of a substantial productivity advantage relative to the UK the foreign owned sector in the ROI does not share NI's problem of relatively high unit costs (O'Malley, 1989). However, in the relatively low productivity indigenous sector there might be scope for restoring cost competitiveness through wage reductions (O'Malley, 1989). Nevertheless, it should be noted that if there is any deficiency in the comparative quality of labour used in the ROI indigenous sector then lower wages would provide a market signal for this position to be reinforced.

Before more detailed recommendations can be made for industrial policy in the ROI research should be conducted to investigate the possible reasons for productivity differences between NI, the ROI and GB. This research would consider such factors as industrial structure, capital intensity (Black, 1977), and management and labour force qualifications.

Productivity and policy in Ireland: conclusions

Efficiency, competitiveness and reduced reliance on public subsidies are all things which matter for the future development of industry in both NI and the ROI. Whilst in principle greater cost competitiveness could be achieved through constraining the rate of wage inflation within the ROI and NI, this would pose great practical problems. However, the IDB and IDA and other relevant development agencies can influence the behaviour of both the externally controlled and indigenously owned sectors and both of these have a role to play in achieving improved competitiveness through higher levels of value-added per head. Externally controlled firms can provide favourable demonstration effects to the other firms within Ireland. They may be able to make the indigenous firms more aware of outside management and product quality standards. Whether the locally owned firms will be able to rise to these standards depends critically on their own stock of management and labour force skills. Such skills should be augmented by public subsidy of training by encouragement of the in-movement into Ireland of widely experienced outsiders (one of the potential benefits of inward investment is the number of highly skilled outsiders which this could bring into the island).

It is important to realise that the performance of NI and ROI industry in the 1990s and the first decades of the twenty-first century will be absolutely critical in determining to what extent certain favourable outcomes are achieved in the overall NI and ROI economies (reduced unemployment and migration and higher living standards). The evidence reviewed here indicates that manufacturing industry in Ireland (which represents the major part of all tradeable goods and services industries) is both relatively small and relatively inefficient (especially when indigenously controlled) as compared to its counterparts in GB, and even more so compared to elsewhere in the industrial world. This has negative implications for the attainment of higher living standards and employment. Certain major Irish industries (such as textiles, clothing, cigarettes, spirits, man-made fibres) can expect unfavourable demand conditions during the 1990s. Such adverse demand shifts will be a function of; the slowing of the UK economy after the over-heating during 1985-88, the effects of the completion of the European Internal Market, and intensified competition from the low wage Newly Industrialised Countries. Other industries can anticipate more buoyant demand prospects during the 1990s (aerospace, telephones, telecommunications, computers and software, motor components, paper, plastics and furniture). However, movements in demand are only half of the story. The question arises as to whether NI and ROI management and labour are sufficiently widely skilled and experienced to achieve the levels of product quality which present German performance suggests will have to be produced by industry in the West during the 1990s (that is, if it wants to head off competition from low labour cost economies).

A number of policy recommendations have been made. What is not a valid option is to attempt to maintain the status quo. This is because the existing type of state aid to industry has reinforced the market profitability signals to firms in such a way as to give them little incentive to move towards German levels of skills and product quality. In the absence of an upgrading of skills and product types Northern Ireland, already the lowest productivity region within a national economy which is itself outclassed by almost every other Western economy, may come to occupy a precarious position between the advanced economies and the Newly Industrialised Countries of the Third World (and perhaps Eastern Europe as well). On the one hand Northern Ireland will be unable to compete in the sorts of sophisticated markets where Germany operates, but on the other with the existing level of wages Northern Ireland will be uncompetitive relative to such countries as Brazil. For their part, policy makers in the ROI face the problem of managing a dualistic manufacturing structure. Thus the multinationals may be doing very well and this to some extent masks the possibility that the indigenous firms in the ROI are facing the same difficulties as their counterparts in NI.

Perhaps one theme above all others has run through the research on which this book is based. This is that there needs to be a much greater awareness of Ireland's position relative to external standards of industrial practise, performance and competitiveness. While GB may present itself as the most obvious standard of comparison we would also wish to stress that Ireland's economic future will only be secure if it can look beyond GB towards the international exemplars of best practise.

Notes

1. Unwarranted in the sense that the NI tradeables sector (i.e. mainly manufacturing) is unable to sell enough extra-regional imports to pay for the import of these services. Whether the high level of public spending in NI can be warranted on grounds other than productive efficiency (e.g. the levels of violence or poverty) is another question (NI Economic Council, 1989).

2. If NI, like the ROI, had to finance its excess of expenditure over output during 1970-89 by borrowing on international capital markets then it would have built up an astronomic level of debt (in practise it is unlikely that even the banks which indulged in the Polish and Brazilian debt debacles of the 1970s would have continued to lend to NI at such levels).

3. The social cost of the ROI's continuing inability to achieve substantial convergence with the level of living standards in GB has been considerable. Conditions of absolute poverty have been intensified by a degree of inequality which may be more substantial than in most other Western societies. Further parallels with a Third World economy are suggested when foreign debt is considered (a per capita level three times that of Mexico; Economist, 1987, January, 18) and the outflows of interest payments have further depressed the ROI's Gross National Product. Unlike NI, the ROI has so far been unable to attract sufficient external subsidisation so as to avoid the penalties of being a low productivity economy (at same time, net transfers from the EC are not inconsiderable; 4.9 per cent of GDP in 1986; Financial Times, 1988, July 21).

4. The need to further expand the size of the ROI manufacturing sector has been recognised by the chairman of the National Economic and Social Council, Padraig O hUiginn "We should have around another 100,000 engaged in industry if we were to have an industrial sector of the relative size of other small countries. We will be unable to generate employment, growth and higher standards of living unless we develop an indigenous sector comparable with... other small economies" (quoted in New Scientist, 1987).

5. The tradeable services in Northern Ireland may have their own special problems (for example, the impact of the Troubles on tourism, and the impact on the financial sector of the dependency on externally controlled firms), though they also have certain areas of revealed comparative advantage (e.g. agricultural development services and health care expertise and training; Financial Times, 1987, October 9; Economist, 1988, March 26). It is therefore unclear to what extent development of the tradeable services could substitute for manufacturing though it would not be unreasonable to aim for a level of service exports per head comparable to the Great Britain regions outside London. Particular emphasis should be placed upon developing those service industries which could absorb those high quality skills which Northern Ireland does appear to produce (for example the output of computer science graduates from the two universities).

The prospects for computer and tourist based services in the ROI may be better than for these industries in NI (tourism already contributes 5 per cent to the ROI's GDP, i.e. more than three times as much as in NI; Coopers and Lybrand Deloitte, 1989). Moreover, banking and finance, itself the fastest growing component of services in most industrial economies, registered a rate of employment growth four times that of the OECD average during the late 1970s-early 1980s. However, it should be recognised that even in the ROI the extent to which services exports and employment can substitute for manufacturing is likely to be small (O'Malley, 1989). Thus in 1987 total employment in IDA-assisted tradeable service projects amounted to only 5700, i.e. less than 3 per cent of the number employed in manufacturing.

6. One of the earliest critics of the Irish attitude to work was Giraldus Cambrensis (twelfth century). "The Irish neither employ themselves in the manufacture of flax or wool or in any kind of trade or mechanical art, but abandon themselves to idleness and are immersed in sloth. Their greatest pleasure is not to work; their greatest wealth is to enjoy liberty". However, while Malthus (1808) blamed "indolent habits of workmen in general" for the comparatively low wages in Ireland he also attributed this to a "deficiency of manufacturing capital". It is also worth noting that an emphasis on incentives as opposed to culture also had its early adherents. Petty (1691) claimed "Their Lazing seems to me to proceed rather from want of Imployment and Encouragement to work". Even some of the Irish themselves have sometimes taken a very dim view of Irish culture and heredity. Despite being a native of Dublin Edward Carson took no care to disguise a view which might today be regarded as racist "The Celts have done nothing in Ireland but create trouble and disorder. Irishmen who have turned out successful are not, in any case I know, of true Celtic origin".

An interesting sidelight on the economic impact of Irish culture is thrown by the reaction of many American employers to the Irish immigrants of the nineteenth century. Because of a perception that the Irish made bad workers "No Irish" signs were common (Majewski,

1989). However, it is probable that discrimination is now much less common in US labour market (Times, 1987, March 20). If this is because the Irish-Americans have successfully absorbed American values towards work and enterprise then this could imply than training and education can in the long run overcome any cultural obstacle to productivity improvements.

7. A number of commentators were not slow to attribute the industrialisation of the Lagan valley area of Ulster to the preponderance of Protestants in that area (especially those of a Scottish, Presbyterian background). Thus the Reverent Henry Cooke told the General Assembly of the Church of Scotland in 1836 "Our Scottish forefathers were planted in the wildest and most barren portions of our lands...Scottish industry has drained its bogs and cultivated its barren wastes, filled its ports with shipping, substituted laws and cities for its hovels and clachans and given peace and order to a land of confusion and blood". In his Political Economy (1832) Thomas Chalmers wrote "The law, the commerce, the industry, the Protestantism, the advanced civilisation of England have elevated the habits and state of the general community there". (i.e. in Ulster.)

Conversely, the comparative lack of development in the rest of Ireland was blamed on the practises and beliefs of a largely Roman Catholic population. Max Weber (1976) writing at the turn of the century and basing his hypothesises on statistical evidence collected in Germany in the 1890s (from the state of Baden) provided a theoretical underpinning for these arguments by suggesting that Protestantism (and especially its Calvinist varieties) provided the ethic necessary to promote the develop of capitalism through its stress predestination and vocation.

8. More doubt is cast on the relevance of Weber's thesis to modern Ireland by the results of Pickles and O'Farrell's (1987) investigation of a large scale sample of recent Irish work histories. While persons with a Church of Ireland background were significantly more likely to found a new business than either Presbyterians or Roman Catholics, there was no statistically significant difference between the measure of entrepreneurship for the other two denominations.

It should also be noted that whatever the validity of Weber's thesis in the past, there have probably always been insurmountable difficulties preventing a satisfactory test of the hypothesis. For example, any investigation of Protestant-Catholic differences in terms of work ethic, capitalist spirit, industriousness, thrift, and commercial honesty is always likely to be confused by other causal factors, e.g. urban-rural differences, the length of a family history of employment in manufacturing industry, minority groups and outsiders.

Nevertheless, even if the Weber thesis has to be placed to one side a number of interesting questions do present themselves to the sociologists of religion and indeed the leaders and members of the churches in Ireland. Increasing emphasis is placed on role of social networks in explaining the growth of small firms (e.g.

these markets provide informal sources of information to businessmen as well as one means of marketing (Mitchell, 1969; Birley and Corrie, 1988). Given the high rate of religious observance in Ireland (Ryan, Fogarty and Lee, 1984) the churches constitute a much more important networking role than their counterparts in comparatively secularised societies such as England and West Germany. One might wish to evaluate the economic impact of this peculiar type of networking. In the case of NI there is also the problem of attempting to reconcile the very high rates of church attendance and extent of adherence to formal Christianity with the prevalence of behaviour which appears to be far from Christian, e.g. negative attitudes towards work and good workmanship, unco-operativeness (see Chapter 15) and widespread social and electoral support for those who practise violence against persons and property.

9. If Britain traded off social stability for lower economic growth it is by no means clear that this was necessarily a bad deal (Johnson, 1972). However, by the 1970s it was increasingly perceived that the continuation of relative economic decline would in the long run undermine the material basis necessary for a good society. Wiener (1981) interprets the policy and practise of "Thatcherism" along these lines though even after ten years of her government it is by no means clear that the relative economic decline has been halted (Crafts, 1988a, 1988b).

10. Too high a wage rate (i.e. one determined without reference to the level of comparative productivity) could be considered along with demand, the Troubles and the role of culture as a possible constraint on the development of manufacturing in Ireland. The scope for a policy of wage cutting or constraint is considered later in this Chapter.

11. By joining the European Monetary System in 1978 the ROI has largely forfeited whatever advantages would accrue to competitiveness from having a free floating currency against Continental trading competitors. ROI's continued membership of the EMS may reflect the perception amongst policy makers that any depreciation against European currencies is more likely to increase domestic inflation than improve cost competitiveness.

APPENDICES

APPENDICES

A Northern Ireland's declining cost competitiveness relative to Great Britain and international competitors

Table A.1 shows that Northern Ireland manufacturing has become less competitive than that of Great Britain in terms of labour costs per unit of output. The extent of catch up by NI wages relative to those in GB was not matched by improvements in comparative productivity. Thus for every pound spent by the NI employer on labour, he was receiving back less output than his GB counterpart. Although Table A.1 shows that NI has regained some cost competitiveness relative to GB since 1978, NI is still uncompetitive by international standards in spite of wage levels which are almost the lowest amongst the developed industrial economies[1]. Table A.2 uses cost data (prepared by the Swedish Employers' Federation using market exchange rates) and comparative productivities estimated by the National Institute of Economic and Social Research (Ray, 1987) to calculate the relative unit costs of Northern Ireland, Great Britain, and seven major OECD economies.

Table A.2 shows that foreign unit labour costs are generally only about two-thirds of those in NI. In other words, in spite of relatively low wages NI manufacturing is not cost competitive.

NI's manufacturing unit labour costs relative to GB
(GB=100)

	1968	1973	1975	1978	1981	1984
Labour costs per employee-hour*	75	83	87	86	89	85
Gross value-added per employee-hour	86	93	90	74	85	84
Relative unit cost	87	89	96	116	104	101

* Average wages and salaries inclusive of social charges, employment taxes and subsidies. Relative unit costs are calculated by dividing the relative level of labour costs by the comparative productivity (in 1968 and 1973 comparative net output per head).

Sources: Labour Cost Survey, Census of Production (various years).

Table A.2
International comparisons of NI's relative unit costs
(GB=100)

	Hourly labour costs		Productivity		Unit costs*	
	1984	1986	1984	1986	1984	1986
USA	194	161	262	265	74	61
Japan	109	129	177	173	62	75
France	114	122	179	179	64	65
Germany	153	173	205	206	75	84
Italy	117	127	156	155	75	83
Belgium	140	149	215	207	70	72
Netherlands	142	156	267	267	53	59
GB	100	100	100	100	100	100
NI	85	na	84	na	101	na

* Unit costs=Hourly labour costs/productivity. Labour costs include all social charges and the productivity measure is output per hour.

Sources: International data, Ray (1987); NI and GB data, Labour Cost Survey.

Notes

1. In 1984 NI average hourly male manufacturing wages were 91 per cent of those in GB. This meant they were less than 50 per cent those in North America, about three-fifths of those in Norway, Denmark and Switzerland (the highest wage European economies) and about 70 per cent those in Japan and Germany (Ray, 1987). The only countries within the Swedish Employer's Federation study with which NI is implied to have roughly equal wages are: France, Italy, Austria and the Republic of Ireland (ROI). (Of the other OECD economies not included in the study our own calculations show NI to have higher wages than Turkey, Greece, Spain and Portugal but lower ones than Australia, New Zealand, Luxembourg and Iceland.) However, when non-wage labour costs (social charges) are included in the comparison then NI's total hourly labour costs are substantially lower than any of the 16 OECD countries included in the Swedish study (with the exception of the ROI whose total labour costs were a few percentage points higher than NI in 1984).

B Public subsidisation of Northern Ireland manufacturing: a comparison with other areas

Tables B.1, B.2, B.3 and B.4 suggest that public subsidies are a very considerable proportion of value-added in Northern Ireland manufacturing; in recent years between one-quarter and one-fifth of the entire GDP of the sector. The data used underestimate both the absolute size of all public support for manufacturing and the extent to which the rate of subsidy exceeds that in GB. This is because grant aid for R and D and labour training, subsidies from the EC and Local Authorities and relief from rates and rents are excluded from this total so as to facilitate comparisons with GB. With the exception of support from local government (Armstrong, 1988), all these additional elements of subsidy are probably larger in NI in relation to output and employment than they are in GB. The subsidy rate remains at about one fifth of manufacturing output even when two loss making engineering giants, Harland and Wolff and Shorts, are excluded.[1] Thus dependence on public aid is widespread and cannot be attributed solely to the activities of publicly owned firms.

Comparison with GB for the years 1981-85 suggests that the NI subsidy rate is between five and ten times greater than that for the rest of the UK. GB regional assistance and industrial policy spending have been in decline throughout 1981-85 and the rate of state support for manufacturing may now be lower than that in West Germany (this is implied by comparing the results in Tables B.2 and B.3).

Table B.1
Rates of subsidy (% of manufacturing GDP, factor cost^2)

	Regional assistance (capital and discretionary grants)		Other grants		Net labour subsidies	
	NI	GB	NI	GB	NI	GB
1978	15.6	1.3	5.1	na	4.3	0.7
1979	14.2	1.2	8.0	1.1	2.3	0.4
1980	15.4	1.2	8.4	na	1.6	1.0
1981	13.2	1.5	8.7	2.0	1.0	0.9
1982	15.0	1.6	9.9	1.8	0.8	0.6
1983	12.3	1.1	10.0	1.2	0.8	0.6
1984	11.0	0.9	9.5	0.9	0.6	0.6
1985	12.0	0.6	8.9	0.9	0.2	0.3

Note: For explanation of categories of subsidy see Appendix E.3.

Sources: Appropriation Accounts (NI); Secretary of State for Trade and Industry (1983); HM Treasury (1986); Shepherd (1987).

Table B.2
Rates of subsidy with and without shipbuilding and aerospace
(% of GDP, factor cost, including or excluding
other transport equipment)

	NI (1)	NI (2)	GB (3)
1978	25.0	24.7	na
1979	25.5	22.1	2.7
1980	24.5	21.2	na
1981	22.9	18.6	4.4
1982	25.7	21.1	4.0
1983	23.1	19.4	2.9
1984	21.1	18.7	2.4
1985	21.1	18.3	1.8

(1) All manufacturing including Short Brothers and Harland and Wolff.
(2) All manufacturing excluding Short Brothers and Harland and Wolff.
(3) Total assistance derived from Table B.1.

Sources: As for Table B.1.

Table B.3
Rate of subsidy to German manufacturing
(% net value-added at factor cost)

1974	1.5
1985	3.2

Sources: Juttesmeier and Lammes (1979); Kiel Institute (1987).

Table B.4
Rates of subsidy in Britain and Ireland
(total assistance as % manufacturing GDP, factor cost, 1985-86)

England	0.5
Wales	4.5
Scotland	3.7
Northern Ireland	18.3
Republic of Ireland	3.6 (16.9)

Note: Total grants include all capital grants and selective assistance and the cost of publically financed land and premises. The estimate in parenthesis for the Republic includes the implicit subsidy of profits given by a corporate profit tax of only 10 per cent as compared to 35 per cent in the UK. (Total profits were estimated from the IDA Survey. ROI grant expenditure recorded in the national accounts was compared to manufacturing GDP as estimated from the same source.)

The NI subsidy rate is for all manufacturing other than Harland and Wolff and Shorts. This was to ensure comparability with the GB results where no attempt was made to apportion Department of Trade and Industry spending (e.g. on shipbuilding, steel, motor vehicles and aerospace) on a regional basis within GB.

Sources: UK regions: Regional Trends 1988; Northern Ireland Appropriation Accounts 1985-86, 1986-7. ROI: National Income and Expenditure 1987; Statistical Abstract 1986; IDA Survey 1986.

Even when comparison is restricted to Scotland, Wales and the Republic which, like NI, have active development agencies and a peripheral location, NI manufacturing again emerges as the most heavily subsidised[3].

Public subsidisation could be thought of as being a policy response to low efficiency in manufacturing firms in the sense that it enables firms to survive in spite of their lack of cost competitiveness. On a like-with-like occupational basis wage costs in NI manufacturing were close to those in GB during 1980-84 (decline in NI's comparative wage rate since 1984 may reflect compositional change and the closure of a few high wage plants more than it does any shift in NI-GB wage relativities at the finely matched level (Harris, 1989)) but productivity levels were only about 80 per cent of those in GB. The rate of public subsidisation in NI would appear to be of the same order of magnitude as NI's shortfall behind GB productivity levels. Since value-added is the means of paying wages and profits, one of the implications of the high rate of subsidisation in NI is that parity in wages can still be attained in spite of a failure in terms of productivity. It is very doubtful that NI as a location has some inherent disadvantage relative to GB which is large enough to justify the huge disparity in subsidy rates (differential costs of transport and energy and the direct damage arising from The Troubles are not large enough). What the subsidies may have done is to allow equal pay for unequal work.

Notes

1. State aid to these publicly owned companies was counted as subsidy even though some of these funds were used to finance capital investment. The rationale for including such state financed investment as a subsidy to value-added is that in the absence of state ownership it is unlikely that Harland and Wolff and Shorts would have been able to borrow similar sums from the private capital market.

2. Because of the difficulties of achieving a reliable apportioning of GDP at market prices between NI and GB, the comparisons of the degree of subsidisation are made in factor cost terms. The administrative costs of industrial policy (e.g. the running costs of the development agencies) are not included in our calculations of the scale of subsidy in NI and GB because we are primarily interested in the extent to which subsidies are inflating the value-added of manufacturing.

3. The rate of subsidy to NI manufacturing is also one of the highest in Western Europe. The European Community Survey of State Aid (1989) suggests that none of the 10 EC members (i.e. excluding Spain and Portugal) for which data was available had a national average rate of subsidy to manufacturing (excluding aid to steel and shipbuilding but inclusive of tax and loan based incentives) as high as that in NI (Financial Times, 1989, November 20). The EC members with rates of support closest to NI were Italy (amounting to a 1981-86 average of 15.8 per cent of value-added, though this estimate has since been revised downwards (Financial Times, 1990, February 28)), Greece (13.9 per cent) and the Republic of Ireland (12.3 per cent). Danish manufacturing received the lowest subsidy rate (1.7 per cent) followed by manufacturing in the UK and Germany (both receiving state aids equivalent to 2.9 per cent).

C The adjustment of the comparative productivity measurements to a per employee-hour basis

If average weekly hours of work differ between NI and GB this would effect the comparative productivity estimate on a per employee-hour basis and cause it to differ from that on a per head basis. In this Appendix Northern Ireland's comparative productivities using these two measures are contrasted.

Table C.1 shows average hours worked per full-time adult manual male[1] in NI as a percentage of the equivalent in GB (only the data for all manufacturing is shown). It can be seen that average hours for all of manufacturing in Northern Ireland varies from a relative low of 93.8 per cent of the GB level in 1961, to a high of 100.9 per cent in 1979. In most years average hours in all manufacturing in NI are less than those in GB. The implication of this is that a productivity comparison in per hour terms will be more favourable to NI than a per head one. However, because the difference in hours worked is small, this adjustment to NI's favour is quite small and in most of the years shown means a gain relative to the GB productivity level of only about one percentage point.

Examination of individual sectors suggest that the effect of an adjustment to a per hour basis is usually not large. In clothing and footwear and all engineering average Northern Ireland hours were longer than GB. Hence the comparative output per hour is worse than that per head (by up to 4 per cent points). In chemicals and man-made fibres, linen and textiles and food, drink and tobacco average hours in NI were consistently lower than those in GB. Hence the comparative output per hour is better than that for output per head (usually the difference is less than 4 per cent points although it is greater than this in 1974 and 1980 for man-made fibres and chemicals, and in 1975 for food, drink and tobacco).

Table C.1
Comparison of average weekly hours worked, 1960-83*

	NI	GB	NI/GB (GB=100)
1960	46.2	47.4	97.5
1961	43.9	46.8	93.8
1962	45.7	46.2	98.9
1963	46.3	46.8	98.9
1964	46.4	46.9	98.9
1965	46.3	46.1	100.4
1966	44.2	45.0	98.2
1967	45.0	45.3	99.3
1968	44.6	45.8	97.4
1969	44.2	45.3	97.6
1970	44.3	44.8	98.9
1971	44.0	43.9	100.2
1972	44.1	43.8	100.8
1973	44.2	44.6	99.1
1974	43.3	44.0	98.4
1975	42.5	42.7	99.5
1976	43.6	43.5	100.2
1977	43.1	43.6	98.9
1978	43.3	43.5	99.5
1979	43.6	43.2	100.9
1980	42.6	45.0	94.7
1981	42.9	43.5	98.6
1982	43.0	43.8	98.2
1983	42.3	43.7	96.8

* Full-time manual males in all manufacturing industries.

Source: October Earnings Survey.

In some of the minor sectors in Northern Ireland there was a larger difference in hours worked as compared to GB. In mineral products NI hours were substantially longer than in GB with the result the comparative productivity per hour was lower than that per head. By contrast, in other manufacturing (rubber and plastics), paper etc and timber and furniture Northern Ireland hours were in some years 10 per cent lower than those in Great Britain. The productivity comparison is therefore better for Northern Ireland when calculated in per hour terms.

Therefore, with the exception of some of the smaller sectors, the difference in average hours worked is generally not large. The implication is that conclusions drawn from per head data as regards comparative levels and rates of growth of productivity are robust. Previous studies (Rostas, 1948; Maddison, 1982; Smith, Hitchens and Davies, 1982) have emphasised that average hours worked in British manufacturing are longer than those in the

USA (and sometimes longer than those in West Germany), since we have shown here that NI's average weekly hours are slightly lower than those in GB there is probably not much to chose between the length of the working week in NI, Germany and USA (i.e. when one considers NI's international comparative productivity little difference is made if one considers output per hour as opposed to output per head[2]).

Notes

1. Unfortunately the time series data as regards female workers are less satisfactory than for males. Given that female workers are a larger proportion of employment in NI manufacturing than in GB, the conclusions drawn from comparisons of males workers only should be treated with caution.

2. In 1986 average weekly hours for all manual workers in manufacturing were 41.6 in the UK, 40.7 in the USA and 40.4 in Germany (Employment Gazette (1981, July; 1988, July); UN Monthly Bulletin of Statistics (1988, July); NI Annual Abstract of Statistics (1986). International differences in total annual hours worked also depend on the length of holidays but data on this subject is likely to unreliable.

D Manufacturing productivity differences within the United Kingdom: Northern Ireland compared to Scotland, Wales and the English regions

In Part 2 we have shown that Northern Ireland's productivity level in manufacturing is about 80 per cent of the average level for Great Britain as a whole. Such a comparison with the GB average does not allow us to say whether NI is lagging most of the GB regions or just one (e.g. South East England). These two possibilities would have different policy implications. If NI were shown to be outperformed by all the other UK regions then this would suggest that some causes of poor productivity levels in Northern Ireland are peculiarly Northern Irish. On the other hand, if NI shares low productivity with a number of other regions then this would indicate that NI is suffering from problems found elsewhere within the UK (though perhaps not to the same intensity). Table D.1 employs the Annual Census of Production data for gross value-added per head in the Standard Regions of the UK.

One of the most striking conclusions to be drawn from this Table is that NI is shown to have lower productivity than other UK regions. Perhaps the most significant fact about the trends in the regional productivities relative to NI is that they cannot fit into a naive framework of a North-South divide in UK economic performance. Scotland and the North maintain productivity levels which are comparatively high relative to NI while comparative productivity in the East and West Midlands falls until it is only about one-tenth higher than NI.

Table D.1
Productivity of GB Standard Regions as a % of NI
(GVA per head, NI=100)

	1951	1963	1975	1985
North	132	136	120	134
Yorks-Humber.	132	121	113	114
North West	136	125	115	127
South West	127	133	112	125
East Midlands	132	120	108	109
West Midlands	138	128	105	113
South East	145*	145	130	135
East Anglia	145*	128	120	132
Scotland	120	129	113	132
Wales	140	150	110	125
Northern Ireland	100	100	100	100

* Data for South East and East Anglia combined.

Sources: 1951, 1963, and 1973 data are estimated by Tyler and Rhodes (1986); 1985 data are derived from the Census of Production.

Regional Trends (1986) presents manufacturing gross value-added per head in 1983 at the more disaggregated level of English and Welsh county and Scottish local authority areas. Thus the NI level of output per head can be compared with 64 spatial areas within GB and it is striking that in all but four of these areas the productivity level exceeds that of NI (the exeptions are; Derbyshire, at a level 98 per cent of NI; Leicestershire, 100 per cent of NI; Powys, 98 per cent of NI and Scottish Borders with 95 per cent of the NI level). The 10 best performing UK areas are; Cumbria, Cheshire, Buckinghamshire, Hampshire, Hertfordshire, Cambridgeshire, Central Scotland, Dumfries and Galloway, Scottish Highlands and Fife. Whereas the NI productivity level was 85 per cent of the UK average it was only between 61 and 73 per cent of the level achieved in each of these regions. Comparison at this level of spatial disaggregation is fair to NI in that the size of NI manufacturing output is considerably greater than that of every Welsh county and Scottish LAA (except Strathclyde) and is about average by the standards of the English counties. In any case, productivity data for smaller areas within the Province are not available for recent years[1].

This appendix suggests Northern Ireland is less productive than almost every other part of the UK. Whilst inter-regional comparisons are complicated by the probability that each of the the UK regions has its own structural bias to high or low comparative productivity, the position of NI so clearly at the bottom of the league is striking and is suggestive of there being factors marking off Northern Ireland from the rest of the UK in productivity terms.

Notes

1. For historical interest, the comparative productivities of the six counties and two cities of Northern Ireland in 1968 (the last year for which these data are disclosed) were (as percentages of the averages for manufacturing as a whole in NI); Londonderry City Borough 50 per cent; County Londonderry 64 per cent; Tyrone 71 per cent; Armagh 71 per cent; Down 76 per cent; Fermanagh 80 per cent; Belfast City Borough 89 per cent; and Antrim 146 per cent.

Given that the average NI manufacturing productivity in 1968 was 84 per cent of the GB level, the implication of these figures is that only County Antrim achieved a productivity level better than the GB average. The productivity gap for the other counties and the cities widens alarmingly (albeit the estimates for the County and City of Londonderry, Tyrone and Fermanagh are based on a limited number of industries within manufacturing). Unfortunately, the lack of published statistics at the county level after 1968 means that one can only speculate about the size and nature of productivity differences within Northern Ireland.

E Description of the data used

E.1 Data used in the calculation of the structural effect

For each year we used the most finely disaggregated data available; for 1935, data by Product Trades given in Isles and Cuthbert (1957); 1968, data by Minimum List Heading (MLH) of the 1968 SIC, some estimated by Harris (1987); 1979 and 1984, data by Activity of the 1980 SIC, some estimated by the authors. More precise details are as follows.

The 1935 productivity data

The 37 Product Trades used in 1935 gave an incomplete coverage of manufacturing in NI and GB; representing 79.8 per cent of NI employment and 72.4 per cent of net output, and 44.4 per cent of GB employment and 42.1 per cent of net output. Thus the structural effect estimated for 1935 by Isles and Cuthbert can only show the effect within a range of industries which represented about three-quarters of all manufacturing in NI and less than half of manufacturing in GB.

The 1968 productivity data

In contrast to the data for 1935, 1968 productivity comparisons were made for every industry as defined by the 1968 SIC, that is, there was complete coverage of employment and output in both NI and GB. Of the total of 143 MLHs NI had a non-negligible output and productivity in 96 (i.e. in 47 industries NI had no production at all). The Business Statistics Office rules on confidentiality prevented the publication of data on output or employment in NI in 24 of the 143 industries. For these industries we have used the estimates made by Harris (1987).

The 1979 productivity data

In 1979 comparisons between NI and GB were possible in 108 industries (termed Activities by the 1980 SIC but broadly comparable with MLHs of the 1968 SIC) and these represented 94 per cent of employment and 98 per cent of gross value-added in NI manufacturing in 1979. Their coverage of employment and GVA in GB manufacturing in 1979 were less complete; 70 per cent and 68 per cent respectively. Thirteen of the 108 comparisons of productivity involved estimation by the authors since the Business Statistical Office had not published NI output and employment data but merged these figures with those of another UK region (usually Wales) so as to withold information about individual firms in NI. In such cases the average productivity of the combination of NI and the other region(s) was known and it was assumed that this average represented a reasonable approximation to the productivity of NI separately (this was especially reasonable in cases where NI represented a large proportion of the multi-regional combination). However, a biased result would occur in cases where NI had a small weight as compared to the other region with which it had been combined. If the other region has a higher productivity level than NI (not improbable as Appendix D shows) then the productivity of the combination of NI with that region will be greater than the actual level of productivity for NI separately. When not disclosed by the Census NI employment was estimated using the Northern Ireland Economic Research Centre (NIERC) employment database. Our estimates of productivity were combined with those for employment to calculate the level of output in NI for each of the 13 industries.

The 1984 productivity data

Productivity comparisons were made for 89 industries in 1984 which represented 93 per cent of employment and 94 per cent of GVA in NI and 88 per cent of employment and 89 per cent of GVA in GB. The Business Statistics Office data were generally more aggregated than in 1979; for example, instead of seven separate Clothing industries there was just one. Fifteen of the 89 comparisons involved estimations similar to those adopted for the 1979 data.

E.2 Data problems

1968 data

The chief problem arising from the 1968 data was how to allow for the complete absence from NI of a large number of industries; 47 out of 143. Since the Isles and Cuthbert method of calculating the

structural effect (see Chapter 4) weights differences in industry
size (for each industry the percentage of total NI employment in
that industry minus the percentage of total GB employment in that
industry) by the productivity levels actually achieved in NI, it
can only measure the effect of NI's structure within the range of
industries which are already in NI. That is, industries such as
branches of mechanical, electrical, electronic engineering, metal
goods and chemicals, which have no output and hence no
productivity in NI add nothing to the size of NI's negative
structural effect. However, the shift-share method (differences
in employment size weighting by GB productivity levels) does allow
these industries to either worsen or improve NI's structural
effect (according to whether they have high or low absolute
levels of output per head in GB). The shift-share calculates the
1968 structural effect to be substantial and negative. By
contrast, the Isles and Cuthbert method produced a substantial
positive structural effect. This difference in sign is due to the
exclusion of the industries absent from NI when the Isles and
Cuthbert's method is used (i.e. within the range of industries
which NI actually had in 1968 there was not a structural
disadvantage relative to GB).

Since measurements of the structural effect are attempts to
estimate the total handicap to comparative productivity imposed by
a region's structure it was held that the positive structural
effect suggested by Isles and Cuthbert was misleading (the 47
industries where NI has no output should not be ignored). Thus
the Isles and Cuthbert calculation of the structural effect was
amended by giving each of the 47 industries which had zero output
in NI a weight equal to the level of productivity achieved by that
industry in GB. In this sense the 1968 Isles and Cuthbert
estimate was a hybrid of the Isles and Cuthbert and the
shift-share method.

1979 data

The chief problem involved in the estimation of the structural
effect in 1979 was the large number of industries where an NI/GB
comparative productivity could not be estimated (45 Activities
mostly in mechanical, electrical engineering, metal goods and
chemicals, hereafter these industries will be referred to as
"unknown industries" as distinct from the 108 "known industries"
where comparisons were possible). One could include the unknown
industries in the calculation of the structural effect by
combining all their output and employment so that they could be
treated as if they were one industry. Whilst it was not possible
to calculate their combined output and employment directly, we did
know the total output and employment of the 108 industries where
data was available and the residual which this left for all
manufacturing was equivalent to the total for the 45 unknown
industries. The weakness of this technique was that the residual
represented a small proportion of All Manufacturing in NI (2 per
cent of GVA and 6 per cent of employment) and therefore the scope
for error in the estimation of its productivity was large. Hence

when the residual was included in the calculation of the structural effect using the method of Isles and Cuthbert it was weighted by its productivity level in GB rather than that implied for NI.

1984 data

In 1984 the nineteen industries for which a comparative productivity could not be estimated were again treated as if they were one industry, the output, employment and productivity of which was estimated as the residual from all manufacturing when all the "known" industries were subtracted. In this case it was reasonable to weight the residual by its productivity level in NI when using the Isles and Cuthbert method.

E.3 Technical notes to tables

Tables in Part 1

Table 1.1: [a] National Censuses of Production net output per head data for the two economies could be compared using average market exchange rates, but this may be an unreliable indicator of price differences between countries. Since the 1950s data were collected on the comparative price of matched products in different economies. When weighted together, these prices provide the basis for the Purchasing Power Parity relationship between Britain and America (this still falls short of the ideal comparison of the level of factory gate prices; see Chapter 1, Note 2). Comparative productivity calculations for a given year can be updated to a more recent year (or projected back further into the past) given data on national changes in the employment and volume indices of output between the two years (subject to the unreliabilities inherent in this procedure; see Appendix G).

[b] Output per employee-hour adjusted to output per head using the difference between British and American average weekly hours (all full-time manual workers in manufacturing).

Table 1.2: [a] Includes extractive and utilities.
[b] UK employment in 1901 (Liesner, 1985); German employment in 1907 (Clark, 1957).
[c] UK employment in 1911 (Liesner, 1985); German employment in 1907 (Clark, 1957).
[d] UK and German employment in 1929 (Liesner, 1985).
[e] Hornby (1958); United States Strategic Bombing (1976). Unweighted average of productivity ratios in the output of airframes, aeroengines, machine tools and military tanks. These activities employed over one-third of manufacturing employment in Britain.
[f] Output per employee-hour adjusted to output per head using the difference between British and German average weekly hours (all full-time manual workers in manufacturing).

Tables in Part 2

Table 3.1 In cases of these two industries there are serious discrepancies in the output and employment estimates from the two Censuses. Comparison with an independent data source (findings of the NIERC employment database) suggest that for instrument engineering the UK Census result may be more reliable. Whilst in rubber and plastics etc the database suggests that the UK estimate can be regarded as the less probable one.

Table 4.5 Some of the data shown are the results of the estimations outlined in Appendix E (e.g. tobacco for 1973-85 and shipbuilding, aircraft and motor vehicles for 1963-73 and 1973-85, and in these cases the results for a single year, either 1973 or 1984, were used to represent the average for the whole period).
   The results for each Census year use the system of industrial classification which was then current. The exception to this are the years 1980-85 where the data were re-estimated on the basis of the 1968 SIC. The reason for doing this was that the new definition in the 1980 SIC had the effect of improving NI's all manufacturing comparative productivity. Thus the extent of long-run productivity convergence would have been exaggerated if that classification had been used.

Table 7.2: * This excludes the substantial migratory flows within the Island; the number of NI residents with birthplaces in the ROI was 46402 in 1971 and 35604 in 1981, the number of ROI residents with NI birthplaces was 26183 in 1971 and 40554 in 1981.

Tables in Part 4

Tables 19.1 and 19.2: 1 Results from 1926 ROI Census were compared with those of the 1924 NI Census and the 1931 and 1936 ROI results with those of NI in 1930 and 1935 respectively. To the extent that productivity (both real and nominal) was growing slowly in the inter-War period any bias in ROI's favour because of these comparisons with NI in an earlier year is likely to be small.

2 There was no disaggregation of the ROI engineering data (that is, excluding all vehicles) in 1926, 1931 and 1936. In 1963 and 1968 motor vehicles and aircraft in the ROI are compared to motor vehicles only in NI. Electrical engineering in both ROI and NI includes the computer industry.

3 The size of units considered are inconsistent (firms of three and more persons in ROI as compared to establishments of either ten or more in NI prior to 1973, and twenty or more after 1973). To the extent that economies of scale are significant one would anticipate a negative bias to the measurement of ROI's productivity relative to NI. When one removes the small firms from the ROI data (as is possible from 1980 onwards) this proves to be the case albeit the size of the adjustment to ROI's comparative productivity is usually small.

Tables in the Appendices

Table B.1 Regional assistance defined as capital grants (SCG in Northern Ireland and RDG in Great Britain), Selective Financial Assistance and public provision of land and premises.

Other grants; in NI these include: grants given by LEDU, assistance to the shipbuilding and aircraft industries, marketing, electricity charges and energy conservation. Whereas in 1978 and 1979 NI firms received a subsidy for their electricity costs from 1980 that subsidy has been paid directly to the Electricity Service. The implied subsidy to manufacturing electricity charges was therefore estimated using the relationship between manufacturing electricity subsidies and total electricity subsidies which could be calculated for 1978 and 1979. In GB the Other grants included: all Department of Trade and Industry spending other than that included under Regional Assistance, and Department of Employment spending on small firms.

Net labour subsidies; Regional Employment Premium net of the Selective Employment Tax.

293

F Northern Ireland's comparative gross value-added: the results for 1979 and 1984

Table F.1 shows comparative GVA per head of NI industries for 1979 and 1984. All comparative productivity levels are assigned a statistical reliablity assessment as follows; **: Good; *: Moderate; Unmarked: Poor.

("Good" means that the extent of any estimation is small and that the industry in NI is large enough for any rounding errors to be small. "Poor" either means extensive estimation, or that the NI industry is very small and liable to rounding errors.

Table F.1
Comparative GVA per head of NI industries
(NI/GB; GB=100)

Activity Headings	1979	1984
2234 Wire	97	..
2245/46/47 Non-ferrous metals	..	66
2310 Stone extraction	135	65**
2330,2396 Miscell. mineral extraction	103	100
2410 Structural clay products	134	125*
2420 Cement, lime and plaster	..	104
2436 Ready mixed concrete	92 }	
		72**
2437 Miscelaneous building products	88** }	

294

	(NI/GB; GB=100)	
	1979	1984
2450 Working of stone	95**	72**
2471/78/79 Glass	153	90*
2489 Ceramic goods	92**	91**
2511,12,13,14,15,16 Miscell. chemicals	269	74**
2513 Fertilisers	27	..
2515 Synthetic rubber	17	..
2562,63,64,65,67,68,69 Other chemicals	..	66*
2551 Paints, varnishes, painter's fillers	79	58
2570 Pharmaceutical products	47	71
2600 Man-made fibres	107**	135
3111 Ferrous metal foundries	92	..
3120 Forging, pressing and stamping	106	72
3137 Bolts, nuts, washers, rivets, chains	54	96
3142 Metal doors, windows etc.	79	47
3166 Metal furniture and safes	80	..
3169 Finished metal products NES	85*	..
3204 Fabricated & constructional steelwork	78 }	69**
3205 Boilers and process plant	67**}	
3211 Agricultural machinery	83	..
3222 Engineers' small tools	97	113
3230 Textile machinery	88**	85**
3244,45,46 Machinery for food, drink, tobacco and chemical indust.	117*	71
3254 Construction & earth-moving equip.	153**}	207**
3255 Mechanical lift & handling equip.	79 }	
3261 Precision chains and transmission	92*	95
3275 Machinery for wood, rubber & plastics industry	109	46
3281 Internal combustion engines (e.g. Marine)	97* }	92**
3284 Refrigerators & ventilators	59**}	
3287 Pumps	138 }	
3289 Mechanical, marine & precision engineering nes.	82**}	
3301/2 Office machinery & data processing equipment	85	58
3410 Insulated wires and cables	160*	84*
3420 Basic electrical equipment	63**	72**
3430 Electrical equipment for industry	..	70
3440 Telecommunications equipment	89	105**
3450 Miscell. electronics (TV & radio)	108	46*
3460 Domestic electrical appliances	101**	81

		(NI/GB; GB=100)	
		1979	1984
3470	Electric lamps & lighting equip.	..	55
3510	Motor vehicles and engines	..	95
3520	Motor vehicle bodies, trailers	85*	74*
3530	Motor vehicle parts	78**	92**
3610	Shipbuilding and repairing	34**	50**
3630	Motor and pedal cycles	29	36
3640	Aerospace equipment manufacturing	98*	101*
3710	Measuring, check & precision instr.	..	53
3720	Medical and surgical equipment	129*	74*
3730	Optical precision instruments	..	94*
3740	Clocks, watches, timing devices	..	102
4110	Organic oils and fats	..	40
4122	Bacon-curing and meat processing	94**⎫	
			106**
4123	Poultry slaughter and processing	120**⎭	
4130	Prep. of milk & milk products	106**	64**
4147	Processing of fruit & vegetables	123	215**
4150	Fish processing	83	40*
4160	Grain milling	61*	85
4196	Bread and flour confectionery	111**	117**
4210	Ice cream, cocoa, choc. confection.	97	73
4221	Compound animal feeds	96**⎫	
			79**
4222	Pet foods and non-compound feeds	80 ⎭	
4180,4239	Starch and miscell. foods	89**	55*
4240	Spirit distilling and compounding	..	112
4270	Brewing and malting	..	81
4283	Soft drinks	54**	79**
4290	Tobacco	81*	78*
4310	Woollen and worsted	102**	64*
4321	Spinning & doubling on cotton system	93**	99**
4322	Weaving cotton, silk & Man-made fibres	99**	..
4340	Spinning & weaving flax, hemp, ramie	79**	116**
4350	Jute and polypropylene yarns	..	141
4363	Hosiery and other weft knitted	110**	..
4364	Warp knitted fabrics	132**	..
4370	Textile finishing	84**	84**
4384	Pile carpets, carpeting rags	97**	127**
4398	Narrow fabrics	75	79
4410	Leather (tanning and dressing)	42	64
4420	Leather goods	107	118
4510	Footwear	75**	173**

	(NI/GB; GB=100)	
	1979	1984
4531 Weatherproof outerwear	99 ⎫	
4532 Men's and boys' outerwear	90** ⎬	
4533 Women's girls' tailored outerwear	60 ⎪	
4534 Work clothing & jeans	65** ⎬	91**
4535 Men's & boys shirts, underwear	101** ⎭	
4536 Women's & girls light outerwear, lingerie	79** ⎫	
4539 Miscellaneous dress industries	93** ⎬	
4556 Canvas goods, sacks, made-up textiles	89 ⎫	
		81**
4557 Household textiles	66** ⎬	
4560 Fur	..	46
4620 Manufacture of semi-finished wood products	..	106
4610 Sawmilling, planing of wood	102**	75**
4630 Builders' carpentry & joinery	101	74**
4640 Wooden containers	83	89
4650 Miscellaneous wooden articles	..	70
4671 Wooden & upholstered furniture	68** ⎫	
		90**
4672 Shop and office fitting	76 ⎬	
4723 Stationery	84** ⎫	
4724 Packaging products of paper & pulp	118** ⎬	91**
4725 Packaging products of board	89** ⎭	
4751 Printing & publish. newspapers	71** ⎫	
4752 Printing & publish. periodicals	63 ⎪	
4753 Printing and publish. books	75 ⎬	80**
4754 Miscell. printing and publishing	77** ⎭	
4811,4812,4820 Rubber products	117**	91**
4832 Plastics semi-manufacture	72 ⎫	
4834 Plastic building products	110** ⎬	95**
4835 Plastics packaging products	110 ⎪	
4836 Plastic products nes.	93 ⎭	
4910 Jewellery and coins	..	49
4920 Musical instruments	..	112
4930 Photographic and cineamatographic laboratories	..	71
4940 Toys and sports goods	..	75
4959 Miscellaneous manufactures nes.	109	..
Average of all above industries	87	82
All manufacturing (Divisions 2-4)	81	82

Note: .. Data for NI not disclosed, industries where NI's output was negligible are not included.

nes. Not elsewhere specified.

G Long run trends in output per head

Trends in productivity

The results presented in Chapter 4 showed that during the period from the early 1950s until the mid-1980s there was some convergence between the level of output attained in NI manufacturing and that achieved by industry in GB. While the extent of this narrowing of the productivity gap was limited (and Chapter 4 indicates the possibility that since 1973 this trend has been reversed i.e. the gap between NI and GB has been widening again in recent years), it does imply that during 1951-86 average productivity growth rates in all manufacturing in NI were higher than those achieved by manufacturing in GB. Table G.1 tests whether this was so by directly comparing trend rates of growth during 1951-86 (as well as appropriate sub-periods suggested by the major recessions of 1973-74 and 1979-80).

NI average productivity growth was indeed higher than GB during this 36 year period though, when the sub-periods are considered separately, it can also be seen that most of this superiority is attributable to very rapid productivity growth during the boom years of 1951-73 (since 1979 NI productivity growth appears to have fallen behind that of GB).

Whilst these results are broadly compatible with those presented in Chapter 4 there is good reason to doubt whether average NI productivity growth was almost one per cent per annum better than that in GB. Indeed, if NI manufacturing had sustained 3.7 per cent per annum productivity growth during 1951-86 while GB managed only 2.8 per cent the implication would be that the productivity gap

should have been entirely closed by 1986. In fact the extent of
convergence measured during this 36 year period by the Census of
production was limited.

Table G.1
Manufacturing output and productivity growth
during the post-war period
(compound growth rates)

	1951-73		1973-79		1979-86		1951-86	
	NI	GB	NI	GB	NI	GB	NI	GB
Output	4.2	3.0	-1.4	-0.9	-1.3	-0.6	2.1	1.6
Productivity	4.5	2.9	1.0	0.7	3.5	4.0	3.7	2.8

Sources: All the output, productivity and employment changes for
each period are calculated independently from the indices of
output and employment (Index of Industrial Production and Census
of Employment).

Similarly, use of the official series for output and employment
change in NI and GB would imply that by the mid-1980s the textiles
and clothing industry in NI should actually have had a higher
level of net output per head than its GB counterpart. In practise,
the Census of Production indicates that the productivity gap
between NI and GB was still substantial.
It should be stressed that these contradictions arise from the
use of two different statistical sources and is not unique to the
experience of NI but can arise in international comparative
projects where the two different statistical bases are used. For
example, Smith (1985) notes that use of the national indices of
manufacturing output and employment from the UK and the USA
implies an increasing American productivity advantage during
1968-77. However, direct calculation of the UK comparative
productivity level from the 1968 and 1977 Censuses suggests the
opposite; Britain has slowly been gaining ground on the United
States. Smith shows that there are strong statistical and
conceptual grounds for preferring comparative productivity level
calculations based directly on the Censuses (for similar reasons
statistical bodies such as the SOEC and the United Nations
International Comparisons Project find it necessary to conduct
periodic comparisons of international price levels rather than use
national series of price change to up-date earlier comparisons).
Since these reasons apply to the use of NI/GB Census-based
comparisons in preference to the projection forward of past
results using the Index of Production, the later are not
considered in detail in this book.

Technical reasons for preferring the Census of Production

The Census of Production produces internally consistent
productivity data because employment and net output data are drawn
from the same sample of firms. By contrast the Index of

Production and the count of employees in employment (Census of Employment) are based on different samples of companies and in our comparisons four different statistical agencies are involved (Department of Employment, Central Statistical Office, Business Statistics Office and the Department of Economic Development (NI)). The sample of firms used in constructing the Index is also smaller and is likely to be less representative than those represented by the Census.

The volume series also suffers from the characteristic difficulties of time series indices. The structure of output in both NI and GB was changing continuously and periodic re-basing may not capture all this.

Perhaps the most significant qualification to its reliability is that the Index of Production gives more indication of movements in gross output per head rather than net output per head. This is because the ideal procedure of "double deflation" is not possible (Smith, Hitchens and Davies, 1982) and as a result net output changes are represented by a variety of proxies, most notably, deflated sales or the number of physical units of output . This use of proxies in turn presents two problems which do not arise if the Census of Production is used to indicate long run trends in comparative productivity.

In the absence of any wholesale price data for NI separately the statistical agencies assume that the price deflator calculated for an industrial activity in GB can be applied to its counterpart in NI. In practise the real rate of wholesale price inflation in NI may differ from that in GB.

Another problem which arises from the Index of Production's reliance on gross output measures is that it is insensitive to long run trends in the net output/gross output ratio. By contrast, the great virtue of the use of Census of Production values of net output is that these can make some allowance for the two dimensions of output; first, the number of physical goods produced, and, second, the amount of work done on bought-in raw materials together with the degree of processing of those materials (Smith, 1985). In other words, productivity changes arising from variations in the ratio of net output to gross output. The Index of Production is essentially an indicator of movements in gross output, whereas the Census values do make allowance for variations in the net output/gross output ratio. Census comparisons will therefore be sensitve to the extent to which the rate of product quality improvement in GB was superior to that in NI. The Index of Production, to the extent that it relies on volume measures, cannot allow for upgrading of product quality. If product quality was improving more rapidly in GB than NI then comparisons of growth rates based on the Index will exaggerate NI's comparative performance.

Bibliography

Ackrill, M. (1988), "British Management and the British Economy 1870s to 1980s", Oxford Review of Economic Policy, vol. 4, no. 1, pp. 59-73.

Albu, A. (1982), "Merchant shipbuilding and marine engineerings", in K. Pavitt (ed), Technical innovation and British economic performance, Science Policy Research Unit, Sussex.

Allen, G.C. (1979), "The British Disease", Hobart Paper, no.67, Institute of Economic Affairs, London.

Allied Irish Bank Review (1981), "Ireland as a Manufacturing Base", no. 24 (April).

Anglo-American Council on Productivity, (1950), Productivity Team Report on Cotton Spinning, Anglo-American Council on Productivity, London.

Armstrong, H.W. (1988), "Variations in Industrial Development Initiatives among District Councils in England and Wales", paper given to, Regional Studies Association Conference- Divided Nation? Regional Policy and Britain's Periphery, (September), Stormont Hotel, Belfast.

Bacon, R.W. and Eltis, W.A (1974), "The Age of US and UK Machinery", National Economic Development Corporation Monograph, no. 3, NEDO, London.

302

Bairoch, P. (1982), "International Industrialisation Levels from 1750 to 1980", Journal of European Economic History, vol. 11, no. 2, pp. 269-333.

Bairoch, P. and Levy-Leboyer, M. (1981), Disparities in Economic Development since the Industrial Revolution, St. Martin's Press, New York.

Baker, T.J. (1988), "Industrial output and wage costs", Quarterly Economic Commentary, October, Economic and Social Research Institute, Dublin.

Bardon, J. (1987), "Industrial Belfast", paper given to, Geography Section of the British Association for the Advancement of Science Meeting, (August 25), Queen's University of Belfast.

Barker, K., Britton, A., Eastwood, F. and Major, R. (1985), " Macroeconomic Policy in Germany and Britain", National Institute Economic Review, no. 114, pp. 69-89.

Barnett, C. (1986), The Audit of War: the Illusion and Reality of Britain as a Great Power, Macmillan, London.

Barnett, C. (1987), The Collapse of British Power, Sutton, Gloucester.

Barrington, T. J. (1975), From Big Government to Local Government: the road to decentralisation, Institute of Public Administration, Dublin.

Barry, F. (1988),"Pluralism and Community", in R. Kearney (ed), Across the Frontiers: Ireland in the 1990s, Wolfhound Press, Dublin, pp. 137-150.

Bauer, P.T. (1982), Equality, The Third World and Economic Delusion, Methuen, London.

Beckett, R. (1987), "Northern Ireland Regional Accounts. Sources and Methods", Policy Planning and Research Unit Occasional Paper, no. 12.

Berndt, E.R. and Wood, D.A. (1986), "Energy Price Shocks and Productivity Growth in UK Manufacturing", Oxford Review of Economic Policy, vol. 2, no. 3, pp. 1-31.

Birch, D.L. (1979), The Job Generation Process, MIT Program on Urban and Regional Change, Cambridge (Massachussetts).

Birley, S. and Corrie, S. (1988), "Social Networks and Entrepreneurship in Northern Ireland", Proceedings of the Enterprise Action Conference, Belfast (September).

Birnie, J.E. (forthcoming), "The Comparative Labour Productivity of Manufacturing in Northern Ireland and the Republic of Ireland",PhD Thesis, Department of Economics, Queen's University of Belfast.

Black, J.B.H. (1987), "Conciliation or Conflict", Industrial Relations Journal, vol. 18, no. 1, pp. 14-25.

Black, W. (1977), "Industrial Development and Regional Policy", in N. Gibson and J.E. Spencer (eds), Economic Activity: in Ireland: a study of two open economies, Gill and Macmillan, Dublin, pp. 40-78.

Blackaby, F. (ed) (1979), De-industrialisation, Heinemann, London.

Blackwell, J. and O'Malley, E. (1984), "The impact of EEC membership on Irish Industry", in P. J. Drudy and D. Mc Aleese (eds), Ireland and the European Community: Irish Studies no.3.

Boakes, K. (1988), "Britain's Productivity Miracle: More to come", Grenfell Montagu Gilt-edged Research Papers.

Borooah, V.K (1987), "The Pathfinder Process: a general comment: by an economist", TSB Business Outlook and Economic Review, vol. 2, no. 3, pp. 29-30.

Borooah, V.K. and Lee, K. (1989), "The Regional Dimension of Competitiveness in Manufacturing: productivity, employment and wages in Northern Ireland and the United Kingdom", Paper prepared for the Department of Economic Development (NI).

Breen, R. and Rottman, D. (1985), " Crime Victimisation in the Republic of Ireland", Economic and Social Research Institute Paper, no. 121, Dublin.

Bridges, S. and Birley, S. (1985), "Small Firms and New Firms: A strategy for Northern Ireland", paper given to, Nineth National Small Firms Policy and Research Conference, Gleneagles.

Britton, A., Eastwood, F. and Major, R. (1986), "Macroeconomic Policy in Italy and Britain", National Institute Economic Review, no. 118, pp. 38-52.

Business and Finance (1989, March 23), "The Threat to US investment".

Business and Finance (1989, April 6), " Transport's critical role".

Business Monitor (1986), Size analyses of UK businesses 1986, Business Statistical Office, Newport.

Cambridge Econometrics and Northern Ireland Economic Research Centre (1988), The UK Regions: Economic Change to the Year 2000, Cambridge Econometrics, Cambridge.

Campaign for Work (1988), Swedish Labour Market Policy, London.

Campbell, A., Sorge, A. and Warner, M. (1990), Microelectronics Product Applications in Great Britain and West Germany: Strategies, Competence and Training, Gower-Avebury, Aldershot.

Canning, D., Moore, B. and Rhodes, J. (1987), "Economic Growth in Northern Ireland: Problems and Prospects", in P. Teague (ed), Beyond the Rhetoric, Lawrence and Wishart, London, pp. 211 -35.

Caves, R.E. and Associates (1968), Britain's Economic Prospects, Brookings Institute, Washington.

Caves, R.E. and Krause, I.B. (eds) (1980), Britain's Economic Performance, Brookings Institute, Washington.

CBI (1987), Absence from Work, CBI, London.

Chambers, D. (1979), "Availability, Supply and Demand for Managers for Industry and Commerce", Report to the Northern Ireland Economic Council, NI Economic Council, Belfast.

Chandler, A.D. (1980), "The Growth of the Transnational Industrial Firm in the United States and the United Kingdom: A Comparative Analysis", Economic History Review, vol. 33, pp. 396-410.

Child, J. and Keiser, A. (1979), "Organisation and Managerial roles in British and West German companies", in C.J. Lammers and D.J. Hickson (ed), Organisations Alike and Unlike, Routledge and Kegan Paul, London, pp. 251-271.

CIP (1973), General Report (Prl 2927), Stationery Office, Dublin.

Clark, C. (1957), The Conditions of Economic Progress, Macmillan, London.

Cogan, J. and Onynenadaum, E. (1981), "Spin-off Companies in the Irish Electronics Industry", Journal of Irish Business and Administrative Research, vol.3, no. 2, October, pp. 3-15.

Coleman, D.C. and MacLeod, C. (1986), "Attitudes and New Techniques: British Businessmen, 1800-1950", Economic History Review, vol. 39, pp. 588-611.

Command Papers (1884), Second Report of the Royal Commission on Technical Instruction, London.

Commission of the European Communities (1988), "The Economics of 1992, Report no. 35, Office for Official Publications of the European Communities, Luxembourg.

Commission on Emigration and Other Population Problems (1954), 1948-54 Reports, Stationery Office, Dublin.

Cooper, C. and Whelan, N. (1973), Science, Technology, and Industry in Ireland, Stationery Office, Dublin.

Cowling, K. (1989), "A New Industrial Strategy: preparing Europe for the turn of the Century", Presidential Address to the European Association for Research in Industrial Economics Conference, (August 30-September 1), Budapest.

CPRS, (Central Policy Review Staff), (1975), The Future of the British Car Industry, HMSO, London.

Crafts, N.F.R. (1988a), "British Economic Growth before and after 1979: a Review of the Evidence, Centre for Economic Policy and Research Discussion Paper, no. 292, CEPR, London.

Crafts, N.F.R. (1988b), "British Economic Growth over the Long-Run", Oxford Review of Economic Policy, vol. 4, no. 1, pp. i-xxi.

Craig, J. (1986), "Crime in Northern Ireland", paper given to, Conference Crime in Ireland: Crisis or Manageable Problems?, National Association of Probation Officers and Officers Branch of the Union of Professional and Technical Civil Servants.

Crotty, R. (1986), Ireland in Crisis: A Study in Capitalist Colonial Undevelopment, Brandon, Dingle.

CSO (1980), "Wholesale Price Index. Principles and Procedures", Studies in Official Statistics, no. 32, HMSO, London.

Cullen, L. M. (1979), "Germination and Growth", in B. Shore (ed), Root and Branch: History of the Allied Irish Bank, Dublin, p58.

Dahrendorf, R. (1957), Class and Conflict in Industrial Society, London.

Daly, A. (1984), "Education, Training and Productivity in the US and Great Britain", National Institute of Economic and Social Research Discussion Paper, no. 63, London.

Daly, A., Hitchens, D.M.W.N., and Wagner, K. (1985), "Productivity, Machinery and Skills in a Sample of British and German Manufacturing Plants", National Institute Economic Review, no. 111, pp. 48-62.

Daly, A. and Jones, D.T. (1980), "The Machine Tool Industry in Britain, Germany and the United States", National Institute Economic Review, no. 92, pp. 53-63.

Daly, M.E. (1981), Social and economic history of Ireland since 1800, Educational Company of Ireland, Dublin.

Davies, S.W. and Caves, R.E (1983), "Inter-Industry analysis of UK-US Productivity Differences", National Institute of Economic and Social Research Discussion Paper, no 61, London.

Davies, S.W. and Caves, R.E (1987), Britain's Productivity Gap, Cambridge University Press, Cambridge.

Department of Commerce (Northern Ireland) (1981), Statistical Abstract for Northern Ireland, HMSO, Belfast.

Department of Commerce (Northern Ireland) (1982), Minutes to the House of Commoms Committee on Trade and Industry, London, Evidence taken on 9 June, pp. 1-44.

Department of Employment (1988), "International Comparisons of Industrial Stoppages for 1986", Employment Gazette, June.

Dow, J.R.C. (1969), "Cyclical developments in France, Germany and Italy since the 1950s", in M. Bronfenbrenner (ed), Is the Business Cycle Obsolete, Wiley-Interscience, New York, pp. 140-96.

Dunning, J.H. (1970), Studies in International Investment, George Allen and Unwin, London.

Dunning, J. and R.D. Pearce (1977), US Industry in Britain, George Allen and Unwin, London.

Dunning, J.H. (1985), "Multinational Enterprises and Industrial Re-structuring in the United Kingdom", Lloyds Bank Review, no. 158, pp. 1-19.

Eatwell, J. (1982), Whatever Happened to Britain, Duckworth, London.

Economist (1983, December 17), "Capital Investment, Level with Japan?"

Economist (1984, June 2), "The Trouble with Ulster: A Survey".

Economist (1987, January 24), "Ireland's Economy".

Economist (1988, March 26), "The Economy. Public Property".

Enderwick, I.P., Gugdin, G., Hitchens, D.M.W.N.(1990), "The role of the firm in manufacturing", in R.I.D. Harris, C.W. Jefferson and J.E. Spencer (eds), The Northern Ireland Economy: a Comparative Study in Economic Development of a Peripheral Region, Longmans, Harlow (forthcoming).

European Management Forum (1981), Report on Industrial Competitiveness, European Management Forum, Geneva.

Fabricant, S. (1942), Employment in Manufacturing 1899-1939, National Bureau of Economic Research, New York.

Ferris, T. (1978), "Alternative Methods of Comparing Productivity and Living Standards in Ireland and other EEC Countries", Irish Banking Review, Spring.

Ferris, T. (1989), "Changes in Productivity and Living Standards: 1971-1986", Irish Banking Review, Spring.

Financial Times (1987, May 13), "Raise the means or tighten the belt".

Financial Times (1987, September 3), "The UK's Skill Shortage".

Financial Times (1987, October 9), "Milking UK Drink Sales with Exotic Desert Tastes".

Financial Times (1987, October 14), "Capital grants to Ulster manufacturing reduced".

Financial Times (1987, December 7), "European Steel, Right to the door of the future".

Financial Times (1988, April 28), "Survey of Textiles".

Financial Times (1988, June 8), "European Man-made Fibres. A long, hard road ahead".

Financial Times (1988, July 21), "A geographical disadvantage".

Financial Times (1988, August 4), "Tipperary "farmer" takes a high flight path".

Financial Times (1988, August 25), "A Success Story called Training".

Financial Times (1988, December 12), "Learning a lesson from history".

Financial Times (1989, January 18), "Time for Caution amid Optimism".

Financial Times (1989, January 20), "Computers "give W Germans competitive edge"".

Financial Times (1989, January 30), "Dagenham's Decline is Genk's Gain".

Financial Times (1989, January 31), "Patchy outlook for clothing manufacturers".

Financial Times (1989, February 2), "Japanese build now to cash later".

Financial Times (1989, March 21), "Boom takes W German mechanical engineers by surprise".

Financial Times (1989, March 22), "The own brand king____Survey of World Textiles".

Financial Times (1989, April 7), "German Giants Shake off the Blues".

Financial Times (1989, August 10), "How Hong Kong can help the UK".

Financial Times (1989, November 20), "Brussels flexs its muscles to a take a swing at state subsidies".

Financial Times (1989, November 21), "A late starter in the race".

Financial Times (1989, November 29), "The need to stay the course".

Financial Times (1989, December 7), "Economic Viewpoint: a win for Germany".

Financial Times (1989, December 19), "Financial Times Top 500".

Financil Times (1990, February 7), "Shorts flies the flag of good employment practise".

Financial Times (1990, February 12), "Control of the inflationary risk".

Financial Times (1990, February 28), "Brussels scales down estimate of Italian state aid to industry".

Finegold, D. and Soskice, D. (1988), "The Failure of Training in Britain: Analysis and Prescription", Oxford Review of Economic Policy, vol. 4, no. 3, pp. 21-53.

Finneston, Sir M. (1980), Engineering Our Future, Command 7794.

Fisher, P. (1987), "The Cost Enviroment of Irish Industry", paper given to, Industry Studies Association, (December), Dublin.

Fitzpatrick, J. and Kelly, J. (1985), "Industry in Ireland: policies, performances and problems", in J. Fitzpatrick and J. Kelly (eds), Perspectives on Irish Industry, IMI, (Irish Management Institute), Dublin, pp. xvii-xlii.

Flood, R. and McCloskey, D. (1981), The Economic History of Britain since 1700. Volume 2: 1860-1970s, Cambridge University Press, Cambridge.

Flux, A.W. (1933), "Industrial productivity in Great Britain and the United States", Quarterly Journal of Economics, November.

Fogarty, M., Ryan, L. and Lee, J. (1984), "Irish Values and Attitudes", in, Irish Report of the European Value Systems Study, Dominican Publications, Dublin.

Fothergill, S. and Gudgin, G. (1979), "The Job Generation Process in Britain", Centre for Enviromental Studies Research Series, no. 32, London.

Fothergill, S. and Guy, N. (1990), "The Closure of Branch Plants in manufacturing during the 1980s", Northern Ireland Economic Research Centre Report, Belfast.

Frankel, M. (1957), British and American manufacturing productivity, Bureau of Economic and Business Research, University of Illinois Press, Urbana.

Galbraith, J. K. (1967), The New Industrial State, Penguin, Hammondsworth.

Gauge and Tool SWP (1981), Toolmaking: a comparison of UK and West German companies, NEDO, London.

Geary, R. C. and Dempsey, M. (1979), "Studies on the adaptation of Irish Industry", Economic and Social Research Institute Memorandum Series, no. 133, Dublin.

Geary, R. C. and Henry, W. (1983), "A Study of Individual Irish Manufacturing Industries", Economic and Social Research Institute Memorandum Series, no. 153, Dublin.

German Chamber of Commerce and Industry (1989), German Companies in Britain, German Chamber of Commerce and Industry, London.

Gibson, N. (1981), "The Northern Ireland Economy: a Personal Perspective II", in S. Harvey and D. Rea (eds), The Northern Ireland Economy: The Future, Decision Partnership, Belfast, pp. 70-81.

Gibson, N. (1989), "Northern Ireland: Time for a fresh look at the province's economy", Financial Times (November 1).

Gleed, I., and Rees R.D. (1979), "The derivation of Regional Capital Stock estimates for UK Manufacturing Industries 1951-73", Journal of the Royal Statistical Society, no. 142, part 3, pp. 330-346.

Glyn, A. and Harrison, J. (1980), The British Economic Disaster, Pluto Press, London.

Gomulka, S. (1971), Inventive Activity, Diffusion and the Stages of Economic Growth, Aarhus, Institute of Economics.

Gudgin, G. (1984), "Employment Creation by Small and Medium Sized Firms in the UK", in X. Greffe (ed), Les P.M.E. Creent-Elles Des Emplois Economica, Paris.

Gudgin, G., Hart, M., Fagg, J., Keegan, R., and D'Arcy E. (1989), "Job generation in manufacturing industry 1973-1986: a comparison of Northern Ireland with the Republic of Ireland and the English Midlands", Northern Ireland Economic Research Centre Report, Belfast.

Gudgin, G. and Healy, T. (1990), "The quality of Management in Northern Ireland", Northern Ireland Economic Research Centre Report, Belfast (forthcoming).

Guinchard, P. (1984), "Productivite et competitivite comparees des grands pays industriels", Economie et Statistique, January.

Handy, C. (1987), The Making of Managers: a Report on Management Education, Training and Development in the United States, West Germany, France and Japan, NEDO, London.

Hannah, L. (1974), "Takeover Bids in Britain before 1850: An Exercise in Business Pre-History", Business History, no. 16, pp. 65-77.

Harris, R.I.D. (1983), "The Measurement of Capital Services in Production for the UK Regions 1968-78", Regional Studies, vol. 17, no. 3, pp. 169-180.

Harris, R.I.D. (1987), "The Structure and Growth of the UK Regional Economy, 1963-1979", Unpublished PhD Thesis, Dept. of Economics, Queen's University of Belfast.

Harris, R.I.D. (1988), "Technological Change and Regional Development in the UK: evidence from the SPRU Database on Innovations", Regional Studies, vol. 22, no. 5, pp. 361-374.

Harris, R.I.D. (1989), "Average earnings in Northern Ireland 1972-1982", in R. Jenkins (ed), <u>Northern Ireland in Social and Economic Life</u>, Avebury in association with the Economic and Social Research Council, Aldershot.

Haughton J. (1987), "The Historical Background", in J. W. O' Hagan (ed), <u>The Economy of Ireland: Policy and Performance</u>, IMI (Irish Management Institute), Dublin.

Hill, T. (1985), <u>Manufacturing Strategy: The Strategic Management of the Manufacturing Function,</u> Macmillan Open University Press, Basingstoke.

Hitchens, D.M.W.N. and Birnie, J.E. (1989a), "The United Kingdom's productivity gap: its size and causes", <u>Omega</u>, vol. 17, no. 3, pp. 209-221.

Hitchens, D.M.W.N. and Birnie, J.E. (1989b), "Economic Development in Northern Ireland: Has Pathfinder lost its way? A Reply", <u>Regional Studies</u>, vol. 23, no. 5, 477-482.

Hitchens, D.M.W.N. and O'Farrell, P.N. (1987), "The Comparative Performance of Small Manufacturing Firms in Northern Ireland and South East England", <u>Regional Studies</u>, vol. 21, no. 6, pp. 543-554.

Hitchens, D.M.W.N. and O'Farrell, P.N. (1988a), "The Comparative Performance of Small Manufacturing Firms located in South Wales and Northern Ireland", <u>Omega</u>, vol. 16, no. 5, pp. 429-438.

Hitchens, D.M.W.N. and O'Farrell, P.N. (1988b), "The Comparative Performance of Small Manufacturing Firms located in the Mid-West of Ireland and Northern Ireland", <u>Economic and Social Review</u>, vol. 19, no. 3, pp. 177-198.

Hitchens, D.M.W.N., Wagner, K. and Birnie, J.E. (1990), "International Managerial Impressions of the Clothing Industry: the results of exchange visits by Northern Ireland and German Clothing Industry Managers", <u>Department of Economics Occasional Paper</u>, Queen's University of Belfast (forthcoming).

HM Treasury (1986),<u> Government Expenditure Plans 1986/87 -1988/89</u>, HMSO, London.

HM Treasury (1987), <u>Economic Progress Report</u>, no. 188.

HM Treasury (1989), "Productivity in the 1980s", <u>Economic Progress Report</u>, no. 201, pp. 4-5.

HM Treasury and Central Statistical Office (1943), <u>Influences Affecting the Level of National Income</u>, CAB 87.13.

Hood, N. and Young, S. (1983), Multinational Investment Strategies in the British Isles, HMSO, London.

Hornby, W. (1958), Factory and Plant, HMSO and Longmans, London.

Hutton, G. (1953), We too can prosper, George Allen and Unwin, London.

IDA (1987), Ireland: The location for successful business, Industrial Development Authority of Ireland, Dublin.

IDB (1985), Report of the Linen Industry Task Force, IDB, Belfast.

Industry Society (1985), Survey of Absence Rates and Attendance Bonuses, London, Peter Rye House.

Ingham, H. and Ingham, M. (1989), "Industrial Change and Strike Activity in the European Community", paper given to the European Association for Research in Industrial Economic Conference, (August 30-September 1), Budapest.

International Comparisons Project (1973), A system of international comparisons of Gross Product and Purchasing Power, John Hopkins University Press, Baltimore.

International Comparisons Project (1977), International comparisons of Real Product and Purchasing, John Hopkins University Press, Baltimore.

International Comparisons Project (1982), World Product and Income: International comparisons of Real Gross Product, John Hopkins University Press, Baltimore.

Irish Times (1989, February 1), "IDA seeks repayment of £1.5 million grant".

Irish Times (1989, March 16), "Making the case for wider state role".

Isles, K. S. and Cuthbert, N. (1957), An Economic Survey of Northern Ireland, HMSO, Belfast.

Jaikumar, R. (1986), "Postindustrial manufacturing", Harvard Business Review, Nov-December, vol. 64, no. 6, pp. 69-76.

Johnson, D. (1985), "The Northern Ireland Economy 1914-39", in L. Kennedy and P. Ollerenshaw (eds), An Economic History of Ulster, Manchester University Press, Manchester.

Johnson, P. (1972), The Offshore Islanders, Weidenfeld and Nicholson, London.

Johnson, P. (1984), A History of the Modern World from 1917 to the 1980s, London, Weidenfeld Paperbacks.

Jones, D. T. (1976), "Output, Employment and Labour Productivity in Europe since 1955", National Institute Economic Review, no. 76, pp. 72-85.

Juttemeier, K. H. and Lamers, K. (1979), "Subventionen in der Bundesrepublik Deutschland", Kieler Diskussionsbeitrage no. 63/64, Kiel.

Kaiser, M. et al (1981), "Fachhochschulabsolventen beim ubergang vom studium zum berlif, Betreib, no. 24, Nurnberg.

Kaldor, N. (1966), Causes of the Slow Rate of Economic Growth of the United Kingdom, An Inaugural Lecture, Cambridge University Press, Cambridge.

Kaldor, M., Sharp, M., and Walker, W. (1986), "Industrial Competition and British Defence", Lloyd's Bank Review, no. 162, pp. 31-49.

Kay, J.A. (1989), "Myths and Realities", in E. Davis (ed.), 1992 Myths and Realities, Centre for Business Strategy London Business School, London Business School.

Kearney, C. (1989), "Training and the Labour Market in Northern Ireland: Patterns and Prospects", paper given to, Conference Europe 1992, Regions and Training, (December 7-8), Marseille.

Keating, P. (1989), "Nationalism and Economic Development in Ireland: a critical view", paper given to, Development Studies Conference, (September 20), Queen's University of Belfast.

Kennedy, K. A. (1971), Productivity and Industrial Growth: The Irish Experience, Clarendon Press, Oxford.

Kennedy, K. A. (1984), "Productivity and Technology: The Employment Dimension", Economic and Social Research Institute Report, no. 169, Dublin.

Kennedy, K. A. and Healy, T. (1985), "Small Scale Manufacturing in Ireland", Economic and Social Research Institute Paper, no. 125, Dublin.

Kennedy, K. A., Giblin, T. and Mc Hugh, D. (1988), The Economic Development of Ireland in the Twentieth Century, Croom Helm, London.

Kennedy, L. and Ollerenshaw, P. (1985), An Economic History of Ulster 1820-1939, Manchester, Manchester University Press.

Kennedy, W.P. (1987), Industrial Structure, Capital Markets and the Origins of British Economic Decline, Cambridge University Press, Cambridge.

Kiel Institute (1987), quoted in The Financial Times (1987, November 5), "In the Clutch of Corporatism".

Kindleberger, C.P. (1975), "Germany's Overtaking of England 1806 -1914 Part I", Weltwirtschfaftliches Archiv, vol. III, pp. 253 -81.

Klinke, R. and Becker, A. (1987), Fuhrungskrafte der bekleidungsindustrie in Bundesrepublik Deutschland, Bundesverband Bekleidungsindustrie, Koln.

Kravis, I.B. (1976), A survey of international comparisons of productivity, Economic Journal, vol. 86, pp. 1-44.

Kurosawa, K. (1982), A Study in International comparisons of Labour Productivity, Japanese Productivity Centre, Tokyo.

Kurt Salmon (1988), Patterns for the future Northern Ireland clothing industry strategy study, Industrial Development Board, Belfast.

Labour Relations Agency (1988), Industrial Relations: The Private Sector, Labour Relations Agency, Belfast.

Lawrence, P. (1980), Managers and Management in West Germany, Croom Helm, London.

Lee, C.H. (1986), The British Economy since 1700, Cambridge University Press, Cambridge.

Lee, J. (1968), "Capital in the Irish Economy", in L.M. Cullen (ed), The Formation of the Irish Economy, Mercier Press, Cork, pp. 55-63.

Lee, J. (1973), The Modernisation of Irish Society 1848-1918, vol. 10, Gill and Macmillan, Dublin.

Leibenstein, H. (1966), "Allocative efficiency VS "X Efficiency"", American Economic Review, vol. 56, June, 392-415

Levitt, M. S. (1985), "The Economics of Defence Spending", National Institute of Economic and Social Research Discussion Paper, London.

Liesner, T. and Economist (1985), Economic Statistics 1900-83, Economist Publications, London.

LWT, (London Weekend Television) (1987), Educating Britain, The Best and the Rest, September 6.

Lyons, F.S.L. (1981), Ireland Since the Famine, Fontana, London.

Maddison, A. (1955), "Output, Employment and Productivity in British Manufacturing over the last half century", Oxford Bulletin of Economic Statistics, November, no. 17, pp. 363-386.

Maddison, A. (1982), The Phases of Capitalist Development, Oxford University Press, Oxford.

Maizels, A. (1963), Industrial Growth and World Trade, An Empirical Study of Trends in Production, consumption and Trade in Manufacturing for 1899-1959 with Future Trends, Cambridge, Cambridge University Press.

Majewski, J. (1988), "The Economics of Race and Discrimination", Economic Affairs, February/March.

Malthus, T.R. (1808), "On the State of Ireland", The Edinburgh Review, no. xii, pp.336-55.

Marshall, A. (1919), Trade and Industry, Macmillan, London.

Marx, K. (1976), Capital Volume I, Penguin, Hammondsworth.

Marx, K. and Engels, F. (1971), Ireland and the Irish Question, Progress Publishers, Moscow.

Mason, C. M. and Harrison, R. T. (1985), "The Geography of Small Firms in the UK: towards a Research Agenda", Progress in Human Geography, no. 9, pp. 1-37.

Matthews, R. C. O. (1969), "Postwar business cycles in the United Kingdom", in M. Bronfenbrenner (ed), Is the business cycle obsolete? Wiley-Interscience, New York.

Matthews, R. C. O. (ed) (1982), Slower Growth in the Western World, Heinemann Educational and National Institute of Economic and Social Research, London.

Matthews, R. C. O., Feinstein, C. H. and Odling-Smee, J. C. (1982), British Economic Growth: 1856-73, Stanford, Stanford University Press.

Matthews, R. C. O. (1988), "Research on Productivity and the Productivity Gap", National Institute Economic Review, no. 124, pp. 66-71.

McAleese, D. (1978), A Profile of Grant-aided Industry in Ireland, Industrial Development Authority of Ireland, Dublin.

McHugh, D. (1989), "The changing face of Irish Industrial Policy", paper to the Development Studies Association, Belfast (20-22 September).

316

Meade, J. (1982), Stagflation: Volume 1, Wage-fixing, George Allen and Unwin, London.

Midland Bank Review (Smith, M.), 1986, "UK Manufacturing: Output and Trade Performance, Autumn, pp. 8-16.

Mishan, E. J. (1984), "GNP-Measurement or Mirage", National Westminster Bank Review, November.

Mitchell, J.C. (1969), "The concept and use of social networks", in J.C. Mitchell (ed), Social Networks in Urban Situations, Manchester University Press, Manchester, pp. 1-50.

Moore, B., Rhodes, J. and Tyler, P. (1977), "The impact of Regional Policy in the 1970s", Centre for Enviromental Studies Review, no. 1, pp. 67-77.

Morishma, M. (1984), Why Japan Succeeded: Japanese Ethos and Western Technology, Cambridge University Press, Cambridge.

Morris, C. (ed) (1985), The Economic System in the UK, Oxford University Press, Oxford.

Muellbauer, J. (1986), "Productivity and Competitiveness of British Manufacturing", Oxford Review of Economic Policy, vol.2, no.3, pp. i-xxv.

Murfin, A. (1987), "Service Industries in the UK economy: background data", mimeo OECD, Paris.

National Economic Development Council and Manpower Services Commission (1984), Competition and Competence: Training and Education in the Federal Republic of Germany, Japan and the United States, NEDO and MSC, London.

National Institute Economic Review (1982), "Special Issue on Britain's Comparative Productivity", no. 101, pp. 9-12.

NEDO (1979), Product design, National Economic Development Council, London.

NEDO (1983), Standards, quality and competitiveness, National Economic Development Council, London.

NEDO (1985), Technological transfer in the UK Food and Drink industry, National Economic Development Council, London.

NESC, (National Economic and Social Council), (1978), "Productivity and Management", Report, no. 43, Government Publications Sales Office, Dublin.

NESC, (National Economic and Social Council), (1989), "Ireland in the European Community: Performance, Prospects and Strategy", Report, no. 88, Government Publications Sales Office, Dublin.

New Ireland Forum (1983), The Costs of the Violence arising from the Northern Ireland Crisis since 1969, Government Stationery Office, Dublin.

New Scientist (1987, August 13), "Two communities get down to business", and, "Ireland defends Europe's regions", no. 1573, pp. 35-40 and pp. 46-51.

News Letter (1987, September 2), "The Rise of Industry, Two Hundred and Fiftieth Anniversary Supplement".

News Letter (1989, March 29), "Terror warning to firms".

Nickell, S. and Wadhani, S. (1987), "Myopia, the Dividend Puzzle and Share Prices", London School of Economics Discussion Paper, no. 272, London.

NI Economic Council (1986a), "Economic Strategy: Industrial Development Linkages", NI Economic Council Report, no. 56, Belfast.

NI Economic Council (1986b), "Demographic Trends in Northern Ireland", NI Economic Council Report, no. 57, Belfast.

NI Economic Council (1987), "Economic Strategy: the clothing industry", NI Economic Council Report, no. 63, Belfast.

NI Economic Council (1988), "The Shipbuilding Industry: its significance to Northern Ireland", NI Economic Council Report, no. 69, Belfast.

NI Economic Council (1989), "Economic Strategy: overall review", NI Economic Council Report, no. 73, Belfast.

NI Economic Council (1990), "The Industrial Development Board for Northern Ireland: Selective Financial Assistance and Economic Development Policy", NI Economic Council Report, no. 79, Belfast.

O'Brien, G. (1918), The Economic History of Ireland in the Eighteenth Century, Maunsel, Dublin and London.

O'Dowd, L. (1987), "Trends and Potential of the Service Sector in Northern Ireland", in P. Teague (ed) (1987), Beyond the Rhetoric, Lawrence and Wishart, London.

OECD (1986), National Accounts, main aggregates vol. 1, 1960-86, OECD, Paris.

OECD (1987a), "Total Factor Productivity", _Economic Outlook_, Paris.

OECD (1987b), _Innovation Policy: Ireland_, OECD, Paris.

OECD (1987c), _National Accounts, main aggregates vol. 1, purchasing power parities supplement_, OECD, Paris.

OECD (1988), _The Newly Industrialised Countries_, OECD, Paris.

O'Farrell, P. N. and O'Loughlin, B. (1980), _An Analysis of New Industry Linkages_, Industrial Development Authority, Dublin.

O'Farrell, P.N. (1986), _Entrepreneurs and Industrial Change_, IMI, (Irish Management Institute), Dublin.

O'Farrell, P.N. and Hitchens, D.M.W.N. (1988a), "The Relative Competitiveness and Performances of Small Manufacturing Firms in Scotland and the mid-West of Ireland: an analysis of Matched Pairs", _Regional Studies_, vol. 22, no. 5, pp. 399-416.

O'Farrell, P.N. and Hitchens, D.M.W.N. (1988b), "Interfirm Comparisons in Industrial Research: the utility of Matched Pairs Design", _Tjidschr.Econ.Soc.Geogr._, no. 79, pp. 63-69.

O'Farrell, P.N. and Hitchens, D.M.W.N (1989a), "The Competitiveness and Performance of Small Manufacturing Firms: an Analysis of Matched Pairs in Scotland and England", _Environment and Planning A_, vol. 21, pp. 1241-63.

O'Farrell, P.N. and Hitchens, D.M.W.N (1989b), _Small Firm Competitiveness and Performance_, Gill and Macmillan, Dublin.

Ollerenshaw, P. (1985), "Industry 1820-1914", in L. Kennedy and P. Ollerenshaw (eds), _An Economic History of Ulster 1820-1939_, Manchester University Press, Manchester.

Olson, M. (1982), _The Rise and Decline of Nations_, Yale University Press, New Haven.

O'Malley, E. (1985a), "The Performance of Irish Indigenous Industry: Lessons for the 1980s", in J. Fitzpatrick and J. Kelly (eds), _Perspectives on Irish Industry_, IMI (Irish Management Institute), Dublin.

O'Malley, E. (1985b), "Industrial Development in the North and South of Ireland, Prospects for an integrated approach", _Administration_, vol. 33, no. 1.

O'Malley, E. (1989), _Industry and Economic Development: the challenge for the latecomer_, Gill and Macmillan, Dublin.

Osborne, R.D. (1985), "Religion and Educational Qualifications in Northern Ireland", Research Paper Number 8, Fair Employment Agency, Belfast.

Osborne, R.D., Cormack, R.J., Miller, R.L. and Williamson, A.P. (1987), "Graduates: geographical mobility and incomes", in R. D. Osborne, R. J. Cormack and R. L Miller (eds), Education and Policy in Northern Ireland, Policy Research Institute, Belfast, pp. 231-44.

Osola, J., (Report, Osola and Associates), (1983), A Critical Review of Industrial Research and Development Facilities in Northern Ireland, Worcester.

Othick, J. (1985), "The Economic History of Ulster: a perspective", in L. Kennedy and P. Ollerenshaw (eds), An Economic History of Ulster 1820-1914, Manchester University Press, Manchester.

Pagnamenta, P. and Overy, R. J (1984), All our working lives.

Paige, D. and Bombach G. (1959), A Comparison of National Output and Productivity in the United Kingdom and United States, OECD, Paris.

Panic, M. (1976), UK and West German Manufacturing Industries, 1954-1972: A Comparison of Performance and Structure, NEDO, London.

Paque, K-H. (1988), "The mixed blessing of labour shortage: German overemployment in the 1960s", Kiel Institute of World Economics Working Paper, no. 82, Kiel.

Parkinson, S. T. (1984), New product development in engineering: a comparison of the British and West German machine tool industries, Cambridge University Press, Cambridge.

Patel, P. and Pavitt, K. (1987), "The Elements of British Technological Competitiveness", National Institute Economic Review, no. 122, pp. 72-83.

Patel, P. and Pavitt, K. (1988), Technological Activities in the Federal Republic of Germany and the UK, Science Policy Research Unit, Sussex.

Pathfinder (Report), (1987), Building a Stronger Economy. The Pathfinder Process, Department of Economic Development, (Northern Ireland), Belfast.

Pavitt, K. and Soete L. (1982), "International Differences in Economic Growth and the International Location of Innovation", in H Giersch (ed), Emerging Technologies, Mohr, Tubingen, pp. 105-133.

320

PEIDA (Consultants), (1984), Transport Costs in Peripheral Regions, Department of Economic Development (NI) and Scottish Office.

PEIDA, Firn, Crichton and Roberts (1986), Manpower, Excellence and Corporate Performance in Scotland, Scottish Development Agency, Edinburgh.

Petty, W. (1691), "Anatomy of Ireland", in C.H. Hill (ed), The Economic Writings of Sir William Petty, Cambridge University Press, Cambridge, pp. 121-231 (published 1899).

Phelps Brown, E. (1973), "Levels and Movements of Industrial Productivity and Real Wages Internationally Compared, 1860 -1970", Economic Journal, vol. 83, no. 329, pp. 58-71.

Pickles, A.R. and O'Farrell, P.N. (1987), "An Analysis of Entrepreneurial Behaviour from Male Work Histories", Regional Studies, vol. 21, no. 5, pp. 425-444.

Piore, M. and Sabel, C. (1984), The Second Industrial Divide, Basic Books, New York.

Platt Report (1944 March-April), Report of the Cotton Textiles Missions to the United States of America, Ministry of Production, London.

Pollard, S. (1982), The Wasting of the British Economy, Croom Helm, London.

Prais, S. J. (1981a), Productivity and Industrial Structure, Cambridge University Press, Cambridge.

Prais, S. J. (1981b), "Vocational qualifications of the labour force in Britain and Germany", National Institute Economic Review, no. 98, pp. 47-59.

Prais, S. J. and Wagner, K. (1983), "Some Practical Aspects of Human Capital Investment", National Institute Economic Review, no. 105, pp. 46-65.

Prais, S. J. and Wagner, K. (1985), "Schooling standards in England and Germany", National Institute Economic Review, no. 112, pp. 53-76.

Prais, S. J. and Wagner, K. (1988), "Productivity and Management: The Training of Foremen in Britain and Germany", National Institute Economic Review, no. 123, pp. 34-47.

Prais, S. J. (1989), "Qualified manpower in engineering in Britain and other industrially advanced countries", National Institute Economic Review, no 127, pp. 76-83.

Pratten, C. F. (1971), Economies of Scale in Manufacturing Industry, Cambridge University Press, Cambridge.

Pratten, C. F. (1976), Labour Productivity Differences within International Companies, Cambridge University Press, Cambridge.

Pratten, C. F. and Atkinson, A. G. (1976), "The Use of Manpower in British Manufacturing Industry", Department of Employment Gazette, no. 84, pp. 571-76.

Pratten, C. F. (1985), Applied Macroeconomics, Oxford University Press.

Pratten, C. F. (1986), "The Importance of Giant Companies", Lloyds Bank Review, no. 159, pp. 33-48.

Pratten, C. F. (1988), "A Survey of the Economies of Scale", in, Research on the Cost of Non-Europe: Basic Findings, vol. 2, Office for Official Publications of the European Communities, Luxembourg.

Pringle, D. (1989), "Partition, Politics and Social Conflict", in R. W. G. Carter and A. J. Parker (eds), Ireland: a contemporary Geographical Perspective, Routledge, Allen and Unwin, London and New York, pp. 23-54.

Quigley, G. (Report), (1976), Economic and Industrial Strategy for Northern Ireland, HMSO, Belfast.

Ray, G. F. (1987), "Labour Costs in Manufacturing", National Institute Economic Review, no. 120, pp. 71-4, and (revised) no. 122, p. 96.

Reward Regional Surveys (1987), Regional Surveys: Cost of Living Report, Reward Regional Surveys, Stone.

Rhodes, J. (1986), "Regional Dimensions of Industrial Decline", in R. Martin and R. Rowthorn (eds), The Geography of De-industrialisation, Macmillan, Basingstoke.

Roberts, A. (1990), Manufacturing into the late 1990s, HMSO, London.

Roper, S., Schofield, A., Gudgin, G. and Tavakoli, M. (1990), "A Guide to the NIERC Model of The Northern Ireland Economy", Northern Ireland Economic Research Centre Report, Belfast.

Rossini, (1988), "Price discrimination in the European clothing sectors, paper given to, Conference of European Association for Industrial Economics, (August 31-September 2), Erasmus University, Rotterdam.

Rostas, L. (1948), Industrial Production, Productivity and Comparative Productivity in British and American Industries, Cambridge, Cambridge University Press.

Rostow, W. W. (1962), The Stages of Economic Growth, Cambridge University Press, Cambridge.

Rothwell, R. (1982), "Innovation in textile machinery", in K. Pavitt (ed), Technical innovation and British economic performance, Science Policy Research Unit, Sussex.

Rottman, D. (1989), "Crime in Geographical Perspective", in R. W. G. Carter and A. J. Parker (eds), Ireland a contemporary Geographical Perspective, Routledge, Allen and Unwin, London and New York, pp. 87-112.

Rowthorn, R. (1975), "What Remains of Kaldor's Laws", Economic Journal, vol. 85, pp. 10-19.

Rowthorn, R. (1981), "Northern Ireland: An Economy in Crisis", Cambridge Joural of Economics, vol. 5, pp. 1-31.

Rowthorn, R. (1986), "De-industrialisation in Britain", in R. Martin and R. Rowthorn (eds), The Geography of De-industrialisation, Macmillan, Basingstoke, pp. 1-29.

Rowthorn, R. (1987), "An Economy in Crisis", in P. Teague (eds), Beyond the Rhetoric, Lawrence and Wishart, London, pp. 111-135.

Rowthorn, R. and Wayne, N. (1988), Northern Ireland: The Political Economy of Conflict, Polity Press, Cambridge.

Roy, A. (1982), "Labour Productivity in 1980: An International Comparison", National Institute Economic Review, no. 101, pp. 26-37.

Ruane, F. (1980), "Optimal Labour Subsidies and Industrial Development in Ireland", Economic and Social Review, vol. 11, no. 2, pp. 77-98.

Ruane, F. (1987), "The Traded Sector: Manufacturing", in J. W. O'Hagan (ed), The Economy of Ireland: Policy and Performance, Irish Management Institute, Dublin.

Rubinstein, W. D. (1981), Men of Property: The very wealthy in Britain since the Industrial Revolution, Croom Helm, London.

Rubinstein, W. D. (1988), "Social Class, social attitudes and British business life", Oxford Review of Economic Policy, vol. 14, no. 1, pp. 51-58.

Salter, W. E. G. (1960), Productivity and Technical Change, Cambridge University Press, Cambridge.

Sanderson, M. (1972), "Research and the Firm in British Industry, 1919-1939", Science Studies, no. 3, pp. 107-51.

Saunders, C. (1978), Engineering in Britain, West Germany and France, Sussex European Papers, Sussex.

Schott, K. and Pick, K. (1984), "The effect of price and non-price factors on UK export performance and import penetration", Discussion Paper 84-01, London.

Secretary of State for Trade and Industry (1983), "Regional Industrial Development", Command 9111, London, HMSO.

Sectoral Development Committee (1983a), "Report and Recommendations on the Clothing and Textiles Industries", Report, no. 1, Government Publications Sales Office, Dublin.

Sectoral Development Committee (1983b), "Report and Recommendations on the Mechanical Engineering Industry", Report, no. 2, Government Publications Sales Office, Dublin.

Sectoral Development Committee (1985a), "Report and Recommendations on the Technological Capacity of Indigenous Irish Industry", Report, no. 8, Government Publications Sales Office, Dublin.

Sectoral Development Committee (1985b), "Report and Recommendations on the Chemical and Pharmaceuticals Industries", Report, no. 9, Government Publications Sales Office, Dublin.

Sectoral Development Committee (1986), "Report and Recommendations on the Electronics Industry", Report, no. 12, Government Publications Sales Office, Dublin.

Shadwell, A. (1906), Industrial efficiency, Longman, Manchester.

Shepherd, J. (1987), "Industrial Support Policies, National Institute Economic Review, no. 122, pp. 59-71.

Silberstone, A. (1987), "The Supply and Demand for Scientists and Engineers in Britain", paper given to the Economics Section, the British Association for the Advancement of Science, Annual Meeting, (August 25), Queen's University of Belfast.

Smith, A.D. (1985), "Changes in Comparative Anglo-American Productivity in Manufacturing Industry", National Institute of Economic and Social Research Discussion Paper, no. 101.

Smith, A.D., Hitchens, D.M.W.N. and Davies, S.W (1982), International Industrial Productivity: A comparison of Britain, America and Germany, Cambridge University Press, Cambridge.

Smith, A. D. and Hitchens, D. M. W. N. (1985), Productivity in Distributive Trades: A comparison of Britain, America and Germany, Cambridge University Press, Cambridge.

SOEC, (Statistical Office of the European Communities), (1981), Structure and activity of industry 1976, Office for Official Publications of the European Communities, Luxembourg.

SOEC (1983), Production statistics: Quarterly statistics No 2, Office for Official Publications of the European Communities, Luxembourg.

SOEC (1986a), Industry Yearbook 1985, Office for Official Publications of the European Communities, Luxembourg.

SOEC (1986b), Structure and Activity of Industry 1981/1982, Office for Official Publications of the European Communities, Luxembourg.

SOEC (1987a), Structure and Activity of Industry 1982/83, Office for Official Publications of the European Communities, Luxembourg.

SOEC (1987b), Industrial production: Quarterly statistics no. 2, Office for Official Publications of the European Communities, Luxembourg.

SOEC (1988), "Appendix", in, Research on the Cost of Non-Europe: Basic Findings, vol. 2, Office for Official Publications of the European Communities, Luxembourg.

Sorge, A. and Warner, M. (1980), "Manpower Training, Manufacturing Organisation and Workplace Relations in Great Britain and West Germany", British Journal of Industrial Relations, p318.

Statistical Abstract 1982-85 (1987), Stationery Office, Dublin.

Statistisches Bundesamt (1988), Statistisches Jahrbuch 1988, Verlag W Kohlhammer, Stuttgart and Mainz.

Steedman, H. (1988), "Vocational Training in France and Britain", National Institute of Economic and Social Research Discussion Paper.

Steedman, H. and Wagner, K. (1987), "A Second look at Productivity, Machinery and Skills in Britain and Germany, National Institute Economic Review, no. 122, pp. 84-95.

Steedman, H. and Wagner, K. (1989), "Productivity, Machinery and Skills: Clothing Manufacturing in Britain and Germany, National Institute Economic Review, no. 128, pp. 40-57.

Stewart, J. (1985), "Aspects of the Financial Behavious of Multinational Companies", in J. Fitzpatrick and J. Kelly (eds), Perspectives on Irish Industry, IMI (Irish Management Institute), Dublin, pp. 167-96.

Storey, D. (1982), Entrepreneurship and the new firm, Croom Helm, London.

Sweeney, G.P. (1989), "Education, Technical Culture and Regional Prosperity", paper given to, Regions and Training Conference, Marseilles (December 7-8).

Swords-Isherwood, N. (1982), "British Management Compared", in K. Pavitt (ed), Technical Innovation and British Economic Performance, Science Policy Research Unit, Sussex, pp. 88-99.

Teague, P. (1987), "Multinational Companies in Northern Ireland: An out-moded model of Industrial development", in P. Teague (ed), Beyond the Rhetoric, Lawrence and Wishart, London, pp. 160-72.

Telesis (Report), (1982), "Review of Industrial Policy", National Economic and Social Councial Report, no. 64, Dublin.

The 1970-75 Development Plan (1969), Report prepared by Professor R Matthew, T Wilson, and J Parkinson for the Northern Ireland Government, HMSO, Belfast.

The Independent (1990, February 8), "At the Bottom of the Class".

The Times (1987, February 16), "Research and Prosperity. Part 1 Left Behind".

The Times (1987, March 20), "When everyone is Irish".

Tilly, R. (1986), "German Banking, 1850-1914: Development Assistance for the Strong", Journal of European Economic History, vol. 15, pp. 113-52.

Tyler, P. and Rhodes, J. (1986), "The Census of Production as an Indicator of Regional Differences in Productivity and Profitability in the UK", Regional Studies, vol. 20, no. 4, pp. 331-39.

Tyler, P., Moore, B. and Rhodes, J. (1988), Geographical Variations in Cost and Productivity, Department of Trade and Industry, London.

Ulster Businessman (1988), "Have they anything to say?"

UN, (United Nations), (1989), Monthly Bulletin of Statistics, February.

United States Strategic Bombing Survey, vol. 1 and 2 (1976), London, Garland Publishing.

Verbrand Deutscher Maschinen und Anlagenbau (1988), Ingenieur -erhebung im maschinen-und anlagenbau, Frankfurt.

Verdoorn, P. J. (1949), "Fattori che regolano lo sviluppo della producttivitta del lavaro", L'Industria.

Vernon, R. (1966) "International Investment and International Trade in the Product Cycle", Quarterly Journal of Economics, vol. LXXX, no. 2, pp. 190-207.

Weber, M. (1976), The Protestant Ethic and the Spirit of Capitalism, George Allen and Unwin, London.

Wenban-Smith, G. C. (1982), "Factors Influencing Recent Productivity Growth: Report on a survey of companies", National Institute Economic Review, no. 101, pp. 57-66.

Whiting, T. (1976), Cyclical Fluctuations in the UK Economy, NEDO, London.

Wiener, M. J. (1981), English Culture and the Decline of the Industrial Spirit 1815-1980, Penguin Books, Hammondsworth.

Williams, E. E. (1896), Made in Germany, in A. Albu (ed, 1973) Heinemann, London.

Wilson, T. (1964), Economic Development in Northern Ireland, Government of Northern Ireland, HMSO, Belfast.

Wilson, T. (1989), Ulster: Conflict and Consent, Blackwell, Oxford.

Yanks, D. et al (1984), Work and Human Values: An International Report on Jobs in the 1980s and 1990s, Aspen Institute for Humanistic Studies, New York.

Zedler, R. (1988), "Standortvorteil: berufsausbildung", in W. Lenske (ed), Qualified in Germany, Koln.